SEX DIFFERENCES

PATRICK C. LEE and ROBERT SUSSMAN STEWART / Editors

SEX DIFFERENCES

CULTURAL AND DEVELOPMENTAL DIMENSIONS

Urizen Books New York

ISBN- 0-916354-22-9
ISBN- 0-916354-23-7

PREFACE AND ACKNOWLEDGMENTS

This collection is an attempt to bring together in one volume a sample of the twentieth century's most influential writing on sex differences. To trace this writing as an individual reader, one would have to search through a voluminous and scattered literature covering seven decades of research and scholarship in the four disciplines of psychoanalysis, anthropology, ethology, and psychology. Thus, there are clear advantages to having the key pieces of the literature drawn together in one place. We have chosen only selections which have contributed importantly to our society's understanding of the differences and similarities between males and females. These include the seminal work of the scholars who laid the foundations of twentieth-century thought on sex differences. Among them are Freud, Horney, Klein, and Deutsch all from the psychoanalytic movement; the anthropologists Malinowski, Linton, and Mead; the ethologists Lorenz and Tinbergen; and Hall, Terman and Miles, Gesell and Ilg, and Tyler, representing psychology. We have also included selections by the most significant current investigators in the field of sex differences who have built upon or altered the foundations of their precursors. These are represented by Kohlberg, Maccoby, Moss, Whiting, Money, the Murphys, and Barry, Bacon, and Child, among others.

Undoubtedly, our selection process has had the unfortunate effect of excluding some authors who would have been included were we allowed unlimited space. However, in the interest of fairness and excellence we adopted two criteria to guide our judgment in making final selections. First, we did *not* attempt to exclude authors who were subsequently shown to be wrong in their thinking on sex differences. The critical criterion was not that one's scholarship be indisputably correct but that it be influential. Such scholarship, rightly or wrongly, creates reality and ultimately meets the most rigorous standard of shaping public consciousness and of being an intellectual force in the area of sex differences. Second, and stemming directly from the first

5

criterion, we required that the anthologized authors have a demonstrated influence on the work of subsequent scholars and researchers. There is little question that the authors we selected from the "classical" era have greatly influenced both the form and substance of later work on sex differences, although not always in intended ways. Similarly, we have little doubt about the importance of the more current authors in shaping the research of their contemporaries and successors.

It is difficult to imagine that our work on this anthology could have proceeded smoothly without the generous assistance of many colleagues who are too numerous to mention. However, some deserve special thanks, and we are happy to acknowledge them by name.

For general intellectual support and the provision of indispensable facilities and services we are indebted to Edmund Sullivan and Clifford Christensen of The Ontario Institute for Studies in Education, and to Peter B. Neubauer of the Child Development Center in New York City. For critical reading of drafts of the anthology's several introductory essays we would like to thank Joanne Chmara of the Ontario Institute for Studies in Education, Joan Clayton of the City University of New York, and our publisher, Michael Roloff. For valuable colleagueship in the study of sex differences over the last few years special thanks must be offered to Nancy Gropper and Gita Kedar Voivodas of Teachers College, Columbia University. We are also grateful to Sigmund Freud Copyrights, Ltd., for permission to quote from the work of Sigmund Freud, to the Melanie Klein Trust for permission to reprint from the works of Melanie Klein, and to the Association for the Advancement of Psychoanalysis for permission to select from the work of Karen Horney. Jeannette Taylor and Ruth Mary Reynolds of the library at the New York Psychoanalytic Institute were particularly helpful in locating research materials and deserve our thanks for this service. For typing, duplicating, and proofreading, Gerald Chiappa has been most generous with his time and talent. Finally, the senior editor extends his warm and personal gratitude to Anne De Renzo for her unwavering confidence in his ability to realize this project.

All of these people deserve considerable credit for the merits of this collection and none are accountable for its faults. The ultimate responsibility for the anthology, of course, lies with the two editors. Growing out of his interest in the cultural and psychological analysis of sex role, the senior editor has organized the sections on anthropology, ethology, and psychology. The associate editor's primary expertise is in psychoanalytic theory, thus he has assumed responsibility for the psychoanalytic section.

Our purpose in editing this book was to try to make sense of the evolving conceptual and social puzzles presented by sex differences. We hope we have had at least a modest success in achieving this purpose.

Patrick C. Lee
Robert Sussman Stewart

New York City
May, 1976

TABLE OF CONTENTS

INTRODUCTION

Patrick C. Lee

The contemporary crisis in sex identity is essentially a conflict between traditional ideas about sex differences and the new realities of sex role. Our society's understanding of the nature of sex differences is derived from the cultural past. But the realities which currently dictate the specific roles and functions of men and women spring from ongoing changes in economics, technology, and social organization. These changes are shaping a new sensibility about sex differences which departs in significant ways from the old sensibility.

This process of change, however, is not occurring in an ideological vacuum. The new sensibility is very much a child of tradition and can be appreciated only in the context of its historical origins. Thus, to understand the contemporary crisis it is necessary, as a first step, to examine the foundations of twentieth-century thinking on sex differences; and, as a second step, to trace this thinking forward through the various transformations it has undergone in arriving at its present state.

In an attempt to take these two steps this anthology has drawn upon two bodies of writings. The first represents the classical twentieth-century literature on sex differences and includes pieces by Sigmund Freud, Karen Horney, Bronislaw Malinowski, Margaret Mead, and G. Stanley Hall, among others. The second represents more recent work in the field of sex differences and selects from the writings of contemporary scholars like John Money, Eleanor Maccoby, Lawrence Kohlberg, and Niko Tinbergen. It is a long way from G. Stanley Hall's expansive social evolutionism to Eleanor Maccoby's incisive ordering of empirical findings—in both chronological and ideological terms. In that interim, the place of the sexes in society has come increasingly under scientific scrutiny, and society, in turn, has recently begun to require greater accountability of the scientific enterprise. The present anthology attempts to capture the evolving contribution science has made to society's understanding of sex differences by charting major twentieth-century developments in the disciplines of psychoanalysis, anthropology, psychology, and ethology.

The Changing Status of the Sexes

By way of introduction to much of the background material presented in this anthology it may be useful to briefly survey the *foreground* of sex differences as they exist in the 1970s in American society. As already mentioned, the status, roles, and functions of the sexes are changing along with technology, economics, and social organization.

Technological Change—Developments in the technologies of work, the household, contraception, and longevity have had far reaching effects on the functional differences between the sexes. Labor-saving machinery and automated systems in the world of work have eliminated the advantage of male strength and size in many industries and occupations, thus tending to homogenize the sexes economically. Labor-saving devices in the household have reduced the amount of time and energy middle and working-class women commit to their traditional domestic responsibilities. Many women use the resulting surplus time for employment outside the home or for self-improvement and education, often combining these activities with raising families. Since 1940, for example, the number of working mothers in the United States has increased eightfold, and they now constitute almost 40 percent of all working women.[1] The technology of birth control, particularly the contraceptive pill, has freed many women from the burden of repeated pregnancies and parents from the inevitability of large families. Moreover, it has given the average woman a degree of control over the consequences of her own sexuality which was unknown in the past, thereby contributing immeasurably to the revolution in sexual mores and to the gradual breakdown of double standards of sexual behavior. Advances in the technology of medical care and nutrition have increased longevity dramatically during the twentieth century. Both men and women are living longer and have more leisure years after retiring from their work and homemaking responsibilities. Since old age is a life stage in which sex differentiation tends to wane, enhanced longevity means that our society now has relatively more people who place relatively less emphasis on differences between the sexes.

Economic Changes—Since 1950 the number of women in the world of work has almost doubled, until they now constitute about 40 percent of the total labor force in the United States. There has also been a modest movement of women into the professions traditionally reserved for men, e.g., medicine and law, although for the vast majority simple employment appears to be a more salient reality than career development. While the domestic technology referred to above might tend to create a "boredom push" of women out of the home into work, it appears that the more important factor has been "income pull." Nearly two-thirds of American working women are single, divorced, widowed, separated, or have husbands who earn less that $7,000 a year. It is safe to conjecture that a large percentage of the remaining third are also working because the standard of living of their families, while not marginal, is such to require two incomes. Men continue to be the main sources of income for American families and continue to work more on the average than women do. But, due to the increasingly technical nature of many contemporary jobs, men require more pre-employment training and/or educational preparation. Consequently, males are entering the job market later than in the past. Moreover, due to changes in technology and in labor practice, work weeks are shorter and retirement ages are earlier than they have been in the past. This has had the net effect of reducing the amount of time men work relative to their life span and, coupled with the increase of working women, has reduced the discrepancy between men and women in sheer amount of time spent at gainful employment. In other words, the experience of formal employment, once almost the exclusive preserve of men, has become something which men and women increasingly share (cf., Neugarten & Datan, 1973). None of this is to say that there has not been discrimination against women in the world of work. It's only to say that, whatever inequities continue to exist, men are working less, women are working more, and the experience of work no longer existentially separates men and women to the degree that it once did.

Changes in the Family—The last two decades have also seen great changes in the family, the basic unit of social organization in Western society. The typical American family is increasingly nuclear and neolocal, in sharp contrast to the traditional extended family which tended to cluster in one community or region. In the absence of the extended familial support system, there has been a convergence of function between husbands and wives, which commonly results in role overlap and occasionally, role reversal. The movement of women into the labor force, as mentioned above, suggests that Talcott Parsons' classic designation of women as "expressive" and men as "instrumental" no longer holds. Women are increasingly assuming instrumental functions as they pursue the family's interests in the outside world. Conversely, the recently emerged concern about "fathering" among men indicates that they are taking on more of the expressive function of maintaining affective ties within the family (see Parsons' selection).

Another phenomenon having a major effect on the structure of the nuclear family is the increased incidence of divorce. In the United States in 1975 there was one divorce for every 2.1 marriages, a dramatic gain of 85 percent over 1960 when the ratio of divorce to marriage was 1 to 3.9. There are now approximately one million divorces and over half a million legal separations annually in the United States which involve well over one million dependent children each year. The accelerated divorce rate is creating two alternative kinds of family. Divorced people who remarry, and most do, are forming a type of nuclear family which has a shifting membership and in which children usually have strong ties to a parent, usually their biological father, who belongs to another family. Those who do not remarry are joining the burgeoning ranks of "single-parent families." There are now over six and a half million single-parent families in the United States which include 14 percent of all American children below eighteen years of age, an increase of 75 percent since 1960. Moveover, during the period 1955 to 1973, single-parent families were increasing at almost twice the rate of two-parent families.

It is evident, then, that novel family forms are increasingly prevalent and that the traditional *complementarity* of sex-divided labor no longer holds in two-parent nuclear families, and is simply dysfunctional in single-parent families, where the remaining parent, usually the mother, must assume both parental roles. Since the family is one of the major societal vehicles for interface between the sexes, changes in its basic structure must inevitably lead to changes in the ways the sexes interact. These, in turn, can be expected to yield new profiles of functional sex differences.

Changing Marriage Customs—New developments in economic practice, social organization, and technology, of course, do not occur in isolated streams, but tend to interact in complex ways which themselves have implications for the ways in which the sexes differ. It is interesting, for example, to note how marriage customs are changing as a result of the interaction between the technology of contraception and the economics of female employment. Widespread earning power among women has provided them a degree of financial independence enjoyed by only a select few in the past. Contraceptive methods designed for female use (as opposed to those designed for males) have given women the prerogative of disassociating their sexual behavior from pregnancy and childbirth, thus freeing them from traditional social and biological constraints on their sexuality. The relative availability of premarital and extramarital sexual partners for both men and women, in turn, has tended to reduce the importance of sex as an incentive to marriage, contributing to the present American trend, evolving over the last fifteen years, toward marrying at a later age.

Economic self reliance has also reduced the need for women to marry in order to be supported by a man. In fact, a woman's real or potential earning power has become a new criterion for female desirability since, as mentioned above, the availability of two incomes is often a prerequisite to the maintenance of an acceptable standard of living. A working wife is an indispensable asset to many men who require long preparation for professional careers; the wives in such arrangements provide support for their husbands as an investment in the economic stability of their own futures. Interestingly enough, these marriages upset the traditional formula in which the man offered material support in return for exclusive sexual rights to the woman. In many contemporary marriages, the reverse almost seems to be the case, at least during the early years of the marriage. These arrangements also allow men to reach "family maturity" prior to "economic maturity," another reversal of the traditional pattern in which young men were expected to be on a sound economic footing before undertaking the responsibilities of marriage and family (cf., Neugarten & Datan, 1973).

Among highly educated and/or talented people there is an increasing incidence of dual-profession and childless "companionate" marriages, in which the functional distinctions between the two sexes are practically nonexistent. These marital arrangements are relatively infrequent, even by contemporary standards, but they are often accorded high visibility by the news media, thus tending to pull the broad spectrum of middle- and working-class arrangements in more "progressive" directions.

Women's Liberation—The technological, social, and economic changes discussed above are primary causes of the new distribution of functions and roles between the sexes. The women's movement is more accurately viewed as an effect of these primary causes and, in turn, as an articulation of the existential status of contemporary women (and, incidentally, of men). It also serves as an intellectual and emotional support system for increasing numbers of women who find themselves bereft of precedent to guide their lives. As women's liberation moves toward organizational maturity, however, it is becoming a social and political force in its own right, designed to bring the legalities of female status into closer correspondence with new economic, social, and technological realities.

Psychological Consequences of Sex-Role Change—These changes, contracted into the relatively brief time-span of one or two generations, have had an enormous impact on the respective psychologies of the sexes. One must ask: How do people *feel* and *think* about these discontinuities in their experience? How do they feel about themselves as men and women? Doubtlessly, the changes have involved psychological dislocation for both sexes. But such dislocations can be viewed both positively, as opening new opportunities for personal growth, and negatively, as closing down familiar routes to personal identity.

For example, one effect of the changes discussed above has been to blur the accepted boundaries between traditional male and female functions. Women are surrendering their traditional expressive primacy in the family and men their instrumental primacy in the world of work and community affairs. It is difficult to imagine that these respective primacies are being abandoned with total equanimity, for, whatever constraints they placed on individual development in the past, at least they offered structure and a sense of order to people's lives. The breakdown of familiar structure is usually accompanied by a degree of anxiety, which may account for the resistance among many men and women to changes in the roles of the two sexes. It may also account for the tentative exhilaration felt by many ordinary people, particularly by women, who sense that new options, once closed to them, are now open.

Another effect of these changes has been the reduction of segregation between the sexes. In the past there has been amazingly little opportunity for the formation of socially accepted relationships between the sexes outside the culturally sanctioned vehicles of courtship, marriage, and family. But today relationships based on friendship, convenience, and occupational interdependence are on the increase in the working world, educational institutions, social clubs, the political arena, and a variety of other cultural settings. Many of these new relationships are built on respect or practical expediency and are free of both the binding intimacy of the culturally sanctioned vehicles, and the conventional propriety once required of male-female interactions which occurred outside these vehicles. It remains to be seen, however, whether widespread sex integration will have an attenuating effect on marriage and family. The statistics on divorce would appear to give little comfort to those committed to marital permanence and family integrity, and suggest that, on balance, the new sex integration may be incompatible with traditional institutions which place a high premium on exclusive personal loyalty. The new modes of cross-sex interaction tend to be *inclusive*, thereby coexisting poorly with modes, such as marriage, that make *exclusive* demands on men and women. Again, the basic questions must be raised: Does the new degree of sex integration provoke an intolerable quantum of jealousy and strain in the average person who has one foot in tradition and the other in contemporary folkways? How well are people accommodating to knowing members of the opposite sex as friends and associates, not only as lovers, spouses, or relatives? Asking the questions in this manner is not meant to prejudge the answers;

it is only to recognize that basic changes do not occur without arousing basic doubts.

It might also be interesting to speculate in passing on the disruptive effect sex integration has had on same-sex "bonding" practices. It is increasingly rare for heterosexual, middle-class women and men to have outlets for association only with members of their own sex, as both sexes have invaded one another's formerly exclusive preserves. Again sex integration has rendered the traditional and exclusive forms of bonding outmoded. It is a matter of conjecture whether such bonding practices formerly served adaptive or superficial functions, but they were at one time very common in American society, particularly among men. Ironically, it is women who are resuscitating such practices in the form of sexually exclusive consciousness-raising groups, thus suggesting that bonding does have a purpose, and that much of that purpose has been lost with the gradual loss of bonding.

Brief mention was made above of the breakdown of the traditional double standard of sexual expression. Birth control technology, along with other changes in sexual attitudes, has conferred more sexual initiative on women. This has proliferated opportunities for sexual experience for both men and women, but it has also had the effect of placing pressure on the two sexes to perform sexually and to compartmentalize sexual *behavior* from affectionate and loving *feelings*. Relative to earlier cultural expectations, women in particular are pressured to be sexually active and to abandon restraints, as the old stigma associated with being sexually expressive has been replaced by the converse stigma of being sexually inhibited. While, in one sense, many women may view this as a desirable hedonistic outcome and a refreshing departure from the Victorian legacy of repressed female sexuality, in another sense it is often felt as an infringement on their freedom of choice and action. Thus, the new "single standard" is in some respects as unsettling and anxiety-producing as the old double standard was unfair and repressive.

From the male perspective, the response to female sexual initiative has run the gamut from acceptance to fear. Many men have welcomed the new initiative because it has freed them from the necessity of unrelenting sexual assertiveness and has allowed them to broaden their sexual repertoire to include more passive forms of expression. However, men may also resent the new female initiative because they view it as a usurpation of their own initiative and, in a broader sense, of their masculinity. Finally, liberated female sexuality has raised questions for many men about their own sexual adequacy. For some, the prospect and/or reality of being sexually outperformed by women constitutes a deep injury to their masculine pride and arouses basic fears about their adequacy as men.

Since the social status of men traditionally has been more valued than that of women, it is natural that men would respond more suspiciously than women to alterations in status arrangements. In fact, many men have a pervasive sense of resentment as they see the social and economic gains of women as encroachments upon their own privileged status. While these apprehensions are real enough in a subjective sense, they do not correspond very well with objective reality. In fact, we are not yet witnessing the dissolution of Western "patriarchy," nor has there been any egregious diminution in the degree of male dominance in American society. At the lower and middle echelons of political, economic, and social control, men are sharing more of their functions with women than they have in the past, but there has been very little sharing at the top levels, and it is improbable that a woman will soon be president of the United States, General Motors, or the National Football League. Thus, the "symbolic" dominance of the male sex promises to be a factor for some time to come. Moveover, as discussed earlier, men stand to benefit from personal relationships with instrumentally competent women because of the potential contribution they can make to one's standard of living. It is also probable that, over the long run, the average man may discover that there are basic human benefits in not having one's self-esteem dependent upon compulsive assertions of dominance, ambition, initiative, and the other ulcer-producing prerogatives of traditional masculinity.

In summary the many changes discussed in this section have had a double-edged effect on the psychological state of men and women. Viewed from one perspective, the changes have ushered in a new era of sex differentiation, one which is full of obvious promise for women and somewhat less obvious (although potentially great) benefit to men. But, from another perspective, the changes have caused considerable psychological dislocation, leaving many people groping anxiously for new and acceptable criteria of sex identity. The sexes continue to differ in significant ways, even while their common humanity makes them essentially similar. However, it is no longer apparent to many people which differences and similarities are operative and which are not. As long as we are socialized to think that such considerations are central to personal identity, they shall continue to play a central role in human psychology.

General Preview of the Anthology

Questions about female identity seem to be the leading edge in the study of sex differences. An overview of research and theoretical writings, such as those sampled in the present anthology, suggests that the study of sex identity is primarily an outgrowth of the conceptual puzzles presented by femininity. Even a quick glance at the titles of the anthologized selections, particularly those in the psychoanalytic section, would seem to indicate that the question of femaleness is the paramount one. Yet, paradoxically enough, psychological and psychoanalytic theories of sex identity have difficulty fitting the findings on female development into their respective theoretical molds, while presenting males as rather straightforward and predictable objects of study. The theories want the two sexes to progress toward different developmental end states, but they also want them to follow parallel rules of development on the separate paths toward mature masculinity and femininity. Unfortunately, boys tend to follow the rules, while girls tend to create theoretical problems. The reason for this female recalcitrance may be that the major developmental theories, as inventions of men, tend to have a "phallocentric" bias. That is, although the theories often use females as the reference point for raising questions about sex-role development, they seem to look to males as the reference point for finding answers.

For example, in presenting cognitive-developmental theory, Kohlberg (1966) mentions more than once that girls do not fit the theory as well as boys do. He postulates that "positive self image" is one of three primary motivators for organization of one's sex identity. But Kohlberg is hard pressed to explain how girls actively decide to become feminine rather than masculine when his own findings indicate that girls view the male role as more powerful, prestigious, and competent than the female role. Thus he resorts to the rather weak argument that girls gravitate toward adult femininity because it is perceived as a superior status to childhood. Whatever else this resolution may suggest, it clearly suggests limited intelligence and judgment on the part of young girls.

Of course, it would be unfair to single out Kohlberg's cognitive-developmental theory as remarkable in this respect. The nature of female identity has mystified many other theorists, including G. Stanley Hall who wrote of woman that " ... her peculiar organs ... are hidden and their psychic reverberations are dim, less localized, more all pervasive" (see Hall selection). This rather lyrical admission of ignorance foreshadowed Erikson's concept of the key to femininity as hidden in an "inner space" and recalls Freud's more dramatic way of expressing his puzzlement when he referred to female sex identity as "a dark continent for psychology" (1926), and as "veiled in an impenetrable obscurity" (1905).

What seems to cause most theoretical concern is that young girls do not follow an unequivocally feminine developmental course, but incorporate decidedly masculine elements at various points in their sex-role development. This is usually viewed as a developmental anomaly or even as an indication of abnormality. It is precisely in this respect that some of the major theories betray a blind spot which fails to see that a developmental outcome so pervasive cannot, by definition, be viewed as anomalous. The theories, even while recognizing that there is a two-tier status system, do not seem to allow that girls also recognize this, and that they have an entirely natural desire to be first in status, like boys. Why should this be viewed as abnormal? Why shouldn't a person want for herself what she quite correctly perceives to be highly valued? One is tempted to suggest that a girl's rejection of the inferior status of "normal" femininity be viewed as *prima facie* evidence of normality, not abnormality.

Freud may have been speaking for all theorists who have lost their way in the conundrums of female development when he reportedly commented to a colleague, Marie Bonaparte: "The great question that has never been answered and which I have not yet been able to answer, despite my thirty years of research into the feminine soul is: What does a woman want?" (Jones, 1955, p. 468). If one might venture to offer a simple answer to a simple question: She probably wants what any person wants, a fair share of the best that life has to offer.

One might also want to paraphrase Freud to ask another question which no theorist has ever seriously raised: How is it that we know so well what men want? It is intriguing to speculate that the anatomical metaphor holds as much for males as it does for females. Just as the latter keep their "essence" hidden in the dim recesses of "inner space," the external genitalia of males may encourage many of us to assume that the essence of masculinity is readily observable, when in fact it is an exceedingly complex and variable phenomenon, and what we think we know about men may be only a fraction of what there is to know. While much of the research and scholarly literature on female identity is replete with stereotypic thinking, it is also characteristic of the literature that the authors feel constrained to justify their stereotypes, to qualify and equivocate, or even to resort to the camouflage of gracious language as a way of softening the impact of their conclusions.

What is equally interesting, however, is the casual and unabashed stereotyping of males in this literature. In discussing the nature of male identity, there is an implicit sureness to stating premises and a relative lack of ambivalence in drawing conclusions. It may be that the assignment to males of characteristics which are presumed to be dominant somehow excuses the offhanded stereotypy to which they are subjected. Males are viewed as assertive, competent, competitive, achieving, risk-taking, and invested in environmental mastery, among other things. All one has to do is look briefly at a random sample of his male acquaintances to realize that this is the stuff of legend and illusion. It certainly has little to do with most real men who live out their lives longing for love and approval, counting their major accomplishments on the fingers of one hand, and hedging all risks with a preoccupation with security. In fact, most discussions of masculinity appear to assume the existence of a denotable masculine ideal, and in this sense they resemble similarly oversimplified discussions of femininity. There is, however, one major difference. Masculinity is assigned a more highly valued status in theory and in reality, thus no apologies are extended to those men who cannot fit the ideal. Femininity is assigned a less valued status, thus excuses and benign puzzlement are offered to those women who refuse to accept their place.

These criticisms do not apply equally, of course, to all who have done scholarly work on sex differences. As a professional group, anthropologists are less ethnocentric than psychologists and psychoanalysts in their approach to sex differences. However, even anthropologists seem to find women more baffling than men. This is probably due to their predilection for those aspects of culture, e.g., government, technology, economics, and social organization, in which males tend to play more salient roles. Since most anthropologists are themselves male, they experience some difficulty in gaining access to local female informants. In many parts of the world people tend to suspect the intentions of a strange male who expresses an interest, however innocent, in observing the daily routines of local women. Ethologists are a different breed altogether since their focus is usually on infra-human subjects. Nevertheless, they are occasionally guilty of anthropomorphic and phallocentric excesses, particularly in their more popular attempts to use findings on animal behavior as a basis for understanding human nature.

Areas of Theoretical Consensus—In any event, despite the problems and limitations outlined above, and despite the different theoretical biases and professional affiliations of the anthologized authors, there seems to be *consensus* among them on the following points:

1. There are functional differences between the sexes.[2] That is, the sexes differ with respect to important aspects of behavior, world-view, preferences, expectations, attitudes, temperament, and/or character. It should be noted that there is also consensus that the sexes have many functional similarities.
2. Sex differences interact with age and/or developmental stage in life. Thus, the pattern of differences between the sexes varies from childhood, through adolescence and adulthood, to old age.
3. There are many males and females who are exceptions to one or more of the normative differences. In other words, functional sex differences are not as steadfast in reality as they

are in the ideal. They appear to be rather flexibily and situationally defined by nature, in both humans and infra-human species.

4. Most functional sex differences are an outgrowth of the interaction of nature with nurture. While some sex differences may be culturally determined and others entirely hereditary, the largest class of functional sex differences is traceable to complex interactions between these two factors.

5. In addition to sex differences in function, there are also sex differences in status, with males almost always being assigned more valued status than females. There are, of course, exotic and intriguing exceptions to this rule, but they are relatively rare.

6. The functional differences between the sexes are complex, multidimensional, and often difficult to understand. This is so despite a common human tendency to view them as simple, unidimensional, and self-evident.

Areas of Nonconsensus—There are also important areas of *nonconsensus* among the anthologized authors, which fall into these three categories:

1. There are differences of opinion on the relative contribution of biology and culture to the interactions which underlie functional sex differences. Some authorities assign a larger role to biological determinants such as heredity and hormonal balance, while others emphasize the influence of cultural factors. Moreover, among those of the culturalist persuasion, there are some who underscore universal cultural practice in the ascription of sex differences, and others who emphasize parochial differences among cultures.

2. There is little consensus on the balance between sex similarities and differences. Some authorities make it clear that they conceptualize sex differences as resting on a broad foundation of common human characteristics, while others perceive the sexes as more different than alike. Another dimension of nonconsensus lies in the balance among which sex differences *do* exist, which *could* exist, and which *should* exist. While the first set of differences usually reflects empirical findings, the second and third sets usually reflect speculations about the potential plasticity of sex differences or prescriptions for the "good society." Apparently social and behavioral scientists are as subject to these latter reflections as anyone else.

3. There is little consensus on the relation of sex differences to sex status. The question is: To what degree are functional differences attibutable to social status differences? Or, to put it in other words, if social status differences between the sexes were removed, which functional differences, if any, would remain?

In a field of study as complex as sex differences, it is inevitable that there would be major areas of nonconsensus. To some degree, these failures in consensus stem from the inherent intractibility of the subject matter itself. Sex differences simultaneously intrigue and confound those who would study them, regardless of disciplinary identification. In another sense, however, failures in consensus may be traceable to the respective natures of the various disciplines. Each discipline has its own bias, methodology, language, and particular way of viewing the universe of sex differences.

Psychoanalysis, for example, has attempted to formulate general laws of the interaction between gender anatomy and individual psychosexual development. Each child is viewed as having primitive sexual fantasies which are organized around differences in gender anatomy. The family is conceptualized as a social framework in which the child is encouraged to harness the energy associated with his or her fantasies and to direct it toward socially desirable ends. During one particularly critical period, commonly referred to as the "Oedipal Complex," boys and girls transform their claim on the opposite-sex parent into an identification with the same-sex parent. This transformation takes place according to two different formulas which, in turn, become the basis for the characteristic personality patterns which differentiate between the two sexes. Thus, psychoanalysis examines the interior, subjective processes of individual sex differentiation.

In rather sharp contrast to the psychoanalytic approach, anthropology focuses on the roles and functions assigned to the sexes by the societies in which they have membership. Each culture is viewed as inventing and maintaining a set of vehicles which define and regulate the interactions between the sexes. As mentioned earlier, these vehicles include prescribed courtship behaviors, marriage customs, kinship and/or family structure, and elaborate systems of division of labor. Within each vehicle the sexes are assigned roles which prescribe some functions while proscribing others. Each individual has to accommodate to these powerful cultural realities to be considered an acceptable member of the society in question.

Psychologists, for the most part, have had little interest in sexuality *per se*. Traditionally, they have focused on a broad spectrum of ways in which the sexes typically differ, including motivational factors like interests and preferences, emotional factors like temperament and stability, and ability factors like intelligence, aptitude, and sensory-motor skills. More recently psychologists, influenced by the social-role bias of anthropologists and the developmental bias of psychoanalysts, have constructed theories which describe the way in which sex-role differences develop as children grow up in a given societal context.

Unlike anthropology, psychoanalysis, and psychology, which are best understood as social sciences, ethology, as a branch of zoology, is one of the life sciences. Like the others, however, its focus is on behavior and its primary methodological tool is direct observation. In a sense ethology stands as a bridge between the social and life sciences. When Niko Tinbergen observes the behavior and habits of seagulls, it is much like Bronislaw Malinowski observing the customs of the Trobriand Islanders. A Tinbergen may use field glasses and a Malinowski may use interview techniques, but, at bottom, both observe their subjects. However, they differ markedly in the way they conceptually organize their observations. Ethologists use evolutionary theory as their conceptual framework, while anthropologists organize their data in terms of a theory of culture, and psychologists and psychoanalysts use theories of individual human development. For the ethologist humankind is only one of many species, and its characteristic patterns of behavior, including those which differ between the sexes, are viewed as outcomes of the evolutionary process. Thus, sex differentiated human behavior is explained according to the same broad principles of behavioral evolution as is that of nonhuman species.

Given these differences in emphasis, methodology, and theoretical frame of reference, it is to be expected that the separate disciplines would have difficulty in coordinating their findings and biases. The full study of sex differences will not be accomplished until a basis for cross-disciplinary communication is found. At present there is no agreement on what that basis should be, but one promising possibility may lie in the notion of sex differences as a patterned phenomenon.

Sex Differences as a Patterned Phenomenon

Functional sex differences in humans are an extremely complex phenomenon. They constitute a *pattern* of shifting valences and tendencies, and the manifest shape of the pattern at any given time and place is a function of the three macro-dimensions of culture, history, and biology and the two micro-dimensions of individual psychology and interpersonal relations. In trying to understand the nature of sex differences, it is important to recognize that they do not occur in isolation, but that they are embedded in a patterned context and have functional meaning only in terms of that context. Sex differences are not a collection of unrelated facts, but are integrated into meaningful configurations by the interplay of these five dimensions.

Culture, the first macro-dimension, establishes norms of acceptable sex-typed behavior and how these interact with the behavioral norms of other societal statuses, e.g., age status, social class status, and status in the family or kinship network. These norms and their patterns of interaction appear to be quite variable from culture to culture, although there are some norms which tend to hold cross-culturally. Even these latter, however, have different *subjective* meanings in different cultures, despite *overt* cross-cultural similarities.

The history of a given cultural group is a second macro-dimension of sex differences. History describes the sequence and substance of economic transformations, changes in technology, the fusing and splitting of cultural groups, patterns of migration, the growth and ebb of ideology, and the rise, decline, and occasional renaissance of means of social organization. Each of these factors has profound influence on the nature of functional sex differences. Examples of the influence of such factors were presented earlier in the discussion of changes in technology, economics, family structure, and marriage customs.

Biologically, sex differences are an outgrowth of modal genetic and hormonal distinctions between the genders. There is a multipotentiality to human biology and a freedom from fixed instinct unknown in other species. Lorenz (1970) refers to this specifically human characteristic as biological "openness." Whatever basic sex differences are emphasized by a particular culture are, of course, biologically given. But in a multipotential species, there are many givens, and which sex differences people adopt are not so much a matter of what is given as it is a choice among the available range of givens. This is not to imply that the choice is always a free one. On the contrary, original cultural choices are usually constrained by ecological realities, and, as human ecology changes, the choices also change, although often at different rates.

In thinking about the interaction of the macro-dimensions of culture and biology, one is often biased toward unidirectional causal formulations such that biology is seen as the cause and limiting condition of culture. However, the converse is as fundamental, for culture is also a determinant and limiting condition of the specific forms human biology takes. In the multipotential human species, culture realizes some sex differences and suppresses others. To a marked degree, mature human biological status is shaped by the work of culture on immature human biology. Thus the two dimensions, through reciprocal interaction, jointly shape the range of sex differences tolerable within a given human society.

At the psychological level, individual development is the key axis of sex identity. Early in life the primal structure of sex identity is laid down in crude, global, and (usually) gender-specific terms. This primary structure is variously referred to as basic "sex-role orientation" (Biller, 1971), "gender identity" (Kohlberg, 1966), or "core gender identity" (Stoller, 1964). It sets the fundamental direction to sex-role development and contributes consistency, stability, and continuity to one's personal pattern of sex-linked characteristics. Subsequent development involves the accumlation of sex-typed behaviors, preferences, and knowledge which become less basic and more dispensable to the degree that the timing of their acquisition is removed from the organization of early structure. These later developmental events allow for situational flexibility and accommodation to trends, fashion, and other pressures for change encountered in adult life.

However, to the best of our knowledge, they usually do not substantially influence one's *basic* sex identity.

A second key factor in the psychological patterning of sex-typed characteristics is one's personal mix of masculine and feminine characteristics. This mix is usually biased toward one identity, but it is very rare that it does not include strong secondary elements of the other identity. Cutting across all levels of individual development is a profile of psychosexual androgyny consisting of male- and female-typed elements which are in some instances synthesized, in others simply coexisting, and in others rigidly compartmentalized within the same person. Again, the basic profile and style of one's personal androgyny is laid down early in life, while subsequent development simultaneously modifies it and is shaped by it.

Modes of social interaction between the sexes is another dimension which contributes immeasureably to the patterning of sex differences. For this reason, continuity in culturally sanctioned vehicles for sex interaction such as courtship practices, marriage customs, and family structure tend to contribute to the stability of sex differences. Changes in these traditional practices and the introduction of new vehicles for sex interaction result in commensurate modifications in functional sex differences. In the present anthology, for example, we have included a selection in which the anthropologist Bronislaw Malinowski describes the family structure of Trobriand Islanders. In another selection the ethologist Konrad Lorenz describes the courtship behavior of Jackdaw birds. What both descriptions have in common is that they depict how the respective species have established patterns of reciprocal and complementary behavior between the sexes. It is inconceivable that functional sex differences in either humans or birds could be understood outside the context provided by these vehicles of interaction.

Finally, it is characteristic of human beings that they relate subjectively to the world. The several dimensions of culture, history, biology, psychology, and interpersonal relations are synthesized at the level of conscious awareness and action. One's personal organization of the contributing elements of sex identity is part of the process of constructing one's self. It is also integral to the ongoing process of finding meaning in one's existence. The resulting pattern is a subjective awareness, above everything else, of who one is as a man or woman occupying a moving place in evolution, history, and culture. In rare moments, it transcends sex identity and becomes an awareness of who one is as a person.

FOOTNOTES

1. Facts and figures cited here and in the following paragraphs are taken from recent official reports of the Women's Bureau of the U.S. Department of Labor and the Census Bureau of the U. S. Department of Commerce.

2. The term "functional" is used here as referring to those sex differences which are not specifically anatomical or physiological in nature. Sex differences in achievement motivation, for example, would be functional. Differences in size are anatomical. Differences in reproductive and childbearing roles are physiological.

REFERENCES

Biller, H.B. *Father, Child, and Sex Role.* Lexington, Massachusetts: Heath Lexington Books, 1971.

Freud, S. "Three Essays on the Theory of Sexuality" (1905). In the *Standard Edition of the Complete Psychological Works of Sigmund Freud,* Volume 7, London: Hogarth Press, 1961, p. 151.

Freud, S. "The Question of Lay Analysis" (1926). In the *Standard Edition of the Complete Psychological Works of Sigmund Freud,* Volume 20, London: Hogarth Press, 1959, p. 212.

Jones, E. *Sigmund Freud: Life and Work,* Volume 2, London: Hogarth Press, 1955.

Kohlberg, L. "A Cognitive-Developmental Analysis of Children's Sex-Role Concepts and Attitudes." In E. E. Maccoby (Ed.) *The Development of Sex Differences.* Stanford: Stanford University Press, 1966.

Lorenz, K. *Studies in Animal and Human Behavior* (Vol. 2). Cambridge, Massachusetts: Harvard University Press, 1970.

Neugarten, B. L., & Datan, N. "Sociological Perspectives on the Life Cycle." In P. B. Baltes & K. W. Schaie (Eds.) *Life-Span Developmental Psychology: Personality and Socialization.* New York: Academic Press, 1973.

Stoller, R. "A Contribution to the Study of Gender Identity." *International Journal of Psychoanalysis,* 1964, *45,* pp. 220-225.

PART ONE

THE PSYCHOANALYTIC DIMENSION

PSYCHOANALYSIS AND SEX DIFFERENCES:
FREUD AND BEYOND FREUD

Robert Sussman Stewart

This introduction is an attempt to trace the evolution of Freud's sexual theories and to see them in relation to his views on the differences between the sexes. That he came to these views from a number of different directions, that he continually re-examined and revised them, and that they led to one of the most heated controversies in the history of the psychoanalytic movement, may explain the nature of the task here and, at least in part, anticipate its complexities.

The First Model: Parallelism and the Oedipus Complex

Freud first outlined his model of the differences between the sexes in the 1905 Edition of *Three Essays on the Theory of Sexuality,* the work which inaugurated his discoveries of childhood psychosexual development and, the cornerstone of his whole framework, the Oedipus Complex. What had drawn him to these discoveries is a difficult issue, one which takes in both the derivation of his libido theory and the completion of his self-analysis. It is, however, clear and relevant that he first understood the Oedipal configuration in the *life of the boy*—in the boy's intense attachment to his mother, out of which came the two most critical determinants of individual development and cultural evolution: the fear of the rival father as castrator and the incest taboo.

There was from the outset, therefore, the "problem" of female sexual development. For if the contest with the father over the mother becomes the driving force in the boy, what is the equivalent in the girl? Freud recognized this difficulty and commented in the *Three Essays* (1905, p. 151) that psychosexual development in men was more accessible to research than that in women, which for him, at that time, still remained "veiled in impenetrable obscurity." The solution he offered, and which he maintained for almost fifteen years, was the solution of "parallelism." He saw the development in boys and in girls as strictly analogous—"the son being drawn towards his mother, the daughter towards her father" (1905, p. 227). Freud knew this to be at best a tentative resolution, but it had the virtue of leaving intact the Oedipus Complex which was, above all else, essential for him.

Yet the problem did not disappear; if anything, it intensified. Although he did not focus on female sexuality as such until the 1920s, he made a number of revisions in the *Three Essays,* taking into account new clinical evidence and the expansion of the theory of psychosexual development to include the pre-Oedipal stages, in particular the "oral" and "anal" stages. Since these pre-Oeidpal stages implied a libidinal attachment to the mother in *both* boys and girls, the "neat parallelism" (his term) would not hold and a new model was needed. As a basis for this new model, Freud postulated the libido itself as "invariably and necessarily of a *masculine nature* (emphasis added), whether it occurs in men or in women and irrespective of whether its object is a man or a woman" (1905, p. 219). This reconceptualization lay behind his major revisions in the theory of sex differences and was published in three papers in the early twenties: "The Infantile Genital Organization" (1923), "The Dissolution of the Oedipus Complex" (1924), and, most critical and central, "Some Psychical Consequences of the Anatomical Distinction Between the Sexes" (1925).

The Second Model: Penis Envy and Anatomical Distinctions

The distinction Freud drew in these new papers was between the nature of adult sexuality and its precursors in childhood, the difference consisting in the fact that for children "only one genital, namely the male one, comes into account. What is present, therefore, is not a primacy of the genitals, but a primacy of the *phallus*" (1923, p. 142). This phallic primacy led Freud to the most controversial of all his notions—that of "penis envy" in girls. If at first both boys and girls think of themselves as similar, then the awareness of the "anatomical distinction" sets off the whole course of differentiation. For the boy, the discovery that the girl has no penis leads to intense castration anxiety—for he must assume that the girl once did have a penis. For the girl, the discovery that the boy has a penis triggers an intense desire to have one herself, a desire which shapes the future of her female development.

There are two considerations here: What led Freud to this concept of penis envy in the first place, and what did he expect to accomplish by it? The answers bring us back to fundamental Oedipal theory. As Freud came to recognize (and here the work of his colleagues becomes crucial to his own theoretical development) the "Oedipus Complex (in little girls) raises one problem more than in boys" (1925, p. 251). The problem is the pre-Oedipal fact that for both boys and girls the mother is the original love object. If the girl takes her mother as a love object, does this not raise serious objections to the basic notion of the love of the parent of the opposite sex?

Freud's way out of this dilemma was to "masculinize" the girl: if she loves her mother, then it is as a boy that she does so. In support of this formulation, Freud saw the girl's "leading erotogenic zone" as located in the clitoris and homologous to the masculine zone of the penis. It is only with the awareness of not having a penis, and with the castration anxiety and penis envy that this awareness gives rise to, that the girl starts the long, complex process of "feminization." She renounces her clitoris, which she sees as inferior, and becomes jealous of her father, while finding herself at the same time attracted to him and to the idea of having his baby, which also means having his phallus. The wish to have a baby moves the girl from her masculine "active" position to her feminine "passive" one, a shift that culminates in the "transfer" of sexual satisfactions from clitoral to vaginal ones.

Freud clearly understood this to be the most difficult task of female sexual development. Failure to accomplish this task accounted for a wide range of conflict and psychopathology in women which he enumerated in his descriptions of female jealousy, passivity, masochism, and narcissism. (According to Freud, the "wound" to a woman's narcissism is at the root of her sense of inferiority.) Yet if these reactions can be resolved—if castration anxiety can move the girl *into* her Oedipus Complex in the way that it moves the boy *out* of his—then the girl can develop into a healthy, normal "feminine" woman.

Critics of Freud and Revisionist Views

The work of a number of colleagues, most of them women, brought Freud to abandon the "neat parallelism" and to revise his views on female sexuality. First of these was Helene Deutsch, trained by Freud and, from the start of her career, a pioneer in feminine psychology. (She was subsequently joined by other pupils of his, namely, Ruth Mack Brunswick, Jeanne Lampl-de Groot, and Marie Bonaparte.) Deutsch investigated the development of women through the whole of their life-cycle, from infancy to old age. She made special studies of homosexuality in women, of masochism, and of the relationship of the reproductive cycle to female psychosexual development.

In doing so, she discovered female sexuality to be far more complex than male sexuality. In that sense, it can be said that she verified Freud's earlier claim of "impenetrable obscurity." At the same time, her investigations produced significant gains and she brought the development of female sexuality to the center of psychoanalytic discussion. In one of her papers presented before the Vienna Psychoanalytic Society she introduced the idea of the "extra step" the girl has to take in the formation of the Oedipus Complex: the renunciation of the mother and transfer to the father. Deutsch was also the first to consider the concept of motherhood as a specific function of female sexuality. In the paper which follows here, she makes a detailed study of the "split" in women between the image of themselves as motherly and creative (the madonna complex) and as sexual and unchaste (the prostitute complex)—a division which she saw as central to some of the most intense conflicts in female sexual development.

Even more extensive than Deutsch's revisions were those proposed in a series of papers written in the 1920s by Karen Horney. Trained under Karl Abraham in Berlin, Horney followed Abraham's focus on the earliest object relations of the pre-Oedipal period. Yet her main concern was not with the development of internalized object theory, but with external "life conditions" which mold the character. For her, the disturbances in human relationships became the crucial agent in the genesis of neurosis. The paper included here, "The Flight from Womanhood," makes clear her interest in cultural factors and indicates her debt to Georg Simmel, whose concept of "social interaction" led her to consider, from the perspective of psychoanalysis, the view that the "whole civilization is a masculine civilization."

Applying this view to Freud himself, she writes: "Psychoanalysis is the creation of a male genius, and almost all those who have developed his ideas have been men. It is only reasonable that they should evolve more easily a *masculine psychology* (emphasis added) and understand more of the development of men than of women." In such a "masculine civilization," according to Horney, women have adapted themselves to the wishes of men and have felt as if their adaptation were "their true nature." She attributed the concept of "penis envy" to the self-evident view of masculine narcissism: "that one half of the human race is discontented with the sex assigned to it and can overcome this discontent only in favorable circumstances ... is decidedly unsatisfactory not only to feminine narcissism but also to biological science."

Horney did not totally deny penis envy in girls; but rather, she gave it a different emphasis, saw it more in relation to the real world, to the girl's sense of her smallness, her inability to see her "hidden" genital (while she could clearly see the boy's penis when he was urinating). In short, she ascribed penis envy to the little girl's actual situation, to the functions of her body rather than to the phantasy of "castration," of having "lost" something. Horney also found clinical evidence to support the theory of the girl's identification with the father, an identification that starts early and in a *womanly* way, not in the masculine way described by Freud. "We can see," she remarks, "that penis envy by no means precludes a deep and wholly womanly attachment to the father." Horney, along with Deutsch, also attributed considerable importance to the role of motherhood in the differences between the sexes. In her view, there is a "blissful consciousness" in birth and motherhood denied to men. "From the biological point of view, woman has in motherhood, or in the capacity for motherhood, a quite indisputable and by no means negligible physiological superiority." Claims for this superiority can be found in the boy's intense envy of motherhood, and with it, envy of pregnancy, of childbirth, of the maternal breasts and suckling. From this line of reasoning she concluded that it is *men who envy women* and not women men, a complete reversal of the Freudian formulation. In the sense that there is a "flight from womanhood," Horney visualized it as a secondary reaction, as a reaction against the little girl's real fear of the adult man, of his big organ, of the dangers of vaginal penetration—dangers reinforced by "male" cultural domination. For her the ultimate goal, which in the end led her to break with Freud, was to "get beyond the subjectivity of the masculine," to "obtain a picture of the mental development of woman that will be more true to the facts of her nature—with its specific qualities and its differences from that of man—than any we have hitherto achieved."

Sex Differences and Early Object Relations

The most extreme reconceptualization of Freud's views emerges in the work of Melanie Klein. She located the source of conflict and development in the earliest years of life—in the first and second year—and moved all of the psychosexual stages (oral, anal, phallic, Oedipal) backward in time to infancy, giving them a new complexity and tying them to the intense attachment to the mother. Like Horney, she did not see the girl as primarily masculine; yet her view was less reality-oriented, focused as it was almost exclusively on internal phantasy life and internalized object relations. Her notion of "splitting" led to the inner image of "good" mother and "bad" mother, an idea which for her had enormous influences on sexual development and differentiation. To this early "splitting," Klein added the notion of infantile guilt reactions, connected to the child's ambivalence, oral and anal-sadistic phantasies and fears of retaliation. The whole internalized struggle centers in both sexes around the mother and takes place in what she described as the "femininity phase." In boys, there is the fear of the mother, the wish to appropriate the contents of her body, the envy of her breasts and of her milk. For Klein, the primary castrating figure is not the father, as it was for Freud, but the mother. Her view of "masculine superiority" closely resembles Horney's. She sees it as a reaction against the boy's identification with his mother, a female identification leading to the boy's "narcissistic over-estimation of the penis." Here again, we have a reversal of Freud's primary phallocentric model. Klein also agreed with Deutsch's view that the girl's genital development is shaped more by oral libido and mothering features than by a renunciation of the clitoris. In addition, she found evidence of early vaginal sensations which initiate the first turning toward the father and toward receptivity, the "taking in" of the penis which she saw as an *active* striving rather than a passive one.

Ego Identity and the Structure of the Self

More recent psychoanalytic views have focused on ego development rather than on instinctual demand, a transformation which attempts to make psychoanalysis a general psychology. Among the most influential of those who have moved in this direction toward an "ego psychology" have been Heinz Hartmann, David Rappaport, and Erik Erikson. Erikson in particular has focused on the nature and functions of the ego and its participation in the formation of a sense of continuous personal "identity." For Erikson, it became clear that one could not speak of "life history" without speaking of history in general. This notion led him to see the whole of the human life-cycle "interwoven throughout" with the life-cycle of the community. He expanded Freud's psychosexual stages of development into "psychosocial" ones. In his view, for example, the oral phase is not organized solely around the infant's "taking," but also around the mother's "giving," so that inner needs must be examined in relation to social realities.

Erikson's focus on identity and "identity crisis" (the failure to form a stable identity) rarely included considerations of sex differences. The one exception came in an empirical study he conducted in 1950 at the University of California on pre-adolescent boys and girls. The children were asked to arrange toy figures and blocks on a table into "an exciting scene from an imaginary moving picture." It was evident to Erikson from the arrangements these children made that there was a direct relation to their sex, for almost invariably, the boys built towers and facades with protrusions, the girls interior scenes or simple enclosures. In short, as he reports in the selection here, the boys emphasized "outer space" and the girls "inner space." It seemed, to Erikson's admitted "surprise," that Freud's "anatomical distinctions" had reasserted themselves. Erikson now had to ask himself again about the contributions of culture. If the sexes *did* experience themselves according to the "groundplan of their bodies," could it be said, after all, that "anatomy is destiny?" His answer is that it *is* destiny, but a destiny that can be modified by the adaptive potentialities of outer and inner space. The use the woman makes of her "inwardness" is the measure of the interaction between her personal history and her cultural history.

A complete reassessment of the whole issue of female sexuality in relation to sex differences is the focus of the paper by William H. Gillespie, one of England's leading psychoanalysts. In what he calls his "jump forward of seventy years," he offers an overview of Freud's earliest findings, the controversies with both Horney and Klein, and, most relevant of all, ends with some comments on the issue of sex differences in the light of current research in physiology. He gives particular attention to the work of Masters and Johnson, which, when it appeared in 1966, introduced many new biophysiological findings about female sexuality. The most important of these centered on the nature of the female orgasm and the evidence revealed that with maturation, the erotogenic zone of the lower third of the vagina does not supplant the clitoral zone, but rather combines with the entire clitoral-labial complex into a "single functional structure." In short, Masters and Johnson seem to have invalidated Freud's "transfer" theory of clitoral gratification as distinct from vaginal gratification. According to the new research, the female orgasm must be seen as a complicated but *unified* response.

Gillespie also mentions the work of Mary Jane Sherfey, who, though she supports Masters and Johnson, maintains that the clitoris is still the "indispensible initiator" of orgasmic reaction, a view closer to Freud's original conception. Gillespie's final discussion addresses itself to the women's movement in relation to Freud's ideas, and though he agrees that Freud's sexual theories can be used to support feminist arguments, he does not himself offer any final judgment. His discussion moves instead toward some of the latest work in phylogenetics. He cites a study by Werner Kemper (1965) which points to the "more complex" development of females in their reporoductive roles. In the evolution from water to land animals, it was the female who had to acquire internal sexual organs, a long and difficult process which may in the end account for the more complicated nature of female sexuality. Perhaps it is not so much "envy" of the man that explains female sexuality as it is the "unfair share" in the reproductive process which evolution has imposed on the female of the species.

Although the future course of the psychoanalytic theory of sex differences is yet to be charted, it seems likely that the current interest in the concepts of narcissism and in the early formation of the structure of the self, may offer some usable formulations. If the emphasis on "self-representations" that Edith Jacobson introduces in *The Self and the Object World* (1964), or Heinz Kohut's notion of the "cohesive self" in *The Analysis of the Self* (1971), come to be understood in their proper context, then the issue of sex differences may recast itself as the issue of individual differences, an issue of self-integration and of a sense of the self as intact. Perhaps then the anatomical distinctions of traditional psychoanalytic theory can be replaced by newer theory and by the distinctions between unified and fractionated selves, whether male or female.

References

Freud, S. "Three Essays on the Theory of Sexuality" (1905). *Standard Edition of the Complete Psychological Works of Sigmund* Freud, Volume 7, London: Hogarth Press, 1961.

Freud, S. "The Infantile Genital Organization" (1923). *Standard Edition of the Complete Psychological Works of Sigmund Freud*, Volume 19, London: Hogarth Press, 1961.

Freud, S. "The Dissolution of the Oedipus Complex" (1924). *Standard Edition of the Complete Psychological Works of Sigmund Freud.* Volume 19, London: Hogarth Press, 1961.

Jacobson, E. *The Self and the Object World.* New York: International Universities Press, 1964.

Kohut, H. *The Analysis of the Self.* New York: International Universities Press, 1971.

Kemper, W. W. *"Neue Beiträge aus der Phylogenese zur Bio-Psychologie der Frau"* (1965). Zentralblatt Psychosomatic Med. 11, pp. 77-82.

Masters, W. H. & Johnson, V. E. *Human Sexual Response,* Boston, Massachusetts: Little, Brown & Co., 1966.

Sherfey, M. J. "The Evolution and Nature of Female Sexuality in Relation to Psychoanalytic Theory." In *Journal of the American Psychoanalytic Association,* 1966, 14, pp. 28-128.

Some Psychical Consequences of the Anatomical Distinction Between the Sexes

Sigmund Freud

*The concise theoretical discussion which follows offers Freud's
most thorough examination of the differences between the sexes.
He takes up here all of the so-called classical formulations he had
outlined in the 1905 edition of* Three Essays on the Theory of
Sexuality, *which were now in need of considerable revision. In the
earlier work, he had anchored the difference between the sexes to
the formation of the Oedipus complex, with the development in
males and females as analogous–"the son being drawn to his
mother, the daughter toward her father." Yet in the decades
which intervened he recognized that this "neat parallelism" did
not hold. "For little girls," he writes below, "the Oedipus complex
raises one problem more than in little boys." Like boys, little girls
also find their original love object in the mother and must, therefore, "shift" from her toward the father. To account for this pre-
Oedipal variation he proposed the "anatomical distinction" of the
present paper, describing both boys and girls as first active and
"masculine"–the girl's investment in the clitoris equal to the boy's
investment in the penis. It is in this so-called "phallic phase" that
children discover one sex lacks a penis, an observation which in
both sexes sets off the whole process of sexual differentiation. According to Freud, it leads to the universal "threat of castration"
for the boy and to "envy of the penis" for the girl. Out of envy, the
girl then transfers her affections to her father, wishes to have his
penis and his baby—a process of "feminization" which is not completed until adolescence with the abandonment of clitoral satisfactions for vaginal ones. Among Freud's most controversial ideas,
these views on female sexual development led to the "great debate"
within psychoanalysis which started in the 1920s and continues to
this day.*

I n my own writings and in those of my followers more and more stress is laid on the necessity that the analyses of neurotics shall deal thoroughly with the remotest period of their childhood, the time of the early efflorescence of sexual life. It is only by examining the first manifestations of the patient's innate instinctual constitution and the effects of his earliest experiences that we can accurately gauge the motive forces that have led to his neurosis and can be secure against the errors into which we might be tempted by the degree to which things have become remodelled and overlaid in adult life. This requirement is not only of theoretical but also of practical importance, for it distinguishes our efforts from the work of those physicians whose interests are focused exclusively on therapeutic results and who employ analytic methods, but only up to a certain point. An analysis of early childhood such as we are considering is tedious and laborious and makes demands both upon the physician and upon the patient which cannot always be met. Moreover, it leads us into dark regions where there are as yet no signposts. Indeed, analysts may feel reassured, I think, that there is no risk of their work becoming mechanical, and so of losing its interest, during the next few decades.

In the following pages I bring forward some findings of analytic research which would be of great importance if they could be proved to apply universally. Why do I not postpone publication of them until further experience has given me the necessary proof, if such proof is obtainable? Because the conditions under which I work have undergone a change, with implications which I cannot disguise. Formerly, I was not one of those who are unable to hold back what seems to be a new discovery until it has been either confirmed or corrected. My *Interpretation of Dreams* (1900) and my "Fragment of an Analysis of a Case of Hysteria" (1905) (the case of Dora) were suppressed by me—if not for the nine years enjoined by Horace—at all events for four or five years before I allowed them to be published. But in those days I had unlimited time before me—"oceans of time" as an amiable author puts it—and material poured in upon me in such quantities that fresh experiences were hardly to be escaped. Moreover, I was the only worker in a new field, so that my reticence involved no danger to myself and no loss to others.

But now everything has changed. The time before me is limited. The whole of it is no longer spent in working, so that my opportunities for making fresh observations are not so numerous. If I think I see something new, I am uncertain whether I can wait for it to be confirmed. And further, everything that is to be seen upon the surface has already been exhausted; what remains has to be slowly and laboriously dragged up from the depths. Finally, I am no longer alone. An eager crowd of fellow-workers is ready to make use of what is unfinished or doubtful, and I can leave to them that part of the work which I should otherwise have done myself. On this occasion, therefore, I feel justified in publishing something which stands in urgent need of confirmation before its value or lack of value can be decided.

In examining the earliest mental shapes assumed by the sexual life of children we have been in the habit of taking as the subject of our investigations the male child, the little boy. With little girls, so we have supposed, things must be similar, though in some way or other they must nevertheless be different. The point in development at which this difference lay could not be clearly determined.

In boys the situation of the Oedipus complex is the first stage that can be recognized with certainty. It is easy to understand, because at that stage a child retains the same object which he previously cathected with his libido—not as yet a genital one—during the preceding period while he was being suckled and nursed. The fact, too, that in this situation he regards his father as a disturbing rival and would like to get rid of him and take his place is a straightforward consequence of the actual state of affairs. I have shown elsewhere[1] how the Oedipus attitude in little boys belongs to the phallic phase, and how its destruction is brought about by the fear of castration—that is, by narcissistic interest in their genitals. The matter is made more difficult to grasp by the complicating circumstance that even in boys the Oedipus complex has a double orientation, active and passive, in accordance with their bisexual constitution; a boy also wants to take his *mother's* place as the love-object of his *father*—a fact which we describe as the feminine attitude.

As regards the prehistory of the Oedipus complex in boys we

are far from complete clarity. We know that that period includes an identification of an affectionate sort with the boy's father, an identification which is still free from any sense of rivalry in regard to his mother. Another element of that stage is invariably, I believe, a masturbatory activity in connection with the genitals, the masturbation of early childhood, the more or less violent suppression of which by those in charge of the child sets the castration complex in action. It is to be assumed that this masturbation is attached to the Oedipus complex and serves as a discharge for the sexual excitation belonging to it. It is, however, uncertain whether the masturbation has this character from the first, or whether on the contrary it makes its first appearance spontaneously as an activity of a bodily organ and is only brought into relation with the Oedipus complex at some later date; this second possibility is by far the more probable. Another doubtful question is the part played by bed-wetting and by the breaking of that habit through the intervention of training measures. We are inclined to make the simple connection that continued bed-wetting is a result of masturbation and that its suppression is regarded by boys as an inhibition of their genital activity—that is, as having the meaning of a threat of castration; but whether we are always right in supposing this remains to be seen. Finally, analysis shows us in a shadowy way how the fact of a child at a very early age listening to his parents copulating may set up his first sexual excitation, and how that event may, owing to its after-effects, act as a starting-point for the child's whole sexual development. Masturbation, as well as the two attitudes in the Oedipus complex, later on become attached to this early experience, the child having subsequently interpreted its meaning. It is impossible, however, to suppose that these observations of coitus are of universal occurrence, so that at this point we are faced with the problem of "primal phantasies."[2] Thus the prehistory of the Oedipus complex, even in boys, raises all of these questions for sifting and explanation; and there is the further problem of whether we are to suppose that the process invariably follows the same course, or whether a great variety of different preliminary stages may not converge upon the same terminal situation.

In little girls the Oedipus complex raises one problem more than in boys. In both cases the mother is the original object; and there is no cause for surprise that boys retain that object in the Oedipus complex. But how does it happen that girls abandon it and instead take their father as an object? In pursuing this question I have been able to reach some conclusions which may throw light precisely on the prehistory of the Oedipus relation in girls.

Every analyst has come across certain women who cling with especial intensity and tenacity to the bond with their father and to the wish in which it culminates of having a child by him. We have good reason to suppose that the same wishful phantasy was also the motive force of their infantile masturbation, and it is easy to form an impression that at this point we have been brought up against an elementary and unanalysable fact of infantile sexual life. But a thorough analysis of these very cases brings something different to light—namely, that here the Oedipus complex has a long prehistory and is in some respects a secondary formation.

The old paediatrician Lindner [1897] once remarked that a child discovers the genital zones (the penis or the clitoris) as a source of pleasure while indulging in sensual sucking (thumb-sucking).[3] I shall leave it an open question whether it is really true that the child takes the newly found source of pleasure in exchange for the recent loss of the mother's nipple—a possibility to which later phantasies (fellatio) seem to point. Be that as it may, the genital zone is discovered at some time or other, and there seems no justification for attributing any physical content to the first activities in connection with it. But the first step in the phallic phase which begins in this way is not the linking-up of the masturbation with the object-cathexes of the Oedipus complex, but a momentous discovery which little girls are destined to make. They notice the penis of a brother or playmate, strikingly visible and of large proportions, at once recognize it as the superior counterpart of their own small and inconspicuous organ, and from that time forward fall a victim to envy for the penis.

There is an interesting contrast between the behaviour of the two sexes. In the analogous situation, when a little boy first catches sight of a girl's genital region, he begins by showing irresolution and lack of interest; he sees nothing or disavows what he has seen, he softens it down or looks about for expedients for bringing it into line with his expectations. It is not until later, when some threat of castration has obtained a hold upon him, that the observation becomes important to him: if he then recollects or repeats it, it arouses a terrible storm of emotion in him and forces him to believe in the reality of the threat which he has hitherto laughed at. This combination of circumstances leads to two reactions, which may become fixed and will in that case, whether separately or together or in conjunction with other factors, permanently determine the boy's relations to women: horror of the mutilated creature or triumphant contempt for her. These developments, however, belong to the future, though not to a very remote one.

A little girl behaves differently. She makes her judgement and her decision in a flash. She has seen it and knows that she is without it and wants to have it.[4]

Here what has been named the masculinity complex of women branches off. It may put great difficulties in the way of their regular development towards femininity, if it cannot be got over soon enough. The hope of some day obtaining a penis in spite of everything and so of becoming like a man may persist to an incredibly late age and may become a motive for strange and otherwise unaccountable actions. Or again, a process may set in which I should like to call a "disavowal," a process which in the mental life of children seems neither uncommon nor very dangerous but which in an adult would mean the beginning of a psychosis. Thus a girl may refuse to accept the fact of being castrated, may harden herself in the conviction that she *does* possess a penis, and may subsequently be compelled to behave as though she were a man.

The psychical consequences of envy for the penis, in so far as it does not become absorbed in the reaction-formation of the masculinity complex, are various and far-reaching. After a woman has become aware of the wound to her narcissism, she develops, like a scar, a sense of inferiority. When she has passed beyond her first attempt at explaining her lack of a penis as being a punishment personal to herself and has realized that that sexual character is a universal one, she begins to share the contempt felt by men for a sex which is the lesser in so important a respect, and, at least in holding that opinion, insists on being like a man.[5]

Even after penis-envy has abandoned its true object, it continues to exist: by an easy displacement it persists in the character-trait of *jealousy*. Of course, jealousy is not limited to one sex and has a wider foundation than this, but I am of opinion that it plays a far larger part in the mental life of women than of men and that that is because it is enormously reinforced from the direction of displaced penis-envy. While I was still unaware of this source of jealousy and was considering the phantasy "a child is being beaten," which occurs so commonly in girls, I constructed a first phase for it in which its meaning was that another child, a rival of whom the subject was jealous, was to be beaten.[6] This phantasy seems to be a relic of the phallic period in girls. The peculiar rigidity which struck me so much in the monotonous formula "a child is being beaten" can probably be interpreted in a special way. The child which is being beaten (or caressed) may ultimately be nothing more nor less than the clitoris itself, so that at its very lowest level the statement will contain a confession of masturbation, which has remained attached to the content of the formula from its beginning in the phallic phase till later life.

A third consequence of penis-envy seems to be a loosening of the girl's relation with her mother as a love-object. The situation as a whole is not very clear, but it can be seen that in the end the girl's mother, who sent her into the world so insufficiently equipped, is almost always held responsible for her lack of a penis. The way in which this comes about historically is often that soon after the girl has discovered that her genitals are unsatisfactory she begins to show jealousy of another child on the ground that her mother is fonder of her, which serves as a reason for her giving up her affectionate relation to her mother. It will fit in with this if the child which has been preferred by her mother is made into the first object of the beating-phantasy which ends in masturbation.

There is yet another surprising effect of penis-envy, or of the discovery of the inferiority of the clitoris, which is undoubtedly the most important of all. In the past I had often formed an impression that in general women tolerate masturbation worse than men, that they more frequently fight against it and that they are unable to make use of it in circumstances in which a man would seize upon it as a way of escape without any hesitation. Experience would no doubt elicit innumerable exceptions to this statement, if we attempted to turn it into a rule. The reactions of human individuals of both sexes are of course made up of masculine and feminine traits. But it appeared to me nevertheless as though masturbation were further removed from the nature of women than of men, and the solution of the problem could be assisted by the reflection that masturbation, at all events of the clitoris, is a masculine activity and that the elimination of clitoridal sexuality is a necessary precondition for the development of femininity. Analyses of the remote phallic period have now taught me that in girls, soon after the first signs of penis-envy, an intense current of feeling against masturbation makes its appearance, which cannot be attributed exclusively to the educational influence of those in charge of the child. This impulse is clearly a forerunner of the wave of repression which at puberty will do away with a large amount of the girl's masculine sexuality in order to make room for the development of her femininity. It may happen that this first opposition to auto-erotic activity fails to attain its end. And this was in fact the case in the instances which I analysed. The conflict continued, and both then and later the girl did everything she could to free herself from the compulsion to masturbate. Many of the later manifestations of sexual life in women remain unintelligible unless this powerful motive is recognized.

I cannot explain the opposition which is raised in this way by little girls to phallic masturbation except by supposing that there is some concurrent factor which turns her violently against that pleasurable activity. Such a factor lies close at hand. It cannot be anything else than her narcissistic sense of humiliation which is bound up with penis-envy, the reminder that after all this is a point on which she cannot compete with boys and that it would therefore be best for her to give up the idea of doing so. Thus the little girl's recognition of the anatomical distinction between the sexes forces her away from masculinity and masculine masturbation on to new lines which lead to the development of femininity.

So far there has been no question of the Oedipus complex, nor has it up to this point played any part. But now the girl's libido slips into a new position along the line—there is no other way of putting it—of the equation "penis-child." She gives up her wish for a penis and puts in place of it a wish for a child: and *with that purpose in view* she takes her father as a love-object.[7] Her mother becomes the object of her jealousy. The girl has turned into a little woman. If I am to credit a single analytic instance, this new situation can give rise to physical sensations which would have to be regarded as a premature awakening of the female genital apparatus. When the girl's attachment to her father comes to grief later on and has to be abandoned, it may give place to an identification with him and the girl may thus return to her masculinity complex and perhaps remain fixated in it.

I have now said the essence of what I had to say: I will stop, therefore, and cast an eye over our findings. We have gained some insight into the prehistory of the Oedipus complex in girls. The corresponding period in boys is more or less unknown. In girls the Oedipus complex is a secondary formation. The operations of the castration complex precede it and prepare for it. As regards the relation between the Oedipus and castration complexes there is a fundamental contrast between the two sexes. *Whereas in boys the Oedipus complex is destroyed by the castration complex, in girls it is made possible and led up to by the castration complex.* This contradiction is cleared up if we reflect that the castration complex always operates in the sense implied in its subject-matter: it inhibits and limits masculinity and encourages femininity. The difference between the sexual development of males and females at the stage we have been considering is an intelligible consequence of the anatomical distinction between their genitals and of the psychical situation involved in it; it corresponds to the difference between a castration that has been carried out and one that has merely been threatened. In their essentials, therefore, our findings are self-evident and it should have been possible to foresee them.

The Oedipus complex, however, is such an important thing that the manner in which one enters and leaves it cannot be without its effects. In boys (as I have shown at length in the paper to which I have just referred [1924] and to which all of my present remarks are closely related) the complex is not simply repressed, it is literally smashed to pieces by the shock of threatened castration. Its libidinal cathexes are abandoned, desexualized and in part sublimated; its objects are incorporated into the ego, where they form the nucleus of the super-ego and give that new structure its characteristic qualities. In normal, or, it is better to say, in ideal cases, the Oedipus complex exists no longer, even in the unconscious; the super-ego has become its heir. Since the penis (to follow Ferenczi [1924]) owes its extraordinarily high narcissistic cathexis to its organic significance for the propagation of the species, the catastrophe to the Oedipus complex (the abandonment of incest and the institution of conscience and morality) may be regarded as a victory of the race over the individual. This is an interesting point of view when one considers that neurosis is based upon a struggle of the ego against the demands of the sexual function. But to leave the standpoint of individual psychology is not of any immediate help in clarifying this complicated situation.

In girls the motive for the demolition of the Oedipus complex is lacking. Castration has already had its effect, which was to force the child into the situation of the Oedipus complex. Thus the Oedipus complex escapes the fate which it meets with in boys: it may be slowly abandoned or dealt with by repression, or its effects may persist far into women's normal mental life. I cannot evade the notion (though I hesitate to give it expression) that for women the level of what is ethically normal is different from what it is in men. Their super-ego is never so inexorable, so impersonal, so independent of its emotional origins as we require it to be in men. Character-traits which critics of every epoch have brought up against women—that they show less sense of justice than men, that they are less ready to submit to the great exigencies of life, that they are more often influenced in their judgements by feelings of affection or hostility—all these would be amply accounted for by the modification in the formation of their super-ego which we have inferred above. We must not allow ourselves to be deflected from such conclusions by the denials of the feminists, who are anxious to force us to regard the two sexes as completely equal in position and worth; but we shall, of course, willingly agree that the majority of men are also far behind the masculine ideal and that all human individuals, as a result of their bisexual disposition and of cross-inheritance, combine in themselves both masculine and feminine characteristics, so that pure masculinity and femininity remain theoretical constructions of uncertain content.

I am inclined to set some value on the considerations I have brought forward upon the psychical consequences of the anatomical distinction between the sexes. I am aware, however, that this opinion can only be maintained if my findings, which are based on a handful of cases, turn out to have general validity and to be typical. If not, they would remain no more than a contribution to our knowledge of the different paths along which sexual life develops.

In the valuable and comprehensive studies on the masculinity and castration complexes in women by Abraham (1921), Horney (1923) and Helene Deutsch (1925) there is much that touches closely on what I have written but nothing that coincides with it completely, so that here again I feel justified in publishing this paper.

Written in 1925, this paper appears in Volume 5 of the *Collected Papers* by Sigmund Freud, Edited by James Strachey, published by Basic Books, Inc., by arrangement with The Hogarth Press Ltd. and the Institute of Psycho-Analysis, London. Reprinted by permission.

FOOTNOTES

1. "The Dissolution of the Oedipus Complex" (1924).
2. Cf. the discussions in the "Wolf Man" analysis (1918), and Lecture XXIII of the *Introductory Lectures* (1916-17).
3. Cf. *Three Essays on the Theory of Sexuality* (1905).
4. This is an opportunity for correcting a statement which I made many years ago. I believed that the sexual interest of children, unlike that of pubescents, was aroused, not by the difference between the sexes, but by the problem of where babies come from. We now see that, at all events with girls, this is certainly not the case. With boys it may no doubt happen sometimes one way and sometimes the other; or with both sexes chance experiences may determine the event.
5. In my first critical account of the "History of the Psycho-Analytic Movement" (1914), I recognized that this fact represents the core of truth contained in Adler's theory. That theory has no hesitation in explaining the whole world by this single point ("organ-inferiority," the "masculine protest," "breaking away from the feminine line") and prides itself upon having in this way robbed sexuality of its importance and put the desire for power in its place! Thus the only organ which could claim to be called

"inferior" without any ambiguity would be the clitoris. On the other hand, one hears of analysts who boast that, though they have worked for dozens of years, they have never found a sign of the existence of a castration complex. We must bow our heads in recognition of the greatness of this achievement, even though it is only a negative one, a piece of virtuosity in the art of overlooking and mistaking. The two theories form an interesting pair of opposites: in the latter not a trace of a castration complex, in the former nothing else than its consequences.

6. " 'A Child is Being Beaten' " (1919).

7. Cf. "The Dissolution of the Oedipus Complex" (1924).

The Flight from Womanhood: The Masculinity-Complex in Women as Viewed by Men and by Women

Karen Horney

Criticism of Freud's views on the development of sex differences came from a number of his own students and from students of his closest colleagues. One of the most outspoken of those who opposed him, and one of the earliest, was Karen Horney. A pupil of Karl Abraham and Hanns Sachs in Berlin, she turned her attention to feminine psychology in the mid-1920s and, in a series of clinical and theoretical papers, took issue with Freud on a number of fronts—a controversy which led, in fact, to her eventual break with Freud and to her resignation from the International Psycho-Analytical Association. She was the first to add a cultural dimension to the sex differences debate, often stating, as she does below, that in so far as psychoanalysis was the creation of a man it is more understandably a "masculine psychology" than a feminine one. She also saw the contribution of social traditions, which force women to "adapt themselves to the wishes of men" and, more important, make them feel this adaptation as "their true nature." Her strongest challenge was to the "phallic phase," which she understood as a reaction to the male "dread of the vagina." In addition, she rejected the idea of "penis envy" as central to character formation in women and reversed the whole concept, offering the alternative view that it is the man who envies the woman, envies her for her capacity in motherhood to create new life, which is, according to Horney, the highest creative form of all.

In some of his latest works Freud has drawn attention with increasing urgency to a certain one-sidedness in our analytical researches. I refer to the fact that till quite recently the minds of boys and men only were taken as objects of investigation.

The reason for this is obvious. Psychoanalysis is the creation of a male genius, and almost all those who have developed his ideas have been men. It is only right and reasonable that they should evolve more easily a masculine psychology and understand more of the development of men than of women.

A momentous step toward the understanding of the specifically feminine was made by Freud himself in discovering the existence of penis envy, and soon after, the work of van Ophuijsen and Abraham showed how large a part this factor plays in the development of women and in the formation of their neuroses. The significance of penis envy has been extended quite recently by the hypothesis of the phallic phase. By this we mean that in the infantile genital organization in both sexes only one genital organ, namely the male, plays any part, and that it is just this that distinguishes the infantile organization from the final genital organization of the adult.[1] According to this theory, the clitoris is conceived as of a phallus, and we assume that little girls as well as boys attach to the clitoris in the first instance exactly the same value as to the penis.[2]

The effect of this phase is partly to inhibit and partly to promote the subsequent development. Helene Deutsch has demonstrated principally the inhibiting effects. She is of the opinion that at the beginning of every new sexual function, e.g., at the beginning of puberty, of sexual intercourse, of pregnancy and childbirth, this phase is reactivated and has to be overcome every time before a feminine attitude can be attained. Freud has elaborated her exposition on the positive side, for he believes that it is only penis envy and the overcoming of it which gives rise to the desire for a child and thus forms the love bond to the father.[3]

The question now arises as to whether these hypotheses have helped to make our insight into feminine development (insight that Freud himself has stated to be unsatisfactory and incomplete) more satisfactory and clear.

Science has often found it fruitful to look at long-familiar facts from a fresh point of view. Otherwise there is a danger that we shall involuntarily continue to classify all new observations among the same clearly defined groups of ideas.

The new point of view of which I wish to speak came to me by way of philosophy, in some essays by Georg Simmel.[4] The point that Simmel makes there and that has been in many ways elaborated since, especially from the feminine side,[5] is this: Our whole civilization is a masculine civilization. The State, the laws, morality, religion, and the sciences are the creation of men. Simmel by no means deduces from these facts, as is commonly done by other writers, an inferiority in women, but he first of all gives considerable breadth and depth to this conception of a masculine civilization: "The requirements of art, patriotism, morality in general and social ideas in particular, correctness in practical judgment and objectivity in theoretical knowledge, the energy and the profundity of life—all these are categories which belong as it were in their form and their claims to humanity in general, but in their actual historical configuration they are masculine throughout. Supposing that we describe these things, viewed as absolute ideas, by the single word 'objective', we then find that in the history of our race the equation objective = masculine is a valid one."

Now Simmel thinks that the reason why it is so difficult to recognize these historical facts is that the very standards by which mankind has estimated the values of male and female nature are "not neutral, arising out of the differences of the sexes, but in themselves essentially masculine. . . . We do not believe in a purely 'human' civilization, into which the question of sex does not enter, for the very reason that prevents any such civilization from in fact existing, namely, the (so to speak) naïve identification of the concept 'human being'[6] and the concept 'man,'[7] which in many languages even causes the same word to be used for the two concepts. For the moment I will leave it undetermined whether this masculine character of the fundamentals of our civilization has its origin in the essential nature of the sexes or only in a certain preponderance of force in men, which is not really bound up with the question of civilization. In any case this is the reason why, in the most varying fields, inadequate achievements are contemptuously called 'feminine,' while distinguished achievements on the part of women are called 'masculine' as an expression of praise."

Like all sciences and all valuations, the psychology of women has hitherto been considered only from the point of view of men. It is inevitable that the man's position of advantage should cause objective validity to be attributed to his subjective, affective relations to the woman, and according to Delius[8] the psychology of women hitherto actually represents a deposit of the desires and disappointments of men.

An additional and very important factor in the situation is that women have adapted themselves to the wishes of men and felt as if their adaptation were their true nature. That is, they see or saw themselves in the way that their men's wishes demanded of them; unconsciously they yielded to the suggestion of masculine thought.

If we are clear about the extent to which all our being, thinking, and doing conform to these masculine standards, we can see how difficult it is for the individual man and also for the individual woman really to shake off this mode of thought.

The question then is how far analytical psychology also, when its researches have women for their object, is under the spell of this way of thinking, insofar as it has not yet wholly left behind the stage in which frankly and as a matter of course masculine development only was considered. In other words, how far has the evolution of women, as depicted to us today by analysis, been measured by masculine standards and how far therefore does this picture fail to present quite accurately the real nature of women.

If we look at the matter from this point of view our first impression is a surprising one. The present analytical picture of feminine development (whether that picture be correct or not) differs in no case by a hair's breadth from the typical ideas that the boy has of the girl.

We are familiar with the ideas that the boy entertains. I will therefore only sketch them in a few succinct phrases, and for the sake of comparison will place in a parallel column our ideas of the development of women.

The Boy's Ideas	*Our Ideas of Feminine Development*
Naïve assumption that girls as well as boys possess a penis	For both sexes it is only the male genital which plays any part
Realization of the absence of the penis	Sad discovery of the absence of the penis
Idea that the girl is a castrated, mutilated boy	Belief of the girl that she once possessed a penis and lost it by castration
Belief that the girl has suffered punishment that also threatens him	Castration is conceived of as the infliction of punishment
The girl is regarded as inferior	
The boy is unable to imagine how the girl can ever get over this loss or envy	

The boy dreads her envy	The girl regards herself as inferior. Penis envy
	The girl never gets over the sense of deficiency and inferiority and has constantly to master afresh her desire to be a man
	The girl desires throughout life to avenge herself on the man for possessing something which she lacks

The existence of this over-exact agreement is certainly no criterion of its objective correctness. It is quite possible that the infantile genital organization of the little girl might bear as striking a resemblance to that of the boy as has up till now been assumed.

But it is surely calculated to make us think and take other possibilities into consideration. For instance, we might follow Georg Simmel's train of thought and reflect whether it is likely that female adaptation to the male structure should take place at so early a period and in so high a degree that the specific nature of a little girl is overwhelmed by it. Later I will return for a moment to the point at which it does actually seem to me probable that this infection with a masculine point of view occurs in childhood. But it does not seem to me clear offhand how everything bestowed by nature could be thus absorbed into it and leave no trace. And so we must return to the question I have already raised—whether the remarkable parallelism I have indicated may not perhaps be the expression of a one-sidedness in our observations, due to their being made from the man's point of view.

Such a suggestion immediately encounters an inner protest, for we remind ourselves of the sure ground of experience upon which analytical research has already been founded. But at the same time our theoretical scientific knowledge tells us that this ground is not altogether trustworthy, but that all experience by its very nature contains a subjective factor. Thus, even our analytical experience is derived from direct observation of the material that our patients bring to analysis in free associations, dreams, and symptoms and from the interpretations we make or the conclusions we draw from this material. Therefore, even when the technique is correctly applied, there is in theory the possibility of variations in this experience.

Now, if we try to free our minds from this masculine mode of thought, nearly all the problems of feminine psychology take on a different appearance.

The first thing that strikes us is that it is always, or principally, the genital difference between the sexes which has been made the cardinal point in the analytical conception and that we have left out of consideration the other great biological difference, namely, the different parts played by men and by women in the function of reproduction.

The influence of the man's point of view in the conception of motherhood is most clearly revealed in Ferenczi's extremely brilliant genital theory.[9] His view is that the real incitement to coitus, its true, ultimate meaning for both sexes, is to be sought in the desire to return to the mother's womb. During a period of contest man acquired the privilege of really penetrating once more, by means of his genital organ, into a uterus. The woman, who was formerly in the subordinate position, was obliged to adapt her organization to this organic situation and was provided with certain compensations. She had to "content herself" with substitutes in the nature of fantasy and above all with harboring the child, whose bliss she shares. At the most, it is only in the act of birth that she perhaps has potentialities of pleasure denied to the man.[10]

According to this view the psychic situation of a woman would certainly not be a very pleasurable one. She lacks any real primal impulse to coitus or at least she is debarred from all direct—even if only partial—fulfillment. If this is so, the impulse toward coitus and pleasure in it must undoubtedly be less for her than for the man. For it is only indirectly, by circuitous ways, that she attains to a certain fulfillment of the primal longing— i.e., partly by the roundabout way of masochistic conversion and partly by identification with the child she may conceive. These, however, are merely "compensatory devices." The only thing in which she ultimately has the advantage over the man is the, surely very questionable, pleasure in the act of birth.

At this point I, as a woman, ask in amazement, and what

about motherhood? And the blissful consciousness of bearing a new life within oneself? And the ineffable happiness of the increasing expectation of the appearance of this new being? And the joy when it finally makes its appearance and one holds it for the first time in one's arms? And the deep pleasurable feeling of satisfaction in suckling it and the happiness of the whole period when the infant needs her care?

Ferenczi has expressed the opinion in conversation that in the primal period of conflict which ended so grievously for the female, the male as victor imposed upon her the burden of motherhood and all it involves.

Certainly, regarded from the standpoint of the social struggle, motherhood *may* be a handicap. It is certainly so at the present time, but it is much less certain that it was so in times when human beings were closer to nature.

Moreover, we explain penis envy itself by its biological relations and not by social factors; on the contrary, we are accustomed without more ado to construe the woman's sense of being at a disadvantage socially as the rationalization of her penis envy.

But from the biological point of view woman has in motherhood, or in the capacity for motherhood, a quite indisputable and by no means negligible physiological superiority. This is most clearly reflected in the unconscious of the male psyche in the boy's intense envy of motherhood. We are familiar with this envy as such, but it has hardly received due consideration as a dynamic factor. When one begins, as I did, to analyze men only after a fairly long experience of analyzing women, one receives a most surprising impression of the intensity of this envy of pregnancy, childbirth, and motherhood, as well as of the breasts and of the act of suckling.

In the light of this impression derived from analysis, one must naturally inquire whether an unconscious masculine tendency to depreciation is not expressing itself intellectually in the above-mentioned view of motherhood. This depreciation would run as follows: In reality women do simply desire the penis; when all is said and done motherhood is only a burden that makes the struggle for existence harder, and men may be glad that they have not to bear it.

When Helene Deutsch writes that the masculinity complex in

women plays a much greater part than the femininity complex in man, she would seem to overlook the fact that the masculine envy is clearly capable of more successful sublimation than the penis envy of the girl, and that it certainly serves as one, if not as the essential, driving force in the setting up of cultural values.

Language itself points to this origin of cultural productivity. In the historic times that are known to us, this productivity has undoubtedly been incomparably greater in men than in women. Is not the tremendous strength in men of the impulse to creative work in every field precisely due to their feeling of playing a relatively small part in the creation of living beings, which constantly impels them to an overcompensation in achievement?

If we are right in making this connection, we are confronted with the problem of why no corresponding impulse to compensate herself for her penis envy is found in woman. There are two possibilities: Either the envy of the woman is absolutely less than that of the man; or it is less successfully worked off in some other way. We could bring forward facts in support of either supposition.

In favor of the greater intensity of the man's envy we might point out that an actual anatomical disadvantage on the side of the woman exists only from the point of view of the pregenital levels of organization.[11] From that of the genital organization of adult women there is no disadvantage, for obviously the capacity of women for coitus is not less but simply other than that of men. On the other hand, the part of the man in reproduction is ultimately less than that of the woman.

Further, we observe that men are evidently under a greater necessity to depreciate women than conversely. The realization that the dogma of the inferiority of women had its origin in an unconscious male tendency could only dawn upon us after a doubt had arisen whether in fact this view were justified in reality. But if there actually are in men tendencies to depreciate women behind this conviction of feminine inferiority, we must infer that this unconscious impulse to depreciation is a very powerful one.

Further, there is much to be said in favor of the view that women work off their penis envy less successfully than men, from a cultural point of view. We know that in the most favorable case this envy is transmuted into the desire for a husband and child, and probably by this very transmutation it forfeits the greater part of its power as an incentive to sublimation. In unfavorable cases, however, as I shall presently show in greater detail, it is burdened with a sense of guilt instead of being able to be employed fruitfully, while the man's incapacity for motherhood is probably felt simply as an inferiority and can develop its full driving power without inhibition.

In this discussion I have already touched on a problem that Freud has recently brought into the foreground of interest:[12] namely, the question of the origin and operation of the desire for a child. In the course of the last decade our attitude toward this problem has changed. I may therefore be permitted to describe briefly the beginning and the end of this historical evolution.

The original hypothesis[13] was that penis envy gave a libidinal reinforcement both to the wish for a child and the wish for the man, but that the latter wish arose independently of the former. Subsequently the accent became more and more displaced on to the penis envy, till in his most recent work on this problem, Freud expressed the conjecture that the wish for the child arose only through penis envy and the disappointment over the lack of the penis in general, and that the tender attachment to the father came into existence only by this circuitous route—by way of the desire for the penis and the desire for the child.

This latter hypothesis obviously originated in the need to explain psychologically the biological principle of heterosexual attraction. This corresponds to the problem formulated by Groddeck, who says that it is natural that the boy should retain the mother as a love object, "but how is it that the little girl becomes attached to the opposite sex?"[14]

In order to approach this problem we must first of all realize that our empirical material with regard to the masculinity complex in women is derived from two sources of very different importance. The first is the direct observation of children, in which the subjective factor plays a relatively insignificant part. Every little girl who has not been intimidated displays penis envy frankly and without embarrassment. We see that the presence of this envy is typical and understand quite well why this is so; we understand how the narcissistic mortification of possessing less than the boy is reinforced by a series of disadvantages arising out of the different pregenital cathexes: the manifest privileges of the boy in connection with urethral erotism, the scoptophilic instinct, and onanism.[15]

I should like to suggest that we should apply the term *primary* to the little girl's penis envy, which is obviously based simply on the anatomical difference.

The second source upon which our experience draws is to be found in the analytical material produced by adult women. Naturally it is more difficult to form a judgment on this, and there is therefore more scope for the subjective element. We see here in the first instance that penis envy operates as a factor of enormous dynamic power. We see patients rejecting their female functions, their unconscious motive in so doing being the desire to be male. We meet with fantasies of which the content is: "I once had a penis; I am a man who has been castrated and mutilated," from which proceed feelings of inferiority that have for after-effect all manner of obstinate hypochondriacal ideas. We see a marked attitude of hostility toward men, sometimes taking the form of depreciation and sometimes of a desire to castrate or maim them, and we see how the whole destinies of certain women are determined by this factor.

It was natural to conclude—and especially natural because of the male orientation of our thinking—that we could link these impressions on to the primary penis envy and to reason *a posteriori* that this envy must possess an enormous intensity, an enormous dynamic power, seeing that it evidently gave rise to such effects. Here we overlooked the fact, more in our general estimation of the situation than in details, that this desire to be a man, so familiar to us from the analyses of adult women, had only very little to do with that early, infantile, primary penis envy, but that it is a secondary formation embodying all that has miscarried in the development toward womanhood.

From beginning to end, my experience has proved to me with unchanging clearness that the Oedipus complex in women leads (not only in extreme cases where the subject has come to grief, but *regularly*) to a regression to penis envy, naturally in every possible degree and shade. The difference between the outcome of the male and female Oedipus complexes seems to me in average cases to be as follows. In boys the mother as a sexual object is renounced owing to the fear of castration, but the male role itself is not only affirmed in further development but is actually over-emphasized in the reaction to the fear of castration. We see this clearly in the latency and prepubertal period in boys and generally in later life as well. Girls, on the other hand, not only renounce the father as a sexual object but simultaneously recoil from the feminine role altogether.

In order to understand this flight from womanhood we must consider the facts relating to early infantile onanism, which is the physical expression of the excitations due to the Oedipus complex.

Here again the situation is much clearer in boys, or perhaps we simply know more about it. Are these facts so mysterious to us in girls only because we have always looked at them through the eyes of men? It seems rather like it when we do not even concede to little girls a specific form of onanism but without more ado describe their autoerotic activities as male; and when we conceive of the difference, which surely must exist, as being that of a negative to a positive, i.e., in the case of anxiety about onanism, that the difference is that between a castration threatened and castration that has actually taken place! My analytical experience makes it most decidedly possible that little girls have a specific feminine form of onanism (which incidentally differs in technique from that of boys), even if we assume that the little girl practices exclusively clitoral masturbation, an assumption that seems to me by no means certain. And I do not see why, in spite of its past evolution, it should not be conceded that the clitoris legitimately belongs to and forms an integral part of the female genital apparatus.

Whether in the early phase of the girl's genital development she has organic vaginal sensations is a matter remarkably difficult to determine from the analytical material produced by adult women. In a whole series of cases I have been inclined to conclude that this is so, and later I shall quote the material upon which I base this conclusion. That such sensations should occur seems to me theoretically very probable for the following reasons. Undoubtedly the familiar fantasies that an excessively large penis is effecting forcible penetration, producing pain and hemorrhage, and threatening to destroy something, go to show that the little girl bases her Oedipus fantasies most realistically (in accordance with the plastic concrete thinking of childhood) on the disproportion in size between father and child. I think too that both the Oedipus fantasies and also the logically ensuing dread of an internal—i.e., vaginal—injury go to show that the vagina as well as the clitoris must be assumed to play a part in the early infantile genital organization of women.[16] One might even infer from the later phenomena of frigidity that the vaginal zone has actually a stronger cathexis (arising out of anxiety and attempts at defence) than the clitoris, and this because the incestuous wishes are referred to the vagina with the unerring accuracy of the unconscious. From this point of view frigidity must be regarded as an attempt to ward off the fantasies so full of danger to the ego. And this would also throw a new light on the unconscious pleasurable feelings that, as various authors have maintained, occur at parturition, or alternatively, on the dread of childbirth. For (just because of the disproportion between the vagina and the baby and because of the pain to which this gives rise) parturition would be calculated to a far greater extent than subsequent sexual intercourse to stand to the unconscious for a realization of those early incest fantasies, a realization to which no guilt is attached. The female genital anxiety, like the castration dread of boys, invariably bears the impress of feelings of guilt and it is to them that it owes its lasting influence.

A further factor in the situation, and one that works in the same direction, is a certain consequence of the anatomical difference between the sexes. I mean that the boy can inspect his genital to see whether the dreaded consequences of onanism are taking place; the girl, on the other hand, is literally in the dark on this point and remains in complete uncertainty. Naturally this possibility of a reality test does not weigh with boys in cases where the castration anxiety is acute, but in the slighter cases of fear, which are practically more important because they are more frequent, I think that this difference is very important. At any rate, the analytical material that has come to light in women whom I have analyzed has led me to conclude that this factor plays a considerable part in feminine mental life and that it contributes to the peculiar inner uncertainty so often met with in women.

Under the pressure of this anxiety the girl now takes refuge in a fictitious male role.

What is the economic gain of this flight? Here I would refer to an experience that all analysts have probably had: They find that the desire to be a man is generally admitted comparatively willingly and that when once it is accepted, it is clung to tenaciously, the reason being the desire to avoid the realization of libidinal wishes and fantasies in connection with the father. Thus the wish to be a man subserves the repression of these feminine wishes or the resistance against their being brought to light. This constantly recurring, typical experience compels us, if we are true to analytical principles, to conclude that the fantasies of being a man were at an earlier period devised for the very purpose of securing the subject against libidinal wishes in connection with the father. The fiction of maleness enabled the girl to escape from the female role now burdened with guilt and anxiety. It is true that this attempt to deviate from her own line to that of the male inevitably brings about a sense of inferiority, for the girl begins to measure herself by pretensions and values that are foreign to her specific biological nature and confronted with which she cannot but feel herself inadequate.

Although this sense of inferiority is very tormenting, analytical experience emphatically shows us that the ego can tolerate it more easily than the sense of guilt associated with the feminine attitude, and hence it is undoubtedly a gain for the ego when the girl flees from the Scylla of the sense of guilt to the Charybdis of the sense of inferiority.

For the sake of completeness I will add a reference to the other gain that, as we know, accrues to women from the process of identification with the father, which takes place at the same time. I know of nothing with reference to the importance of this process itself to add to what I have already said in my earlier work.

We know that this very process of identification with the father is one answer to the question of why the flight from feminine wishes in regard to the father always leads to the adoption of a masculine attitude. Some reflections connected with what has already been said reveal another point of view that throws some light on this question.

We know that whenever the libido encounters a barrier in its development an earlier phase of organization is regressively activated. Now, according to Freud's latest work, penis envy forms the preliminary stage to the true object love for the father. And so this train of thought suggested by Freud helps us to some comprehension of the inner necessity by which the libido flows back precisely to this preliminary stage whenever and insofar as it is driven back by the incest barrier.

I agree in principle with Freud's notion that the girl develops toward object love by way of penis envy, but I think that the nature of this evolution might also be pictured differently.

For when we see how large a part of the strength of primary penis envy is accrued only by retrogression from the Oedipus complex, we must resist the temptation to interpret in the light of penis envy the manifestations of so elementary a principle of nature as that of the mutual attraction of the sexes.

Whereupon, being confronted with the question of how we should conceive psychologically of this primal, biological principle, we would again have to confess ignorance. Indeed, in this respect the conjecture forces itself more and more strongly upon me that perhaps the causal connection may be the exact converse and that it is just the attraction to the opposite sex, operating from a very early period, which draws the libidinal interest of the little girl to the penis. This interest, in accordance with the level of development reached, acts at first in an autoerotic and narcissistic manner, as I have described before. If we view these relations thus, fresh problems would logically present themselves with regard to the origin of the male Oedipus complex, but I wish to postpone these for a later paper. But, if penis envy were the first expression of that mysterious attraction of the sexes, there would be nothing to wonder at when analysis discloses its existence in a yet deeper layer than that in which the desire for a child and the tender attachment to the father occur. The way to this tender attitude toward the father would be prepared not simply by disappointment in regard to the penis but in another way as well. We should then instead have to conceive of the libidinal interest in the penis as a kind of "partial love," to use Abraham's term.[17] Such love, he says, always forms a preliminary stage to true object love. We might explain the process too by an analogy from later life: I refer to the fact that admiring envy is specially calculated to lead to an attitude of love.

With regard to the extraordinary ease with which this regression takes place, I must mention the analytical discovery[18] that in the associations of female patients the narcissistic desire to possess the penis and the object libidinal longing for it are often so interwoven that one hesitates as to the sense in which the words "desire for it"[19] are meant.

One word more about the castration fantasies proper, which have given their name to the whole complex because they are the most striking part of it. According to my theory of feminine development, I am obliged to regard these fantasies also as a secondary formation. I picture their origin as follows: When the woman takes refuge in the fictitious male role, her feminine genital anxiety is to some extent translated into male terms—the fear of vaginal injury becomes a fantasy of castration. The girl gains by this conversion, for she exchanges the uncertainty of her expectation of punishment (an uncertainty conditioned by her anatomical formation) for a concrete idea. Moreover, the castration fantasy, too, is under the shadow of the old sense of guilt—and the penis is desired as a proof of guiltlessness.

Now these typical motives for flight into the male role— motives whose origin is the Oedipus complex—are reinforced and supported by the actual disadvantage under which women labor in social life. Of course we must recognize that the desire to be a man, when it springs from this last source, is a peculiarly suitable form of rationalization of those unconscious motives. But we must not forget that this disadvantage is actually a piece of reality and that it is immensely greater than most women are aware of.

Georg Simmel says in this connection that "the greater importance attaching to the male sociologically is probably due to his position of superior strength," and that historically the relation of the sexes may be crudely described as that of master and slave. Here, as always, it is "one of the privileges of the master that he has not constantly to think that he is master, while the position of the slave is such that he can never forget it."

Here we probably have the explanation also of the underestimation of this factor in analytical literature. In actual fact a girl is exposed from birth onward to the suggestion—inevitable, whether conveyed brutally or delicately—of her inferiority, an experience that constantly stimulates her masculinity complex.

There is one further consideration. Owing to the hitherto purely masculine character of our civilization, it has been much harder for women to achieve any sublimation that would really satisfy their nature, for all the ordinary professions have been filled by men. This again must have exercised an influence upon women's feelings of inferiority, for naturally they could not accomplish the same as men in these masculine professions and so it appeared that there was a basis in fact for their inferiority. It seems to me impossible to judge to how great a degree the unconscious motives for the flight from womanhood are reinforced by the actual social subordination of women. One might conceive of the connection as an interaction of psychic and social factors. But I can only indicate these problems here, for they are so grave and so important that they require a separate investigation.

The same factors must have quite a different effect on the man's development. On the one hand they lead to a much stronger repression of his feminine wishes, in that these bear the stigma of inferiority; on the other hand it is far easier for him successfully to sublimate them.

In the foregoing discussion I have put a construction upon certain problems of feminine psychology, which in many points differs from current views. It is possible and even probable that the picture I have drawn is one-sided from the opposite point of view. But my primary intention in this paper was to indicate a possible source of error arising out of the sex of the observer, and by so doing to make a step forward toward the goal that we are all striving to reach: to get beyond the subjectivity of the masculine or the feminine standpoint and to obtain a picture of the mental development of woman that will be more true to the facts of her nature—with its specific qualities and its differences from that of man—than any we have hitherto achieved.

From the *International Journal of Psycho-Analysis,* Volume VII (1926), pages 324-329. Reprinted by permission.

FOOTNOTES

1. Freud, "The Infantile Genital Organization of the Libido." *Collected Papers*, Vol. II, No. XX.
2. H. Deutsch, *Psychoanalyse der weiblichen Sexualfunktionen* (1925).
3. Freud, "Einige psychische Folgen der anatomischen Geschlechtsunterschiede," *Intern. Zeitschr. f. Psychoanal.*, XI (1925).
4. Georg Simmel, *Philosophische Kultur.*
5. Cf. in particular Vaerting, *Männliche Eigenart im Frauenstaat und Weibliche Eigenart im Männerstaat.*

6. German *Mensch.*
7. German *Mann.*
8. Delius, *Vom Erwachen der Frau.*
9. Ferenczi, *Versuch einer Genitaltheorie* (1924).
10. Cf. also Helene Deutsch, *Psychoanalyse der Weiblichen Sexualfunktionen;* and Groddeck, *Das Buch vom Es.*
11. K. Horney, "On the Genesis of the Castration Complex in Women," *Int. J. Psycho-Anal.,* Vol. V (1924).
12. Freud, *"Über einige psychische Folgen der anatomischen Geschlechtsunterschiede."*
13. Freud, "On the Transformation of Instincts with Special Reference to Anal Erotism," *Collected Papers,* Vol. II, No. XVI.
14. Groddeck, *Das Buch vom Es.*
15. I have dealt with this subject in greater detail in my paper "On the Genesis of the Castration Complex in Women."
16. Since the possibility of such a connection occurred to me, I have learned to construe in this sense—i.e., as representing the dread of vaginal injury—many phenomena that I was previously content to interpret as castration fantasies in the male sense.
17. Abraham, *Versuch einer Entwicklungsgeschichte der Libido* (1924).
18. Freud referred to this in *The Taboo of Virginity.*
19. German, *Haben-Wollen.*

Early Stages of the Oedipus Conflict

Melanie Klein

The most radical psychoanalytic views on sex differences came from the theoretical formulations of Melanie Klein. She first worked in Berlin, then in London (where the so-called "Kleinian School" became established) and developed these views out of intensive clinical work with disturbed children. What she saw in her young patients was the very early onset of Oedipal conflicts— often in the first year of life. (For Freud the Oedipus complex did not arise until the child's fourth or fifth year.) In such cases, the Oedipus configuration had a primitive, oral coloration, overcast with cannibalistic and destructive phantasies towards the parents which, according to Klein, filled the infant with dread and fear of retaliation. Although she did not focus on cultural conditioning as Horney did, Melanie Klein joined her in disputing Freud's notion of the phallic phase. Rather than infantile "masculine" activities in girls and boys, she hypothesized a "femininity-complex" in infants of both sexes—a complex drawn out of intense identification with the mother and with the desire to "rob" the contents of the mother's body: to take from her the "hidden babies" and the "hidden penis." To this "penis envy" in boys she also added the idea of "envy of the breast," and, on somewhat similar lines to Horney, considered the boy's masculinity as a compensation for his wish to have a baby and for his frustrated maternal desires.

In my analyses of children, especially of children between the ages of three and six, I have come to a number of conclusions of which I shall here present a summary.

I have repeatedly alluded to the conclusion that the Oedipus complex comes into operation earlier than is usually supposed. In my paper, "The Psychological Principles of Early Analysis," I discussed this subject in greater detail. The conclusion which I reached there was that the Oedipus tendencies are released in consequence of the frustration which the child experiences at weaning, and that they make their appearance at the end of the first and the beginning of the second year of life; they receive reinforcement through the anal frustrations undergone during training in cleanliness. The next determining influence upon the mental processes is that of the anatomical difference between the sexes.

The boy, when he finds himself impelled to abandon the oral and anal positions for the genital, passes on to the aim of *penetration* associated with possession of the penis. Thus he changes not only his libido-position, but its *aim*, and this enables him to retain his original love-object. In the girl, on the other hand, the *receptive* aim is carried over from the oral to the genital position: she changes her libido-position, but retains its aim, which has already led to disappointment in relation to her mother. In this way receptivity for the penis is produced in the girl, who then turns to the father as her love-object.

The very onset of the Oedipus wishes, however, already becomes associated with incipient dread of castration and feelings of guilt.

The analysis of adults, as well as of children, has familiarized us with the fact that the pregenital instinctual impulses carry with them a sense of guilt, and it was thought at first that the feelings of guilt were of subsequent growth, displaced back on to these tendencies, though not originally associated with them. Ferenczi assumes that, connected with the urethral and anal impulses, there is a "kind of physiological forerunner of the super-ego," which he terms "sphincter-morality." According to Abraham, anxiety makes its appearance on the cannibalistic level, while the sense of guilt arises in the succeeding early anal-sadistic phase.

My findings lead rather further. They show that the sense of guilt associated with pregenital fixation is already the direct effect of the Oedipus conflict. And this seems to account satisfactorily for the genesis of such feelings, for we know the sense of guilt to be in fact a result of the introjection (already accomplished or, as I would add, in process of being accomplished) of the Oedipus love-objects: that is, a sense of guilt is a product of the formation of the super-ego.

The analysis of little children reveals the structure of the super-ego as built up of identifications dating from very different periods and strata in the mental life. These identifications are surprisingly contradictory in nature, excessive goodness and excessive severity existing side by side. We find in them, too, an explanation of the severity of the super-ego, which comes out specially plainly in these infant analyses. It does not seem clear why a child of, say, four years old should set up in his mind an unreal, phantastic image of parents who devour, cut and bite. But it *is* clear why in a child of about *one year* old the anxiety caused by the beginning of the Oedipus conflict takes the form of a dread of being devoured and destroyed. The child himself desires to destroy the libidinal object by biting, devouring and cutting it, which leads to anxiety, since awakening of the Oedipus tendencies is followed by introjection of the object, which then becomes one from which punishment is to be expected. The child then dreads a punishment corresponding to the offence: the super-ego becomes something which bites, devours and cuts.

The connection between the formation of the super-ego and the pregenital phases of development is very important from two points of view. On the one hand, the sense of guilt attaches itself to the oral- and anal-sadistic phases, which as yet predominate; and, on the other, the super-ego comes into being while these phases are in the ascendant, which accounts for its sadistic severity.

These conclusions open up a new perspective. Only by strong repression can the still very feeble ego defend itself against a super-ego so menacing. Since the Oedipus tendencies are at first chiefly expressed in the form of oral and anal impulses, the question of which fixations will predominate in the Oedipus development will be mainly determined by the degree of the repression which takes place at this early stage.

Another reason why the direct connection between the pregenital phase of development and the sense of guilt is so important is that the oral and anal frustrations, which are the prototypes of all later frustrations in life, at the same time signify *punishment* and give rise to anxiety. This circumstance makes the frustration more acutely felt, and this bitterness contributes largely to the hardship of all subsequent frustrations.

We find that important consequences ensue from the fact that the ego is still so little developed when it is assailed by the onset of the Oedipus tendencies and the incipient sexual curiosity associated with them. The infant, still undeveloped intellectually, is exposed to an onrush of problems and questions. One of the most bitter grievances which we come upon in the unconscious is that these many overwhelming questions, which are apparently only partly conscious and even when conscious cannot yet be expressed in words, remain unanswered. Another reproach follows hard upon this, namely, that the child could not understand words and speech. Thus his first questions go back beyond the beginnings of his understanding of speech.

In analysis both these grievances give rise to an extraordinary amount of hate. Singly or in conjunction they are the cause of numerous inhibitions of the epistemophilic impulse: for instance, the incapacity to learn foreign languages, and further, hatred of those who speak a different tongue. They are also responsible for direct disturbances in speech, etc. The curiosity which shows itself plainly later on, mostly in the fourth or fifth year of life, is not the beginning, but the climax and termination, of this phase of development, which I have also found to be true of the Oedipus conflict in general.

The early feeling of *not knowing* has manifold connections. It unites with the feeling of being incapable, impotent, which soon results from the Oedipus situation. The child also feels this frustration the more acutely because he *knows nothing* definite about sexual processes. In both sexes the castration complex is accentuated by this feeling of ignorance.

The early connection between the epistemophilic impulse and sadism is very important for the whole mental development. This instinct, activated by the rise of the Oedipus tendencies, at first mainly concerns itself with the mother's body, which is assumed to be the scene of all sexual processes and developments. The child is still dominated by the anal-sadistic libido-position which impels him to wish to *appropriate* the contents of the body. He thus begins to be curious about what it contains, what it is like, etc. So the epistemophilic instinct and the desire to take possession come quite early to be most intimately connected with one another and at the same time with the sense of guilt aroused by the incipient Oedipus conflict. This significant connection ushers in a phase of development in both sexes which is of vital importance, hitherto not sufficiently recognized. It consists of a very early identification with the mother.

The course run by this "femininity" phase must be examined separately in boys and girls, but, before I proceed to this, I shall show its connection with the previous phase, which is common to both sexes.

In the early anal-sadistic stage the child sustains his second severe trauma, which strengthens his tendency to turn away from the mother. She has frustrated his oral desires, and now she also interferes with his anal pleasures. It seems as though at this point the anal deprivations cause the anal tendencies to amalgamate with the sadistic tendencies. The child desires to get possession of the mother's faeces, by penetrating into her body, cutting it to pieces, devouring and destroying it. Under the influence of his genital impulses, the boy is beginning to turn to his mother as a love-object. But his sadistic impulses are fully at work, and the hate originating in earlier frustrations is powerfully opposed to his object-love on the genital level. A still greater obstacle to his love is his dread of castration by the father, which arises with the Oedipus impulses. The degree to which he attains the genital position will party depend on his capacity for tolerating this anxiety. Here the intensity of the oral-sadistic and anal-sadistic fixations is an important factor. It affects the degree of hatred which the boy feels towards the mother; and this, in its turn, hinders him to a greater or lesser extent in attaining a positive relation to her. The sadistic fixations exercise also a decisive influence upon the formation of the super-ego, which is coming into being whilst these phases are in the ascendant. The more cruel the super-ego the more terrifying will be the father as castrator, and the more tenaciously, in the child's flight from his genital impulses, will he cling to the sadistic levels, from which levels his Oedipus tendencies, too, in the first instance, take their colour.

In these early stages all the positions in the Oedipus development are cathected in rapid succession. This, however, is not noticeable, because the picture is dominated by the pregenital impulses. Moreover, no rigid line can be drawn between the active heterosexual attitude which finds expression on the anal level and the further stage of identification with the mother.

We have now reached that phase of development of which I spoke before under the name of the "femininity-phase." It has its basis on the anal-sadistic level and imparts to that level a new content, for faeces are now equated with the child that is longed for, and the desire to rob the mother now applies to the child as well as to faeces. Here we can discern two aims which merge with one another. The one is directed by the desire for children, the intention being to appropriate them, while the other aim is motivated by jealousy of the future brothers and sisters whose appearance is expected, and by the wish to destroy them in the mother. (A third object of the boy's oral-sadistic tendencies inside the mother is the father's penis.)

As in the castration complex of girls, so in the femininity complex of the male, there is at bottom the frustrated desire for a special organ. The tendencies to steal and destroy are concerned with the organs of conception, pregnancy and parturition, which the boy assumes to exist in the mother, and further with the vagina and the breasts, the fountain of milk, which are coveted as organs of receptivity and bounty from the time when the libidinal position is purely oral.

The boy fears punishment for his destruction of his mother's body, but, besides this, his fear is of a more general nature, and here we have an analogy to the anxiety associated with the castration-wishes of the girl. He fears that his body will be mutilated and dismembered, and this dread also means castration. Here we have a direct contribution to the castration complex. In this early period of development the mother who takes away the child's faeces signifies also a mother who dismembers and castrates him. Not only by means of the anal frustrations which she inflicts does she pave the way for the castration complex: in terms of psychic reality she *is* also already the *castrator*.

This dread of the mother is so overwhelming because there is combined with it an intense dread of castration by the father. The destructive tendencies whose object is the womb are also directed with their full oral- and anal-sadistic intensity against the father's penis, which is supposed to be located there. It is upon this penis that the dread of castration by the father is focused in this phase. Thus the femininity-phase is characterized by anxiety relating to the womb and the father's penis, and this anxiety subjects the boy to the tyranny of a super-ego which devours, dismembers and castrates and is formed from the image of father and mother alike.

The incipient genital positions are thus from the beginning crisscrossed by and intermingled with the manifold pregenital tendencies. The greater the preponderance of sadistic fixations, the more does the boy's identification with his mother correspond to an attitude of rivalry towards the woman, with its blending of envy and hatred; for, on account of his wish for a child, he feels himself at a disadvantage and inferior to the mother.

Let us now consider why the femininity complex of men seems so much more obscure than the castration complex in women, with which it is equally important.

The amalgamation of the desire for a child with the epistemophilic impulse enables a boy to effect a displacement on to the intellectual plane; his sense of being at a disadvantage is then concelaed and over-compensated by the superiority he deduces from his possession of a penis, which is also acknowledged by girls. This exaggeration of the masculine position results in excessive protestations of masculinity. In her paper, "Die Wurzel des Wissbegierde," Mary Chadwick (1925), too, has traced the man's narcissistic over-estimation of the penis, and his attitude of intellectual rivalry towards women, to the frustration of his wish for a child and to the displacement of this desire on to the intellectual plane.

A tendency in boys to express excessive aggression, which very frequently occurs, has its source in the femininity complex. It goes with an attitude of contempt and "knowing better," and is highly asocial and sadistic; it is partly determined by an attempt to mask the anxiety and ignorance which lie behind it. In part it coincides with the boy's protest (originating in his fear of castration) against the feminine rôle, but it is rooted also in his dread of his mother, whom he intended to rob of the father's penis, her children and her female sexual organs. This excessive aggression unites with the pleasure in attack which proceeds from the direct, genital Oedipus situation, but it represents that part of the situation which is by far the more asocial factor in character-formation. This is why a man's rivalry with women will be far more asocial than his rivalry with his fellow-men, which is largely prompted through the genital position. Of course, the quantity of sadistic fixations will also determine the relationship of a man to other men when they are rivals. If, on the contrary, the identification with the mother is based on a more securely established genital position, on the one hand his relation to women will be positive in character, and on the other the desire for a child and the feminine component, which play so essential a part in men's work, will find more favourable opportunities for sublimation.

In both sexes one of the principal roots of inhibitions in work is the anxiety and sense of guilt associated with the femininity phase. Experience has taught me, however, that a thorough analysis of this phase is, for other reasons as well, important from a therapeutic point of view, and should be of help in some obsessional cases which seem to have reached a point where nothing more could be resolved.

In the boy's development the femininity-phase is succeeded by a prolonged struggle between the pregenital and the genital positions of the libido. When at its height, in the third to the fifth year of life, this struggle is plainly recognizable as the Oedipus conflict. The anxiety associated with the femininity-phase drives the boy back to identification with the father; but this stimulus in itself does not provide a firm foundation for the genital position, since it leads mainly to repression and over-compensation of the anal-sadistic instincts, and not to overcoming them. The dread of castration by the father strengthens the fixation to the anal-sadistic levels. The degree of constitutional genitality also plays an important part as regards a favourable issue, i.e. the attainment of the genital level. Often the outcome of the struggle remains undecided, and this gives rise to neurotic troubles and disturbances of potency.[1] Thus the attainment of complete potency and reaching the genital position will in part depend upon the favourable issue of the femininity-phase.

I will now turn to the development of girls. As a result of the process of weaning, the girl-child has turned from the mother, being impelled more strongly to do so by the anal deprivations she has undergone. Genital trends now begin to influence her mental development.

I entirely agree with Helene Deutsch (1925), who holds that the genital development of the woman finds its completion in the successful displacement of oral libido on to the genital. Only, my results lead me to believe that this displacement begins with the first stirrings of the genital impulses and that the oral, receptive aim of the genitals exercises a determining influence in the *girl's turning to the father*. Also I am led to conclude that not only an unconscious awareness of the vagina, but also sensations in that organ and the rest of the genital apparatus, are aroused as soon as the Oedipus impulses make their appearance. In girls, however, onanism does not afford anything like so adequate an outlet for these quantities of excitation as it does in boys. Hence the accumulated lack of gratification provides yet another reason for more complications and disturbances of female sexual development. The difficulty of obtaining full gratification by masturbation may be another cause, besides those indicated by Freud, for the girl's repudiation of onanism, and this may partly explain why, during her struggle to give it up, manual masturbation is generally replaced by pressing the legs together.

Besides the receptive quality of the genital organ, which is brought into play by the intense desire for a new source of gratification, envy and hatred of the mother who possesses the father's penis seem, at the period when these first Oedipus impulses are stirring, to be a further motive for the little girl's turning to the father. His caresses have now the effect of a seduction and are felt as "the attraction of the opposite sex."[2]

In the girl, identification with the mother results directly from' the Oedipus impulses: the whole struggle caused in the boy by his castration anxiety is absent in her. In girls as well as boys this identification coincides with the anal-sadistic tendencies to rob and destroy the mother. If identification with the mother takes place predominantly at a stage when oral- and anal-sadistic tendencies are very strong, dread of a primitive maternal super-ego will lead to the repression and fixation of this phase and interfere with further genital development. Dread of the mother, too, impels the little girl to give up identification with her, and identification with the father begins.

The little girl's epistemophilic impulse is first roused by the Oedipus complex; the result is that she discovers her lack of a penis. She feels this lack to be a fresh cause of hatred of the mother, but at the same time her sense of guilt makes her regard it as a punishment. This embitters her frustration in this direction, and, in its turn, exercises a profound influence on the whole castration complex.

This early grievance about the lack of a penis is greatly magnified later on, when the phallic phase and the castration complex are fully active. Freud has stated that the discovery of the lack of a penis causes the turning from the mother to the father.

My findings show, however, that this discovery operates only as a reinforcement in this direction: it is made at a very early stage in the Oedipus conflict, and penis-envy succeeds the wish for a child, which again replaces penis-envy in later development. I regard the deprivation of the breast as the most fundamental cause of the turning to the father.

Identification with the father is less charged with anxiety than that with the mother; moreover, the sense of guilt towards her impels to over-compensation through a fresh love-relation with her. Against this new love-relation with her there operates the castration complex which makes a masculine attitude difficult, and also the hatred of her which sprang from the earlier positions. Hate and rivalry of the mother, however, again lead to abandoning the identification with the father and turning to him as the object to love and be loved by.

The girl's relation to her mother causes her relation to her father to take both a positive and a negative direction. The frustration undergone at his hands has as its very deepest basis the disappointment already suffered in relation to the mother; a powerful motive in the desire to possess him springs from the hatred and envy against the mother. If the sadistic fixations remain predominant, this hatred and its over-compensation will also materially affect the woman's relation to men. On the other hand, if there is a more positive relation to the mother, built up on the genital position, not only will the woman be freer from a sense of guilt in her relation to her children, but her love for her husband will be strongly reinforced, since for the woman he always stands at one and the same time for the mother who gives what is desired and for the beloved child. On this very significant foundation is built up that part of the relation which is connected exclusively with the father. At first it is focused on the act of the penis in coitus. This act, which also promises gratification of the desires that are now displaced on to the genital, seems to the little girl a most consummate performance.

Her admiration is, indeed, shaken by the Oedipus frustration but unless it is converted into hate, it constitutes one of the fundamental features of the woman's relation to the man. Later, when full satisfaction of the love-impulses is obtained, there is joined with this admiration the great gratitude ensuing from the long-pent-up deprivation. This gratitude finds expression in the greater feminine capacity for complete and lasting surrender to one love-object especially to the "first love."

One way in which the little girl's development is greatly handicapped is the following. Whilst the boy does in reality *possess* the penis, in respect of which he enters into rivalry with the father, the little girl has only the *unsatisifed* desire for motherhood, and of this, too, she has but a dim and uncertain, though a very intense, awareness.

It is not merely this uncertainty which disturbs her hope of future motherhood. It is weakened far more by anxiety and sense of guilt, and these may seriously and permanently damage the maternal capacity of a woman. Because of the destructive tendencies once directed by her against the mother's body (or certain organs in it) and against the children in the womb, the girl anticipates retribution in the form of destruction of her own capacity for motherhood or of the organs connected with this function and of her own children. Here we have also one root of the constant concern of women (often so excessive) for their personal beauty, for they dread that this too will be destroyed by the mother. At the bottom of the impulse to deck and beautify themselves there is always the motive of *restoring* damaged comeliness, and this has its origin in anxiety and sense of guilt.[3]

It is probable that this deep dread of the destruction of internal organs may be the psychic cause of the greater susceptibility of women, as compared with men, to conversion-hysteria and organic diseases.

It is this anxiety and sense of guilt which is the chief cause of the repression of feelings of pride and joy in the feminine rôle, which are originally very strong. This repression results in depreciation of the capacity for motherhood, at the outset so highly prized. Thus the girl lacks the powerful support which the boy derives from his possession of the penis, and which she herself might find in the anticipation of motherhood.

The girl's very intense anxiety about her womanhood can be shown to be analogous to the boy's dread of castration, for it certainly contributes to the checking of her Oedipus impulses. The course run by the boy's castration anxiety concerning the penis which *visibly* exists is, however, different; it might be termed more *acute* than the more chronic anxiety of the girl concerning her internal organs, with which she is necessarily less familiar.

Moreover, it is bound to make a difference that the boy's anxiety is determined by the paternal and the girl's by the maternal super-ego.

Freud has said that the girl's super-ego develops on different lines from that of the boy. We constantly find confirmation of the fact that jealousy plays a greater part in women's lives than in men's, because it is reinforced by deflected envy of the male on account of the penis. On the other hand, however, women especially possess a great capacity, which is not based merely on an over-compensation, for disregarding their own wishes and devoting themselves with self-sacrifice to ethical and social tasks. We cannot account for this capacity by the blending of masculine and feminine traits which, because of the human being's bisexual disposition, does in individual cases influence the formation of character, for this capacity is so plainly maternal in nature. I think that in order to explain how women can run so wide a gamut from the most petty jealousy to the most self-forgetful loving-kindness, we have to take into consideration the peculiar conditions of the formation of the feminine super-ego. From the early identification with the mother in which the anal-sadistic level so largely preponderates, the little girl derives jealousy and hatred and forms a cruel super-ego after the maternal imago. The super-ego which develops at this stage from a father-identification can also be menacing and cause anxiety, but it seems never to reach the same proportions as that derived from the mother-identification. But the more the identification with the mother becomes stabilized on the genital basis, the more will it be characterized by the devoted kindness of a bountiful mother-ideal. Thus this positive affective attitude depends on the extent to which the maternal mother-ideal bears the characteristics of the pregenital or of the genital stage. But when it comes to the active conversion of the emotional attitude into social or other activities, it would seem that it is the paternal ego-ideal which is at work. The deep admiration felt by the little girl for the father's genital activity leads to the formation of a paternal super-ego which sets before her active aims to which she can never fully attain. If, owing to certain factors in her development, the incentive to accomplish these aims is strong enough, their very impossibility of attainment may lend an impetus to her efforts which, combined with the capacity for self-sacrifice which she derives from the maternal super-ego, gives a woman, in individual instances, the capacity for very exceptional achievements on the intuitive plane and in specific fields.

The boy, too, derives from the feminine phase a maternal super-ego which causes him, like the girl, to make both cruelly primitive and kindly identifications. But he passes through this phase to resume (it is true, in varying degrees) identification with the father. However much the maternal side makes itself felt in the formation of the super-ego, it is yet the *paternal* super-ego which from the beginning is the decisive influence for the man. He too sets before himself a figure of an exalted character upon which to model himself, but, because the boy *is* "made in the image of" his ideal, it is not unattainable. This circumstance contributes to the more sustained and objective creative work of the male.

The dread of injury to her womanhood exercises a profound influence on the castration complex of the little girl, for it causes her to over-estimate the penis which she herself lacks; this exaggeration is then much more obvious than is the underlying anxiety about her own womanhood. I would remind you here of the work of Karen Horney, who was the first to examine the sources of the castration complex in women in so far as those sources lie in the Oedipus situation.

In this connection I must speak of the importance for sexual development of certain early experiences in childhood. In the paper which I read at the Salzburg Congress in 1924, I mentioned that when observations of coitus take place at a later stage of development they assume the character of traumata, but that if such experiences occur at an early age they become fixated and form part of the sexual development. I must now add that a fixation of this sort may hold in its grip not only that particular stage of development, but also the super-ego which is then in process of formation, and may thus injure its further development. For the more completely the super-ego reaches its zenith in the genital stage, the less prominent will be the sadistic identification in its structure and the more likely will be the securing of mental health and the development of a personality on an ethically high level.

There is another kind of experience in early childhood which strikes me as typical and exceedingly important. These experiences often follow closely in time upon the observations of coitus and are induced or fostered by the excitations set up thereby. I refer to the sexual relations of little children with one another, between brothers and sisters or playmates, which consist in the most varied acts: looking, touching, performing excretion in common, fellatio, cunnilingus and often direct attempts at coitus. They are deeply repressed and have a cathexis of profound feelings of guilt. These feelings are mainly due to the fact that this love-object, chosen under the pressure of the excitation due to the Oedipus conflict, is felt by the child to be a substitute for the father or mother or both. Thus these relations, which seem so insignificant and which apparently no child under the stimulus of the Oedipus development escapes, take on the character of an Oedipus relation actually realized, and exercise a determining influence upon the formation of the Oedipus complex, the subject's detachment from that complex and upon his later sexual relations. Moreover, an experience of this sort forms an important fixation-point in the development of the super-ego. In consequence of the need for punishment and the repetition-compulsion, these experiences often cause the child to subject himself to sexual traumata. In this connection I would refer you to Abraham (1927), who showed that experiencing sexual traumata is one part of the sexual development of children. The analytic investigation of these experiences, during the analysis of adults as well as of children, to a great extent clears up the Oedipus situation in its connection with early fixations, and is therefore important from the therapeutic point of view.

To sum up my conclusions: I wish first of all to point out that they do not, in my opinion, contradict the statements of Professor Freud. I think that the essential point in the additional considerations which I have advanced is that I date these processes earlier and that the different phases (especially in the initial stages) merge more freely into one another than was hitherto supposed.

The early stages of the Oedipus conflict are so largely dominated by pregenital phases of development that the genital phase, when it begins to be active, is at first heavily shrouded and only later, between the third and fifth years of life, becomes clearly recognizable. At this age the Oedipus complex and the formation of the super-ego reach their climax. But the fact that the Oedipus tendencies begin so much earlier than we supposed, the pressure of the sense of guilt which therefore falls upon the pregenital levels, the determining influence thus exercised so early upon the Oedipus development on the one hand and that of the super-ego on the other, and accordingly upon character-formation, sexuality and all the rest of the subject's development—all these things seem to me of great and hitherto unrecognized importance. I found out the therapeutic value of this knowledge in the analyses of children, but it is not confined to these. I have been able to test the resulting conclusions in the analysis of adults and have found not only that their theoretical correctness was confirmed but that their therapeutic importance was established.

Written in 1928 and published in *Love, Guilt and Reparation and Other Works 1921-1945* (Volume I, *The Writings of Melanie Klein*), Delacorte Press/Seymour Lawrence, 1975, pages 186–198. Reprinted by permission.

FOOTNOTES

1. Cf. here W. Reich: *"Die Funktion des Orgasmus"* (1927).
2. We regularly come across the unconscious reproach that the mother has seduced the child whilst tending it. This reproach goes back to the period when genital desires come to the fore and the Oedipus tendencies are awakening.
3. Cf. Hárnik's (1928) paper at the Innsbruck Psycho-Analytical Congress: *"Die ökonomischen Beziehungen zwischen dem Schuldgefühl und dem weiblichen Narzissmus."*

Motherhood and Sexuality

Helene Deutsch

Among the earliest of Freud's women students, Helene Deutsch stands as the "pioneer" of feminine psychology. From the start of her psychiatric career in 1912, she took the development of women as her chief interest and was the first to explore the full female "life cycle"–from prepuberty to the onset of old age. Her course at the Vienna Psycho-Analytic Institute on "The Psychic Development in Women" (out of which this paper originates) was a landmark in psychoanalytic education. Although she never broke from Freud, as Karen Horney did, Deutsch continued to criticize Freud's views and called his attention to the "pre-Oedipal" attachment to the mother–in both girls and boys. It was also her idea that it is the girl who must take the "extra step" in her development as she shifts from the love of her mother to the love of her father. In the present paper, she focuses on the distinction between motherhood and sexuality and on its connection to frigidity and sexual inhibitions in females. According to Deutsch, this "split" in women, between the image of themselves as "madonna," on the one hand, and "prostitute," on the other, is the source of some of the most intense conflict in the whole of feminine sexual development.

S exual inhibition, in men and women alike, to the best of our knowledge takes its origin in the castration complex and the Oedipus complex. As we use the term here, "sexual inhibition" designates a state of blocking in the obtainment of sexual gratification: a partial or complete inability to love, unaccompanied however by neurotic symptoms. The inhibition has many forms and degrees of intensity. It may present itself as a total inability to gratify the sexual impulse, an inability even to feel any conscious sexual urgency or longing; or the inhibition may be less severe, so that there may be response and gratification, but this only under certain restrictive conditions, as for example in many men who require an inferiority of some sort in the object of their sexual wishes.

To discuss the various forms of sexual frigidity in women would take us beyond the limits set for this report. In general it may be said that the unconscious determinants of frigidity correspond to those of impotence in men. Frigidity, like impotence, also originates in the development of the castration complex and the Oedipus complex. Its most frequent cause is a protest against the assumption of the passive feminine role—in other words, the masculinity complex.

I am inclined to ascribe the widespread distribution of frigidity to the masochistic elements in the female libido. Fear of masochistic gratification, and the possibility of obtaining sublimated gratification from motherhood, often deflect female sexuality from normal forms of gratification (Deutsch, 1930). Granting this assumption, motherhood would have to be regarded as antagonistic to sexual gratification, a view which ill agrees with other conclusions based on other authentic observations. Nevertheless, from the analyses of neurotic women and girls we have learned of the intimate association between the neurotic repudiation of the female erotic response and impaired capacity for maternity. It is, indeed, a matter of frequent observation that sterility and frigidity have the same roots, and we have often had the satisfactory experience of observing, as the result of analysis, the appearance of a ready consent to conception and a restoration of the previously impaired sexual response. Curiously enough, the latter often develops subsequently to the former.

However, there is not always so intimate an association between motherhood and a positive sexual response. There are various possible grades of detachment of the one from the other, which may lead to conditions in the love life that can be described as neurotic. This is a parallel to the already-mentioned split in the love life of men who disregard chaste and pure women as sexual objects and are sexually aroused only by notorious low-class women. Freud (1910-1918) described this type of reaction and its variations, and showed how it is determined by the Oedipus complex. Of the antithetical pair, "mother" and "prostitute," the mother is rejected as taboo, and only the prostitute is accepted. Analysis reveals that this separation maintained in the conscious mind is abrogated in the deeper layers of the unconscious. For there was a time—marked by the boy's discovery of sexual secrets—when the mother herself was depreciated and accused of unfaithfulness.

This split in the love life of men has its parallel in the love life of women, but with this difference: the woman's own ego takes the place of the man's object. The woman is herself "mother" or "prostitute," and the whole inner conflict represents the struggle between the two tendencies, which appear to be contrary, but which, ultimately, in this case too converge in the single idea of the unworthy mother.

The formulation of this unconscious thought runs somewhat as follows: Since I have discovered my mother's role as a sexual object, I can only think of her as a base and besmirched creature. If I am like my mother—that is, if I identify myself with her—I am as base and soiled as she. I am quite as much a prostitute.

From the compulsion to identify herself with the mother as well as to diverge from her by acquiring the opposite tendency (i.e., the desire to be different from the mother) there result numerous possibilities in the psychic structure.

Let us start with the pre-Oedipal relationship and its significance for the girl's later life. Following Freud's account, we may speak of an identification with the *active* mother, which as yet had no relation to the Oedipus complex. In this identification the child tries herself out in the role of mother, and displaces her own childish role onto another object, perhaps a younger child in the family, or a doll, or an adult who is willing to assume the role in play. In such play the child makes others suffer or enjoy what she has suffered or enjoyed at the hands of her mother; or she betrays her unfulfilled wishes by imputing to the fantasied child things that were refused her by her mother. If the libido remains attached to the original active and passive roles of the mother-child relationship, this play will be continued into later life under the guise of homosexuality. In the analyses of homosexual women, the pre-Oedipal libidinal components appear repeatedly; nevertheless, one discovers as a rule (this is true at least for my cases) that the women showing such an obdurate mother attachment had developed a regular, perhaps even an unusually strong Oedipus complex in childhood. Indeed, it is usually the difficulties arising out of the Oedipus complex that force the little girl to retreat to the pre-Oedipal mother relationship.

This is not the place for a further discussion of female homosexuality. I merely wish to draw attention to the fact that it is one way for the pre-Oedipal mother relationship to secure its continued existence. Even in this relationship, as mentioned above, it is possible to discover the father's role in the libidinal economy, but in the last analysis the situation is independent of the man; and in libidinal relationships only the roles of mother and child are taken into account, without reference to men. There are various causes and various results of such a repudiation of men.

Numerous possible ways of identifying with the mother are to be found. In analytic work we are most apt to encounter the identification that leads to the normal feminine attitude. The little girl wants to be loved by the father just as her mother is, and like the mother, she wants to have a child by the father (passive identification). This wish can be realized in later life, provided she succeeds in exchanging her infantile object, her father, for another man. Otherwise, she runs into neurotic disturbances, among which we must reckon, along with others, difficulties of conception, of pregnancy and of labor. Instead of a *successful* identification with her mother, the little girl develops a spiteful rivalry, which may result in a grave sense of guilt. Weighed down by this, she renounces the maternal role once and for all, and replaces it with symptoms which betray the wish and the reason for its nonfulfillment. In still another possible development, the mother identification is maintained, the idea of having a child is acceptable, and only the part of the man as a sexual partner is denied. The girl wants to be a mother and to have a child, but quite by herself, by immaculate conception or parthenogenesis. I have described this type of wish fantasy elsewhere (1925), but at that time I understood only one of its components, the one due to the masculinity complex. Its formula is: "I have a child, but quite by herself, by immaculate conception or parthenogenesis. I have described this type of wish fantasy elsewhere show, this fantasy contains the fulfillment of various wishes, and betrays the influence of the Oedipus complex in many ways;

among others, it serves to relieve the sense of guilt by denying the father's share in the child's origin. But the *most important* component is expressed in the formula: "What a man can do, I can," which directly replaces the missing penis by another enlargement of the body-ego, namely, by the self-conceived child.

But what I originally neglected when dealing with this fantasy, I now want to make good, for it belongs to the theme of mother-child relationship. From this point of view, the fantasy is another variety of the mother-child relationship that is expressed in homosexuality. It excludes the troublesome man, and in identification, the active role as originally played with dolls is carried on in relation to the self-created fantasy child. Moreover, the original high evaluation of the mother is thereby revived. The fantasy serves as the mother's expiation. It is a counterpart of the prostitution fantasy and a variant of the part of the family romance which might be stated: "I am not my mother's child, for my mother doesn't do such things." Neither does the mother "do such things" in the parthenogenetic fantasy; she has not only borne the child herself, but conceived it by herself—whereas, according to the family romance, the mother has borne no children at all. The parthenogenetic fantasy is an expression of the longing both in boys and girls, which has given rise to the myth of immaculate conception. For the woman it is a matter of identification with the immaculate mother, whose maternity is perpetuated in her ego, with a denial of sexuality, just as she has denied sexuality to her own mother. This, then, is another way for the woman to assent to motherhood while denying sexuality. She may succeed in doing this in a variety of ways.

The first way is indicated by the pre-Oedipal mother-child relationship; the maternal libido, which is firmly lodged in a mother identification, reaches out to an individual of the same sex, and the man's role in the libidinal economy is reduced to zero.

The second possible way depends on the marked masochistic tendencies, so dominant in the female libido. They may attain such great satisfaction from motherhood—from the role of a *mater dolorosa*—that, due to this gratification, direct sexual satisfaction becomes insignificant.

The third form of asexual motherhood is the parthenogenetic, in its various versions. Paradoxical as it may seem, this structure, too, is closely related to masochism—paradoxical, because the masculinity complex is admittedly very important in its determination. I have observed, however, that when the child conceives her mother's sexual experience as something very masochistic, she also develops a strong tendency to deny this experience. It is usually the child's marked sadistic components that account for such a conception of coitus. The mother, according to this conception, endures great suffering, and her inferior position is regarded as an extreme degradation. Now there are two possibilities: either the identification with the mother will be rejected, or the mother's role as sexual object will be denied (by the above-described mechanism), and the child will identify herself with the asexual mother. If the little girl's passive-feminine wish has a marked masochistic stamp, sexuality will be rejected in apprehension of the fulfillment of her dangerous masochistic wish, but the wish for the asexual parthenogenetically produced child will be retained.

We encounter this split between motherhood and sexuality quite as often in the neuroses as in the life patterns. We find it in the phenomenon discussed at the beginning of this article, where both trends are present in one and the same individual, but existing quite separately with no possibility of symbiosis. Either of these components may completely dominate the conscious life, while the other remains hidden in the unconscious until brought to consciousness by analysis. The genius of a great artist was able to perceive with an intuitive flash what the painstaking effort of analysis has disclosed. In his book *Two Women*, Balzac gives a masterful description of these two opposing tendencies in the female psyche. Two women relate their experiences to each other in letters. They represent contrary types, but each discovers deep within her the hidden longing for something else, for the opposite. The longing is in itself evidence of the fact that the something else is present, even though in a rudimentary form, and repressed. It would seem, indeed, that in this case, Balzac had made use of a favorite literary mechanism—the personification of two opposing psychic reactions. The two women represent, in fact, the opposing tendencies of *one woman*. Opposing tendencies are characteristic of the feminine mind and belong, as a matter of fact, to the normal psyche. Only a marked preponderance of the one or the other leads to complications and neurotic difficulties.

The Baroness Louise de Macumère is the courtesan type, the devotee of love, whose only aim in life is the pursuit of passion, the enjoyment of intense erotic experiences. Her friend, Renée de l'Estorade, on the other hand, is completely given over to her motherhood, even in her relations with her husband. Louise writes: "We are both of us women, I a most blissful love goddess, you the happiest of mothers." . . . "Nothing can be compared to the delights of love." . . . "You, my dear friend, must describe for me the joys of motherhood, so that I may partake of motherhood through you."

And yet, even in the midst of her ecstasy in love relationships, a voice within cries out: "A childless woman is a monstrosity; we are born to be mothers." . . . "I, too, want to be able to sacrifice myself, and I am often absorbed these days in gloomy thoughts—will there never be a little one to call me mother?"

However, this flicker of motherhood is extinguished in the flame of passionate love, and Louise is consumed in this fire without ever having fulfilled her womanhood—in the sense of becoming a mother.

The motherly Madame de l'Estorade writes on the other hand: "My one real happiness (and how precious that was!) lay in my certainty that I had given renewed life to this poor man, even before I had borne him a child!" (i.e., motherhood even in her love relations with her husband).

Desire for children and motherhood completely filled this woman's emotional life. In her repudiation of sexuality she admitted no other feeling beyond motherhood. And yet she writes to her erotic friend: "I had to renounce the pleasures of love and passionate joys for which I long and can only experience through you, the nocturnal meeting on the starlit balcony, the passionate yearning and unbridled effusions of love."

Thus the longing for the enjoyments of love lurks within the virtuous Renée just as the longing for motherhood lurks within the erotic Louise. She even betrays to us that a vigorous protest and hate against the unborn and newborn child can arise in spite of her self-sacrificing motherhood, a hate whose origin lies in the renunciation of erotic satisfaction, in a curtailment of the ego's expectation of erotic fulfillment. The maternal Madame de l'Estorade holds her child on her lap and writes her frivolous friend: "Marriage has brought me motherhood, and so I am happy, too." But a little later: "Everyone talks about the joy of being a mother! I alone can not feel it; I am almost ashamed to confess to you my total lack of feeling." ... "I should like to know at just what point this joy of motherhood puts in its appearance. Good-bye, my happy friend, through whom I relive and enjoy those rapturous delights of love, jealousy at a wayward glance, the secret whisper in the ear." ...

In a word, one is the mother longing for passion, the other the devotee of love who longs for motherhood. No clinical example could describe the phenomenon of cleavage between motherhood and erotism in a more lucid or gripping way than Balzac's portrayal of these two opposite and complementary types. I do not know the sources of Madame de l'Estorade's unbending motherhood—whether it springs from identification with the pre-Oedipal mother, or with the later mother whose sexuality she attempts to deny. But I can speak more definitely about my own patients. They were more radical in repressing sexuality and in splitting off their maternal feelings. Madame de l'Estorade, even though clearly sexually anesthetic, has nevertheless borne a family and has satisfied her maternal feelings on her real and living children. The women under discussion are incapable even of this solution. They transfer their maternal feelings to objects other than their own children—to other women's children or to adults to whom they extend their maternal protection. Many choose a profession or work which offers an outlet for their maternal feelings.

One of my patients was a German midwife. She had chosen this work (which was very unusual for one of her social class) in order to keep on having children—many, many children—and the weaker they were and the more in need of protection, the more she liked them. Her own fear of childbirth played an important role for her; she had to leave the situation of danger to the other woman before she could identify herself with the mother in possession of a child. She was a highly qualified and well-trained midwife, and capable of unlimited self-sacrifice in her work. She came into analysis because of certain strange difficulties in the line of duty. "A patient is in labor" was a battle cry for her, to which she responded like the Germans of old with great fervor (at least inwardly). The agonies of childbirth as seen in other women aroused a curious mixture of feelings of anxiety and pleasure in her. The moment of the child's birth, when she could take it over and give it its first attention, was an ecstatic experience for her. No work was too hard for her; she could stand sleepless nights without fatigue. What she could not endure was the knowledge that a labor was going on when she could not be present; it was intolerable to her to have to miss a delivery. Since it was physically impossible for her to be on hand at every birth in a maternity hospital, she developed a state of excitement and exhaustion which brought her to analysis.

The symptoms in themselves are explanatory. Her profession was intended to free her from an oppressive sense of guilt in relation to her mother: out of her original fantasies of killing her mother and the newborn child arose her urge to rescue lives. Death and birth are closely associated in her childhood fantasies. As a child she certainly heard about pain and danger at the times of her mother's numerous deliveries. This was responsible also for her extremely masochistic conception of the female role in the sexual act. Her own masochistic wishes had manifested themselves during puberty in very sanguinary fantasies of violation. So great a danger for her ego lay in the fulfillment of these fantasies that she completely renounced her sexuality, and she could give expression to her maternal feelings only in the manner described. In her choice of work, then, she was serving two masters: her sense of guilt, and her masochism; she satisfied the latter by means of identification. I have in my possession a photograph of her with eight newborn babies in her arms—an ideal representation of motherhood.

In analysis I have come to know many professional women who were able to satisfy very warm and intense maternal feelings in their work, but who were prevented from having children of their own by a repudiation of their mothers' sexuality together with their own.

I should like to cite one of my own cases as an example of motherhood gone astray. Balzac's Louise as a patient would probably have resembled my case, a woman who sought treatment for nymphomania. From her fifteenth year on, she had given herself to any youth on hand; she was always unhappy and unsatisfied, but curiously enough, despite her puritanical upbringing, quite impenitent. Only extracts from her history can be cited here. The patient was twice forced into a respectable, middle-class marriage by friends who wanted to save her from a prostitute's life. Both marriages were, of course, unsuccessful. She had never had children. She was incapable of conceiving, and did not want children. The words "motherhood" and "motherliness" aroused her abhorrence and disgust, and this spread to all words ending in "hood" or "liness." An absolutely unmotherly woman, one would say. And yet—to betray at the outset the key to her long analysis—in her instinctual life she was nothing else but mother. All the youths to whom she gave herself represented her three younger brothers: she was always wanting to give her brothers something; she used to try taking them into her arms when they were little in the hope of attaining a genital union with them; in this she identified herself with her mother, from whom, at the same time, she took away the children.

In this case one can put the responsibility for the whole neurotic picture on the developmental processes of the pre-Oedipal phase and an overstrong primary mother attachment. She was the only child for six long years—an extremely petted and pampered girl. Then she had to live through three of her mother's pregnancies in quick succession, and the withdrawal of her mother's love in favor of the newborn children. At these times she was always told the fiction of the child growing under the heart, and she was filled with bitter disappointment. The relationship between the little boys and her mother had in her mind a libidinal-sexual character; the mother-child unity (the child in the womb or at the breast) in which she in her childhood jealousy had wanted to play both roles, should accordingly be genitally satisfied in later life. She remained frigid because her fantasies excluded sexuality, and her feelings of guilt were kept in apparent abeyance, because by virtue of her maternal devotion she could deny her hostility toward the youngsters and thereby relieve her sense of guilt.

This case points to various psychic situations in which motherhood either completely denies sexuality, or uses it for its own ends (as in this case) to the detriment of sexual satisfaction; or sexuality may be accepted, but only under conditions which set aside and repudiate motherhood, as mentioned at the beginning of this paper; or, contrariwise, these very conditions must serve to satisfy the demands of motherhood. This may be expressed in the object choice—for example, in the acceptance exclusively of boyish, helpless men as love objects.

As an illustration I may cite another case from literature which made a great impression on me. It is taken from the book, *Aunt Tula,* by the well-known Spanish author, Miguel de Unamuno. Aunt Tula is obsessed with motherhood. Her whole relation to the world is maternal—and nothing but maternal. She regards anything that approaches sensuality or the erotic as despicable or ugly; but to the act of reproduction in another woman she gives the kind of attentive care that a farmer bestows on his crops, or a gardener on his flowers. Yet, it is only the product, the fruit that ripened under her watchful care, which she appropriates as her own, and to which she devotes herself in complete absorption. In this way she gains mental possession of a life which someone else has brought forth in pain. Aunt Tula is the psychological twin sister of our German midwife—only she is still more ruthless in the asexuality of her motherhood. She retains a lifelong hold on the children some other woman has borne for her, and—again more thoroughly consistent than the midwife—she cruelly lets the woman die after she has exhausted her function of childbearing. She even makes a child of the man: she kills his erotic attachment to her, and with iron determination steers him to another woman.

The author has described the complete severance of motherhood from erotism with fine poetical skill and power. One might very well ask how it is possible for a man to obtain such insight into the innermost depths of a woman's psyche.

Aunt Tula lets her sister marry the man whom she herself loves and by whom she is beloved. She arranges the marriage, urges them to have a child, and then takes complete charge of it. She drives her weak sister on from one childbirth to another until the sister dies from exhaustion and leaves the children to the care of Aunt Tula, their spiritual mother. Aunt Tula lives in her brother-in-law's house as the mother of his children and directs his sexual passion onto the servant, the "debased sexual object," who, in turn, is let slowly die after she has repeatedly borne children for Aunt Tula. Aunt Tula lays stress on her role as spiritual mother, and never lets the children imagine for a moment that she—the spiritual mother—conceived them in her body and gave them birth. The consciousness of the corporeal mother must always be present in the home, lest the pure, true motherhood of Aunt Tula be stained with a suspicion of physical participation. Occasionally the repressed longing breaks through and Aunt Tula leaves the village, where she lives with her widowed brother-in-law, for the noisy city. "There is no real purity in the country. Purity develops only where people herd together in a dirty jumble of houses, where they can isolate themselves better. The city is a cloister of lonely people. But in the country the land brings everybody together, the earth on which nearly everyone lies down to sleep. And as for the animals—they are the ancient serpents of paradise. Back to the city!" But of the man who desires her she says, "He is still very childish in many ways. How may she bring him to be one of her children?"

Once again the unspiritual longing breaks the bonds of her spiritual motherhood. "She took her little nephew who was whining with hunger and shut herself in a room with him. Then she drew out one of her shriveled, virginal breasts—it was flushed and trembling as in a fever, shaken as it was by the heavy pounding of her heart—and she pushed the nipple into the baby's soft pink mouth, but his whining only grew the worse as his pale lips sucked on the tremulous desiccated nipple."

Aunt Tula's refusal to admit that she ever had a father who was co-responsible for her conception is masterfully drawn, and it agrees closely with our analytic knowledge. In her mind the really great and beloved father is Don Primitivo, her mother's brother and foster father. It is clearly brought out how Aunt Tula in her fantasy life had wanted to keep her mother's purity intact, just as she preserves her own, and that her relationship to the children is a repetition of her reaction in her relationship to her own mother. It is easy, therefore, for us to understand the following comments which Aunt Tula makes to her sister about Don Primitivo. "Always still and quiet with hardly a spoken word for us, he consecrated our life to the cult of the Holy Virgin, the Mother of God, and at the same time to the cult of our own mother and grandmother, his sister and mother respectively. He gave us a mother with a rosary, and you he taught how to be a mother." The fantasy of the mother's immaculate conception, of motherhood without a father, can be clearly recognized here—as a matter of fact the book describes Aunt Tula's memories of her childhood games with dolls which already contained the essence of the subsequent developments in this direction. One could continue thus to quote the entire book, which is to be warmly recommended to psychoanalytic readers.

From a course of lectures on "The Psychic Development of Women," delivered at the Vienna Psychoanalytic Institute, Summer, 1932. Published in *Neuroses and Character Types;* International Universities Press, 1965, pages 190-202. Reprinted by permission.

Inner and Outer Space: Reflections on Womanhood

Erik H. Erikson

Erik Erikson has been most noted for his theoretical contribution on "identity" and "identity crises." Although he saw these as crystallizing in adolescence, he related both to the entire life cycle, a cycle which he outlined in depth and which led him to extend Freud's "psychosexual" stages of development to "psychosocial" ones. For Erikson, the Ego, "prime mover" of identity formation, must continually mediate between inner needs and outer realities—realities that vary from one historical moment to another and from culture to culture. Rarely, though, did he take up the issue of sex differences—with this exception: his famous "Guidance Study" at the University of California. Conducted shortly after World War II, the experiment used preadolescent boys and girls (ages ten, eleven, and twelve) who were asked to construct "an exciting scene from an imaginary moving picture" and who were given toy blocks, people, and animals with which to do so. Consistently, the girls built "interior scenes"—either a configuration of furniture without walls or simple, low enclosures. The boys, on the other hand, built elaborate walls and façades—"exterior scenes" with protrusions and high towers. These projections of inner and outer space marked significant sex differences according to what Erikson called "the experience of the groundplan of the human body." In the discussion below, which was part of the Daedalus *symposium on "The Woman in America," Erikson re-evaluates these findings nearly two decades later. He connects the theme of "inner space" to Freud's classical views on female sexuality, yet he argues against too "anatomical" an interpretation, pointing instead to a number of relevant social and cultural implications—in particular, to the adaptive possibilities of woman's "inwardness," which exists with all of its positive and negative potentials and which is rooted in the core of female identity.*

1

There are a great number of practical reasons for an intensified awareness of woman's position in the modern world: reasons concerning the availability of women for jobs in which *they are needed* and of their employability in jobs which *they need* in view of intensified industrial competition, international and national. But I believe that there are deeper and darker reasons. The ubiquity of nuclear threat, the breakthrough into outer space, and increasing global communication are all bringing about a total change in the sense of geographic space and of historical time, and thus they necessitate a redefinition of the identity of the sexes within a new image of man. I cannot go here into the alliances and oppositions of the two sexes in previous styles of war and peace. This is a history as yet to be written and, indeed, discovered. But it is clear that the danger of man-made poison dropping invisibly from outer space into the marrow of the unborn in the wombs of women has suddenly brought one major male preoccupation, namely, the "solution " of conflict by periodical and bigger and better wars to its own limits. The question arises whether such a potential for annihilation as now exists in the world should continue to exist without the representation of the mothers of the species in the councils of image-making and of decision.

The frantic and diffused preoccupation with the differences between the sexes and the question as to what kind of woman, now that equality assumes a new and world-wide importance, should be mass manufactured in the future in place of the types now favored by the mass media also reflect a widespread sense on the part of both sexes that a great psychological counterforce has been neglected in what has purported to be progress toward a technological millennium. The special dangers of the nuclear age clearly have brought male leadership close to the limit of its adaptive imagination. The dominant male identity is based on a fondness for "what works" and of what man can make, whether it helps to build or to destroy. For this very reason the all too obvious necessity to sacrifice some of the possible climaxes of technological triumph and of political hegemony for the sake of the mere preservation of mankind is not in itself an endeavor enhancing the male sense of identity. True, an American president felt impelled to say, and said with deep feeling: "A child is not a statistic"; yet the almost desperate urgency of his pleas made clear enough the need for a new kind of political and technological ethics. Maybe if women would only gain the determination to represent as image providers and law givers what they have always stood for privately in evolution and in history (realism of householding, responsibility of upbringing, resourcefulness in peacekeeping, and devotion to healing), they might well be mobilized to add an ethically restraining, because truly supranational, power to politics in the widest sense.

This, I think, many men and women hope openly and many more, secretly. But their hope collides with dominant trends in our technological civilization, and with deep inner resistances as well. Self-made man, in "granting" a relative emancipation to women, could offer only his self-made image as a model to be equaled; and much of the freedom thus won by women now seems to have been spent in gaining access to limited career competition, standardized consumership, and strenuous one-family homemaking. Thus woman, in many ways, has kept her place within the typologies and cosmologies which men have had the exclusive opportunity to cultivate and to idolize. In other words, even where equality is closer to realization it has not led to equivalence, and equal rights have by no means secured equal representation in the sense that the deepest concerns of women find expression in their public influence or, indeed, their actual role in the game of power. In view of the gigantic one-sidedness which is threatening to make man the slave of his triumphant technology, the now fashionable discussion, by women and by men, as to whether woman could and how she might become "fully human" in the traditional sense is really a cosmic parody, and for once one is nostalgic for gods with a sense of humor. The very question as to what it is to be "fully human" and who has the right to grant it to whom indicates that a discussion of the male and female elements in the potentialities of human nature must include rather fundamental issues.

An interdisciplinary symposium, therefore, cannot avoid exploring certain emotional reactions or resistances which hinder concerted discussion. We all have observed the fact that it seems almost impossible to discuss women's nature or nurture without awaking the slogans (for and against) of the all too recent struggle for emancipation. Moralistic fervor outlives changed conditions, and feminist suspicion watches over any man's attempt to help define the uniqueness of womanhood. Yet it still seems to be amazingly hard for the vast majority of women to say clearly what they feel most deeply, and to find the right words for what to them is most acute and actual, without saying too much or too little, and without saying it with defiance or apology. Some who observe and think vividly and deeply do not seem to have the courage of their native intelligence, as if they were somehow afraid on some final confrontation to be found to have no "real" intelligence. Even successful academic competition has, in many, failed to correct this. Thus women are tempted quickly to go back to "their place" whenever they feel out of place. I would also think that a major problem exists in the relationship of leading women to each other and to their women followers. As far as I can judge, "leading" women are all too often inclined to lead in too volatile, moralistic, or sharp a manner (as if they agreed to the proposition that only exceptional and hard women can think) rather than to inform themselves of and to give voice to what the mass of undecided women are groping to say and are willing to stand by, and thus what use they may wish to make of an equal voice in world affairs. Here, maybe, countries in the stages of rapid development or urgent recovery are more fortunate, for immediate needs are more obvious, and free choices restricted.

On the other hand, the hesitance of many men to respond to the new "femininist" alarm, as well as the agitated response of others, may suggest explanations on many levels. No doubt there exists among men an honest sense of wishing to save at whatever cost a sexual polarity, a vital tension and an essential difference which they fear may be lost in too much sameness, equality, and equivalence, or at any rate in too much self-conscious talk. Beyond this, the defensiveness of men (and here we must include the best educated) has many facets. Where men desire, they want to awake desire, not empathize or ask for empathy. Where they do not desire, they find it hard to empathize, especially where empathy makes it necessary to see the other in yourself and yourself in the other, and where therefore the horror of diffused delineations is apt to kill both joy in otherness and sympathy for sameness. It also stands to reason that where dominant identities depend on being dominant, it is hard to grant real equality to the dominated. And, finally, where one feels exposed, threatened, or cornered, it is difficult to be judicious.

For all of this there are age-old psychological reasons, upon only a very few of which will I be able to throw light with my essay. But even a limited report, in the present climate, calls for an acknowledgment from the onset that ambivalences and ambiguities of ancient standing are apt to be temporarily aggravated rather than alleviated by attempts to share partial insight in these matters.

2

There is another general consideration which must precede the discussion of a subject which is so incompletely formulated and which always retains an intense actuality. Every discussant will and must begin where he feels his own field has succeeded or failed to do justice to the issue as he sees it, that is, where he feels he is coming from and going within his own advancing discipline. But since the intricacies of his discipline and of his position in it cannot be intimately known to all discussants, he is apt to be confronted with the remark which a Vermont farmer made to a driver who asked him for directions: "Man, if I wanted to go where you want to go, I wouldn't start here."

Here is where I am, and where I intend to go. In my preface to the book which grew out of the Youth issue of *Daedalus*, I pointed out that that extraordinary symposium failed to develop fully—although Bruno Bettelheim made a determined start—the problem of the identity of female youth. This is a severe theoretical handicap. For the student of development and practitioner of psychoanalysis, the stage of life crucial for the understanding of womanhood is the step from youth to maturity, the state when the young woman relinquishes the care received from the parental family and the extended care of institutions of education, in order to commit herself to the love of a stranger and to the care to be given to his and her offspring. In the *Daedalus* issue on Youth, I suggested that the mental and emotional ability to receive and to give *Fidelity* marks the conclusion of adolescence, while adulthood begins with the ability to receive and give *Love* and *Care*. If the terms here capitalized sound shockingly virtuous in a way reminiscent of moralistic values, I offer no apology: to me, they represent human strengths which are not a matter of moral or esthetic choice, but of stark necessity in individual development and social evolution. For the strength of the generations (and by this I mean a basic disposition *underlying* all varieties of human value systems) depends on the process by which the youths of the two sexes find their respective identities, fuse them in love and marriage, revitalize their respective traditions, and together create and "bring up" the next generation. Here whatever sexual differences and dispositions have developed in earlier life become polarized with finality because they must become part of the whole process of production and procreation which marks adulthood. But how, then, does a woman's identity formation differ by dint of the fact that her somatic design harbors an "inner space" destined to bear the offspring of chosen men and, with it, a biological, psychological, and ethical commitment to take care of human infancy? Is not the disposition for this commitment (whether it be realized in actual motherhood or not) the core problem of *female* fidelity?

The psychoanalytic psychology of women, however, does not "start here." In line with its originological orientation, i.e., the endeavor to infer the meaning of an issue from its origins, it begins with the earliest experiences of differentiation, largely reconstructed from women patients necessarily at odds with their womanhood and with the permanent inequality to which it seemed to doom them. However, since the psychoanalytic method could be developed only in work with acutely suffering individuals, whether adults or children, it was necessary to accept clinical observation as the original starting point for investigating what the little girl, when becoming aware of sex-differences, can *know* as observable fact, can *feel* because it causes intense pleasure or unpleasant tension, or may *infer* or *intuit* with the cognitive and imaginative means at her disposal. Here it would be as unfair as it would be easy to extract quotations from psychoanalysts who were much too circumspect not to offer at least on the margins of their discourses extensive modifications of Freud's position. Nevertheless, I think it is fair to say that the psychoanalytic view of womanhood has been strongly influenced by the fact that the first and basic observations were made by clinicians whose task it was to understand suffering and to offer a remedy; and that they by necessity had to understand the female psyche with male means of empathy, and to offer what the ethos of enlightenment dictated, namely, the "acceptance of reality." It is in line with this historical position that they saw, in the reconstructed lives of little girls, primarily an attempt to observe what could be seen and grasped (namely, what was there in boys and hardly there in girls) and to base on this observation "infantile sexual theories" of vast consequence.

From this point of view, the most obvious fact, namely that children of both sexes sooner or later "know" the penis to be missing in one sex, leaving in its place a woundlike aperture, has led to generalizations concerning women's nature and nurture. From an adaptive point of view, however, it does not seem reasonable to assume that observation and empathy, except in moments of acute or transitory disturbance, would so exclusively focus on what is *not* there. The female child under all but extreme urban conditions is disposed to observe evidence in older girls and women and in female animals of the fact that an inner-bodily space—with productive as well as dangerous potentials—does exist. Here one thinks not only of pregnancy and childbirth, but also of lactation, and of all the richly convex parts of the female anatomy which suggest fullness, warmth, and generosity. One wonders, for example, whether girls are quite as upset by observed symptoms of pregnancy or of menstruation as are (certain) boys, or whether they absorb such observation in the rudiments of a female identity—unless, of course, they are "protected" from the opportunity of comprehending the ubiquity and the meaning of these natural phenomena. Now, no doubt, at various stages of childhood observed data will be interpreted with the cognitive means then available, will be perceived in analogy with the organs then most intensely experienced, and will be endowed with the impulses then prevailing. Dreams, myths, and cults attest to the fact that the vagina has and retains (for both sexes) connotations of a devouring mouth as well as an eliminating sphincter, in addition to being a bleeding wound. However, the cumulative experience of being and becoming a man or a woman cannot, I believe, be entirely dependent

upon fearful analogies and phantasies. Sensory reality and logical conclusion are given form by kinesthetic experience and by
series of memories which "make sense"; and in this total actuality the existence of a *productive inner-bodily space* safely set in
the center of female form and carriage has, I think, a reality
superior to that of the missing organ.

This whole controversy has, I am sure, little to do with the
starting point of most participants in this symposium. If I
nevertheless start from here, it is because I believe that a future
formulation of sex-differences must at least include post-
Freudian insights in order not to succumb to the repressions and
denials of pre-Freudian days.

3

Let me present here an observation which makes my point
wordlessly. Since it has already been presented on a number of
other occasions, I should admit that I am the kind of clinical
worker in whose mind a few observations linger for a long time.
Such observations are marked by a combination of being surprised by the unexpected and yet somehow confirmed by something long awaited. For this same reason, I am apt to present
such observations to various audiences, hoping each time that
understanding may be deepened.

It was in the observation of preadolescent children that I was
enabled to observe sex-differences in a nonclinical setting. The
children were Californian boys and girls, aged ten, eleven, and
twelve years, who twice a year came to be measured, inter-
viewed, and tested in the "Guidance Study" of the University of
California. It speaks for the feminine genius of the director of
the study, Jean Walker Macfarlane, that for over more than two
decades the children (and their parents) not only came with reg-
ularity, but confided their thoughts with little reservation and,
in fact, with much "zest"—to use Jean Macfarlane's favorite
word. That means, they were confident of being appreciated as
growing individuals and eager to reveal and to demonstrate
what (so they had been convincingly told) was useful to know
and might be helpful to others. Since this psychoanalyst, before

joining the California study, had made it his business to interpret play-behavior—a nonverbal approach which had helped him
to understand better what his small patients were not able to
communicate in words—it was decided that he would test his
clinical hypotheses by securing a number of play-constructions
from each child. Over a span of two years, I saw 150 boys and
150 girls three times and presented them, one at a time, with
the task of constructing a "scene" with toys on a table. The toys
were rather ordinary: a family; some uniformed figures (policeman, aviator, Indian, monk, etc.); wild and domestic animals;
furniture; automobiles. But I also provided a variety of blocks.
The children were asked to imagine that the table was a moving
picture studio; the toys, actors and props; and they themselves,
moving picture directors. They were to arrange on the table "an
exciting scene from an imaginary moving picture," and then tell
the plot. This was recorded, the scene photographed, and the
child complimented. It may be necessary to add that no "interpretation" was given.

The observer then compared the individual constructions with
about ten years of data in the files to see whether it provided
some key to the major determinants of the child's inner development. On the whole this proved helpful, but that is not the
point to be made here. The experiment also made possible a
comparison of all play constructions with each other.

A few of the children went about the task with the somewhat
contemptuous attitude of one doing something which was not
exactly worth the effort of a young person already in his teens,
but almost all of these bright and willing youngsters in somber
jeans and gay dresses were drawn to the challenge by that eagerness to serve and to please which characterized the whole
population of the study. And once they were "involved," certain
properties of the task took over and guided them.

It soon became evident that among these properties the spatial
one was dominant. Only half of the scenes were "exciting," and
only a handful had anything to do with moving pictures. In fact,
the stories told at the end were for the most part brief and in no
way comparable to the thematic richness evidenced in verbal
tests. But the care and (one is tempted to say) esthetic responsibility with which the children selected blocks and toys and then
arranged them according to an apparently deeply held sense of

spatial propriety was astounding. At the end, it seemed to be a sudden feeling of "now it's right" which made them come to a sense of completion and, as if awakening from a wordless experience, turn to me and say, "I am ready now,"—meaning: to tell you what this is all about.

I, myself, was most interested in defining the tools and developing the art of observing not only imaginative themes but also spatial configurations in relation to stages of the life cycle, and, of course, in checking psychoanalytic assumptions concerning the sources and forms of neurotic tension in prepuberty. Sex-differences thus were not the initial focus of my interest in spatial behavior. I concentrated my attention on how these constructions-in-progress moved forward to the edge of the table or back to the wall behind it; how they rose to shaky heights or remained close to the table surface; how they were spread over the available space or constricted to a portion of the space. That all of this "says" something about the constructor is the open secret of all "projective techniques." This, too, cannot be discussed here. But soon I realized that in evaluating a child's play-construction, I had to take into consideration the fact that girls and boys used space differently, and that certain configurations occurred strikingly often in the constructions of one sex and rarely in those of the other.

The differences themselves were so simple that at first they seemed a matter of course. History in the meantime has offered a slogan for it: the girls emphasized inner and the boys outer space.

This difference I was soon able to state in such simple configurational terms that other observers, when shown photographs of the constructions without knowing the sex of the constructor (nor, indeed, having any idea of my thoughts concerning the possible meaning of the differences), could sort the photographs according to the configurations most dominant in them, and this significantly in the statistical sense. These independent ratings showed that considerably more than two-thirds of what I subsequently called male configurations occurred in scenes constructed by boys, and more than two-thirds of the "female" configurations in the constructions of girls. I will here omit the finer points which still characterized the atypical scenes as clearly built by a boy or by a girl. This, then, is typical: the girl's scene is an *interior* scene, represented either as a configuration of furniture without any surrounding walls, or by a *simple enclosure* built with blocks. In the girl's scene, people and animals are mostly *within* such an interior or enclosure, and they are primarily people or animals in a *static* (sitting, standing) position. Girls' enclosures consist of *low walls;* i.e., only one block high, except for an occasional elaborate *doorway.* These interiors of houses with or without walls were, for the most part, expressly *peaceful.* Often, a little girl was playing the piano. In a number of cases, however, the *interior was intruded* by animals or dangerous men. Yet the idea of an intruding creature did not necessarily lead to the defensive erection of walls or the closing of doors. Rather the majority of these intrusions have an element of humor and of pleasurable excitement.

Boys' scenes are either houses with *elaborate walls* or *façades with protrusions* such as cones or cylinders representing ornaments or cannons. There are *high towers*; and there are *exterior scenes.* In boys' constructions more people and animals are *outside* enclosures or buildings, and there are more *automotive objects* and *animals moving* along streets and intersections. There are elaborate automotive *accidents*, but also traffic channeled or arrested by the *policeman.* While high structures are prevalent in the configurations of the boys, there is also much play with the danger of collapse or *downfall; ruins* were exclusively boys' constructions.

The male and female spaces, then, were dominated, respectively, by height and downfall and by strong motion and its channelization or arrest; and by static interiors which were open or simply enclosed, and peaceful or intruded upon. It may come as a surprise to some, and seem a matter of course to others, that here sexual differences in the organization of a play space seem to parallel the morphology of genital differentiation itself: in the male, an *external* organ, *erectible* and *intrusive* in character, serving the channelization of *mobile* sperm cells; *internal* organs in the female, with vestibular *access,* leading to *statically expectant* ova. The question is, what *is* really surprising about this, and what only too obvious, and in either case, what does it tell us about the two sexes?

4

Since I first presented these data a decade and a half ago to workers in different fields, some standard interpretations have not yielded an iota. There are, of course, derisive reactions which take it for granted that a psychoanalyst would want to read the bad old symbols into this kind of data. And indeed, Freud did note more than half a century ago that "a house is the only regularly occurring symbol of the (whole) human body in dreams." But there is quite a methodological step (not to be specified here) from the occurrence of a symbol in dreams and a configuration created in actual space. Nevertheless, the purely psychoanalytic or somatic explanation has been advanced that the scenes reflect the preadolescent's preoccupation with his own sexual organs.

The purely "social" interpretation, on the other hand, denies the necessity to see anything symbolic or, indeed, somatic in these configurations. It takes it for granted that boys love the outdoors and girls the indoors, or at any rate that they see their respective roles assigned to the indoors of houses and to the great outdoors of adventure, to tranquil feminine love for family and children and to high masculine aspiration.

One cannot help agreeing with both interpretations—up to a point. Of course, whatever social role is associated with one's physique will be expressed thematically in any playful or artistic representation. And, of course, under conditions of special tension or preoccupation with one part of the body, that body part may be recognizable in play-configurations. The spokesmen for the anatomical and for the social interpretations are thus both right if they insist that neither possibility may be ignored. But this does not make either exclusively right.

A pure interpretation in terms of social role leaves many questions unanswered. If the boys thought primarily of their present or anticipated roles, why, for example, is the policeman their favorite toy, traffic stopped dead a frequent scene? If vigorous activity outdoors is a determinant of the boys' scenes, why did they not arrange *any* sports field on the play table? (One tomboyish girl did.) Why did the girls' love for home life not result in an increase in high walls and closed doors as guarantors of intimacy and security? And could the role of playing the piano in the bosom of their families really be considered representative of what these girls (some of them passionate horseback riders and all future automobilists) wanted to do most or, indeed, thought they should pretend they wanted to do most? Thus the boys' *caution outdoors* and the girls' *goodness indoors* in response to the explicit instruction to construct an *exciting movie scene* suggested dynamic dimensions and acute conflicts not explained by a theory of mere compliance with cultural and conscious roles.

I would suggest an altogether more inclusive interpretation, according to which a profound difference exists between the sexes in the experience of the groundplan of the human body. The spatial phenomenon observed here would then express two principles of arranging space which correspond to the male and female principles in body construction. These may receive special emphasis in prepuberty, and maybe in some other stages of life as well, but they are relevant throughout life to the elaboration of sex-roles in cultural space-times. Such an interpretation cannot be "proven," of course, by the one observation offered here. The question is whether it is in line with observations of spatial behavior in other media and at other ages; whether it can be made a plausible part of a developmental theory; and whether, indeed, it gives to other sex-differences closely related to male and female structure and function a more convincing order. On the other hand, it would not be contradicted by the fact that other media of observation employed to test male and female performance might reveal few or no sexual differences in areas of the mind which have the function of securing verbal or cognitive agreement on matters dominated by the mathematical nature of the universe and the verbal agreement of cultural traditions. Such agreement, in fact, may have as its very function the *correction* of what differentiates the experience of the sexes, even as it also corrects the idiosyncrasies separating other classes of men.

The play-constructing children in Berkeley, California, will lead us into a number of spatial considerations, especially concerning feminine development and outlook. Here I will say little about men; their accomplishments in the conquest of geographic space and of scientific fields and in the dissemination of ideas speak loudly for themselves and confirm traditional values of masculinity. Yet the play-constructing boys in Berkeley may give us pause: on the world scene, do we not see a supremely gifted yet somewhat boyish mankind playing with history and technology, and this following a male pattern as embarrassingly simple (if technologically complex) as the play-constructions of the preadolescent? Do we not see the themes of the toy microcosm dominating an expanding human space: height, penetration, and speed; collision, explosion—and cosmic super-police? In the meantime, women have found their identities in the care suggested in their bodies and in the needs of their issue, and seem to have taken it for granted that the outer world space belongs to the men.

5

Many of the original conclusions of psychoanalysis concerning womanhood hinge on the so-called genital trauma, i.e., the little girl's sudden comprehension of the fact that she does not and never will have a penis. The assumed prevalence of envy in women; the assumption that the future baby is a substitute for the penis; the interpretation that the girl turns from the mother to the father because she finds that the mother not only cheated her out of a penis but has been cheated herself; and finally the woman's disposition to abandon (male) activity and aggressivity for the sake of a "passive-masochistic" orientation: all of these depend on "the trauma," and all have been built into elaborate explanations of femininity. They all exist; and their psychic truth can be shown by psychoanalysis, although it must always be suspected that a special method bares truths especially true under the circumstances created by the method, here the venting in free association of hidden resentments and repressed traumata. These truths, however, assume the character of very partial truths within a theory of feminine development which would assume the early relevance of the productive interior and would thus allow for a shift of theoretical emphasis from the loss of an external organ to a sense of vital inner potential; from a hateful contempt of the motehr to a solidarity with her and other women; from a "passive" renunciation of male activity to the purposeful and competet activity of one endowed with ovaries and a uterus; and from a masochistic pleasure in pain to an ability to stand (and to understand) paid as a meaningful aspect of human experience in general, and of the feminine role in particular. And so it is, in the "fully feminine" woman, as such outstanding writers as Helene Deutsch have recognized even though their nomenclature was tied to the psychopathological term "masochism" (a word which is derived from the name of an Austrian man and novelist who described the perversion of being sexually aroused and satisfied by having pain inflicted on him, even as the tendency to inflict it has been named after the Marquis de Sade).

When this is seen, much now dispersed data will, I believe, fall into line. However, a clinician must ask himself in passing what kind of thinking may have permitted such a nomenclature to arise and to be assented to by outstanding women clinicians. This thinking is, I believe, to be found not only in the psychopathological beginnings of psychoanalysis, but also in the original analytic-atomistic method employed by it. In science, our capacity to think atomistically corresponds to the nature of matter to a high degree and thus leads to the mastery over matter. But when we apply atomistic thinking to man, we break him down into isolated fragments rather than into constituent elements. In fact, when we look at man in a morbid state, he is already fragmented; so that in psychopathology an atomizing mind meets a phenomenon of fragmentation and is apt to mistake fragments for atoms. In psychoanalysis we repeat for our own encouragement (and as an argument against others) that human nature can best be studied in a state of partial breakdown or, at any rate, of marked conflict because—so we say—a conflict delineates borderlines and clarifies the forces which collide on these borderlines. As Freud himself put it, we see a crystal's structure only when it cracks. But a crystal, on the one hand, and an organism or a personality, on the other, differ in the fact that one is inanimate and the other an organic whole which cannot be broken up without a withering of the parts. The ego (in the psychoanalytic sense of a guardian of inner continuity) is in a pathological state more or less inactivated; that is, it loses its capacity to organize personality and experience and to relate itself to other egos in mutual activation. To that extent its irrational defenses are "easier to study" in a state of conflict and isolation than is the ego of a person in vivid interaction with other persons. Yet I do not believe that we can entirely reconstruct the ego's normal functions from an understanding of its dysfunctions, nor that we can understand all vital conflict as neurotic conflict. This, then, would characterize a post-Freudian position: the complexes and conflicts unearthed by psychoanalysis in its first breakthrough to human nature are recognized as existing; they do threaten to dominate the developmental and accidental crises of life. But the freshness and wholeness of experience and the opportunities arising with a resolved crisis can, in an ongoing life, transcend trauma and defense. To illustrate this, let me briefly remark on the often repeated statement that the little girl at a given stage "turns to" her father, whereas in all preceding stages she had been attached to the mother. Actually, Freud insisted only that a theoretical libido was thus turning from one "object" to another, a theory which was, at one time, scientifically pleasing because it corresponded to a simple and (in principle) measurable transfer of energy. Developmentally seen, however, the girl turns to the father at a time when she is quite a different person from the one she was when primarily dependent on her mother. She has normally learned the nature of an "object relationship," once and for all, from the mother. The relationship to the father, then, is of a different kind, in that it happens when the girl has learned to trust (and does not need to retest) basic relationships. She autonomously develops a new form of love for a being who in turn is, or should be, ready to be responsive to the budding (and teasing) woman in her. The total process thus has many more aspects than can be condensed in the statement that the girl turns her libido from the mother to the father. Such transfer can, in fact, be reconstructed only where the ego has been inactivated in some of its capacity to reorganize experience in line with emotional, physical, and cognitive maturation; and only then can it be said that the girl turns to the father *because* she is disappointed in the mother over what the mother has seemingly refused to give her, namely, a penis. Now, no doubt, some unavoidable or excessive disappointment, and the expectation that a new relationship will make up for all the deficiencies of all the old ones, play an eminent role in all changes of attachment from an old to a new person or activity. But in any healthy change the fresh opportunities of the new relationship will outweigh the repetitious insistence on old disappointment.

No doubt, also, new attachments prepare new disappointments. The increasing commitment to an inner-productive role will cause in the small woman such phantasies as must succumb to censorship and frustration, for example, in the insight that no daughter may give birth to her father's children. No doubt also the very importance of the promises and the limitations of the inner productive space exposes women to a sense of specific loneliness, to a fear of being left empty or deprived of treasures, of remaining unfulfilled and of drying up. This, no less than the strivings and disappointments of the little "Oedipus" are fateful ingredients of the human individual and of the whole race. For this very reason it seems decisive not to misinterpret these feelings as totally due to a resentment of not being a boy or of having been mutilated.

It will now be clear why and in what way the children's play constructions evoked in me a response combining the "unexpected and yet awaited." What was unexpected was the domination of the whole space by the sex-differences—a dominance going far beyond the power of any "symbolism" or a "representation" of the morphology of sex organs. The data was "awaited," above all, as nonclinical and nonverbal support of pervasive clinical and developmental impressions concerning the importance of the "inner space" throughout the feminine life cycle. For, as pointed out, clinical observation suggests that in female experience an "inner space" is at the center of despair even as it is the very center of potential fulfillment. Emptiness is the female form of perdition—known at times to men of the inner life (whom we will discuss later), but standard experience for all women. To be left, for her, means to be left empty, to be drained of the blood of the body, the warmth of the heart, the sap of life. How a woman thus can be hurt in depth is a wonder to many a man, and it can arouse both his empathic horror and his refusal to understand. Such hurt can be re-experienced in each menstruation; it is crying to heaven in the mourning over a child; and it becomes a permanent scar in the menopause. Clinically, this "void" is so obvious that generations of clinicians must have had a special reason for not focusing on it. Maybe, even as primitive men banned it with phobic avoidances and magic rituals of purification, the enlightened men of a civilization pervaded by technological pride could meet it only with the interpretation that suffering woman wanted above all what man had, namely, exterior equipment and traditional access to "outer" space. Again, such envy exists and is aggravated in some cultures; but the explanation of it in male terms or the suggestion that it be borne with fatalism and compensated for by a redoubled enjoyment of the feminine equipment (duly certified and accepted as second rate) has not helped women to find their places in the modern world. For it made of womanhood an ubiquitous compensation neurosis marked by a repetitive insistence on being "restored."[1]

6

In approaching the place of sexual differentiation in basic social organization, I will also call on a visual and nonverbal impression.

Recent motion pictures taken in Africa by Washburn and deVore[2] demonstrate vividly the morphology of basic baboon organization. The whole wandering troop in search of food over a certain territory is so organized as to keep within a safe inner space the females who bear future offspring within their bodies or carry their growing young. They are protectively surrounded by powerful males who, in turn, keep their eyes on the horizon, guiding the troop toward available food and guarding it from potential danger. In peacetime, the strong males also protect the "inner circle" of pregnant and nursing females against the encroachments of the relatively weaker and definitely more importunate males. Once danger is spotted, the whole wandering configuration stops and consolidates into an inner space of safety and an outer space of combat. In the center sit the pregnant females and mothers with their newborns. At the periphery are the males best equipped to fight or scare off predators.

I was impressed with these movies not only for their beauty and ingenuity, but because here I could see in the Bush configurations analogous to those in the Berkeley play structures. The baboon pictures, however, can lead us one step further. Whatever the morphological differences between the female and the male baboons' bony structures, postures, and behaviours, they are adapted to their respective tasks of harboring and defending the concentric circles, from the procreative womb to the limits of the "productive" and defensible territory. Thus morphological trends "fit" given necessities and are therefore elaborated by basic social organization. And it deserves emphasis that, even among the baboons, the greatest warriors display a chivalry which permits the female baboons, for example, to have weaker shoulders and lesser fighting equipment.

Whether, when, and in what respects, then, a female in any setting is "weaker" is a matter to be decided not on the basis of comparative tests of isolated muscles, capacities, or traits but on that of the functional fitness of each item as part of an organism which, in turn, fits into an ecology of divided function.

Human society and technology has, of course, transcended evolutionary arrangement, making room for cultural triumphs and liberties as well as for physical and psychological maladaptation on a large scale. But when we speak of biologically given strengths and weaknesses in the human female, we may yet have to accept as one measure of all difference the biological rockbottom of sexual differentiation. In this, the woman's productive inner space may well remain the principal criterion, whether she chooses to build her life partially or wholly around it or not. At any rate, many of the testable items on the long list of "inborn" differences between human males and females can be shown to have a meaningful function within an ecology which is built, as any mammalian ecology must be, around the fact that the human foetus must be carried inside the womb for a given number of months; and that the infant must be suckled or, at any rate, raised within a maternal world best staffed at first by the mother (and this for the sake of her own awakened motherliness as well as for the newborn's needs), with a gradual addition of other women. Here years of specialized womanhours of work are involved. It makes sense, then, that the little girl, the bearer of ova and of maternal powers, tends to survive her birth more surely and is a tougher creature, to be plagued, to be sure, by many small ailments, but more resistant to some man-killing diseases (for example, of the heart) and with a longer life expectancy. It also makes sense that she is able earlier than boys to concentrate on details immediate in time and space, and has throughout a finer discrimination for things seen, touched, and heard. To these she reacts more vividly, more personally, and with greater compassion. More easily touched and touchable, however, she is said also to recover faster, ready to react again and elsewhere. That all of this is essential to the "biological" task of reacting to the differential needs of others, especially infants, will not appear to be a farfetched interpretation; nor will it, in this context, seem a deplorable inequality that in the employment of larger muscles she shows less vigor, speed, and coordination. The little girl also learns to be more easily content within a limited circle of activities and shows less resistance to control and less impulsivity of the kind that later leads boys and men to "delinquency." All of these and more certified "differences" could be shown to have corollaries in our play constructions.

Now it is clear that much of the basic schema suggested here as female also exists in some form in all men and decisively so in men of special giftedness—or weakness. The inner life which characterizes some artistic and creative men certainly also compensates for their being biologically men by helping them to specialize in that inwardness and sensitive indwelling (the German *Innigkeit*) usually ascribed to women. They are prone to cyclic swings of mood while they carry conceived ideas to fruition and toward the act of disciplined creation. The point is that in women the basic schema exists within a *total optimum configuration* such as cultures have every reason to nurture in the majority of women, and this for the sake of collective survival as well as individual fulfillment. It makes little sense, then, when discussing basic sex-differences to quote the deviations and accomplishments (or both) of exceptional men or women without an inclusive account of their many-sided personalities, their special conflicts and their complex life histories. On the other hand, one should also emphasize (and especially so in a post-Puritan civilization which continues to decree predestination by mercilessly typing individuals) that successive stages of life offer growing and maturing individuals ample leeway for free variation in essential sameness.

Thus only a total configurational approach—somatic, historical, individual—can help us to see the differences of functioning and experiencing in context rather than in isolated and senseless comparison. Woman, then, is not "more passive" than man simply because her central biological function forces her or permits her to be active in a manner tuned to inner-bodily processes, or because she may be gifted with a certain intimacy and contained intensity of feeling, or because she may choose to dwell in the protected inner circle within which maternal care can flourish. Nor is she "more masochistic" because she must accept inner periodicities (Benedek) in addition to the pain of childbirth, which is explained in the Bible as the eternal penalty for Eve's delinquent behavior and interpreted by writers as recent as de Beauvoir as "a hostile element within her own body." Taken together with the phenomena of sexual life and motherhood, it is obvious that woman's knowledge of pain makes her a "dolorosa" in a deeper sense than one who is addicted to small pains. She is, rather, one who "takes pains" to understand and alleviate suffering, and who can train others in the forbearance necessary to stand unavoidable pain. She is a "masochist," then, only when she exploits pain perversely or vindictively, which means that she steps out of, rather than deeper into, her female function. By the same token, a woman is pathologically passive only when she becomes too passive within a sphere of efficacy and personal integration which includes her disposition for female activity.

One argument, however, is hard to counter. Woman, through the ages (at any rate, the patriarchal ones), has lent herself to a variety of roles conducive to an exploitation of masochistic potentials: she has let herself be incarcerated and immobilized, enslaved and infantilized, prostituted and exploited, deriving from it at best what in psychopathology we call "secondary gains" of devious dominance. This fact, however, could be satisfactorily explained only within a new kind of biocultural history which (and this is one of my points) would first have to overcome the prejudiced opinion that woman must be, or will be, what she is or has been under particular historical conditions.

7

Am I saying, then, that "anatomy is destiny"? Yes, it is destiny, insofar as it determines the potentials of physiological functioning and its limitations. But anatomy also, to an extent, codetermines personality configurations. The modalities of woman's commitment and involvement, for better *and* for worse, also reflect the groundplan of her body. We may mention only woman's capacity on many levels of existence to (actively) include, to accept, to "have and hold"—but also to hold on, and to hold in. She may be protective with high selectivity, and overprotective without discrimination. That she must protect means that she must rely on protection—she may demand overprotection. She too has her organ of intrusion, the nipple which nurses; and her wish to succor can, indeed, become intrusive and oppressive. It is, in fact, of such exaggerations and deviations that many men and also women think when the unique potentials of womanhood are discussed.

In all of this, however, the problem is not whether a woman is "more so" than a man, but how much she varies within womanhood and what she makes of it within the leeway of her stage of life and of her historical and economic opportunities. For man, in addition to having a body, is *some*body; which means he is an indivisible personality *and* a defined member of a group. In this sense Napoleon's dictum that *History is destiny*, which was, I believe, to be counterpointed by Freud's dictum that destiny lies in anatomy (and one often must know what a man tried to counterpoint with his most one-sided dicta) is equally valid. In other words: anatomy, history, and personality are our *combined destiny*.

Men, of course, have shared and taken care of some of the concerns for which women stand: each sex can transcend itself to feel and to represent the concerns of the other. For even as real women harbor a legitimate as well as a compensatory masculinity, so real men can partake of motherliness—if permitted to do so by powerful mores.

In search of an observation which bridges biology and history, an extreme historical example comes to mind in which women elevated their procreative function to a style of life when their men seemed totally defeated.

This story was highlighted for me on two occasions when I participated in conferences in the Caribbean and learned of family patterns prevailing throughout the islands. Churchmen have had reason to deplore, and anthropologists to explore, the pattern of Caribbean family life, obviously an outgrowth of the slavery days of plantation America, which extended from the northeast coast of Brazil through the Caribbean half-circle into the southeast of the present United States. Plantations, of course, were agricultural factories owned and operated by gentlemen whose cultural and economic identity had its roots in a supraregional upper class. They were worked by slaves, that is, by men who, being mere equipment, were put to use when and where necessary, and who often had to relinquish all chance of becoming the masters of their families and communities. Thus the women were left with the offspring of a variety of men who could give neither provision nor protection, nor provide any identity except that of a subordinate species. The family system which ensued is described in the literature in terms of circumscriptions: the rendering of "sexual services" between persons who cannot be called anything more definite than "lovers"; "maximum instability" in the sexual lives of young girls, who often "relinquish" the care of their offspring to their mothers; and mothers and grandmothers who determine the "standardized mode of co-activity" which is the minimum requirement for calling a group of individuals a family. These are, then, called "household groups"—single dwellings occupied by people sharing a common food supply. These households are "matrifocal," a word understating the grandiose role of the all-powerful grandmother-figure, who will encourage her daughters to leave their infants with her, or at any rate to stay with her as long as they continue to bear children. Motherhood thus became community life; and where churchmen could find little or no morality, and casual observers little or no order at all, the mothers and grandmothers had to become fathers and grandfathers, in the sense that they exerted the only continuous influence resulting in an ever newly improvised set of rules for the economic obligations of the men who had fathered the children. They upheld the rules of incestuous avoidance. Above all, so it seems to me, they provided the only superidentity which was left open after the enslavement of the men, namely, that of the worthwhileness of a human infant irrespective of his parentage. It is well known how many little white gentlemen benefited from the extended fervor of the nurturant Negro woman—southern mammies, creole das, or Brazilian babas. This phenomenal caring is, of course, being played down by the racists as mere servitude, while the predominance of personal warmth in Caribbean women is decried by moralists as Af-

rican sensualism or idolized as true femininity by refugees from
"Continental" womanhood. One may, however, see at the roots of
this maternalism a grandiose gesture of human adaptation
which has given the area of the Caribbean (now searching for a
political and economic pattern to do justice to its cultural unity)
both the promise of a positive maternal identity and the threat
of a negative male one: for the fact that identity relied on the
mere worth of being born has undoubtedly weakened economic
aspiration in many men.

That this has been an important historical issue can be seen in
the life of Simón Bolívar. This "liberator of South America"
originated in the coastal region of Venezuela, which is one an-
chorpoint of the great Caribbean half-circle. When in 1827
Bolívar liberated Caracas and entered it in triumph, he recognized the Negress Hipolita, his erstwhile wetnurse, in the crowd.
He dismounted and "threw himself in the arms of the Negress
who wept with joy." Two years earlier, he had written to his sister: "I enclose a letter to my mother Hipolita so that you give
her all she wants and deal with her as if she were my mother;
her milk fed my life, and I knew no other father than she"
(translation not mine). Whatever personal reason can be found
for Bolívar's attitude toward Hipolita (he had lost his mother
when he was nine, etc.) is amply matched by the historical significance of the fact that he could play up this relationship as a
propaganda item within that often contradictory ideology of race
and origin which contributed to his charisma throughout the
continent he conquered.

That continent does not concern us here. But as for the Caribbean area, the matrifocal theme explains much of a certain dis-
balance between extreme trustfulness and weakness of initiative
which could be exploited by native dictators as well as by foreign
capital and has now become the concern of the erstwhile colonial
masters as well as of the emancipated leaders of various island
groups. Knowing this, we may understand that the bearded
group of men and boys who have taken over one of the islands
represents a deliberately new type of man who insists on proving
that the Caribbean male can earn his worth in production as
well as in procreation without the imposition of "continental"
leadership or ownership.

This transformation of a colorful island area into an inner

space structured by woman is an almost clinical example to be applied with caution. And yet it is only one story out of that unofficial history which is as yet to be written for all areas and eras: of how women have attempted to balance the official history of territories and domains, markets and empires; the history of women's quiet creativity in preserving and restoring what official history had torn apart. Some stirrings in contemporary historiography, such as attempts to describe closely the everyday atmosphere of a given locality in a given historical era, seem to bespeak a growing awareness of a need for, shall we say, an integrated history.

8

We speak of anatomical, historical, and psychological facts; and yet, it must be clear that facts reliably ascertained by the methods of these three fields by the same token lose a most vital interconnection. Man is, at one and the same time, part of a somatic order of things, and part of a personal and of a social one. To avoid identifying these orders with established fields, we may call them Soma, Psyche, and Polis, and yet know that each can be hyphenated with the other to designate new fields of inquiry such as psycho-somatic and psycho-social. Each order guards a certain intactness and also offers a leeway of optional or at least workable choices; while man lives in all three and must work out their complementarities and contradictions.

Soma is the principle of the *organism*, living its *life cycle*. But the female Soma is not only comprised of what is within a woman's skin (and clothes). It includes a mediatorship in evolution, genetic as well as socio-genetic, by which she creates in each child the somatic (sensual, and sensory) basis for his physical, cultural, and individual identity. This mission, once a child is conceived, must be completed. It is woman's unique job. But no woman lives or needs to live only in this extended somatic sphere. She must make (or else neglect) decisions as a citizen and worker, and of course, as an individual; and the modern world offers her even greater leeway in choosing, planning, or renouncing her somatic tasks more knowingly and responsibly.

The sphere of *citizenship* I call Polis because I want to emphasize that it reaches as far as the borderlines of what one has recognized as one's "city," and it is clear that modern communication makes such a communality ever larger if not global. In this sphere women can be shown to share with men a close sameness of intellectual orientation and capacity for work and leadership. "Political" equality, however, can live up to this fact only by encompassing for women a position in the political sphere which goes beyond an occasional voice (whispered or shouted) and a periodic vote for male politicians and for issues exclusively determined by men. It even goes beyond the active participation in politics and government. In this sphere, too, the influence of women will not be fully actualized until it reflects without apology the facts of the "inner space" and the potentialities and needs of the feminine psyche. It is as yet unpredictable what the tasks and roles and opportunities and job specifications will be once women are not merely adapted to male jobs but when they learn to adapt jobs to themselves. Such a revolutionary reappraisal may even lead to the insight that jobs now called masculine force men, too, to inhuman adjustments.

In the sphere of Psyche, psychoanalysis has come to understand an organizing principle called ego.[3] Ego-organization mediates between somatic and personal experience and political actuality in the widest sense. To do so it uses psychological mechanisms common to both sexes—a fact which makes intelligent communication, mutual understanding, and social organization possible. It is in the ego that the equivalence of all truly individualized experience has its organizing center, for the ego is the guardian of the *indivisibility of the person*. No doubt militant individualism has inflated this core of individuality to the point where it seemed altogether free of somatic and social considerations. However, psychoanalysis is making it clear that the active strength of the ego (and especially the identity within the individuality) is inseparable from the power of somatic development and of social organization. Here, then, the fact that a woman, whatever else she may also be, never is not-a-woman, creates unique relations between her individuality, her bodily intimacy, and her productive potentials, and demands that feminine ego-strength be studied and defined in its own right.

It should be clear, then, that I am using my definitions concerning the central importance of woman's procreative task not in a renewed attempt to "doom" every woman to perpetual motherhood and to deny her the equivalence of individuality and the equality of citizenship. But since a woman is never not-a-woman, she can see her long-range goals only in those modes of activity which include and integrate her natural dispositions. An emancipated woman thus does not necessarily accept comparisons with more "active" male proclivities as a measure of her equivalence, even if and after it has become quite clear that she can match man's performance and competence in most spheres of achievement. True equality can only mean the right to be uniquely creative.

We may well hope, therefore, that there is something in woman's specific creativity which has waited only for a clarification of her relationship to masculinity (including her own) in order to assume her share of leadership in those fateful human affairs which so far have been left entirely in the hands of gifted and driven men, and often of men whose genius of leadership eventually has yielded to ruthless self-aggrandizement. Mankind now obviously depends on new kinds of social inventions and on institutions which guard and cultivate that which nurses and nourishes, cares and tolerates, includes and preserves.

Before he left Harvard, Paul Tillich in a conversation expressed uneasiness over the clinical preoccupation with an "adaptive ego" which, he felt, might support (these are my words) further attempts at manufacturing a mankind feeling so "adapted" that it would be unable to face "ultimate concerns." I agreed that psychoanalysis was in danger of becoming part of such vain streamlining of existence; but that in its origin and essence, it intends to *free* man for "ultimate concerns." For such concerns can begin to be ultimate only in those rare moments and places where neurotic resentments end and where mere adaptation is transcended. I think he agreed. One may add that man's Ultimate has too often been visualized as an infinity which begins where the male conquest of outer spaces ends, and a domain where an even more omnipotent and omniscient Being must be submissively acknowledged. The Ultimate, however, may well be found also in the Immediate, which has so largely been the domain of woman and of the inward mind. Such considerations would lead us to the *temporal* aspects (here neglected throughout) of the space-time experience of womanhood.

From *Daedalus*, Journal of the American Academy of Arts and Sciences, Boston, Massachusetts, Spring 1964, *The Woman in America*, pages 582-606. Reprinted by permission.

FOOTNOTES

1. The question of the innermost extent of the woman's total sexual response can not be discussed here.
2. Three films taken in Kenya, 1959: "Baboon Behavior," "Baboon Social Organization," and "Baboon Ecology."
3. The term ego—in all but narrow professional circles—is fighting a losing battle against its popular and philosophical namesakes, the inflated and the self-centered and self-conscious "egos." Nevertheless, the term must be used as long as the concept represents an important trend in psychoanalytic theory.

Woman and Her Discontents: A Reassessment of Freud's Views on Female Sexuality

William H. Gillespie

One of today's leading English psychoanalysts, William H. Gillespie has been President of the British Psycho-Analytic Society and, from 1959 until 1963, served as President of the International Psycho-Analytical Association. In the selection which follows, he offers a broad historical survey of Freud's views on female sexual development and sex differentiation, reconsiders the criticisms of Karen Horney, Melanie Klein, and Ernest Jones, and relates the entire inquiry to current clinical and biological research. In particular, Gillespie points to the research of Masters and Johnson on the physiological functions of female orgasm and to their conclusion which shows the "integral nature of the clitoral-vaginal complex of organs." Such recent studies, and their extensive findings, reconfirm the need to reexamine Freud's earlier conceptualization of the clitoris as essentially a "male" organ and the vagina as essentially a "female" one. Gillespie also introduces relevant work in phylogenetics and bio-psychology and raises a number of stimulating questions about the evolution of female sexual development. Was it not, he asks, the female who had to evolve internal sexual organs as water animals gradually turned into land animals (the female fish, for example, like the male, expels her reproductive product out of her body and into the water), and could this not explain the more complicated nature of female sexuality? Although Freud came to the subject of women from a different direction, he may have had, Gillespie concludes, a better grasp of the complexities of their development than his critics previously realized.

The vast dimensions of the subject of female sexuality have obliged me to limit my field rather carefully. I have therefore taken as my starting point Freud's own views on female sexuality. As we all know, Freud was a true scientist and his career was a voyage of discovery, during which new vistas kept presenting themselves; and so, of course, we have to reckon with Freud's changing views, for some of them were altered quite radically in his later years. Some, however, were retained relatively unchanged, and it is these steadfastly held opinions that led to a controversy, which became particularly lively in the 1920s. The opposition was led largely by women analysts, but they had the powerful support of Ernest Jones. This controversy is part of the intellectual environment in which Melanie Klein's lines of thought and clinical activity took shape, and so one begins to appreciate how far-reaching have been its consequences.

I have attempted to discover some of the germs of Freud's views on female sexuality by scrutinizing his early published works and the correspondence with Fliess. The first important statements emerged in 1894-95, in Draft G of the Fliess papers (Freud, 1950a) and in the paper on anxiety neurosis published on 15 January, 1895 (Freud, 1895). Draft G is remarkable for the so-called sexual diagram; the same ideas are presented purely verbally in the 1895 paper, where Freud makes it quite clear that his view of the sexual process applies, in the first instance, to men. I will quote:

In the sexually mature male organism sexual excitation is produced—probably continuously—and periodically becomes a stimulus to the psyche.... This somatic excitation is manifested as a pressure on the walls of the seminal vesicles, which are lined with nerve endings; thus this visceral excitation will develop continuously, but it will have to reach a certain height before it is able to overcome the resistance of the intervening path of conduction to the cerebral cortex and express itself as a psychical stimulus. When this has happened, however, the group of sexual ideas which is present in the psyche becomes supplied with energy and there comes into being the psychical state of libidinal tension which brings with it an urge to remove that tension. A psychical unloading of this kind is only possible by means of what I shall call *specific* or *adequate* action. This adequate action consists, for the male sexual instinct, in a complicated spinal reflex act which brings about the unloading of the nerve-endings, and in all the psychical preparations which have to be made in order to set off that reflex. Anything other than the adequate action would be fruitless, for once the somatic sexual excitation has reached threshold value it is turned continuously into psychical excitation, and something must positively take place which will free the nerve-endings from the load of pressure on them—which will, accordingly, remove the whole of the existing somatic excitation and allow the subcortical path of conduction to re-establish its resistance (pp. 108–109).

This view seems to depend on a close analogy with that other vesicle, the urinary bladder; in principle the difference would reside in the more complicated specific action required in the sexual act.

Freud goes on to say:

... in essentials this formula is applicable to women as well, in spite of the confusion introduced into the problem by all the artificial retarding and stunting of the female sexual instinct. ... Where women are concerned, however, we are not in a position to say what the process analogous to the relaxation of the seminal vesicles may be (p. 109).

Freud's inability to discover a female analogue to the seminal vesicles is surely damaging to the theory. Another point to which I would draw attention, however, is his remark about the "artificial retarding and stunting of the sexual instinct," for it shows how much, at this early date, Freud was alive to the importance of social factors in producing effects that might be mistakenly attributed to inherent differences between the sexes. Similar remarks can be found in other parts of his early writings. For example, in Draft G he writes:

Women become anaesthetic more easily because their whole upbringing works in the direction of not awakening somatic sexual excitation, but of changing all excitations which might otherwise have that effect into psychical stimuli. ... This is necessary because, if there were a vigorous somatic sexual excitation, the psychical sexual group would soon acquire such strength intermittently that, as in the case of men, it would bring the sexual object into a favourable position by means of a specific reaction. But women are required to leave out the arc of the specific reaction: instead, permanent specific actions are required of them which entice the male into the specific action (p. 204). [Note the word "required."]

I think that what Freud says here about the "permanent specific actions" required of women which entice the male into the specific action is particularly interesting in connection with fairly recent work by one of our British colleagues, Dr. Michael, whose investigations of rhesus monkeys (Michael, 1968) have shown that the male's sexual activity or lack of it varies, not with his own hormonal state but with that of his female partner. Considerations like this, which in a way Freud had anticipated by more than a half-century, just as he anticipated the discovery of sexual hormones themselves—such considerations should make one suspicious of formulations which ascribe sexual activity to the male and passivity to the female, a trap which Freud continually found himself escaping by a hairsbreadth.

Already in 1897 (Freud, 1950*b*) Freud's exposition of the origins of repression foreshadowed the views about the role of the clitoris which were to play so important a part in his theory. The "something organic" in repression is a question of the abandonment of former sexual zones, i.e., the regions of the anus and of the mouth and throat, which originally instigate something analogous to the later release of sexuality. Memories of excitations of these abandoned sexual zones, thanks to "deferred action" (i.e., the intensification due to sexual maturing)—such memories give rise not to libido but to unpleasure, analogous to disgust—"just as we turn away our sense organ . . . [from a stinking object] in disgust, so do our preconsciousness and our conscious sense turn away from the memory. This is *repression*" (p. 269). If psychically bound this leads to rejection *(Verwerfung)*, the affective basis for morality, shame, etc. Disgust appears earlier in little girls than in boys, but the main distinction emerges at puberty, when a further sexual zone is (wholly or in part) extinguished in females which persists in males, that is, the region of the clitoris. "Hence the flood of shame . . . till the new, vaginal, zone is awakened."

It was, of course, in the *Three Essays*, published eight years later (Freud, 1905) that Freud elaborated all this more fully. He writes there:

If we are to understand how a little girl turns into a woman, we must follow the further vicissitudes of this excitability of the clitoris. Puberty, which brings about so great an accession of libido in boys, is marked in girls by a fresh wave of *repression*, in which it is precisely clitoridal sexuality that is affected. What is thus overtaken by repression is a piece of masculine sexuality. . . . When at last the sexual act is permitted and the clitoris itself becomes excited, it still retains a function: the task, namely, of transmitting the excitation to the adjacent female sexual parts, just as—to use a simile—pine shavings can be kindled in order to set a log of harder wood on fire.... When erotogenic susceptibility to stimulation has been successfully transferred by a woman from the clitoris to the vaginal orifice, it implies that she has adopted a new leading zone for the purpose of her later sexual activity.... The fact that women change their leading erotogenic zone in this way, together with the wave of repression at puberty, which, as it were, puts aside their childish masculinity, are the chief determinants of the greater proneness of women to neurosis and especially to hysteria. These determinants, therefore, are intimately related to the essence of femininity (pp. 220-221).

I hope you will forgive me if I now make a jump forward of 70 years. The subject will be the same, but the approach that of observation and physiological inquiry, which by 1965 had caught up with the Freud of 1895. I am referring to the clinical researches of Masters & Johnson (1966). This work has, I believe, aroused criticism and resistance in many people, sometimes rationalized as disapproval of scientific scopophilia. Sexual matters continue to be in some ways taboo, despite all appearances to the contrary, and for my part I see Masters & Johnson's bold and direct approach to the subject of human sexual activity as something quite analogous to Freud's own attitude in defying Victorian convention by handling these matters verbally with patients; and so I experience some of the hostile criticism of Masters & Johnson as *déjà vu*. What they have described are facts, unless the contrary is proved by further research; the theories that may be built on these facts are, of course, an entirely different matter; they have been used, for example, by Sherfey (1966) to support an extreme feminist point of view.

At this point I am not discussing feminism but the significance of clitoris and vagina in female sexuality. With the help of special apparatus Masters & Johnson were able to make direct observations on the changes in the female genitalia during sexual activity. These showed that: "The female's physiologic responses to effective sexual stimulation ... develop with consistency, regardless of the source of the psychic or physical sexual stimulation." But note carefully that they are speaking of physiological, not psychological responses. They also observe that actual orgasmic experiences are initiated in both sexes by similar muscle components. As regards the clitoris during intravaginal coitus, it is kept in a state of continuous stimulation through the transmitted effect of alternate penile thrust and withdrawal even though, as Sherfey says, it is not being touched and appears to have vanished, owing to its erection and retraction into the swollen clitoral hood. Sherfey adds:

Furthermore, it is also obvious why the thrusting movements of the penis will necessarily create simultaneous stimulation of the lower third of the vagina, labia minora, and clitoral shaft and glans as an integrated, inseparable functioning unit with the glans being the most important and, in far the majority of instances, the indispensable initiator of the orgasmic reaction.

With this last remark in mind, namely, that the glans of the clitoris is generally the indispensable initiator of orgasm, let us return to the *Three Essays* and note that Freud had expressed just the same thought when he wrote of: "transmitting the excitation to the adjacent female sexual parts, just as . . . pine shavings can be kindled in order to set a log of harder wood on fire." But there is a vital difference, and I suspect that it is betrayed by Freud's phrase "the adjacent *female* sexual parts" (my italics) —does not this mean, even if unintentionally, that the clitoris is *not* a female sexual part, and that it must therefore be given up? Does not Freud's theory of the pseudo-male clitoris which has to be given up imply an insistence that the female *must* be castrated—it is "required of her," to use his phrase? After all, this female castration is actually practised in certain cultures. If I may be permitted to misquote Scripture: From her that hath not shall be taken away even that which she hath. And so Freud, having expressed so beautifully, by his simile of kindling, this true insight into the function of the clitoris, at once extends his concept in a different direction—mistakenly, I submit. He assumes that the transfer to excitation from the clitoris to the adjacent sexual parts is not merely a matter of topography but one of maturational development. He says:

before this transference can be effected, a certain interval of time must elapse, during which the young woman is anaesthetic. This anaesthesia may become permanent if the clitoridal zone refuses to abandon its excitability. . . . They are anaesthetic at the vaginal orifice but are by no means incapable of excitement originating in the clitoris or even in other zones (p. 221).

And from this there arises the unrealistic and idealized concept of vaginal orgasm, about which I have written elsewhere (Gillespie, 1969).

With the knowledge at his disposal at the turn of the century, to say nothing of the paternalistic cultural background against which he was working, combined with Victorian prudery, the amazing thing is not Freud's erroneous conclusion but the fact that he was able to achieve so much insight into female sexuality. Often, over the years, he expressed the difficulty he found in exploring this "dark continent." It is a corner of precisely this darkness on which Masters & Johnson have been able to throw some light, in a highly literal sense, with their illuminated phallus and colour cinematography.

Freud did not make public any comprehensive revision of his views until the appearance of his very important paper on "Some Psychical Consequences of the Anatomical Distinction between the Sexes" (Freud, 1925), although already in "The Sexual Theories of Children" (Freud, 1908) he is speaking of the castration complex and female penis envy, one of the main themes of the later paper. Now the visual discovery of the penis begins to assume a leading place. "She has seen it [the penis] and knows that she is without it and wants to have it. Here what has been named the masculinity complex of women branches off" (Freud, 1925, pp. 252–253). And Freud explains how the hope of obtaining a penis may persist indefinitely and account for strange actions; or its absence may be disavowed and so she may behave as though she were a man. Alternatively, she remains aware of the wound to her narcissism and develops a sense of inferiority, which she may extend to womankind in general, in this way showing at least one male characteristic. She becomes in general more prone to jealousy than a man. Her loving relationship with her mother becomes loosened, for she holds her mother responsible for her inferior equipment. She also turns against masturbation for the same narcissistic reason. But through the equation "penis-child" she is able to give up the wish for a penis of her own; with the wish for a child in view she takes her father as a love object and her mother becomes the object of her jealousy. So she reaches her Oedipus complex in this roundabout way and has "turned into a little woman"—*faute de mieux*, one feels obliged to add. To quote again: *"Whereas in boys the Oedipus complex is destroyed by the castration complex, in girls it is made possible and led up to by the castration complex"* (p. 256, Freud's italics). Ideally, in the boy, the Oedipus complex exists no longer, the superego has become its heir. So what of the female superego? Freud says:

I cannot evade the notion (though I hesitate to give it expression) that for women the level of what is ethically normal is different from what it is in men. Their super-ego is never so inexorable, so impersonal, so independent of its emotional origins as we require it to be in men....We must not allow ourselves to be deflected from such conclusions by the denials of the feminists (pp. 257, 258).

Of course the feminists and their latter-day counterparts of the women's liberation movement have done much more than deny Freud's conclusions; they have counter-attacked vigorously and denounced Freud as a male chauvinist. But what should concern us is not whether Freud's views give offense—this they have always done in one way or another—but whether they are correct. The essential point concerns the nature of femininity. Is it something natural to the female child, or is it something that she has to learn to accept, after failing to achieve a more desirable condition? And if it is true that many females in our culture are reluctant to accept their role as feminine women, is this because that role is inherently unattractive for anatomical and physiological as well as for psychological reasons; or is it because society, dominated by men as the feminists maintain, has decreed that the feminine role is to be weak, submissive and enslaved? The feminists would say that Freud, with his scientific authority, has supported powerfully the male chauvinistic forces from which liberation must be achieved. Some of his remarks can easily be used to support this view of his attitude to female development and its deviations from *his* idea of the normal or desirable. For example, in his last comments on the subject (Freud, 1940), he says: "It does little harm to a woman if she remains in her feminine Oedipus attitude. . . . She will choose her husband for his paternal characteristics and be ready to recognize his authority" (p. 194). How very convenient for a paternalistic husband, one can hear the feminists say.

For the present let us postpone any attempt to assess Freud's attitude and alleged antifemale prejudice and let us consider briefly some of the criticisms and attempted rebuttals of Freud's views that have been made by other psychoanalysts, mostly women. Perhaps the most outspoken, and one of the earliest, was Karen Horney (1926, 1932, 1933). For her, the "undiscovered" vagina is the denied vagina; vaginal erotism is primary and not a derivative of oral erotism (in this she opposes the views of both Helene Deutsch and Melanie Klein). It is only anxiety that prevents the seeking of pleasure in the vagina—anxiety connected with the size of the father's penis, with observations of female vulnerability, and with injury caused by masturbation, either physically or in fantasy. Ernest Jones (1933) repeatedly cites Horney with approval and explicitly endorses her concept of the denied vagina. Of course Jones's paper covers a very much wider field and is greatly influenced by the views of Melanie Klein. It is a masterly piece of work and cannot readily be summarized.

No doubt it is equally impossible to summarize Klein's views; but they have been so influential and are in important respects so much at variance with Freud's earlier views that some attempt should be made to compare the two. Klein's conception of female sexual development was clearly formulated already in 1932 and, so far as I know, never fundamentally changed. She agrees with Freud to the extent that the girl wants to have a penis and hates her mother for not giving her one. What she wants, however, is not to be masculine through possessing a penis of her own, but to incorporate her father's penis as an oral object to replace the disappointing mother's breast. So far from being an outcome of her castration complex, this wish is the result of her dominant feminine instinctual components and the most fundamental expression of her Oedipal tendencies, for these are orally rooted. Here Klein differs from Horney, who believed in *primary* early vaginal erotism. Although Helene Deutsch also held that the father's penis as an object derives from the mother's breast, she believed that all this, together with the emergence of the vagina, occurs only at sexual maturity. Klein disagrees with Freud's view that the girl's sexuality is essentially masculine and clitoris-oriented until puberty. She holds that after an initial breast-dominated phase common to both sexes, the boy passes next through a feminine phase with an oral-sucking fixation on the father's penis, just like the girl. So—it is the boy who is feminine, not the girl who is masculine!

According to Klein, the clitoris overshadows the vagina in early sexuality because of the girl's fears concerning the inside of her body, for she unconsciously knows of the vagina. In this area Klein is very much in agreement with Horney. Klein, however, adds that although clitoral masturbation fantasies are at first largely pregenital, the later fantasies centered on the father's penis assume a genital and vaginal character and thus, *to begin with*, take a feminine direction—"being often accompanied, it would seem, by vaginal sensations." Here I would remind you of Masters & Johnson and Sherfey, who stress the integral nature of the clitoral-vaginal complex of organs. It was not possible for Freud to know of this, and I believe this led him to a false antithesis between clitoris and vagina.

Klein agrees with Freud that there is a difference between the girl's superego and the boy's, but for her the difference is of another kind. The impulsion to introject the paternal imago, represented by the father's penis, is much stronger in the girl because vaginal introjection is added to oral introjection, and so she is more at the mercy of a very potent superego. Later on, in coitus, she attempts to introject a "good" penis to counteract the introjected "bad" penis. She is thus more dependent on her objects, and this dependence is increased by her lack of a penis of her own.

In "Female Sexuality" (1931) Freud criticized some of the views I have been discussing, but strangely failed (as Strachey points out) to take note of the fact that these writers were in part reacting to his own paper (Freud, 1925) on the anatomical distinction. By this time he had discovered the intensity and long duration of the little girl's attachment to her mother, so that the pre-Oedipal phase in females gains a new importance; he freely admits his inability to see his way through any case completely, and likewise the possibility that women analysts may have the advantage of him here. However, he still feels justified in assuming that for many years the vagina is virtually non-existent and may not produce any sensations before puberty—and from this there follows the theory of two phases, first masculine, then feminine. He also notes that the clitoris, with its virile character, continues to function in later life in some obscure way. Some of this obscurity has now, I think, been removed by Masters & Johnson. Essentially, then, Freud holds fast to his theory of a normal masculine phase based on the clitoral zone, and a consequent feeling of being a castrated creature when this phase has to be abandoned, and the superior male organ has to be acknowledged. But the girl rebels against this and may develop a feeling of general revulsion against sexuality, or she may cling assertively to her masculinity, or thirdly, by a circuitous route she may arrive at the normal female attitude, taking her father as her object. Her Oedipus complex, having been created, not destroyed, by the castration fantasy, itself escapes destruction. The pre-Oedipal attachment to the mother is far more important in women than in men, and their struggles with their husbands essentially repeat the struggle with the mother rather than with the father. The girl emerges from the phase of mother-attachment with the reproach, not only that the mother did not give her a penis, but also that she did not give her enough milk.

It may perhaps be agreed that in this paper on female sexuality Freud is feeling his own way rather than accepting uncritically what was being urged by his analytic opponents. Nevertheless, a few of these independent conclusions do seem to show Freud moving slightly closer to them—for example, the enormous importance for the girl of the initial relationship with her mother, and the possibly equivalent reproaches that she was not given a penis and was not given enough milk, which surely suggests that behind all the fuss about the penis there lies an earlier concern with the breast. It is interesting to note, in passing, that Freud resisted the temptation to conclude that the girl's strong ambivalence towards her mother is due to her inability to direct her hostility on to her father, as the boy does, for he says that this conclusion would be premature before we have studied the pre-Oedipal stage in boys—something which he does not seem to have accomplished subsequently. This is hard to reconcile with his statements about the great obscurity of female sexual development. In the "New Introductory Lecture on Femininity" (1933) Freud expresses himself more confidently in that he simply inculpates the castration complex for the girl's specific and greater hostility to the mother, as well as for her greater proneness to envy and jealousy. In general, this lecture recapitulates earlier formulations, and the same may be said of Chapter 7 in *An Outline of Psychoanalysis* (Freud, 1940).

The need for limitation has led me to exclude two very important subjects from my discussion of Freud's views—namely narcissism and masochism. To discuss them adequately would require at least two further papers. I have also been unable to consider properly the very interesting and thought-provoking contributions of our French colleagues (Chasseguet-Smirgel, 1964), for example Grunberger's point that, since the origin of narcissism is to be found in the mother's love for her baby, the fact that, as he alleges, every mother is ambivalent towards her girl baby helps to account for female complaints about being a woman, and for women being narcissistic before all else. Chasseguet-Smirgel herself also stresses the narcissistic wound inflicted on the little girl by an onmipotent mother, and her inability to overcome this as the boy does with the help of his penis; so that penis envy really arises out of the need to cope with the omnipotent mother. Turok stresses the anal level of the conflict with the mother, who takes control of the girl's sphincter and demands possession of her stool. I think Turok would probably agree that what this stands for is the girl's internal, female sexual world. Penis envy is a manifestation of repression of the true underlying anal conflict, and the idealized penis represents the value of what she has lost all hope of having in herself, namely female genital maturity.

Before returning to Freud for a final attempt to bring together and review his theories, I want to say a few words on a phylogenetic theme; my attention was drawn to it first by David Attenborough's television program on courtship and mating among animals. It was a beautiful and remarkable film, and it aroused in me the thought—how is it that we can observe and have rather intimate knowledge of the sexual lives and practices of so many species of land and aquatic animals, in such striking contrast to the little that we really know and have observed in the case of the human animal? And in view of this discrepancy how can one despise and condemn the attempts, however imperfect, of researchers like Masters & Johnson? One of the pictures that specially intrigued me was that of a male and a female fish expelling their sexual products into the same piece of water, first one, then immediately the other, in each case with what *could* be interpreted as orgastic wrigglings. Then, whilst I was preparing this paper, I received a reprint from Werner Kemper of Berlin of a paper (Kemper, 1965) with a title that could be translated "New Contributions from Phylogenetics to Female Bio-psychology." To my delight, he describes there this very phenomenon of fish reproduction, including the "convulsive movements of manifestly *(offensichtlich)* orgastic nature." Kemper's thesis is that there are four other important reasons, besides those listed by Freud, why female sexual development is so much more complicated and leads so much more frequently to dissatisfaction than is the case in the male. These are phylogenetic in nature, and the first of the four is illustrated by the fishes mentioned above, together with the well-authenticated assumption that life—and so our ancestors—began in the sea (and of course Kemper is well acquainted with Ferenczi's "Thalassa"). The point is that the female fish appears to enjoy an orgasm in no way different from the male's; in each case it is a matter of orgastic pleasure in the act of expulsion of a bodily product *(Ausstossungslust)*. The male creature, who now appears as the arch-conservative, has had the good fortune to be able to preserve this way of sexual life right through his development into a land animal, a viviparous mammal, and finally man himself; but not so the female, who has been "required" (if I may use Freud's word in this connection) by the process of evolution to develop a vagina and uterus out of her cloaca, and to get what sexual pleasure she can from taking the male's sexual product into it in the service of internal impregnation. Hers is the plastic, adaptive sex, but she has been obliged to give up the pleasure that her fish-ancestress had shared with her male partner. Is it too fanciful to suggest that the lack of female orgasm, which is, I believe, the rule in most mammals, can be understood in this sense; and to suggest that the human female, in our day at least, has learned again how to have an orgasm with the aid of just those muscle groups that go into action during male orgasm? And I would add too that the fact that nearly simultaneous orgasm is generally an essential factor in producing ultimate pleasure could readily be seen as a reflection of the fact that, in the case of fishes, near-synchronicity is of the essence, for without this condition fertilization will not occur. The suggestion arising from all these ideas is that woman's dissatisfaction with her role is rooted a great deal more deeply than mere envy of the male's possession of imposing external genitalia. As Decter (1973) has convincingly argued, the extreme exponents of women's liberation are going far beyond the demand for a fair deal from men; they are demanding to be liberated from that unfair share in the reproductive process which evolution has imposed on the female of the viviparous species.

If we return now to Freud's early formulations, we can see that from the beginning he perceived that human society as we know it has imposed various requirements on the female, such as the demand that she leave out the arc of the male specific reaction and develop instead permanent specific enticing actions calculated to induce the specific reaction in the male. He also observed that frigidity often depends on a woman's marrying without love; that is, on social pressure.

A little later, however, he began to stress the overriding importance of the clitoris in childhood sexuality, which he declared to be masculine in both sexes. In this case it is inevitable that the little girl should compare herself unfavorably to the male, with very damaging consequences to her narcissism. Thus, behind the social factors which he had earlier recognized, he felt sure from this point onwards that there is an unavoidable problem for the female based on the slogan that anatomy is destiny, and he held fast to this conviction to the end. Despite Freud's belief in the essentially masculine (i.e., phallic and active) nature of the little girl's sexual strivings, he admitted that she shows characteristics that are clearly feminine. This is a point that has been emphasized by a number of analytic critics of his theory, beginning perhaps with Horney. However, when we take into account the more recent work such as the observations of Stoller (1968) on transsexualism and related problems, it becomes clear that in this area we need to be very cautious in coming to firm conclusions, since gender identity is independent of genetic sex; indeed even the anatomical sex does not necessarily correspond to the genetic constitution, and without the appropriate hormonal influence at a certain stage of embryonic development the genetic male will develop into a female, though the genetic female continues as such with or without the appropriate hormones. Thus we cannot confidently draw any conclusions about the significance of so-called feminine behavior in little girls, since the type of behavior that a child exhibits is determined to such an important degree by what is expected of it by parents who assume, or who wish, its sex to be this or that.

A striking change was introduced into Freud's thinking when, with his recognition of the vital importance of early attachment to the mother and its difference in the two sexes, he abandoned the notion of parallelism between male and female development. Nevertheless, he clung persistently to his conviction of the crucial influence of the girl's traumatic discovery of the penis, just as he continued to stress the boy's traumatic discovery of the no-penis. In both sexes these discoveries belied the initial assumption that everyone is like oneself anatomically. Freud seems not to have considered seriously the possibility that the occurrence of such sudden traumatic discoveries might depend on current conventions of child rearing. Nowadays it can seldom happen that a child is prevented from seeing the bodies of children of the opposite sex—a prohibition that was common in Freud's time and indeed in my own. It would be interesting to hear the comments of child analysts on this point.

At one place, (1933, Lecture 33), Freud admits that some may accuse him of an *idée fixe* in believing in the influence of lack of a penis on the configuration of femininity. You may well ask—am I making this accusation? If you insist that I answer yes or no I should find myself in difficulty. It does seem to me that Freud overemphasized the traumatic effect resulting from the visual impression of the unfamiliar genitals of the other sex, and I cannot help comparing Freud's unshakable belief in this idea with his earlier traumatic theory of neurosis, produced by sexual seduction. It was many years before he recognized this error, and many more years before he admitted it publicly. Is it not possible that his theory of a castration complex resulting from a traumatic visual experience is a kind of residue from the neurosis theory, something that he clung to as if it were a treasure saved from the wreckage?

Why indeed should the little girl be so disturbed and so overcome by inextinguishable envy at the mere sight of an unexpected excrescence on the little boy's body? If it were a matter of witnessing an adult erection, that would be different, but this is not what Freud had in mind. Surely we must agree that the girl's reaction is not the result merely of recognizing that he has something that she does not possess, but much more the result of her fantasies about it, based, on the most obvious and superficial level, on its urinary capacities, which would seem to offer more ego control and narcissistic gratification in the function. I would agree that the problem of where the female is hiding her penis is a big one for the boy, and I would suggest that this teasing conundrum constitutes an important ingredient in the impression of female insincerity and the dark obscurity in which she hides her sexuality; when Freud speaks of these things one senses a certain feeling of frustration and annoyance. When the clitoris is finally discovered as the answer to the problem, its diminutive size and lack of any obvious function lead naturally to the view that it is merely a vestigial penis, and that the girl's valuation of it shows that she is trying, in a pitifully inadequate way, to be a boy. The boy—and in this context I suggest that Freud had retained some of his boyishness, just like the rest of us chauvinist males—the boy in this way has his revenge for the female's insincere concealment—a concealment compounded of anatomy and prudery.

But the essence of the matter is that even if one admits the justice of these criticisms, Freud was in a much deeper sense right, if it be conceded that when he talks of the penis he is no more talking simply of a concrete anatomical organ than is Melanie Klein when she talks of the breast. I know that when one feels tempted to say that the penis stands for many less concrete things, rather than the other way round, one is in danger of going the way of Jung. Nevertheless, I think one is justified in saying that the anatomical difference between the sexes is important not so much for itself but because it is the outward and visible sign of the vastly more extensive differences in the reproductive roles which evolution has decreed shall be allotted to men and to women. Whatever psychological significance, if any, one may be prepared to attach to the contrast between a female fish and a woman, it cannot be denied that the evolutionary process that has produced the mammals has called for a profound internalization of female sexuality, and that this has had very far-reaching psychological consequences, some of which take the form of resentment and dissatisfaction with the female role. Other consequences, of course, are of an opposite kind and can afford intense satisfactions which men cannot share except by identification and empathy. There is clearly a difference of opinion in analytic circles between those who would agree with Freud that the girl who settles for femininity does so only because she gives up the hopeless struggle to be a man, and others who hold that femininity is a primary thing, but has to be abandoned for a time out of fear of the mother, and that the girl's masculine clitoral sexuality is temporarily substituted for it. But it seems to me that the meaning of the clitoris is still somewhat obscure, for Masters & Johnson have demonstrated that it plays an important part in normal female sexual excitement and orgasm. Does this mean that Freud was mistaken in assuming that the clitoris is necessarily associated with masculine, penetrative strivings: Is it not possible that its excitement leads normally to the wish to be penetrated vaginally, so producing further stimulation of the clitoris as well as of the vagina? This is one of the many questions that I must leave unanswered.

From the *International Review of Psycho-Analysis,* Vol. 2, Part 1 (1975), pages 1-9. Reprinted by permission.

REFERENCES

CHASSEGUET-SMIRGEL, J. (ed.) (1964). *Female Sexuality: New Psychoanalytic Views.* Ann Arbor: Michigan Univ. Press, 1970.

DECTER, M. (1973). *The New Chastity.* London: Wildwood House.

FREUD, S. (1895). "On the grounds for detaching a particular syndrome from neurasthenia under the description 'anxiety neurosis.'" *Standard Edition* 3.

FREUD, S. (1905). *Three essays on the theory of sexuality. Standard Edition* 7.

FREUD, S. (1908). "On the sexual theories of children." *Standard Edition* 9.

FREUD, S. (1925). "Some psychical consequences of anatomical distinction between the sexes." *Standard Edition* 19.

FREUD, S. (1931). "Female sexuality." *Standard Edition* 21.

FREUD, S. (1933). *New introductory lectures on psycho-analysis,* "Femininity." *Standard Edition* 22.

FREUD, S. (1940). *An outline of psycho-analysis. Standard Edition* 23.

FREUD, S. (1950*a*). Extracts from the Fliess Papers. Draft G. Melancholia. *Standard Edition* 1.

FREUD, S. (1950*b*). Extracts from the Fliess Papers. Letter 75. *Standard Edition* 1.

GILLESPIE, W. H. (1969). "Concepts of vaginal orgasm." *Int. J. Psycho-Anal.* 50, 495–497.

HORNEY, K. (1926). "The flight from womanhood." *Int. J. Psycho-Anal.* 7, 324–339.

HORNEY, K. (1932). "The dread of woman." *Int. J. Psycho-Anal.* 13, 348–360.

HORNEY, K. (1933). "The denial of the vagina." *Int. J. Psycho-Anal.* 14, 57–70.

JONES, E. (1933). "The phallic phase." *Int. J. Psycho-Anal.* 14, 1–33.

KEMPER, W. W. (1965). *"Neue Beiträge aus der Phylogenese zur Bio-Psychologie der Frau." Z. psychosom. Med.* 11, 77–82.

KLEIN, M. (1932). *The Psycho-Analysis of Children.* New York: Norton.

MASTERS, W. H. & JOHNSON, V. E. (1966). *Human Sexual Response.* Boston, Mass.: Little, Brown.

MICHAEL, R. P. (1968). "Gonadal hormones and the control of primate behaviour." In R. P. Michael (ed.), *Endocrinology and Human Behaviour.* London: Oxford Univ. Press.

SHERFEY, M. J. (1966). "The evolution and nature of female sexuality in relation to psychoanalytic theory." *J. Am. rsychoanal. Ass.* 14, 28–128.

STOLLER, R. (1968). *Sex and 'ender.* New York: Science House.

PART TWO

THE ANTHROPOLOGICAL DIMENSION

ANTHROPOLOGY AND SEX DIFFERENCES

Patrick C. Lee

For the anthropologist male-female dimorphism is a psycho-biological constant to which every known human society has made accommodations. Although anthropologists have a secondary interest in biological sex differences, their primary interest is in the patterned accommodations human beings have made to these differences. Taken collectively, these accommodations are known as "sex role," and they include whatever behaviors, attitudes, values, and expectations a given society regards as appropriate for either males or females, but not for both. The basic questions anthropologists raise about sex role are these: How variable versus universal are sex roles across human cultures? What means are used to teach and persuade members of a culture to assume the sex role which corresponds to their biological sex? In what ways is sex role adaptive and in what ways is it maladaptive? How does sex role fit into the total pattern of a given culture? One or more of these questions is addressed in each of the selections to follow and it may be useful to introduce the anthropology of sex differences by briefly considering each question in turn.

How variable versus universal are sex roles across cultures? There is considerable evidence indicating the diversity of sex role among societies. In her classic study of three New Guinea societies (see selection), Mead found marked variation in "sex-temperament." The Arapesh prescribed a mild and responsive temperamental style for both sexes, while the Mundugumor socialized both sexes to approximate an aggressive, vitriolic temperamental type. In the third society, the Tchambuli, women were expected to be competent and detached, while men were to be dependent and nurturant. In addition to temperament, Linton (see selection) noted that the *functions* assigned to sexes differ among societies. Even such functions as hunting, manual labor, farming, tending domestic animals, cooking, housekeeping, and child rearing are not the universal province of one sex, but are often assigned to different sexes in different societies. One of Malinowski's findings in his study of Trobriand society (see selection) was that fathers did not exercise authority over their children, but related to them in playful and nurturant ways, a behavioral pattern not often found among European fathers. The ethnographic literature is full of instances of variability in sex role and, for the most part, it tends to accurately reflect reality. But it would be a mistake to conclude that human sex role is an infinitely malleable phenomenon or that there are no universal tendencies.

In fact there are some universal practices, although they appear to be negative rather than positive. For example, there is no known society in which women are unequivocally the dominant sex, although there are some in which they share dominance with men. More specifically, in most societies men have clear control of the political and military apparatus, and there are no known societies in which women have such control. Even among the mild mannered Arapesh, as described by Mead, the men were the warriors, and the emotionally dependent Tchambuli men were headhunters before this practice was outlawed by a colonial administration (cf., Munroe & Munroe, 1975, pp. 116-122). Barry, Bacon, and Child (see selection) found that, with one exception, no society in their sample fostered achievement and self-reliance in females more so than in males. To the degree that these personal characteristics contribute to dominance, this finding is supportive of the near-universal dominance of males over females. Moreover, Whiting and Whiting (1975) in their "six cultures study" also found that boys tend to seek dominance more than girls do and are significantly more aggressive than girls, both physically and verbally. Again, these results support the cross-cultural hypothesis that where dominance is assumed by only one of the sexes, that sex is invariably male. It does appear, then, that there is cross-cultural *consensus,* if not unanimity, on some aspects of sex role.

It remains an open question, however, whether these near-universal sex-role characteristics are genetic givens or are a function of near-universal cultural practice. The exceptions and variations would seem to argue against the genetic hypothesis, although some anthropologists think that some behaviors, e.g., touching and rough-and-tumble-play, are innate characteristics of girls and boys, respectively (Whiting & Edwards, 1973). Other anthropologists reserve judgment in the absence of compelling evidence one way or the other (e.g., Murdock, 1949; Munroe & Munroe, 1975). Still others see consensual agreement on sex role as reflective not of biological programming per se, but as a culturally invented elaboration of those sex differences, e.g., childbearing and nursing, which *are* biologically universal (e.g., D'Andrade, 1966).

The second question, regarding how children are socialized to an "appropriate" sex-role identity, is one which has been investigated more extensively by psychologists than by anthropologists. However, anthropologists have also raised this question and they have tended to focus on the family as the primary vehicle for training boys and girls to assume their respective sex roles. The family is a universal cultural institution, although its particular form varies among cultures (cf., Murdock, 1949). In Western culture the typical family is "nuclear," that is, a unit consisting of two parents and their children. The nuclear family usually recognizes itself as part of two larger kinship networks, but its economy, primary loyalty, place of residence, and membership are viewed as essentially autonomous of the larger networks. Parsons (see selection) has theorized that sex-role identity is formed in the nuclear family as a function of the family's efforts to maintain its own integrity and stability as a social unit. According to Parsons, if the father and mother assume, respectively, "instrumental" and "expressive" leadership, and if they present a united front to the children, then it is almost inevitable that their sons will gravitate toward instrumental competence while their daughters will identify with the expressive role. It is only when the complementary leadership of the parents ceases to be collaborative that deviations in sex-role identity take place. One may not agree with the *inevitability* of Parsons' analysis, but it does stand as a useful descriptive model of what seems to happen in Western nuclear families.

Although the nuclear family is universal, it is an autonomous unit in only 25 percent of human societies. In the majority of societies its economy, loyalty, and membership are incorporated into larger extended familial networks (Murdock, 1949). These other family types yield rather different versions of sex role from the Western nuclear type. For example, Malinowski (see selection) found that among the matrilineal Trobriand Islanders, the child's primary allegiance was to his mother's kin rather than to his nuclear family of origin. Thus the authority figure in the child's life was not the father, but the uncle, and the primary incest taboo was between brother and sister, not between mother and son. This family constellation allowed for the formation of broadly defined sex roles. Each boy, for example, would grow up to be authoritarian and instrumentally demanding in his role as uncle but expressively playful and nurturant in his role as father. Each girl would learn to be deferent toward her brother, but to assume a roughly egalitarian status vis-a-vis her husband. Murphy and Murphy (see selection) found that, although the Mundurucú were patrilineal, they were matrilocal, that is, the nuclear family located in the village or living compound of the mother's kinfolk. Since the women under such an arrangement inevitably spent the major part of their waking hours working in the company of other women to whom they were related by kinship, they formed fast bonding alliances which tended to overide their allegiance to their respective nuclear families. This female bond gave them considerable *de facto* power vis-à-vis the men who had official power, but were not kinfolk to one another. Thus, young girls identified with a role and reference group which assigned them functional equality with males.

Burton and Whiting (see selection) studied yet another family arrangement, one in which young children were essentially segregated from adult males, including their fathers, during the first few years of life. They found that such living arrangements presented particular problems to young boys who were expected to assume a male identity essentially in the absence of male identification models. In patrilocal societies this problem was overcome by subjecting the male adolescent to harsh initiation rites which tended to expunge his early identification with his mother. In *matrilocal* societies, however, where the female role has relatively more prestige, the problem was overcome by allowing males to retain important aspects of their primary female identification. Burton and Whiting found, for example, that in most of these societies adult males were expected to experience labor pains when their wives were giving birth. This phenomenon, commonly called "couvade," is a clear indication that female behaviors were incorporated into the male sex-role repertoire.

It seems safe to conclude that family structure greatly influences the structure of sex role, the social status of the sexes, and the patterns of interaction between the sexes. Analysis of family structure helps to clarify not only how the sex roles differ within a culture, but also how the interactions between the sexes differ from culture to culture.

In considering the third question about the degree to which sex role has made human society adaptive, one is immediately caught in a welter of qualifications and relativities. For example, how much sex role distinction is needed for adaptability . . . to what end is sex role adaptive . . . what options does sex role close down . . . what efficiencies does it incorporate . . . how do these efficiencies change over time? Like the questions already entertained these cannot be definitively answered. Nevertheless, a few considerations are in order.

Linton (see selection) distinguishes between ascribed and achieved status. Most societies cannot afford to socialize all individuals open-endedly so they can fairly compete or qualify for achieved statuses. So human beings are arbitrarily divided into ascribed categories on the basis of some physical or social characteristic which is usually apparent from birth, e.g., sex, race, and/or social class membership. By ascribing one role to females, for example, and another to males, there is an automatic economy of socialization energy. By ascribing these roles from birth, society ensures that the child will have the primary and sustained exposure to role expectations prerequisite to the easy acceptance of one's adult role. If these roles prescribe functions and temperamental dispositions which correspond to the basic physiology of sex, then they would appear to have further adaptive value. Thus, as we saw earlier, there are near-universal tendencies for males to be dominant, achievement-oriented, and self-reliant, while women tend to be nurturant and domestically oriented in their functions. These functional and temperamental characteristics conveniently fit the physiological facts of female childbearing and nursing and of male size and degree of muscularity. Finally, there are economic and kinship factors which tend to dictate the degree of sex-role differentiation found in a given society. As Barry, Bacon, and Child found (see selection), where economic requirements such as hunting large animals or tending large livestock prevail, there is a need for the superior strength, mobility, and motor skill of men. Where social organization, e.g., the extended family, provides a ready supply of women to stand in for each other during periods of illness or dysfunction, there is no need for men to learn female-typed functions. Under both these conditions there is a tendency for sex roles to be sharply differentiated in the service of adaptability.

There are other arguments that could be raised on behalf of

the adaptive value of sex-role differentiation, but the above will suffice. It is clear that the adaptive process in the past has not respected individual talent or predilection, although, as Linton notes, most societies have created some achieved statuses for people of extraordinary talent. Thus, exceptionally talented or resourceful women occasionally have risen to prominent positions despite the near-universal social handicaps under which they labor. It should also be added that cultural adaptation often violates its own depersonalized code that what is functional gets priority. In fact those persons who benefit by the adaptive process, so called, often have a vested interest in maintaining standard ways of adaptation even after they have become dysfunctional. Thus, it is apparent that in modern, industrialized society, traditional notions of sex role are increasingly maladaptive. Technological developments as well as fundamental changes in social organization, particularly in the dynamics of the nuclear family, have reduced the importance of male large motor skills and increased the need that males and females share expressive and instrumental functions. To use Linton's and Parsons' terms again, modern society is full of achieved statuses which are begging for instrumental talent, and of alienating influences which make expressive competence a personal resource of incalculable value for both males and females.

The fourth question about the ways in which sex role is interwoven into the total fabric of cultural role prescriptions is explicitly and lucidly treated by Linton in his selection. Therefore, little need be said about it here except to mention that sex role is a patterned phenomenon. It cannot really be understood except in the context of its interactions with other social roles, statuses, and codes defining lineage and kinship. The selections by Malinowski and the Murphys indicate how different kinship systems make for different patterns of sex role.

One final point should be made. With important exceptions, two in the present anthology, the bulk of anthropological field work has been carried out by men and has focused on the male-dominated sphere of day to day living. Local women have either been ignored or given minimal treatment (Murphy & Murphy, 1974, pp. viii-ix). There are, of course, practical reasons for this oversight, not the least being that traditional societies are usually reluctant to let male anthropologists have free access to their women. In many parts of the world, it is inconceivable to the local people that an adult male would have anything other than a sexual interest in an adult woman to whom he is not married or related. Another reason has to do with the male ethnocentrism shared by most male anthropologists. When social scientists are interested in the nature of *people*, their reference point is men; when studying the *sexes*, however, women are usually the reference point of inquiry. Thus the anthropology of women *as people* has not yet been compiled, and it may be that when accomplished it will change some of the answers to our four questions. In the meantime, female anthropoligists like Margaret Mead and Yolanda Murphy have provided us with some first insights into the day-to-day experience of women.

References

D'ANDRADE, R. G. "Sex differences and cultural institutions." In E. E. Maccoby (Ed.), *The Development of Sex Differences*. Stanford, California: Stanford University Press, 1966.

MUNROE, R. L., & MUNROE, R. H. *Cross-Cultural Human Development*. Monterey, California: Brooks Cole, 1975.

MURDOCK, G. P. *Social Structure*. New York: Macmillan, 1949.

MURPHY, Y., & MURPHY, R. F. *Women of the Forest*. New York: Columbia University Press, 1974.

WHITING, B. B. & EDWARDS, C. P. "A cross-cultural analysis of sex differences in the behavior of children aged three through 11." *Journal of Social Psychology,* 1973, *91;* pp. 171–188.

WHITING, B. B., & WHITING, J. W. M. *Children of Six Cultures: A Psycho-Cultural Analysis*. Cambridge, Massachusetts: Harvard University Press, 1975.

THE FAMILY IN FATHER-RIGHT AND MOTHER-RIGHT
and
THE COMPLEX OF MOTHER-RIGHT

Bronislaw Malinowski

Although he received a doctorate in physics and mathematics in his native Poland, Bronislaw Malinowski soon developed an interest in anthropology and migrated to London for formal studies in his newly adopted discipline. After doing field work in the Trobriand Islands during the first World War, he returned to England and eventually rose to a preeminence in anthropology that was rivaled only by his contemporaries A. R. Radcliffe-Brown and Franz Boas. He is generally recognized as the founder of "psychological functionalism" and, as such, was a forerunner of the later "culture and personality" school, of which Margaret Mead is a charter member. This school, in turn, is closely related to what is now known as "psychological anthropology," an approach represented by John W. M. Whiting.

Malinowski's stay among the Trobriand Islanders set a new standard for field work which holds to the present day. He spent four years in the field, learned the Trobriand language, lived among the indigenous people themselves, came to know the difference between the espoused norms and actual behaviors of his hosts, and established as a principle that a given society be understood on its own terms and as an integrated whole, that is, not in terms of other cultures or in piecemeal fashion. He viewed culture, quite simply, as a way of life and maintained that a culture was not thoroughly studied until one comprehended its adherents' way of life.

We have reprinted two selections from Malinowski's book, **Sex and Repression in Savage Society** *(1927). Malinowski's basic point is that the Oedipal complex, as described by Freud, is not a biological universal, but is merely a specific case of the "family complex," which is determined by culturally invented rules of lineage. Matrilineal Trobriand and patrilineal European societies, therefore, have different family complexes. These, in turn, make for different interaction patterns between the sexes in the two societies and, ultimately, for the development of sex-role identities among Trobriand children which differ greatly from those of European children.*

THE FAMILY IN FATHER-RIGHT AND MOTHER-RIGHT

The best way to examine this first problem—in what manner the "family complex" is influenced and modified by the constitution of the family in a given society—is to enter concretely into the matter, to follow up the formation of the complex in the course of typical family life, and to do it comparatively in the case of different civilizations. I do not propose here to survey all forms of human family, but shall compare in detail two types, known to me from personal observation: the patrilineal family of modern civilization, and the matrilineal family of certain island communities in North-Western Melanesia. These two cases, however, represent perhaps the two most radically different types of family known to sociological observation, and will thus serve our purpose well. A few words will be necessary to introduce the Trobriand Islanders of North-Eastern New Guinea (or North-Western Melanesia) who will form the other term of our comparison, besides our own culture.

These natives are matrilineal, that is, they live in a social order in which kinship is reckoned through the mother only, and succession and inheritance descend in the female line. This means that the boy or girl belongs to the mother's family, clan and community: the boy succeeds to the dignities and social position of the mother's brother, and it is not from the father but from the maternal uncle or maternal aunt, respectively, that a child inherits its possessions.

Every man and woman in the Trobriands settles down eventually to matrimony, after a period of sexual play in childhood, followed by general licence in adolescence, and later by a time when the lovers live together in a more permanent intrigue, sharing with two or three other couples a communal "bachelor's house." Matrimony, which is usually monogamous, except with chiefs, who have several wives, is a permanent union, involving sexual exclusiveness, a common economic existence, and an independent household. At first glance it might appear to a superficial observer to be the exact pattern of marriage among ourselves. In reality, however, it is entirely different. To begin with, the husband is not regarded as the father of the children in the sense in which we use this word; physiologically he has nothing to do with their birth, according to the ideas of the natives, who are ignorant of physical fatherhood. Children, in native belief, are inserted into the mother's womb as tiny spirits, generally by the agency of the spirit of a deceased kinswoman of the mother.[1] Her husband has then to protect and cherish the children, to "receive them in his arms" when they are born, but they are not "his" in the sense that he has had a share in their procreation.

The father is thus a beloved, benevolent friend, but not a recognized kinsman of the children. He is a stranger, having authority through his personal relations to the child, but not through his sociological position in the lineage. Real kinship, that is identity of substance, "same body," exists only through the mother. The authority over the children is vested in the mother's brother. Now this person, owing to the strict taboo which prevents all friendly relations between brothers and sisters, can never be intimate with the mother, or therefore with her household. She recognizes his authority, and bends before him as a commoner before a chief, but there can never be tender relations between them. Her children are, however, his only heirs and successors, and he wields over them the direct *potestas*. At his death his worldly goods pass into their keeping, and during his lifetime he has to hand over to them any special accomplishment he may possess—dances, songs, myths, magic and crafts. He also it is who supplies his sister and her household with food, the greater part of his garden produce going to them. To the father, therefore, the children look only for loving care and tender companionship. Their mother's brother represents the principle of discipline, authority, and executive power within the family.[2]

The bearing of the wife towards her husband is not at all servile. She has her own possessions and her own sphere of influence, private and public. It never happens that the children see their mother bullied by the father. On the other hand, the father is only partially the bread-winner, and has to work mainly for his own sisters, while the boys know that when they grow up they in turn will have to work for their sisters' households.

Marriage is patrilocal: that is, the girl goes to join her husband in his house and migrates to his community, if she comes from another, which is in general the case. The children therefore grow up in a community where they are legally strangers, having no right to the soil, no lawful pride in the village glory; while their home, their traditional centre of local patriotism, their possessions, and their pride of ancestorship are in another place. Strange combinations and confusion arise, associated with this dual influence.

From an early age boys and girls of the same mother are separated in the family, owing to the strict taboo which enjoins that there shall be no intimate relations between them, and that above all any subject connected with sex should never interest them in common. It thus comes about that though the brother is really the person in authority over the sister, the taboo forbids him to use this authority when it is a question of her marriage. The privilege of giving or withholding consent, therefore, is left to the parents, and the father—her mother's husband—is the person who has most authority, in this one matter of his daughter's marriage.

The great difference in the two family types which we are going to compare is beginning to be clear. In our own type of family we have the authoritative, powerful husband and father backed up by society.[3] We have also the economic arrangement whereby he is the bread-winner, and can—nominally at least—withhold supplies or be generous with them at his will. In the Trobriands, on the other hand, we have the independent mother and her husband, who has nothing to do with the procreation of the children, and is not the bread-winner, who cannot leave his possessions to the children, and has socially no established authority over them. The mother's relatives on the other hand are endowed with very powerful influence, especially her brother, who is the authoritative person, the producer of supplies for the family, and whose possessions the sons will inherit at his death. Thus the pattern of social life and the constitution of the family are arranged on entirely different lines from those of our culture.

THE ANTHROPOLOGICAL DIMENSION / 165

THE COMPLEX OF MOTHER-RIGHT

We have been comparing the two civilizations, the European and the Melanesian, and we have seen that there exist deep differences, some of the forces by which society moulds man's biological nature being essentially dissimilar. Though in each there is a certain latitude given to sexual freedom, and a certain amount of interference with and regulation of the sex instinct, yet in each the incidence of the taboo and the play of sexual liberty within its prescribed bounds are entirely different. There is also a quite dissimilar distribution of authority within the family, and correlated with it a different mode of counting kinship. We have followed in both societies the growth of the average boy or girl under these divergent tribal laws and customs. We have found that at almost every step there are great differences due to the interplay between biological impulse and social rule which sometimes harmonize, sometimes conflict, sometimes lead to a short bliss, sometimes to an inequilibrium fraught, however, with possibilities for a future development. At the final stage of the child's life-history, after it has reached maturity, we have seen its feelings crystallize into a system of sentiments towards the mother, father, brother, sister, and in the Trobriands, the maternal uncle, a system which is typical of each society, and which, in order to adapt ourselves to psycho-analytic terminology, we called the "Family Complex" or the "nuclear complex."

Now allow me to restate briefly the main features of these two "complexes." The Oedipus complex, the system of attitudes typical of our patriarchal society, is formed in early infancy, partly during the transition between the first and second stages of childhood, partly in the course of the latter. So that, towards its end, when the boy is about five or six years old, his attitudes are well formed, though perhaps not finally settled. And these attitudes comprise already a number of elements of hate and suppressed desire. In this, I think, our results do not differ to any extent from those of psycho-analysis.[4]

In the matrilineal society at that stage, though the child has developed very definite sentiments towards its father and mother, nothing suppressed, nothing negative, no frustrated desire forms a part of them. Whence arises this difference? As we saw, the social arrangements of the Trobriand matriliny are in almost complete harmony with the biological course of development, while the institution of father-right found in our society crosses and represses a number of natural impulses and inclinations. To trace it more in detail, there is the passionate attachment to the mother, the bodily desire to cling close to her, which in patriarchal institutions is in one way or another broken or interfered with; the influence of our morality, which condemns sexuality in children; the brutality of the father, especially in the lower [socio-economic] strata, the atmosphere of his exclusive right to mother and child acting subtly but strongly in the higher strata, the fear felt by the wife of displeasing her husband—all these infleucnes force apart parents and children. Even where the rivalry between father and child for the mother's personal attention is reduced to a minimum, or to naught, there comes, in the second period, a distinct clash of social interests between father and child. The child is an encumbrance and an obstacle to the parental freedom, a reminder of age and decline and, if it is a son, often the menace of a future social rivalry. Thus, over and above the clash of sensuality, there is ample room for social friction between father and child. I say advisedly "child" and not "boy," for, according to our results, the sex difference between the children does not play any great part at this stage, nor has a closer relation between father and daughter as yet made its appearance.

All these forces and influences are absent from the matrilineal society of the Trobriands. First of all—and that has, *bien entendu,* nothing to do with matriliny—there is no condemnation of sex or of sensuality as such, above all, no moral horror at the idea of infantile sexuality. The sensuous clinging of the child to his mother is allowed to take its natural course till it plays itself out and is diverted by other bodily interests. The attitude of the father to the child during these two early periods is that of a near friend and helper. At the time when our father makes himself pleasant at best by his entire absence from the nursery, the Trobriand father is first a nurse and then a companion.

The development of pre-sexual life at this stage also differs in Europe and Melanesia; the repressions of the nursery among us, especially in the higher classes, develop a tendency towards clandestine inquisitions into indecent things, especially excretory functions and organs. Among the savages we find no such period. Now this infantile pre-genital indecency establishes distinctions between the decent-indecent, the pure-impure, and the indecent, parent-proof compartment reinforces and gives additional depth to the taboo which is suddenly cast over certain relations to the mother, that is to the premature banishment from her bed and bodily embraces.

So that here also the complications of our society are not shared by the children in the Trobriands. At the next stage of sexuality we find a no less relevant difference. In Europe there is a latency period more or less pronounced, which implies a breach of continuity in the sexual development and, according to Freud, serves to reinforce many of our repressions and the general amnesia, and to create many dangers in the normal development of sex. On the other hand, it also represents the triumph of other cultural and social interests over sexuality. Among the savages at this stage, sex in an early genital form—a form almost unknown among ourselves—establishes itself foremost among the child's interests, never to be dislodged again. This, while in many respects it is culturally destructive, helps the gradual and harmonious weaning of the child from the family influences.

With this we have entered already into the second half of the child's development, for the period of sexual latency in our society belongs to this part. When we consider these two later stages which form the second half of the development, we find another profound difference. With us during this early period of puberty, the Oedipus complex, the attitudes of the boy towards his parents, only solidify and crystallize. In Melanesia, on the other hand, it is mainly during this second epoch, in fact almost exclusively then, that any complex is formed. For only at this period is the child submitted to the system of repressions and taboos which begin to mould his nature. To these forces he responds, partly by adaptation, partly by developing more or less repressed antagonisms and desires, for human nature is not only malleable but also elastic.

The repressing and moulding forces in Melanesia are twofold—the submission to matriarchal tribal law, and the prohibitions of exogamy. The first is brought about by the influence of the mother's brother, who, in appealing to the child's sense of honour, pride and ambition, comes to stand to him in a relation in many respects analogous to that of the father among us. On the other hand, both the efforts which he demands and the rivalry between successor and succeeded introduce the negative elements of jealousy and resentment. Thus an "ambivalent" attitude is formed in which veneration assumes the acknowledged dominant place, while a repressed hatred manifests itself only indirectly.

The second taboo, the prohibition of incest, surrounds the sister, and to a lesser degree other female relatives on the maternal side, as well as clanswomen, with a veil of sexual mystery. Of all this class of women, the sister is the representative to whom the taboo applies most stringently. We noted that this severing taboo, entering the boy's life in infancy, cuts short the incipient tenderness towards his sister which is the natural impulse of a child. This taboo also, since it makes even an accidental contact in sexual matters a crime, causes the thought of the sister to be always present, as well as consistently repressed.

Comparing the two systems of family attitudes briefly, we see that in a patriarchal society, the infantile rivalries and the later social functions introduce into the attitude of father and son, besides mutual attachment, also a certain amount of resentment and dislike. Between mother and son, on the other hand, the premature separation in infancy leaves a deep, unsatisfied craving which, later on, when sexual interests come in, is mixed up in memory with the new bodily longings, and assumes often an erotic character which comes up in dreams and other fantasies. In the Trobriands there is no friction between father and son, and all the infantile craving of the child for its mother is allowed gradually to spend itself in a natural, spontaneous manner. The ambivalent attitude of veneration and dislike is felt between a man and his mother's brother, while the repressed sexual attitude of incestuous temptation can be formed only towards his sister. Applying to each society a terse, though somewhat crude formula, we might say that in the Oedipus complex there is the repressed desire to kill the father and marry the mother, while in the matrilineal society of the Trobriands the wish is to marry the sister and to kill the maternal uncle.

With this, we have summarized the results of our detailed inquiry, and given an answer to the first problem set out at the beginning, that is, we have studied the variation of the nuclear complex with the constitution of the family, and we have shown in what manner the complex depends upon some of the features of family life and sexual morals.

We are indebted to psycho-analysis for the discovery that there exists a typical configuration of sentiments in our society, and for a partial explanation, mainly concerned with sex, as to why such a complex must exist. In the foregoing pages we were able to give an outline of the nuclear complex of another society, a matrilineal one, where it has never been studied before. We found that this complex differs essentially from the patriarchal one, and we have shown why it must differ and what social forces bring it about. We have drawn our comparison on the broadest basis, and, without neglecting sexual factors, we have also systematically drawn in the other elements. The result is important, for, so far, it has never been suspected that another type of nuclear complex might be in existence. By my analysis, I have established that Freud's theories not only roughly correspond to human psychology, but that they follow closely the modification in human nature brought about by various constitutions of society. In other words, I have established a deep correlation between the type of society and the nuclear complex found there. While this is in a sense a confirmation of the main tenet of Freudian psychology, it might compel us to modify certain of its features, or rather to make some of its formulae more elastic. To put it concretely, it appears necessary to draw in more systematically the correlation between biological and social influences; not to assume the universal existence of the Oedipus complex, but in studying every type of civilization, to establish the special complex which pertains to it.

From Bronislaw Malinowski. *Sex and Repression in Savage Society.* London: Routledge & Kegan Paul; Atlantic Highlands, New Jersey: Humanities Press, Inc., 1927, pages 8-13, 74-82. Reprinted by permission.

FOOTNOTES

1. See the writer's *The Father in Primitive Psychology* (Psyche Miniatures), 1927, and "Baloma, Spirits of the Dead," *Journ. R. Anthrop. Inst.,* 1916.
2. For an account of the strange economic conditions of these natives, see the writer's "Primitive Economics" in *Economic Journal,* 1921, and *Ar-*

gonauts of the Western Pacific, chapters ii and vi. The legal side has been fully discussed in *Crime and Custom in Savage Society,* 1926.

3. I should like to mention that although under "our own" civilization I am here speaking about the European and American communities in general, I have in mind primarily the average type of continental family, as this was the material on which the conclusions of psycho-analysis were founded. Whether among the higher social strata of the Western European or of the North American cities we are now slowly moving towards a condition of mother-right more akin to the legal ideas of Melanesia than to those of Roman Law and of continental custom, I do not dare to prophesy. If the thesis of this book be correct, some modern developments in matters of sex ("petting parties," etc.), as well as the weakening of the patriarchal system, should deeply modify the configurations of the sentiments within the family.

4. I have come to realize since the above was written that no orthodox or semi-orthodox psycho-analyst would accept my statement of the "complex," or of any aspect of the doctrine.

SELECTIONS FROM "THE STUDY OF MAN"

Ralph Linton

Ralph Linton began his career as an archeologist, but during his first field trip to the Marquesas in 1920 his interest shifted from ancestral relics to the living Marquesans themselves. His simultaneous grasp of archeology and cultural anthropology was not uncommon among his generation of American anthropologists, who often brought two or three disciplines to bear during their diaspora into the field in the 1920s and 1930s. This was a romantic era in American anthropology, as Franz Boas dispatched his students to every hinterland on the globe to capture "pure cultures" before they disappeared or were irretrievably contaminated by contact with the more imperial cultures.

Linton eventually settled at the University of Wisconsin, while retaining close ties with the University of Chicago. Although he was an independent figure, he had strong conceptual sympathies with Malinowski, in that both viewed culture as an elaborated response to basic human needs, unlike other anthropologists who either ignored culture altogether (e.g., A. R. Radcliffe-Brown) or saw it as an entity which transcended the individual human being, (e.g., A. L. Kroeber). Indicative of the high esteem granted to Linton, George P. Murdock wrote, "For Ralph Linton the author feels only the most profound respect. In him the historical, functional, and psychological approaches are welded into a harmonious synthesis which typifies modern cultural anthropology at its best" (1949, p. xv). As the following selections from the Study of Man *(1936) will show, he was also an excellent writer whose books combined balance, scholarship, and readability.*

In the first selection, Linton discusses sex role and its interaction with other culturally prescribed roles. In the second selection, he describes the interaction between sex, dominance, and control of resources. The third selection discusses various forms of marital arrangements and the consequences they have for husband-wife relationships.

Status and Role

I n all societies certain things are selected as reference points for the ascription of status. The things chosen for this purpose are always of such a nature that they are ascertainable at birth, making it possible to begin the training of the individual for his potential statuses and rôles at once. The simplest and most universally used of these reference points is sex. Age is used with nearly equal frequency, since all individuals pass through the same cycle of growth, maturity, and decline, and the statuses whose occupation will be determined by age can be forecast and trained for with accuracy. Family relationships, the simplest and most obvious being that of the child to its mother, are also used in all societies as reference points for the establishment of a whole series of statuses. Lastly, there is the matter of birth into a particular socially established group, such as a class or caste. The use of this type of reference is common but not universal. In all societies the actual ascription of statuses to the individual is controlled by a series of these reference points which together serve to delimit the field of his future participation in the life of the group.

The division and ascription of statuses with relation to sex seems to be basic in all social systems. All societies prescribe different attitudes and activities to men and to women. Most of them try to rationalize these prescriptions in terms of the physiological differences between the sexes or their different rôles in reproduction. However, a comparative study of the statuses ascribed to women and men in different cultures seems to show that while such factors may have served as a starting point for the development of a division the actual ascriptions are almost entirely determined by culture. Even the psychological characteristics ascribed to men and women in different societies vary so much that they can have little physiological basis. Our own idea of women as ministering angels contrasts sharply with the ingenuity of women as torturers among the Iroquois and the sadistic delight they took in the process. Even the last two generations have seen a sharp change in the psychological patterns for women in our own society. The delicate, fainting lady of the middle eighteen-hundreds is as extinct as the dodo.

When it comes to the ascription of occupations, which is after all an integral part of status, we find the differences in various societies even more marked. Arapesh women regularly carry heavier loads than men "because their heads are so much harder and stronger." In some societies women do most of the manual labor; in others, as in the Marquesas, even cooking, housekeeping, and baby-tending are proper male occupations, and women spend most of their time primping. Even the general rule that women's handicap through pregnancy and nursing indicates the more active occupations as male and the less active ones as female has many exceptions. Thus among the Tasmanians sealhunting was women's work. They swam out to the seal rocks, stalked the animals, and clubbed them. Tasmanian women also hunted opossums, which required the climbing of large trees.

Although the actual ascription of occupations along sex lines is highly variable, the pattern of sex division is constant. There are very few societies in which every important activity has not been definitely assigned to men or to women. Even when the two sexes coöperate in a particular occupation, the field of each is usually clearly delimited. Thus in Madagascar rice culture the men make the seed beds and terraces and prepare the fields for transplanting. The women do the work of transplanting, which is hard and back-breaking. The women weed the crop, but the men harvest it. The women then carry it to the threshing floors, where the men thresh it while the women winnow it. Lastly, the women pound the grain in mortars and cook it.

When a society takes over a new industry, there is often a period of uncertainty during which the work may be done by either sex, but it soon falls into the province of one or the other. In Madagascar, pottery is made by men in some tribes and by women in others. The only tribe in which it is made by both men and women is one into which the art has been introduced within the last sixty years. I was told that during the fifteen years preceding my visit there had been a marked decrease in the number of male potters, many men who had once practised the art having given it up. The factor of lowered wages, usually advanced as the reason for men leaving one of our own occupations when women enter it in force, certainly was not operative here. The field was not overcrowded, and the prices for men's and women's products were the same. Most of the men who had given up the trade were vague as to their reasons, but a few said frankly that they did not like to compete with women. Apparently the entry of women into the occupation had robbed it of a certain amount of prestige. It was no longer quite the thing for a man to be a potter, even though he was a very good one.

The use of age as a reference point for establishing status is as universal as the use of sex. All societies recognize three age groupings as a minimum: child, adult, and old. Certain societies have emphasized age as a basis for assigning status and have greatly amplified the divisions. Thus in certain African tribes the whole male population is divided into units composed of those born in the same years or within two- or three-year intervals. However, such extreme attention to age is unusual, and we need not discuss it here.

The physical differences between child and adult are easily recognizable, and the passage from childhood to maturity is marked by physiological events which make it possible to date it exactly for girls and within a few weeks or months for boys. However, the physical passage from childhood to maturity does not necessarily coincide with the social transfer of the individual from one category to the other. Thus in our own society both men and women remain legally children until long after they are physically adult. In most societies this difference between the physical and social transfer is more clearly marked than in our own. The child becomes a man not when he is physically mature but when he is formally recognized as a man by his society. This recognition is almost always given ceremonial expression in what are technically known as puberty rites. The most important element in these rites is not the determination of physical maturity but that of social maturity. Whether a boy is able to breed is less vital to his society than whether he is able to do a man's work and has a man's knowledge. Actually, most puberty ceremonies include tests of the boy's learning and fortitude, and if the aspirants are unable to pass these they are left in the child status until they can. For those who pass the tests, the cer-

monies usually culminate in the transfer to them of certain secrets which the men guard from women and children.

The passage of individuals from adult to aged is harder to perceive. There is no clear physiological line for men, while even
women may retain their full physical vigor and their ability to
carry on all the activities of the adult status for several years
after the menopause. The social transfer of men from the adult
to the aged group is given ceremonial recognition in a few cultures, as when a father formally surrenders his official position
and titles to his son, but such recognition is rare. As for women,
there appears to be no society in which the menopause is given
ceremonial recognition, although there are a few societies in
which it does alter the individual's status. Thus Comanche women, after the menopause, were released from their disabilities
with regard to the supernatural. They could handle sacred objects, obtain power through dreams and practice as shamans, all
things forbidden to women of bearing age.

The general tendency for societies to emphasize the individual's first change in age status and largely ignore the second is no
doubt due in part to the difficulty of determining the onset of old
age. However, there are also psychological factors involved. The
boy or girl is usually anxious to grow up, and this eagerness is
heightened by the exclusion of children from certain activities
and knowledge. Also, society welcomes new additions to the most
active division of the group, that which contributes most to its
perpetuation and well-being. Conversely, the individual who enjoys the thought of growing old is atypical in all societies. Even
when age brings respect and a new measure of influence, it
means the relinquishment of much that is pleasant. We can see
among ourselves that the aging usually refuse to recognize the
change until long after it has happened.

In the case of age, as in that of sex, the biological factors involved appear to be secondary to the cultural ones in determining the content of status. There are certain activities which cannot be ascribed to children because children either lack the
necessary strength or have not had time to acquire the necessary
technical skills. However, the attitudes between parent and child
and the importance given to the child in the family structure
vary enormously from one culture to another. The status of the
child among our Puritan ancestors, where he was seen and not

heard and ate at the second table, represents one extreme. At the other might be placed the status of the eldest son of a Polynesian chief. All the *mana* (supernatural power) of the royal line converged upon such a child. He was socially superior to his own father and mother, and any attempt to discipline him would have been little short of sacrilege. I once visited the hereditary chief of a Marquesan tribe and found the whole family camping uncomfortably in their own front yard, although they had a good house built on European lines. Their eldest son, aged nine, had had a dispute with his father a few days before and had tabooed the house by naming it after his head. The family had thus been compelled to move out and could not use it again until he relented and lifted the taboo. As he could use the house himself and eat anywhere in the village, he was getting along quite well and seemed to enjoy the situation thoroughly.

The statuses ascribed to the old in various societies vary even more than those ascribed to children. In some cases they are relieved of all heavy labor and can settle back comfortably to live off their children. In others they perform most of the hard and monotonous tasks which do not require great physical strength, such as the gathering of firewood. In many societies the old women, in particular, take over most of the care of the younger children, leaving the younger women free to enjoy themselves. In some places the old are treated with consideration and respect; in others they are considered a useless incumbrance and removed as soon as they are incapable of heavy labor. In most societies their advice is sought even when little attention is paid to their wishes. This custom has a sound practical basis, for the individual who contrives to live to old age in an uncivilized group has usually been a person of ability and his memory constitutes a sort of reference library to which one can turn for help under all sorts of circumstances.

In certain societies the change from the adult to the old status is made more difficult for the individual by the fact that the patterns for these statuses ascribe different types of personality to each. This was the case among the Comanche, as it seems to have been among most of the Plains tribes. The adult male was a warrior, vigorous, self-reliant, and pushing. Most of his social relationships were phrased in terms of competition. He took what he could get and held what he had without regard to any abstract rights of those weaker than himself. Any willingness to arbitrate differences or to ignore slights was a sign of weakness resulting in loss of prestige. The old man, on the other hand, was expected to be wise and gentle, willing to overlook slights and, if need be, to endure abuse. It was his task to work for the welfare of the tribe, giving sound advice, settling feuds between the warriors, and even preventing his tribe from making new enemies. Young men strove for war and honor, old men strove for peace and tranquillity. There is abundant evidence that among the Comanche the transition was often a difficult one for the individual. Warriors did not prepare for old age, thinking it a better fate to be killed in action. When waning physical powers forced them to assume the new rôle, many of them did so grudgingly, and those who had strong magic would go on trying to enforce the rights which belonged to the younger status. Such bad old men were a peril to young ones beginning their careers, for they were jealous of them simply because they were young and strong and admired by the women. The medicine power of these young men was still weak, and the old men could and did kill them by malevolent magic. It issignificant that although benevolent medicine men might be of any age in Comanche folklore, malevolent ones were always old.

Before passing on, it might be well to mention still another social status which is closely related to the foregoing. This is the status of the dead. We do not think of the dead as still members of the community, and many societies follow us in this, but there are others in which death is simply another transfer, comparable to that from child to adult. When a man dies, he does not leave his society; he merely surrenders one set of rights and duties and assumes another. Thus a Tanala clan has two sections which are equally real to its members, the living and the dead. In spite of rather half-hearted attempts by the living to explain to the dead that they are dead and to discourage their return, they remain an integral part of the clan. They must be informed of all important events, invited to all clan ceremonies, and remembered at every meal. In return they allow themselves to be consulted, take an active and helpful interest in the affairs of the community, and act as highly efficient guardians of the group's mores. They carry over into their new status the conservatism characteristic of the aged, and their invisible presence and constant watchfulness does more than anything else to ensure the good behavior of the living and to discourage innovations. In a neighboring tribe there are even individual statuses among the dead which are open to achievement. Old Betsileo men and women will often promise that, after their deaths, they will give the living specific forms of help in return for specified offerings. After the death of one of these individuals, a monument will be erected and people will come to pray and make offerings there. If the new ghost performs his functions successfully, his worship may grow into a cult and may even have a priest. If he fails in their performance, he is soon forgotten.

Biological relationships are used to determine some statuses in all societies. The mere fact of birth immediately brings the individual within the scope of a whole series of social patterns which relate him to his parents, either real or ascribed, his brothers and sisters, and his parents' relatives. The biological basis for the ascription of these family statuses is likely to blind us to the fact that the physiological factors which may influence their content are almost exactly the same as those affecting the content of sex and age statuses. While there is a special relationship between the young child and its mother, based on the child's dependence on nursing, even this is soon broken off. After the second year any adult woman can do anything for the child that its mother can do, while any adult male can assume the complete rôle of the father at any time after the child is conceived. Similarly, the physiological factors which might affect the statuses of uncle and nephew, uncle and niece, or brother and sister are identical with those affecting the relations of persons in different age or sex groupings. This lack of physiological determinants may be responsible in part for the extraordinarily wide range of variation in the contents of the statuses ascribed on the basis of biological relationships in various societies.

Actually, the statuses associated with even such a close biological relationship as that of brother and sister are surprisingly varied. In some societies the two are close intimates. In others they avoid each other carefully and cannot even speak to each other except in the presence of a third party who relays the questions and answers. In some systems the eldest child ranks the others regardless of sex and must be respected and obeyed by them. In others the question of dominance is left to be settled by the children themselves, while in still others the youngest child ranks all those who preceded him. Practically every possible arrangement is represented in one society or another, suggesting that we have here a free field for variation, one in which one arrangement will work quite as well as another. The same sort of wide variation is found in the content of all the other statuses based on blood relationship with the exception of those relating to mother and child, and even here there is a fair degree of variation. There are a number of societies in which there is a more or less conscious attempt to break up the child's habits of dependence upon the mother and to alienate the child from her in order to bring it into closer association with its father's relatives. The child is taught that its mother really is not a member of the family, and hostility between mother and child is encouraged.

The factor of social class or caste rarely if ever replaces the factors of sex, age, and biological relationship in the determination of status. Rather, it supplements these, defining the rôles of individuals still more clearly. Where the class system is strong, each class becomes almost a society in itself. It will have a series of sex, age, and relationship statuses which are peculiar to its members. These will differ from the statuses of other classes even when both are determined by the same biological factors. Not only is the commoner debarred from the occupation of aristocratic statuses, but the aristocrat is similarly debarred from the occupation of common statuses. It may be mentioned in passing that this arrangement is not always entirely to the advantage of the members of the upper class. During the nineteenth century the aristocratic prohibition against engaging in trade condemned many aristocrats to genteel poverty.

Feudal Europe offers an excellent example of the ascription of statuses on the basis of social class. A man born into the noble class could look forward to being a bachelor, in the technical sense of a boy beginning his training for knighthood, a squire, and lastly a knight and lord of a manor. The performance of the rôles connected with the final status required a long and arduous training both in the use of arms and in administration. The woman born into the same class could also look forward to being lady of a manor, a task which entailed special knowledge and administrative ability fully on a par with that of her husband. A man born into the peasant class could look forward only to becoming a tiller of the soil. He would pass through no statuses corresponding to those of bachelor or squire, and although he might be trained to the use of weapons, these would be different weapons from those used by the knight. The woman born in this class could only look forward to becoming a simple housewife, and her necessary training for this status was limited to a knowledge of housekeeping and baby-tending. The third class in medieval society, the burghers, also had its own series of statuses, the boy looking forward to becoming first an apprentice and then a master training apprentice in turn. All these divergent, class-determined statuses were mutually interdependent, and all contributed to the successful functioning of medieval society. The noble provided protection and direction, the peasant provided food, and the burgher took care of trade and manufactures.

Ascribed statuses, whether assigned according to biological or to social factors, compose the bulk of all social systems. However, all these systems also include a varying number of statuses which are open to individual achievement. It seems as though many statuses of this type were primarily designed to serve as baits for socially acceptable behavior or as escapes for the individual. All societies rely mainly on their ascribed statuses to take care of the ordinary business of living. Most of the statuses which are thrown open to achievement do not touch this business very deeply. The honored ones are extremely satisfying to the individuals who achieve them, but many of them are no more vital to the ordinary functioning of the society than are honorary degrees or inclusions in "Who's Who" among ourselves.

Most societies make only a grudging admission of the fact that a limited number of statuses do require special gifts for their successful performance. Since such gifts rarely manifest themselves in early childhood, these statuses are, of necessity, thrown open to competition. At the same time, the pattern of ascribing all vital statuses is so strong that all societies limit this competition with reference to sex, age, and social affiliations. Even in our own society, where the field open to individual achievement is theoretically unlimited, it is strictly limited in fact. No woman can become President of the United States. Neither could a Negro nor an Indian, although there is no formal rule on this point, while a Jew or even a Catholic entering the presidential race would be very seriously handicapped from the outset. Even with regard to achievable statuses which are of much less social importance and which, perhaps, require more specific gifts, the same sort of limited competition is evident. It would be nearly if not quite impossible for either a woman or a Negro to become conductor of our best symphony orchestra, even if better able to perform the duties involved than any one else in America. At the same time, no man could become president of the D. A. R., and it is doubtful whether any man, unless he adopted a feminine *nom de plume,* could even conduct a syndicated column on advice to the lovelorn, a field in which our society assumes, *a priori*, that women have greater skill.

These limitations upon the competition for achieved statuses no doubt entail a certain loss to society. Persons with special talents appear to be mutants and as such are likely to appear in either sex and in any social class. At the same time, the actual loss to societies through this failure to use their members' gifts to the full is probably a good deal less than persons reared in the American tradition would like to believe. Individual talent is too sporadic and too unpredictable to be allowed any important part in the organization of society. Social systems have to be built upon the potentialities of the average individual, the person who has no special gifts or disabilities. Such individuals can be trained to occupy almost any status and to perform the associated rôle adequately if not brilliantly. The social ascription of a particular status, with the intensive training that such ascription makes possible, is a guarantee that the rôle will be performed even if the performance is mediocre. If a society waited to have its statuses filled by individuals with special gifts, certain statuses might not be filled at all. The ascription of status sacrifices the possibility of having certain rôles performed superlatively well to the certainty of having them performed passably well.

. . .

THE RAW MATERIALS FOR SOCIETY

The human male, like most if not all primates, is sexually active at all seasons. The female, although her interest is probably more cyclic, is also capable of responding to his advances at any time. This is also characteristic of primates as an order, and it has been noted that among many of the lower primates the females, even at times of diminished sexual interest, use sexual advances as a means of placating the male. It is further characteristic of *Homo sapiens* as a species that the males are, on the average, larger and heavier than the females and able to dominate them physically. Whether the feminists like it or not, the average man can thrash the average woman. Continuity of sexual activity does not in itself make for permanence of mated relationships. It ensures the active interest of the partners in each other, but it also leads each of them to have an active interest in all individuals of the opposite sex. However, the combination of continuous sexual activity and male dominance does make for the continuity of sexual partnerships. In such a species as the baboons, the males are jealous of each other and try to restrict the attentions of their female partners to themselves. At the same time, the males are actively interested in all females and try to collect and hold as many of them as possible. Whether the females object to this arrangement we do not know, but at least they are in no position to do anything about it. The double standard is probably as old as the primate order.

In man also the combination of continuous sexual activity and male dominance makes for the continuity of sexual partnerships. Practically all societies have tacitly recognized the existence of these tendencies and capitalized them to a greater or less degree in their formal organization. Through the institution of marriage, sexual partnerships are given social recognition and made still more permanent, thus increasing their utility as a basis for the assignment of activities to individuals. In a very large number of societies marriage has become a means of assuring male assistance to the woman and her children.

The male tendency to accumulate and hold females, which springs from the same background, is much more difficult for society to capitalize. In fact it is a liability rather than an asset. With a sex ratio balanced as it is by a normal birth-rate, the male's collecting tendencies can be exercised only at the expense of other males. Moreover, man's continuity of sexual interest is reflected in a jealousy which gives conflicts over women an unusually high emotional content. Machiavelli (1513), long ago noted that a ruler could do almost anything with his subjects as long as he did not interfere with their women or their religion, but that when he began to tamper with these his end was only a matter of time. All societies inhibit the male's tendency to collect females to some degree, setting limits to the competition for them and, through marriage, assuring the male of the possession of those which he has already gathered. Any society which failed to do this would be constantly disrupted by fights.

The direct expression of any one of the tendencies arising from continuous sexual activity and male dominance can be inhibited, and all of them are inhibited by one social system or another. At the same time, such inhibition requires the development of a series of compensating patterns, even if these do nothing more than to provide the individual with intensive inhibitory training. Thus among the Comanche sexual jealousy between brothers or even close friends was socially deprecated and rarely shown. Compensation for the individual was provided by another social pattern, that of wife exchange. In such exchanges the rights of the husband were fully recognized and he was compensated for restraining his jealousy partly by the social approval of his generosity, partly by his expectation of a return in kind. An older brother would loan his wife freely to his unmarried younger brother, but the latter would return the compliment after his marriage. If the younger brother did not live up to his obligation, the older brother would, in the words of an informant, "never feel the same about him again." Other societies encourage sexual jealousy and use it as an aid to the enforcement of faithfulness upon one or both partners to a marriage, but this pattern also entails inhibitions. The partners must restrain their roving tendencies, and society must aid them in this by providing special training and compensations.

Culture plays such an important part in both the inhibition and encouragement of jealousy that it may very well be asked whether jealousy is one of the innate qualities of human beings. It is certainly present in the lower primates, and there seems to be a good deal of evidence that it is also characteristic of our own species. It appears sporadically even in those societies which reprehend it most severely. Thus in the Marquesas Islands both men and women enjoy an unusual degree of sexual freedom both before and after marriage. Both sexes begin to have intercourse at a very early age and are almost completely promiscuous until marriage, which is rather late. There is thus little opportunity for an early conditioning to the idea of exclusive sexual possession of any individual by another. Moreover, group marriage is, or rather was, the normal form, so that even after marriage there were few exclusive partnerships. The restrictions were further relaxed by frequent periods of license and by the regular practice of sexual hospitality. Any manifestation of sexual jealousy still exposes the individual to ridicule, and the natives rarely show any signs of it when sober. However, when they are drunk such jealousy promptly manifests itself and leads to numerous fights among both the men and the women. These are considered breaches of good manners, and the participants are ashamed of themselves when they become sober again.

The physical superiority of the human male has had a much greater effect on the development of social institutions than we usually realize. In combination with the differing rôles of the two sexes in reproduction and the early care of offspring, it has led to the delegation to men of the tasks of hunting and defense. Under uncivilized conditions both of these are of primary importance to the group's survival, and the social importance of males has been increased accordingly. In practically all societies the actual business of ruling is carried on by men. The official head of a society may be a woman, but the exercise of the powers which go with the position are nearly always delegated to some man or group of men. Similarly, male control of the family unit is nearly universal. There are certain societies in which women are officially recognized as dominant in the marriage relationship, but this is not incompatible with more inclusive patterns of male dominance. We are so accustomed to think of marriage as the core of the family that we are likely to jump to the conclusion that a social system under which a woman rules her husband and dismisses him at will is dominated by women. Actually, in most of these so-called matriarchies ultimate control is still vested in the males. A woman may dominate her husband, but she is normally dominated in turn by some male relative, usually her mother's brother or her own brother. Although a husband may have no control over his own wife and children, he will control some other woman and her children, thus evening the account.

It is questionable whether there is any society in existence which is actually dominated by women. Nevertheless, it is possible to imagine a situation in which this might come to be the case. Economic considerations are of great importance in the organization of all social systems. We all recognize that even in our own society the ultimate control of the family is vested in the partner who makes the greatest contribution to its support.

The poor man who marries a rich wife is under his wife's thumb no matter what the theoretical relation of husband and wife may be in that particular society. When any group becomes mainly dependent for its subsistence on an occupation or series of occupations carried on exclusively by women, the social importance of women will be increased and their actual if not their theoretical position in the society correspondingly raised. If the inheritance of property necessary to the particular industry is involved, the position of women will be still further strengthened.

It is a general rule that property is inherited by the sex to whom it will be most useful. Thus in our own society if a man died leaving a son and a daughter, a dress-suit and a sewing-machine, and no will, there would be no question as to which child would get which. In a group in which agriculture is exclusively a woman's occupation, land will tend to pass from mother to daughter rather than from mother to son. If the group comes to depend mainly on agriculture, the women will be in the position of rich wives to poor husbands. They will own both the main natural resource of the group and the means of exploiting it. Given such a condition, women will have an actual dominance which may in time achieve social recognition. This was the case among the Iroquois, frequently cited as an example of strong matriarchal organization. However, in spite of the very important rôle of women in Iroquois society and their control of its economic basis, even here actual rule outside the family was carried on by men. Although men made little economic contribution they took care of defense, which was equally necessary to the survival of the group, and thus balanced their economic deficiencies. Actually, cases of extreme dependence upon women even in economic matters are rare. The activities assigned to the two sexes in any society are usually well balanced in their social importance, and this gives the physical superiority of the male a chance to assert itself.

MARRIAGE

Polyandry is quite rare. It seems to be rather uniformly correlated with hard economic conditions and a necessity for limiting population. Ethical concepts aside, the most effective method of limitation is female infanticide. The number of women of child-bearing age in any group determines the possible rate of increase, while the number of men has no effect on this rate. Polyandry, as an institution, serves to provide the surplus males with mates and also to ensure to the conjugal group the economic contributions of several males. Under certain conditions this last factor may be as important as the first. Any social worker will testify that even in our own society hard times often result in what is essentially a polyandrous arrangement, although the secondary husband is usually known as a boarder.

In most polyandrous societies the plural husbands are usually a group of actual or socially ascribed brothers. Tibetan polyandry is one of the classic examples. In Tibet all arable land has long since passed into family holdings. Many of these holdings have become so small that they barely suffice to support a conjugal group and could not do so if they were further subdivided. It has become customary for one son from each family to go into religious life, thus relinquishing his claim on the family land. The other sons marry a single wife, work the family holding for the support of this woman and her children, and pass the holding on to the children intact. In spite of female infanticide, the position of women is high. The wife usually takes charge of the finances of the family and may dominate her spouses. That Tibetan polyandry is primarily due to hard economic conditions seems to be proved by the fact that it is characteristic only of the lower classes. Tibetans of higher economic status tend to be monogamous, while rich nobles are sometimes polygynous.

Polygyny, i.e., plurality of wives, is considered the most desirable form of marriage in a very large part of the world's societies. It does not seem to be directly correlated with any particular set of economic conditions or even with the primary dependence of the society on the labor of either men or women. It exists alike in societies in which women do most of the work and every wife is an added asset to the conjugal group and in those in which men carry the economic burden and each wife is an added liability. Although such factors do not seem to influence the ideal pattern, they naturally limit its exercise. Where wives are an asset, even a poor man can be polygynous unless the bride-price is prohibitive, and actual plurality of wives tends to be common. Where wives are a liability, few men can afford the luxury of an extra wife. Thus, although the Greenland Eskimo permit polygyny, only a very good hunter can support more than one woman, and only about one man in twenty has a second wife. The same holds for most Mohammedan communities. Although a man is allowed four wives and an unlimited number of concubines by Koranic law, poor families are nearly always monogamous and only the rich can take the full number of wives permitted.

One factor which unquestionably does make for polygyny is a shortage of men. Systematic male infanticide is almost unknown. It would have no effect on population increase and would weaken the power of the group for offense or defense even if it had no economic consequences. However, due to the more active life of men and the ascription to them of the more hazardous occupations, uncivilized groups usually show a surplus of women. Warfare, of course, contributes to this situation, but its effects are probably secondary in most cases to those of the occupational dangers. Although uncivilized tribes are usually at war with some one, the actual losses are surprisingly small. Thus a chief of the Mahafaly, in southwestern Madagascar, in telling me of an important war which had cost his people a large piece of territory, said that his tribe *had had eight men killed!*

It seems probable that the widespread occurrence of polygyny derives more from the general primate tendency for males to collect females than from anything else. The other factors involved are only contributory causes. At the same time, polygyny does not necessarily imply a high degree of male dominance in the marriage relationship or even a low position of women in the society. Polygynous societies are as variable in this respect as are monogamous ones. While there are a few cases in which the wives are completely dependent upon the husband, in most instances their rights are well guarded. When the plural wives are congenial, the women of a polygynous household may form a block, presenting a solid front against the husband and even dominating him. The situation existing in polygynous families in Madagascar, which is typical for a large part of Africa as well, is about as follows.

There are some differences in the family arrangements from one tribe to another, but the basic patterns are nearly the same everywhere. A man's first marriage is normally a love match, although there are a few tribes which require marriage with the daughter of a father's sister. In either case, the first wife ranks all subsequent wives and is the unquestioned head of the women's half of the conjugal group. The first plural marriage usually takes place three or four years after the original union and is, in a surprisingly large number of cases, instigated by the first wife. Women work in the fields as well as in the house, and when there are small children they often find the burden exceedingly heavy. No female help can be hired, and even the purchase of a slave woman is not a satisfactory solution. (Slavery has, of course, been terminated by French rule. We are discussing conditions of fifty years ago.) The husband would be entitled to use such a slave as a concubine, thus giving the wife as much cause for jealousy as would another wife, while the slave's interest in the establishment would be less and her cooperation less wholehearted. The best solution is for the husband to marry another wife, and his failure to do so is either an admission of poverty or a sign of indifference to the first wife's interests.

Second wives are drawn from the women who are not attractive enough to be chosen as first wives, from widows and from divorcées. A man must marry his brother's widow if she has children, his first wife having no say in the matter. Otherwise, he must have his wife's permission for the second marriage. Actually, they usually talk over the possibilities and finally agree on some woman who will be acceptable to both. In at least one case a man married a second wife because his first wife insisted on it. The woman was a close friend of hers whom the husband rather disliked. For all subsequent marriages the husband must have the permission of all his previous wives. As the number increases it becomes more difficult to get this, and the husband often has to resort to bribery, making the other wives gifts of money or cattle. The only exception to this rule is when the husband is detected in an affair with an unmarried woman. If it seems to be serious, his wives may insist upon his marrying her on the principle that she should share in the labors of the household. Needless to say, her position after the marriage is not a happy one, and this curious form of revenge is a rather strong incentive to good behavior. Chiefs do not have to have their wives' permission for plural marriages, and they are the only men who collect large numbers of wives. Very few commoners have more than three.

When a man has three wives, each wife will have a separate house for herself and her children. The first wife usually keeps the original dwelling, and the husband considers her house as his real home and keeps most of his belongings there. However, he is required to spend one day with each wife in succession. If he spends one wife's day with another wife, it constitutes adultery under native law and entitles the slighted wife to a divorce with alimony amounting to one third of the husband's property other than land. Such an offense is considered more serious than misconduct with a woman outside the conjugal group, and the husband will be lucky if he escapes with a liberal gift to the offended wife. Conversely, adultery in our use of the term is considered the affair only of the wife on whose day the offense was committed. The other wives will be sure to tell her about it if they discover it first, but unless the husband is having a real affair they are more likely to make fun of her than to sympathize. Theoretically the injured wife is entitled to a divorce with alimony, but she will be ridiculed if she claims one on grounds of a single offense and is usually satisfied with a moderate gift.

For purposes of cultivation, the husband's land is divided among the wives as equally as possible. Each wife works her section and can claim the husband's assistance on her day. This economic claim over the husband goes so far that if he hunts or fishes on that day the wife has a right to half his take or to half the money received from the sale of any surplus. From the produce of her section of land each woman feeds herself and her children, also the husband on the day he is with her. If there is a surplus to be sold, one half of the proceeds go to the husband as ground rent. The other half is the property of the wife, and she usually banks it with her own family. In a well-organized conjugal group the women usually take turns working on the land while one of them remains at home to cook and tend the children. The whole family will eat first at one house and then at another, so that, if there are three wives, cooking and dishwashing will fall to the portion of any one of them only on every third day. In many cases the plural wives become strongly attached to each other, while there is always a tendency for the female part of the group to present a united front toward the husband. Wives will not infrequently carry on love affairs with the full knowledge of their fellow-wives without fear of betrayal. The female half of the family is thus able to control family policies to a considerable degree, and hen-pecked husbands are by no means unknown. If the husband tries to coerce one wife, the rest will resent it and make his life miserable by those unofficial methods with which all women are familiar. The wives receive added power from the fact that the husband is theoretically in complete control and cannot appeal for outside help without making himself ridiculous.

The condition just described may be extreme, but there are few polygynous systems in which the position of the male is really better than it is under monogamy. If the plural wives are not congenial, the family will be torn by feuds in which the husband must take the thankless rôle of umpire, while if they are congenial he is likely to be confronted by an organized feminine opposition. Among the sub-human primates the male can dominate a group of females because these females are unable to organize among themselves. He can deal with them in detail. The human male cannot dominate his wives in the same degree, since they can and do organize for both defense and offense. If all a man's wives want a particular thing, they can work on him in shifts and are fairly certain to get what they want.

The only form of marriage which is recognized and permitted in all social systems is monogamy. It coexists with all the other forms, although it is the preferred form in a relatively small number of societies. In those groups which recognize it as an alternative, its social significance varies according to what the preferred form may be. Thus in a polyandrous society monogamous unions may bring the members a certain prestige. A man who can support a conjugal group without help must be richer and more able than the average. Conversely, in a polygynous society monogamous unions may mean loss of prestige. If a man has only one wife, it will be tacitly assumed that he is too poor to buy or support a second. When this attitude is present, the first wife often feels the situation keenly and does all that she can to bring about a second marriage. She may not enjoy having a rival in the family, but she enjoys still less the idea that she is married to a failure.

An actual analysis of marriage in various societies shows that there are very few groups in which plurality of spouses is the general condition. Even when polygyny is the ideal, there are usually only a few men who can afford to have more than one wife. Thus among the Eskimo plural unions stand to monogamous ones in the ratio of about one to twenty. In the non-Christian civilizations such as those of India, China, or Islam, the ratio is almost as low. Although economic factors are mainly responsible for this condition, all groups can also show certain unions which are monogamous by preference. When the partners find complete emotional satisfaction in each other, they prefer not to admit additional spouses even when there is social pressure for them to do so. Such unions seem to provide the maximum of happiness to the parties involved.

There is no absolute scale against which the advantages and disadvantages of the various forms of marriage can be measured. Each form is an integral part of a particular economic and social system and, as such, will function better in connection with that system than with any other. Our own form of marriage works very well in its present setting, yet when it has been introduced into other societies the results have often been catastrophic. As far as the happiness of the individuals involved is concerned, there are a few persons in all societies who would not be content under any form of permanent mating, and a few at the opposite end of the scale who are able to find complete contentment in enduring monogamous unions. The bulk of all populations appear to fall between these two extremes. They can be conditioned to accept any type of union as natural and will find contentment in it as long as the other partners are not actively uncongenial.

From Ralph Linton. *The Study of Man.* New York: Appleton-Century-Crofts, 1936, pages 115-123, 127-129, 135-139, 182-188. Reprinted by permission of Prentice-Hall, Inc.

REFERENCES

MACHIAVELLI, N. *The Prince* (1513). In *Great Books of the Western World,* Volume 23, edited by R. M. Hutchins. Chicago: Encyclopaedia Britannica, 1952.

MURDOCK, G. P. *Social Structure.* New York: The Free Press, 1949.

THE STANDARDIZATION OF SEX-TEMPERAMENT

Margaret Mead

Unlike Malinowski and Linton who discovered cultural anthropology after their advanced studies, Margaret Mead turned to cultural anthropology while still an undergraduate at Barnard College. From there she went to Columbia University where her doctoral work was guided by Ruth Benedict and Franz Boas. This was a most fortunate combination of mentors, for in Boas she had exposure to the massive erudition of the primary source figure in American anthropology as it is known today; while in Benedict she found a specific intellectual direction, ultimately known as the "culture and personality" approach, and one which she formed as it was forming her.

Gifted with great vigor and an extraordinary sense of mission, Mead is one of those few academic personalities who have transcended disciplinary boundaries and become public figures in the larger society. In her case the wide recognition is deserved as she has written, taught, and lectured prolifically and profoundly on most subjects which have been of concern to contemporary humanity: Race and racism, cultural relativity, warfare and peace, sex and sex role, the gap between generations, the care and education of children, the impact of technological change on culture, and, perhaps most importantly, the relevance of human culture as we know it to the realities of the modern human condition, as we are only beginning to know it.

She is now Curator of Ethnology at the American Museum of Natural History and Adjunct Professor of Anthropology at Columbia University. During her career she has made numerous field expeditions, particularly to the South Pacific regions of Bali, Samoa, and New Guinea. It was during her field work in the latter setting that she collected the data and developed the ideas which appeared in Sex and Temperament in Three Primitive Societies *(1935). The selection below is one of the final chapters of that book.*

We have now considered in detail the approved personalities of each sex among three primitive peoples. We found the Arapesh—both men and women—displaying a personality that, out of our historically limited preoccupations, we would call maternal in its parental aspects, and feminine in its sexual aspects. We found men, as well as women, trained to be co-operative, unaggressive, responsive to the needs and demands of others. We found no idea that sex was a powerful driving force either for men or for women. In marked contrast to these attitudes, we found among the Mundugumor that both men and women developed as ruthless, aggressive, positively sexed individuals, with the maternal cherishing aspects of personality at a minimum. Both men and women approximated to a personality type that we in our culture would find only in an undisciplined and very violent male. Neither the Arapesh nor the Mundugumor profit by a contrast between the sexes; the Arapesh ideal is the mild, responsive man married to the mild, responsive woman; the Mundugumor ideal is the violent aggressive man married to the violent aggressive woman. In the third tribe, the Tchambuli, we found a genuine reversal of the sex-attitudes of our own culture, with the woman the dominant, impersonal, managing partner, the man the less responsible and the emotionally dependent person. These three situations suggest, then, a very definite conclusion. If those temperamental attitudes which we have traditionally regarded as feminine—such as passivity, responsiveness, and a willingness to cherish children—can so easily be set up as the masculine pattern in one tribe, and in another be outlawed for the majority of women as well as for the majority of men, we no longer have any basis for regarding such aspects of behaviour as sex-linked. And this conclusion becomes even stronger when we consider the actual reversal in Tchambuli of the position of dominance of the two sexes, in spite of the existence of formal patrilineal institutions.

The material suggests that we may say that many, if not all, of the personality traits which we have called masculine or feminine are as lightly linked to sex as are the clothing, the manners, and the form of head-dress that a society at a given period assigns to either sex. When we consider the behaviour of the typical Arapesh man or woman as contrasted with the behaviour of the typical Mundugumor man or woman, the evidence is overwhelmingly in favour of the strength of social conditioning. In no other way can we account for the almost complete uniformity with which Arapesh children develop into contented, passive, secure persons, while Mundugumor children develop as characteristically into violent, aggressive, insecure persons. Only to the impact of the whole of the integrated culture upon the growing child can we lay the formation of the contrasting types. There is no other explanation of race, or diet, or selection that can be adduced to explain them. We are forced to conclude that human nature is almost unbelievably malleable, responding accurately and contrastingly to contrasting cultural conditions. The differences between individuals who are members of different cultures, like the differences between individuals within a culture, are almost entirely to be laid to differences in conditioning, especially during early childhood, and the form of this conditioning is culturally determined. Standardized personality differences between the sexes are of this order, cultural creations to which each generation, male and female, is trained to conform. There remains, however, the problem of the origin of these socially standardized differences.

While the basic importance of social conditioning is still imperfectly recognized—not only in lay thought, but even by the scientists specifically concerned with such matters—to go beyond it and consider the possible influence of variations in hereditary equipment is a hazardous matter. The following pages will read very differently to one who has made a part of his thinking a recognition of the whole amazing mechanism of cultural conditioning—who has really accepted the fact that the same infant could be developed into a full participant in any one of these three cultures—than they will read to one who still believes that the minutiae of cultural behaviour are carried in the individual germ-plasm. If it is said, therefore, that when we have grasped the full significance of the malleability of the human organism and the preponderant importance of cultural conditioning, there are still further problems to solve, it must be remembered that these problems come *after* such a comprehension of the force of conditioning; they cannot precede it. The forces that make children born among the Arapesh grow up into typical Arapesh personalities are entirely social, and any discussion of the variations which do occur must be looked at against this social background.

With this warning firmly in mind, we can ask a further question. Granting the malleability of human nature, whence arise the differences between the standardized personalities that different cultures decree for all of their members, or which one culture decrees for the members of one sex as contrasted with the members of the opposite sex? If such differences are culturally created, as this material would most strongly suggest that they are, if the new-born child can be shaped with equal ease into an unaggressive Arapesh or an aggressive Mundugumor, why do these striking contrasts occur at all? If the clues to the different personalities decreed for men and women in Tchambuli do not lie in the physical constitution of the two sexes—an assumption that we must reject both for the Tchambuli and for our own society—where can we find the clues upon which the Tchambuli, the Arapesh, the Mundugumor, have built? Cultures are man-made, they are built of human materials; they are diverse but comparable structures within which human beings can attain full human stature. Upon what have they built their diversities?

We recognize that a homogeneous culture committed in all of its gravest institutions and slightest usages to a co-operative, unaggressive course can bend every child to that emphasis, some to a perfect accord with it, the majority to an easy acceptance, while only a few deviants fail to receive the cultural imprint. To consider such traits as aggressiveness or passivity to be sex-linked is not possible in the light of the facts. Have such traits, then, as aggressiveness or passivity, pride or humility, objectivity or a preoccupation with personal relationships, an easy response to the needs of the young and the weak or a hostility to the young and the weak, a tendency to initiate sex-relations or merely to respond to the dictates of a situation or another person's advances—have these traits any basis in temperament at all? Are they potentialities of all human temperaments that can be developed by different kinds of social conditioning and which will not appear if the necessary conditioning is absent?

When we ask this question we shift our emphasis. If we ask why an Arapesh man or an Arapesh woman shows the kind of personality that we have considered in the first section of this book, the answer is: Because of the Arapesh culture, because of the intricate, elaborate, and the unfailing fashion in which a culture is able to shape each new-born child to the cultural image.

And if we ask the same question about a Mundugumor man or woman, or about a Tchambuli man as compared with a Tchambuli woman, the answer is of the same kind. They display the personalities that are peculiar to the cultures in which they were born and educated. Our attention has been on the differences betwen Arapesh men and women as a group and Mundugumor men and women as a group. It is as if we had represented the Arapesh personality by a soft yellow, the Mundugumor by a deep red, while the Tchambuli female personality was deep orange, and that of the Tchambuli male, pale green. But if we now ask whence came the original direction in each culture, so that one now shows yellow, another red, the third orange and green by sex, then we must peer more closely. And leaning closer to the picture, it is as if behind the bright consistent yellow of the Arapesh, and the deep equally consistent red of the Mundugumor, behind the orange and green that are Tchambuli, we found in each case the delicate, just discernible outlines of the whole spectrum, differently overlaid in each case by the monotone which covers it. This spectrum is the range of individual differences which lie back of the so much more conspicuous cultural emphases, and it is to this that we must turn to find the explanation of cultural inspiration, of the source from which each culture has drawn.

There appears to be about the same range of basic temperamental variation among the Arapesh and among the Mundugumor, although the violent man is a misfit in the first society and a leader in the second. If human nature were completely homogeneous raw material, lacking specific drives and characterized by no important constitutional differences between individuals, then individuals who display personality traits so antithetical to the social pressure should not reappear in societies of such differing emphases. If the variations between individuals were to be set down to accidents in the genetic process, the same accidents should not be repeated with similar frequency in strikingly different cultures, with strongly contrasting methods of education.

But because this same relative distribution of individual differences does appear in culture after culture, in spite of the divergence between the cultures, it seems pertinent to offer a hypothesis to explain upon what basis the personalities of men and women have been differently standardized so often in the history of the human race. This hypothesis is an extension of that advanced by Ruth Benedict in her *Patterns of Culture*. Let us assume that there are definite temperamental differences between human beings which if not entirely hereditary at least are established on a hereditary base very soon after birth. (Further than this we cannot at present narrow the matter.) These differences finally embodied in the character structure of adults, then, are the clues from which culture works, selecting one temperament, or a combination of related and congruent types, as desirable, and embodying this choice in every thread of the social fabric—in the care of the young child, the games the children play, the songs the people sing, the structure of political organization, the religious observance, the art and the philosophy.

Some primitive societies have had the time and the robustness to revamp all of their institutions to fit one extreme type, and to develop educational techniques which will ensure that the majority of each generation will show a personality congruent with this extreme emphasis. Other societies have pursued a less definitive course, selecting their models not from the most extreme, most highly differentiated individuals, but from the less marked types. In such societies the approved personality is less pronounced, and the culture often contains the types of inconsistencies that many human beings display also; one institution may be adjusted to the uses of pride, another to a casual humility that is congruent neither with pride nor with inverted pride. Such societies, which have taken the more usual and less sharply defined types as models, often show also a less definitely patterned social structure. The culture of such societies may be likened to a house the decoration of which has been informed by no definite and precise taste, no exclusive emphasis upon dignity or comfort or pretentiousness or beauty, but in which a little of each effect has been included.

Alternatively, a culture may take its clues not from one temperament, but from several temperaments. But instead of mixing together into an inconsistent hotchpotch the choices and emphases of different temperaments, or blending them together into a smooth but not particularly distinguished whole, it may isolate each type by making it the basis for the approved social personality for an age-group, a sex-group, a caste-group, or an occupational group. In this way society becomes not a monotone with a few discrepant patches of an intrusive colour, but a mosaic, with different groups displaying different personality traits. Such specializations as these may be based upon any facet of human endowment—different intellectual abilities, different artistic abilities, different emotional traits. So the Samoans decree that all young people must show the personality trait of unaggressiveness and punish with opprobrium the aggressive child who displays traits regarded as appropriate only in titled middle-aged men. In societies based upon elaborate ideas of rank, members of the aristocracy will be permitted, even compelled, to display a pride, a sensitivity to insult, that would be deprecated as inappropriate in members of the plebeian class. So also in professional groups or in religious sects some temperamental traits are selected and institutionalized, and taught to each new member who enters the profession or sect. Thus the physician learns the bed-side manner, which is the natural behaviour of some temperaments and the standard behaviour of the general practitioner in the medical profession; the Quaker learns at least the outward behaviour and the rudiments of meditation, the capacity for which is not necessarily an innate characteristic of many of the members of the Society of Friends.

So it is with the social personalities of the two sexes. The traits that occur in some members of each sex are specially assigned to one sex, and disallowed in the other. The history of the social definition of sex-differences is filled with such arbitrary arrangements in the intellectual and artistic field, but because of the assumed congruence between physiological sex and emotional endowment we have been less able to recognize that a similar arbitrary selection is being made among emotional traits also. We have assumed that because it is convenient for a mother to wish to care for her child, this is a trait with which women have been more generously endowed by a carefully teleological process of evolution. We have assumed that because men hunted, an activity requiring enterprise, bravery, and initiative, they have been endowed with these useful attitudes as part of their sex-temperament.

Societies have made these assumptions both overtly and implicitly. If a society insists that warfare is the major occupation for the male sex, it is therefore insisting that all male children display bravery and pugnacity. Even if the insistence upon the differential bravery of men and women is not made articulate, the difference in occupation makes this point implicitly. When, however, a society goes further and defines men as brave and women as timorous, when men are forbidden to show fear and women are indulged in the most flagrant display of fear, a more explicit element enters in. Bravery, hatred of any weakness, of flinching before pain or danger—this attitude which is so strong a component of *some human* temperaments has been selected as the key to masculine behaviour. The easy unashamed display of fear or suffering that is congenial to a different temperament has been made the key to feminine behaviour.

Originally two variations of human temperament, a hatred of fear or willingness to display fear, they have been socially translated into inalienable aspects of the personalities of the two sexes. And to that defined sex-personality every child will be educated, if a boy, to suppress fear, if a girl, to show it. If there has been no social selection in regard to this trait, the proud temperament that is repelled by any betrayal of feeling will display itself, regardless of sex, by keeping a stiff upper lip. Without an express prohibition of such behaviour the expressive unashamed man or woman will weep, or comment upon fear or suffering. Such attitudes, strongly marked in certain temperaments, may by social selection be standardized for everyone, or outlawed for everyone, or ignored by society, or made the exclusive and approved behaviour of one sex only.

Neither the Arapesh nor the Mundugumor have made any attitude specific for one sex. All of the energies of the culture have gone towards the creation of a single human type, regardless of class, age, or sex. There is no division into age-class for which different motives or different moral attitudes are regarded as suitable. There is no class of seers or mediums who stand apart drawing inspiration from psychological sources not available to the majority of the people. The Mundugumor have, it is true, made one arbitrary selection, in that they recognize artistic ability only among individuals born with the cord about their necks, and firmly deny the happy exercise of artistic ability to those less unusually born. The Arapesh boy with a tinea infection has been socially selected to be a disgruntled, antisocial individual, and the society forces upon sunny co-operative children cursed with this affliction a final approximation to the behaviour appropriate to a pariah. With these two exceptions no emotional rôle is forced upon an individual because of birth or accident. As there is no idea of rank which declares that some are of high estate and some of low, so there is no idea of sex-difference which declares that one sex must feel differently from the other. One possible imaginative social construct, the attribution of different personalities to different members of the community classified into sex-, age-, or caste-groups, is lacking.

When we turn however to the Tchambuli, we find a situation that while bizarre in one respect, seems nevertheless more intelligible in another. The Tchambuli have at least made the point of sex-difference; they have used the obvious fact of sex as an organizing point for the formation of social personality, even though they seem to us to have reversed the normal picture. While there is reason to believe that not every Tchambuli woman is born with a dominating, organizing, administrative temperament, actively sexed and willing to initiate sex-relations, possessive, definite, robust, practical and impersonal in outlook, still most Tchambuli girls grow up to display these traits. And while there is definite evidence to show that all Tchambuli men are not, by native endowment, the delicate responsive actors of a play staged for the women's benefit, still most Tchambuli boys manifest this coquettish play-acting personality most of the time. Because the Tchambuli formulation of sex-attitudes contradicts our usual premises, we can see clearly that Tchambuli culture has arbitrarily permitted certain human traits to women, and allotted others, equally arbitrarily, to men.

From Margaret Mead. *Sex and Temperament in Three Primitive Societies.* New York: William Morrow & Co., 1935, pages 279-288. Reprinted by permission of Margaret Mead and William Morrow & Co., Inc. Copyright 1935, 1950, 1963 by Margaret Mead.

REFERENCE

BENEDICT, R. F. *Patterns of Culture.* Boston: Houghton Mifflin, 1934.

FAMILY STRUCTURE AND THE SOCIALIZATION OF THE CHILD

Talcott Parsons

Talcott Parsons is the only bona fide sociologist to contribute a selection to this anthology. His scope, however, has never been limited to sociology, as he has studied, at one time or another, economics, psychoanalysis, psychology, and cultural anthropology, the latter with Malinowski in London. Parsons once described himself as an "incurable theorist" and, indeed, his life's work bears out this label. He has always worked toward a total theory of human society and has shown great imagination in his efforts to synthesize the best of the above disciplines into a coherent whole.

Our particular interest in Parsons, however, lies in his analysis of the oedipal, nuclear family as a small social system. The central constructs of his analysis are female expressiveness and male instrumentality. Unlike Freud, he did not conceptualize these as extensions of anatomical differences, but as societal givens. According to Parsons the larger society requires that the family protect its integrity as the basic social unit and prepare children for the eventual assumption of adult roles. The family meets these demands by having the mother maintain its internal expressive bonds and the father manage its instrumental ties to the external social order. This complementarity of function reduces competition between the parents and enables them to present a united, sex-differentiated front to the children. Thus, the children are encouraged to assume functional roles which correspond to the roles of their same sex parents. In the selection below, taken from Family, Socialization and Interaction Process *(1955), Parsons first describes the basic role structure of the nuclear family, then the dynamics of sex-role formation within this structure.*

Parsons spent the greater part of his career as professor of sociology at Harvard University. A past president of the American Sociological Association, he is generally regarded as one of the great theoretical sociologists of the Twentieth Century.

THE SOCIAL STRUCTURES IMPINGING ON THE CHILD

L et us now turn to the problems of the structure of the systems of social interaction which are relevant to this paradigm of socialization. Though it stands, in its most critical significance, in the middle of a series, the nuclear family may conveniently be used as the point of reference for our analysis, because of the general clarity of relationships here.

The structure of the nuclear family can be treated as a consequence of differentiation on two axes, that of hierarchy or power and that of instrumental vs. expressive function. If this is correct and relevant, it follows that so far as this aspect of its differentiation is concerned the family contains four fundamental *types* of status-role. This basic four-role pattern can be modified by a variety of factors such as stage of the family cycle, age-differential of husband and wife, interval between their ages and those of children, number, assortment by sex, and interval between children. All these and others may prove significant for more refined analyses, but there seems little doubt that these two axes of differentiation as symbolized by the two great differentiations of generation (during the pre-adult period of children) and sex, overshadow other bases of differentiation within what in any sense may be considered a "typical" nuclear family.

This role structure may then be roughly represented by the four-fold table of Figure 1. The father role is, *relative to the others*, high both on power and on "instrumentality"—hence low on "expressiveness." The mother role is high on power and on "expressiveness," thus low in instrumentality. The son role is low on power but high on instrumentality, the daughter role low on power but high on expressiveness—hence low on instrumentality.[1]

As has already been pointed out, these distinctions are of course relative. They are defined in terms of amount and mode of influence on the functioning of the family as a social system. The power axis of this differentiation is, as we interpret it, simply the quantitative degree of such influence. This makes its interpretation relative to the generation difference almost obvious; surely the adult can affect the affairs of the family as a system more than can a small child. Of course with maturation of the child his power grows, and the inequality vis-à-vis his parents is

FIGURE 1

Basic Role-Structure of the Nuclear Family

Instrumental Priority	Expressive Priority
Instrumental superior	*Expressive superior*
Father (husband)	*Mother (wife)*
Instrumental inferior	*Expressive inferior*
Son (brother)	*Daughter (sister)*

Superior +

power

Inferior −

lessened. But the basic point is clear.[2] The instrumental-expressive distinction we interpret[3] as essentially the differentiation of function, and hence of relative influence, in terms of "external" vs. "internal" functions of the system. The area of instrumental function concerns relations of the system to its situation outside the system, to meeting the adaptive conditions of its maintenance of equilibrium, and "instrumentally" establishing the desired relations to *external* goal-objects. The expressive area concerns the "internal" affairs of the system, the maintenance of integrative relations between the members, and regulation of the patterns and tension levels of its component units.

We must remember that the four paramount familial roles of father, mother, son and daughter are interpreted here to be differentiated on a generically significant basis. Therefore, particularly in relating them to extrafamilial roles it will be important to think in these more generic terms. For these purposes we may refer to them as the roles of instrumental superiority, expressive superiority, instrumental inferiority and expressive inferiority respectively. The latter two mean of course instrumentally specialized *but* inferior to father, similarly with expressively specialized but inferior to mother.

We spoke above of the social systems in which the child was involved as constituting some kind of a series, of which increasing structural differentiation must be one primary aspect. Can we now suggest a more precise idea of the nature of this series and hence of what kind of transition is involved in passage from one point in the series to another? In this connection the fact that there are *four* role types which have a "primary" order of structural differentiation from each other in the nuclear family is extraordinarily suggestive. For one major aspect of differentiation is increasing complexity and one aspect of increasing complexity in turn is increasing *number* of differentiated parts of a system. The obvious series of which the number four is a step in increasing complexity is one of binary division. By binary division a four-unit system can be derived from one of two units, and two in turn can be derived from one by dividing the one. Moving in the other direction by the same principle, four divide into eight, eight into sixteen, etc. We wish to use this principle as our working assumption in analyzing the series of social structures in which the child comes to be progressively integrated in the course of the socialization process.

On the assumption, then, that the four-role family structure is a stage in a series of structures whose complexity increases progressively on the binary principle, what concrete meaning can be given to the terms of the series in both directions from four as the point of reference? Moving toward decreasing complexity the subsystem mother-child comes immediately to mind. Leaning on very widespread views in the field of child development, we have above suggested that the Oedipal crisis constitutes the transition from primary integration of the child with the mother as a love-object to integration in the family in such a way that, vis-à-vis ego father and siblings acquire much greater and more independent significance for his interaction. We, therefore, postulate that the two-member unit of the series is the mother-child system (in the mother's role as mother of *this particular* child, of course). This is to be considered as a social system in the strictest sense.[4]

What then could be the one-member system which is the end of the series? It clearly cannot be either the mother or the child as "individuals," since we are talking about systems of *social* interaction. Psychoanalytic theory gives us a very important clue here, in speaking of the "mother-child *identity*"[5] which is the referent of Freud's discussion of "primary identification." Essentially, we interpret this to mean a system of interaction on an authentically socio-cultural—i.e., meaningfully symbolic—level in which one member of the system has so little autonomy that his independent influence on the behavior of the *system*—as *actor,* note, not as a "condition" which influences the mother—may be treated as secondary. This is not, however, to say that it is not a social system in the sense that his "responsiveness" or lack of it is indifferent to the mother. Then for theoretical purposes it may be assumed that mother and child "act as one" not in the special meaning of "action in concert" which is characteristic of differentiated social collectivities, but in a special and more radical sense. It is, however, a true social system in that there is "double contingency" and the points of view of both parties must be taken into account.[6]

What in turn may lie back of this "identity" at the stage of oral dependency, we will treat as pre- or proto-social. Until the oral dependency stage is reached, the child cannot be said to have become integrated in any social system. He is more or less only an "organism" in the sense of not being *socialized,* i.e., as seen from the point of view of an observer. To his mother he is a person in process of becoming. Furthermore, we must not be understood as holding that this "identity" with the mother is given at birth and is an expression of constitutional factors. On the contrary, we conceive it in its essentials as a product of *learning.* It is the end-product of the first major phase of the socialization process. Mother and child by this time—we have suggested on the eve of language-learning—constitute an authentic social system, but one of a very special sort, a kind of limiting case of the concept social system.

SEX ROLE, EROTICISM AND THE INCEST TABOO

With this framework in mind, let us come back to the problem of sex-role assumption and the Oedipus complex in Freud's sense. Let us start with the relevant aspects of the structure of the nuclear family as a social system. The mother-child, pre-Oedipal system is of course a subsystem of this. The question is how this subsystem can, by a process of transformation, be absorbed into the larger system, through change in the structure of the roles, without disorganizing the family as a system. Maturation of the child and the cultural demands as to what kind of behavior is appropriate for a "big" boy or girl, make simple maintenance of the pre-Oedipal status quo untenable. We will first assume that inertia will operate in the motivational systems of both mother and child, but more prominently the latter, because a lesser proportion of the mother's personality is invested in this particular subsystem. Regardless of the sex of the child, the "line of least resistance" would be to move the child into a role analogous to that of the husband (father). This would make it possible to preserve primary solidarity with the mother, especially advantageous of course for the child.

This of course is blocked by two main circumstances. The more obvious of course is that the role of husband is, in the normal case, already occupied, and this tendency would bring the child into direct competition with the father. In general, in view of the power situation, the outcome of such competition can hardly be in doubt, unless the mother is in such conflict with her husband that *she* gives the child priority over him. Something approaching this obviously does sometimes happen.[7] The second main reason is what, from the instrumental-expressive point of view, is the "tandem" relation of the three roles. The father-role is the more instrumental in the superordinate family system, the mother-role the more expressive, but in the mother-child system the mother-role is the more instrumental, the child-role the more expressive. Then one could say that assumption of the father role was particularly difficult for the child. Nevertheless the facts about children's, particularly of course, boys' deep sense of rivalry with their fathers, and jealousy of the father's position with the mother, seems to fit this situation and suggest that in fact there is a strong trend in this direction which has to be dealt with by strong counteracting forces. That the trend should be stronger for the boy is understandable in view of his developing masculine identification.

A second possibility, of course is that the child should attempt to take the role of the mother in relation to the father, again regardless of the sex of the child. That this is very much a possibility is indicated by the fact that the mother as object has been thoroughly internalized, and therefore the mother-role in relation to a child is in fact a need-disposition of the child's personality. In particular certain nurturant aspects of this role can relatively easily be generalized to other objects, as can the showing of love-solidarity. Again, because of developing feminine identification, it is particularly easy for a girl to embark on this path, which is the development of an "electra" complex in relation to her father.

A further consideration derives from the reciprocity of the mother-child relation in erotic as in other respects. The mother in fact *has* an erotic attachment to her child the renunciation of which she tends to resist. She may, hence tend to "aid and abet" the child in his "bid" for a "husband role." The erotic attachment of a father to his child is likely to be considerably weaker, but the components of it are clearly present as precipitates of his own developmental history and to some degree in his actual role. Hence he also may tend—unless there are adequate countermotives—to encourage the child's erotic interest in him.

On the basis of these considerations, we suggest that from the family point of view the primary function of the repression of eroticism is to prevent the assumption of either parental role by the child or its encouragement by the parent. In the mechanisms involved on the social system level two points stand out. The first is the very general fact about groups, which Bales has brought out, namely that the stability of a small group is highly dependent, both on the differentiation of instrumental and expressive leadership roles and on a coalition of the instrumental and expressive leaders.[8] From this point of view denial of the child's impulses to assume either of the parental roles vis-à-vis the other (equally of the parents' complementary impulses) is a protection of the integration of the family as a system against a disruptive tendency. Secondly, the erotic relation between the marriage partners, is a primary symbolic focus of their solidarity. It both symbolizes the differentiation of their roles in the family system, and their integration with each other. The child's earlier erotic attachment to the mother can be defined as non-competitive with her attachment to the father, but beyond a certain point, particularly where the child's role becomes sufficiently active, this non-competitiveness tends to break down.[9] It is a well-known principle of differentiation of social structures, that competitive pressures can be eased by qualitative differentiation of roles (this was probably first stated by Durkheim). It can then be argued that repression of the child's eroticism has the function for the family of protecting the integration of the family as a system by enforcing a clear differentiation of roles. As the child grows in relative power and independence,[10] his role is forced in the direction of greater qualitative differentiation from that of either parent, particularly in relation to the other.

What then, of the situation with respect to the child's personality? We have suggested above that a primary function of eroticism is as a vehicle of expressive generalization. At the oral stage it serves to bind together into a single complex the meanings of various segmental gratifications of which the mother is the agent. We may go on to suggest that, at the love-dependency stage this generalizing significance is extended in that erotic pleasure forms a link between the dependency and the autonomy sub-systems, thus serves to integrate the personality. Erotic stimulation, that is, particularly at this stage that type associated with diffuse pleasure on affectionate bodily contact, is a pleasure-gratification source. But *giving* such pleasure is also a manifestation of love as distinguished from nurturance, and serves as a symbolic acceptance-reward.

There is, however, in this generalizing function of eroticism, an inherent link to the more expressive aspect of the child's personality. In this wider respect it is associated with dependency. But the imperative developmental need at the Oedipal stage is to build up the instrumental side, cognitive powers and knowledge, instrumental skills, independent responsibility and the like. The erotic need, precisely because of its paramount expressive significance, can be the most serious barrier to progress in this direction, it can serve as the primary focus of the inertia of the older personality system.

Thus we have, anchored in their roles in and responsibility for the family as a system, in both the normal parents powerful motivation not to allow the child to build up and extend his relations to them on an erotic basis. This motivation above all depends on the stability of the coalition between them and on the importance in their personalities of their extra-familial roles. "Seduction" of a child into erotic reciprocity by either parent is presumably very generally associated with disturbance in the marital relationship. On the child's side we have serious resistance to giving up his erotic investments, but at the same time, with proper parental functioning, powerful rewards for development of the instrumental side of his personality.

Finally, it is of the greatest importance that this erotic need-disposition is repressed, but *not* extinguished. It presumably has some of the characteristics of "addiction."[11] It re-emerges as a critical aspect of the adult personality, but only when certain further conditions have been fulfilled. These conditions, we feel, involve successful carrying through of two further major steps in personality development beyond the Oedipal stage. After we have sketched our interpretation of what happens in these steps we will return to this subject.

Now we can approach the question of the differences between the sexes with respect to erotic development. These result, on the above interpretation, from a combination of two factors, first having to fit as a "latency period" child into the family as a system, and second the operation, at this phase, of sex-role identification. We spoke above of sex-role identification as one of three identifications which have to be learned by the child at this period. Perhaps the most important difference of the sexes at this point lies in the fact that, as shown in Figure 2, for the boy neither of the two sub-identifications, leaving out the family as a family, coincides, personnel-wise, with the pre-Oedipal identification with the mother, whereas for the girl, one of them does. We noted that there are, in the family system, two sub-collectivities to which a given member *cannot* belong. From the boy's point of view, i.e., both by sex and by generation, the mother belongs to both. From the girl's point of view she is excluded only by generation. Then we can say that the boy has to undergo at this stage a *double* "emancipation." In common with his sister he has to recognize that, in a sense not previously so important, he must not pretend to adulthood, he is unequivocally a child. But as differentiated from her, he must substitute a new identification with an unfamiliar and in a very important sense threatening object, the father, at the expense of his previous solidarity with his mother. He must renounce his previous dependency in a more radical sense. The girl, on the other hand, though she must internalize the father as object, does so only in his role as instrumental leader of the family as a system, not in the dual role which includes sex-role-model as well. Similarly, she remains categorized with her mother by sex, which coincides with the previous a-sexual (but not non-erotic) mother-child solidarity. Put a little differently, the boy must proceed farther and more radically on the path away from expressive primacy toward instrumental primacy. He is, therefore, subjected to greater strain.

FIGURE 2 *Basis of Sex-Role Identification in the Nuclear Family*

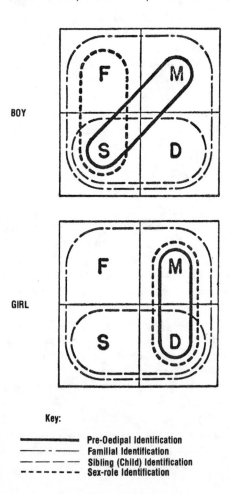

Key:

—————— Pre-Oedipal Identification
———·——— Familial Identification
—— —— —— Sibling (Child) Identification
- - - - - - - - Sex-role Identification

The impact of sex-role assumption is, in our society certainly, sharply emphasized in the differentiation of play interests in the early latency period. The girl, we must say, tends to act out symbolically precisely the *instrumental* aspect of the pre-Oedipal mother role. Playing with dolls and playing "house" in the sense of household chores seem to provide the principal content. It is strikingly notable that in the main pattern no adult masculine object is present, she herself is the "mother" and her doll is the child, but there is no father in the picture. Does this not suggest that she is symbolically acting out the mother role in the *pre-Oedipal* situation where the separate identity of the father as object was not prominent? One might say that if there were a father-doll the girl would be forced into the role of "wife" which is just what she is under pressure to avoid.

The boy, correspondingly, tends to attempt to act out what are symbolic representatives of the instrumental aspects of adult masculine roles. These are notably nonfamilial in content. He plays with trains, cars, airplanes. He more or less explicitly assumes relatively tangible adult masculine roles such as fireman or soldier. He puts great emphasis on physical prowess. But his play is a less exact copy of the specific father role than his sister's is of the mother. This may well be explained, partly at least, by two facts. First the mother role is far more uniform than the masculine occupational role; the girl has a rather specific role-model stereotype. Secondly, being, as we have suggested, under less acute strain, the girl is less driven to the kinds of symbols which tangibly express compulsively tinged sex-qualities. Thus both the difficulty of understanding many middle-class occupations—their remoteness, and the fact that not involving physical prowess or skills, they do not patently symbolize masculinity—may prevent the urban middle-class boy from so directly emulating his father as the girl does her mother. But it is nevertheless conspicuous that the boy's play-world at this stage seems to be almost wholly devoid of adult feminine figures, as the girl's is of masculine.

The girl on the other hand faces the opposite difficulty. The boy, we have just held, is under heavy pressure to achieve a degree and rate of emancipation from his dependency on his mother which puts him under severe strain. He must, as we have pointed out, move the farthest from his initial position. The girl, on the other hand, retains her sex-role identification with the mother, and of course also her categorization as child in common with her siblings regardless of sex. The problem here seems to be the obverse of that with the boy; it is how to push her hard and far enough to renounce dependency. It is further, socially more acceptable for a girl to maintain dependency than for a boy. Hence we would suppose that imperfections of adjustment would in boys tend to be manifested more in reaction-formation to dependency needs, in girls more in overt dependency. Furthermore one would expect girls and women to be more readily open to the directly regressive types of deviation from the normal pattern of development.

These considerations seem to underlie the fact that, probably even cross-culturally, but certainly in our society, the "Oedipus" complex is a much more pronounced storm-center than is the "Electra" complex. In terms of the relations of the parents to child care the family is a fundamentally asymmetrical system, and this fact is reflected in these circumstances. This seems to explain why boys develop such a pronounced "tenderness" taboo and a variety of similar phenomena. It does not, however, imply that in the longer run strain is not relatively equally distributed between the sexes.

If this general analysis is correct, then the most fundamental difference between the sexes in personality type is that, relative to the total culture as a whole, the masculine personality tends more to the predominance of instrumental interests, needs and functions, presumably in whatever social system both sexes are involved, while the feminine personality tends more to the primacy of expressive interests, needs and functions. We would expect, by and large, that other things being equal, men would assume more technical, executive and "judicial" roles, women more supportive, integrative and "tension-managing" roles. However, this is at best an extremely broad formula and other things very often are not equal.

From Talcott Parsons and Robert F. Bales. *Family, Socialization and Interaction Process.* New York: The Free Press, 1955, pages 45-49, 94-101. Reprinted with permission of Macmillan Publishing Co., Inc. Copyright 1955 by The Free Press of Glencoe.

FOOTNOTES

1. It is probably correct to say that cross-culturally these four roles are the only ones within the nuclear family which are consistently and always symbolically differentiated, usually but not always through kinship terminology. Thus dress, personal names, etc., may supplement this. I know of no case where both parents are called exclusively by the same term. Siblings of both sexes are to be sure sometimes terminologically identified, but in such cases the discrimination will be made by other symbolic devices. There may of course be collective terms like "parents" and "children." In many "classificatory" systems of course family members may be classified with other kin (e.g., father and father's brothers), and finally distinctions may be made within such a category as between older and younger brother. But no known symbolic system *fails* to distinguish these four categories from each other.

2. Professor Albert J. Reiss (in private correspondence) raises the question of whether "dependency" does not confer power which is sometimes equal to or superior to that of the person on whom dependency exists. He suggests that in these terms the child may be as powerful as the parent. We think that this problem involves the discrimination between two phenomena both of which are sometimes referred to as power. We have used the term as meaning "relative importance in carrying out the functional performance of the system." If we accept socialization of the child into the values and roles of the society as the relevant family function, there can be no question that the child—so long as he is a child—cannot be the equal of his parents. The other meaning is "ability to cause trouble by threatening to disrupt the system." In this sense the child, and other persons or groups in dependent positions have considerable "power." We are not primarily concerned here with definitions but only with preventing confusion caused by possible misunderstanding of our usage.

3. Cf. *Working Papers;* Chap. V, pp. 189 ff. of Parsons & Bales, *Family, Socialization and Interaction Process.* The Free Press, 1955.

4. It might be useful to compare it with the therapist-patient system, since the latter is a two-member system which has been subjected to relatively intensive sociological analysis.

5. Cf. especially E. H. Erikson, *Childhood and Society* (New York: W. W. Norton and Co., 1950).

6. Thus the child can fulfill the mother's expectations or withhold his compliance, and he can both ask and protest.

7. In a seminar discussion Anna Freud was asked why the marriage solidarity of two parents was important to the development of the Oedipal child. One principal reason, she said, was that it prevented the child from playing the role of spouse with either parent. She illustrated with the case of a five-year-old child of divorced parents who clearly was trying to be both a "husband" to her mother and a "wife" to her father—she saw both of them regularly.

8. First reported by Bales in *Working Papers*, Chap. IV, and will be further developed in Chap. V of Parsons & Bales, 1955, *op. cit.*

9. This problem seems to be classically illustrated in Freud's famous case of "Little Hans." Hans' neurosis broke out after a summer spent at a resort with his mother. During the week Hans slept in the same bed with his mother, but on the week-ends the father arrived and displaced Hans as the mother's bedfellow. Could anything be better calculated to define the situation as one of rivalry?

10. In general this argument assumes a family system—in the most general sense, including the role of the incest taboo—as given. The problem then concerns the reasons for the universality of the conditions on which both family and incest taboo depend The relation of the taboo to the stability of the family was strongly emphasized by Malinowski (Introduction to H. Ian Hogbin, *Law and Order in Polynesia*, Christophers, 1934). A more general consideration of problems of the incest taboo will be found in Parsons, "The Incest Taboo in Relation to Social Structure and the Socialization of the Child," *British Journal of Sociology*, June, 1954.

11. Cf. R. L. Solomon and L. C. Wynne on the unextinguishability of fear reactions in dogs once sufficiently firmly established in "Traumatic Avoidance Learning: the Principles of Anxiety, Conservation and Partial Irreversibility," *Psychological Review*, November 1954.

A CROSS-CULTURAL SURVEY OF SOME SEX DIFFERENCES IN SOCIALIZATION

Herbert Barry III / Margaret K. Bacon / and Irvin L. Child

At first glance the following study might be interpreted as demonstrating the "universality," thus the biological inevitability, of certain sex differences. But a closer reading indicates that, despite the authors' selection of variables on which one might expect the sexes to differ, particularly the sexes in small-scale, nonliterate societies, the findings were mixed. Girls tended to be socialized toward nurturance, and boys toward achievement and self-reliance, while the results on obedience and responsibility were less than compelling.

In the second part of the study, the authors try to categorize cultures according to one characteristic, in this case degree of sex differentiation in child-rearing practice; then to see if those cultures similarly categorized share other characteristics in common. Correlation analyses of this sort represent a sound first step toward the discovery of principles of cultural patterning. Basically, the authors found marked sex differentiation in those societies which either relied upon the ready availability of superior male strength, and/or had a ready supply of female substitutes to assume child-rearing functions when the primary caregiver was unavailable.

This study is a fine example of the large-sample cross-cultural analyses which can be made when abundant ethnographic data are available and when they are carefully categorized. The Human Relations Area files of Yale University and the categories previously developed by George P. Murdock were of great assistance to the authors in this respect.

Herbert Barry, a psychologist, is professor of pharmacology at the University of Pittsburgh. Margaret Bacon is professor of anthropology at Livingston College of Rutgers University, and Irvin Child holds his professorship in the Psychology Department of Yale University.

I n our society, certain differences may be observed between the typical personality characteristics of the two sexes. These sex differences in personality are generally believed to result in part from differences in the way boys and girls are reared. To the extent that personality differences between the sexes are thus of cultural rather than biological origin, they seem potentially susceptible to change. But how readily susceptible to change? In the differential rearing of the sexes does our society make an arbitrary imposition on an infinitely plastic biological base, or is this cultural imposition found uniformly in all societies as an adjustment to the real biological differences between the sexes? This paper reports one attempt to deal with this problem.[1]

DATA AND PROCEDURES

The data used were ethnographic reports, available in the anthropological literature, about socialization practices of various cultures. One hundred and ten cultures, mostly nonliterate, were studied.[2] They were selected primarily in terms of the existence of adequate ethnographic reports of socialization practices and secondarily so as to obtain a wide and reasonably balanced geographical distribution. Various aspects of socialization of infants and children were rated on a 7-point scale by two judges (Mrs. Bacon and Mr. Barry). Where the ethnographic reports permitted, separate ratings were made for the socialization of boys and girls. Each rating was indicated as either confident or doubtful; with still greater uncertainty, or with complete lack of evidence, the particular rating was of course not made at all. We shall restrict the report of sex difference ratings to cases in which both judges made a confident rating. Also omitted is the one instance where the two judges reported a sex difference in opposite directions, as it demonstrates only unreliability of judgment. The number of cultures that meet these criteria is much smaller than the total of 110; for the several variables to be considered, the number varies from 31 to 84.

The aspects of socialization on which ratings were made included:

1. Several criteria of attention and indulgence toward infants.
2. Strength of socialization from age 4 to 5 years until shortly before puberty, with respect to five systems of behavior; strength of socialization was defined as the combination of positive pressure (rewards for the behavior) plus negative pressure (punishments for lack of the behavior). The variables were:

   a Responsibility or dutifulness training. (The data were such that training in the performance of chores in the productive or domestic economy was necessarily the principal source of information here; however, training in the performance of other duties was also taken into account when information was available.)
   b Nurturance training, i.e., training the child to be nurturant or helpful toward younger siblings and other dependent people.
   c Obedience training.
   d Self-reliance training.
   e Achievement training, i.e., training the child to orient his behavior toward standards of excellence in performance, and to seek to achieve as excellent a performance as possible.

Where the term "no sex difference" is used here, it may mean any of three things: a) the judge found separate evidence about the training of boys and girls on this particular variable, and judged it to be identical; b) the judge found a difference between the training of boys and girls, but not great enough for the sexes to be rated a whole point apart on a 7-point scale; c) the judge found evidence only about the training of "children" on this variable, the ethnographer not reporting separately about boys and girls.

SEX DIFFERENCES IN SOCIALIZATION

On the various aspects of attention and indulgence toward infants, the judges almost always agreed in finding no sex differ-

ence. Out of 96 cultures for which the ratings included the infancy period, 88 (92%) were rated with no sex difference by
either judge for any of those variables. This result is consistent
with the point sometimes made by anthropologists that "baby"
generally is a single status undifferentiated by sex, even though
"boy" and "girl" are distinct statuses.

On the variables of childhood socialization, on the other hand,
a rating of no sex difference by both judges was much less
common. This finding of no sex difference varied in frequency from
10% of the cultures for the achievement variable up to 62% of
the cultures for the obedience variable, as shown in the last column of Table 1. Where a sex difference is reported, by either one
or both judges, the difference tends strongly to be in a particular
direction, as shown in the earlier columns of the same table.
Pressure toward nurturance, obedience, and responsibility is
most often stronger for girls, whereas pressure toward achievement and self-reliance is most often stronger for boys.

For nurturance and for self-reliance, all the sex differences are
in the same direction. For achievement there is only one exception to the usual direction of difference, and for obedience only
two; but for responsibility there are nine. What do these exceptions mean? We have reexamined all these cases. In most of
them, only one judge had rated the sexes as differently treated
(sometimes one judge, sometimes the other), and in the majority
of these cases both judges were now inclined to agree that there
was no convincing evidence of a real difference. There were exceptions, however, especially in cases where a more formal or
systematic training of boys seemed to imply greater pressure on
them toward responsibility. The most convincing cases were the
Masai and Swazi, where both judges had originally agreed in
rating responsibility pressures greater in boys than in girls. In
comparing the five aspects of socialization we may conclude that
responsibility shows by far the strongest evidence of real variation in the direction of sex difference, and obedience much the
most frequently shows evidence of no sex difference at all.

In subsequent discussion we shall be assuming that the obtained sex differences in the socialization ratings reflect true sex
differences in the cultural practices. We should consider here two
other possible sources of these rated differences.

1. The ethnographers could have been biased in favor of seeing

the same pattern of sex differences as in our culture. However, most anthropologists readily perceive and eagerly report novel and startling cultural features, so we may expect them to have reported unusual sex differences where they existed. The distinction between matrilineal and patrilineal, and between matrilocal and patrilocal cultures, given prominence in many ethnographic reports, shows an awareness of possible variations in the significance of sex differences from culture to culture.

2. The two judges could have expected to find in other cultures the sex roles which are familiar in our culture and inferred them from the material on the cultures. However, we have reported only confident ratings, and such a bias seems less likely here than for doubtful ratings. It might be argued, moreover, that bias has more opportunity in the case ambiguous enough so that only one judge reported a sex difference, and less opportunity in the cases where the evidence is so clear that both judges agree. Yet in general, as may be seen in Table 1, the deviant cases are somewhat more frequent among the cultures where only one judge reported a sex difference.

The observed differences in the socialization of boys and girls are consistent with certain universal tendencies in the differentiation of adult sex role. In the economic sphere, men are more frequently allotted tasks that involve leaving home and engaging in activities where a high level of skill yields important returns; hunting is a prime example. Emphasis on training in self-reliance and achievement for boys would function as preparation for such an economic role. Women, on the other hand, are more frequently allotted tasks at or near home that minister most immediately to the needs of others (such as cooking and water carrying); these activities have a nurturant character, and in their pursuit a responsible carrying out of established routines is likely to be more important than the development of an especially high order of skill. Thus training in nurturance, responsibility, and, less clearly, obedience, may contribute to preparation for this economic role. These consistencies with adult role go beyond the economic sphere, of course. Participation in warfare, as a male prerogative, calls for self-reliance and a high order of skill where survival or death is the immediate issue. The childbearing which is biologically assigned to women, and the child care which is socially assigned primarily to them, lead to nurturant behavior and often call for a more continuous responsibility than do the tasks carried out by men. Most of these distinctions in adult role are not inevitable, but the biological differences between the sexes strongly predispose the distinction of role, if made, to be in a uniform direction.[3]

The relevant biological sex differences are conspicuous in adulthood but generally not in childhood. If each generation were left entirely to its own devices, therefore, without even an older generation to copy, sex differences in role would presumably be almost absent in childhood and would have to be developed after puberty at the expense of considerable re-learning on the part of one or both sexes. Hence, a pattern of child training which foreshadows adult differences can serve the useful function of minimizing what Benedict termed "discontinuities in cultural conditioning" (1).

The differences in socialization between the sexes in our society, then, are no arbitrary custom of our society, but a very widespread adaptation of culture to the biological substratum of human life.

TABLE 1 RATINGS OF CULTURES FOR SEX DIFFERENCES OF FIVE VARIABLES OF CHILDHOOD SOCIALIZATION PRESSURE

Variable	Number of Cultures	Both Judges Agree in Rating the Variable Higher in		One Judge Rates No Difference; One Rates the Variable Higher in		Percentage of Cultures with Evidence of Sex Difference in Direction of		
		Girls	Boys	Girls	Boys	Girls	Boys	Neither
Nurturance	33	17	0	10	0	82%	0%	18%
Obedience	69	6	0	18	2	35%	3%	62%
Responsibility	84	25	2	26	7	61%	11%	28%
Achievement	31	0	17	1	10	3%	87%	10%
Self-reliance	82	0	64	0	6	0%	85%	15%

VARIATIONS IN DEGREE OF SEX DIFFERENTIATION

While demonstrating near-universal tendencies in direction of difference between the socialization of boys and girls, our data do not show perfect uniformity. A study of the variations in our data may allow us to see some of the conditions which are associated with, and perhaps give rise to, a greater or smaller degree of this difference. For this purpose, we classified cultures as having relatively large or small sex difference by two different methods, one more inclusive and the other more selective. In both methods the ratings were at first considered separately for each of the five variables. A sex difference rating was made only if both judges made a rating on this variable and at least one judge's rating was confident.

In the more inclusive method the ratings were dichotomized, separately for each variable, as close as possible to the median into those showing a large and those showing a small sex difference. Thus, for each society a large or a small sex difference was recorded for each of the five variables on which a sex difference rating was available. A society was given an over-all classification of large or small sex difference if it had a sex difference rating on at least three variables and if a majority of these ratings agreed in being large, or agreed in being small. This method permitted classification of a large number of cultures, but the grounds for classification were capricious in many cases, as a differnce of only one point in the rating of a single variable might change the over-all classification of sex difference for a culture from large to small.

In the more selective method, we again began by dichotomizing each variable as close as possible to the median; but a society was now classified as having a large or small sex difference on the variable only if it was at least one step away from the scores immediately adjacent to the median. Thus only the more decisive ratings of sex difference were used. A culture was classified as having an over-all large or small sex difference only if it was given a sex difference rating which met this criterion on at least two variables, and only if all such ratings agreed in being large, or agreed in being small.

We then tested the relation of each of these dichotomies to 24 aspects of culture on which Murdock has categorized the customs of most of these societies[4] and which seemed of possible significance for sex differentiation. The aspects of culture covered include type of economy, residence pattern, marriage and incest rules, political integration, and social organization. For each aspect of culture, we grouped Murdock's categories to make a dichotomous contrast (sometimes omitting certain categories as irrelevant to the contrast). In the case of some aspects of culture, two or more separate contrasts were made (e.g., under form of marriage we contrasted monogamy with polygyny, and also contrasted sororal with nonsororal polygyny). For each of 40 comparisons thus formed, we prepared a 2 × 2 frequency table to determine relation to each of our sex-difference dichotomies. A significant relation was found for six of these 40 aspects of culture with the more selective dichotomization of overall sex difference. In four of these comparisons, the relation to the more inclusive dichotomization was also significant. These relationships are all given in Table 2, in the form of phi coefficients, along with the outcome of testing significance by the use of x^2 or Fisher's exact test. In trying to interpret these findings, we have also considered the nonsignificant correlations with other variables, looking for consistency and inconsistency with the general implications of the significant findings. We have arrived at the following formulation of results:

TABLE 2/CULTURE VARIABLES CORRELATED WITH LARGE SEX DIFFERENCES IN
SOCIALIZATION, SEPARATELY FOR TWO TYPES OF SAMPLE

Variable	More Selective Sample		More Inclusive Sample	
Large animals are hunted	.48*	(34)	.28*	(72)
Grain rather than root crops are grown	.82**	(20)	.62*	(43)
Large or milking animals rather than small animals are kept	.65*	(19)	.43*	(35)
Fishing unimportant or absent	.42*	(31)	.19	(69)
Nomadic rather than sedentary residence	.61**	(34)	.15	(71)
Polygyny rather than monogamy	.51*	(28)	.38**	(64)

*$p<.05$.
**$p<.01$.
Note—The variables have been so phrased that all correlations are positive. The phi coefficient is shown, and in parentheses, the number of cases on which the comparison was based. Significance level was determined by x^2, or Fisher's exact test where applicable, using in all cases a two-tailed test.

1. Large sex difference in socialization is associated with an economy that places a high premium on the superior strength, and superior development of motor skills requiring strength, which characterize the male. Four of the correlations reported in Table 2 clearly point to this generalization: the correlations of large sex difference with the hunting of large animals, with grain rather than root crops, with the keeping of large rather than small domestic animals, and with nomadic rather than sedentary residence. The correlation with the unimportance of fishing may also be consistent with this generalization, but the argument is not clear.[5] Other correlations consistent with the generalization, though not statistically significant, are with

large game hunting rather than gathering, with the hunting of large game rather than small game, and with the general importance of all hunting and gathering.

2. Large sex difference in socialization appears to be correlated with customs that make for a large family group with high cooperative interaction. The only statistically significant correlation relevant here is that with polygyny rather than monogamy. This generalization is, however, supported by several substantial correlations that fall only a little short of being statistically significant. One of these is a correlation with sororal rather than nonsororal polygyny; Murdock and Whiting (4) have presented indirect evidence that co-wives generally show smoother cooperative interaction if they are sisters. Correlations are also found with the presence of either an extended or a polygynous family rather than the nuclear family only; with the presence of an extended family; and with the extreme contrast between maximal extension and no extension of the family. The generalization is also to some extent supported by small correlations with wide extension of incest taboos, if we may presume that an incest taboo makes for effective unthreatening cooperation within the extended family. The only possible exception to this generalization, among substantial correlations, is a near-significant correlation with an extended or polygynous family's occupying a cluster of dwellings rather than a single dwelling.[6]

In seeking to understand this second generalization, we feel that the degree of social isolation of the nuclear family may perhaps be the crucial underlying variable. To the extent that the nuclear family must stand alone, the man must be prepared to take the woman's role when she is absent or incapacitated, and vice versa. Thus the sex differentiation cannot afford to be too great. But to the extent that the nuclear family is steadily interdependent with other nuclear families, the female role in the household economy can be temporarily taken over by another woman, or the male role by another man, so that sharp differentiation of sex role is no handicap.

The first generalization, which concerns the economy, cannot be viewed as dealing with material completely independent of the ratings of socialization. The training of children in their economic role was often an important part of the data used in rating socialization variables, and would naturally vary according to the general economy of the society. We would stress, however, that we were by no means using the identical data on the two sides of our comparison; we were on the one hand judging data on the socialization of children and on the other hand using Murdock's judgments on the economy of the adult culture. In the case of the second generalization, it seems to us that there was little opportunity for information on family and social structure to have influenced the judges in making the socialization ratings.

Both of these generalizations contribute to understanding the social background of the relatively small difference in socialization of boys and girls which we believe characterizes our society at the present time. Our mechanized economy is perhaps less dependent than any previous economy upon the superior average strength of the male. The nuclear family in our society is often so isolated that husband and wife must each be prepared at times to take over or help in the household tasks normally assigned to the other. It is also significant that the conditions favoring low sex differentiation appear to be more characteristic of the upper segments of our society, in socioeconomic and educational status, than of lower segments. This observation may be relevant to the tendency toward smaller sex differences in personality in higher status groups (cf. Terman and Miles, 8).

The increase in our society of conditions favoring small sex difference has led some people to advocate a virtual elimination of sex differences in socialization. This course seems likely to be dysfunctional even in our society. Parsons, Bales, *et al.* (5) argue that a differentiation of role similar to the universal pattern of sex difference is an important and perhaps inevitable development in any social group, such as the nuclear family. If we add to their argument the point that biological differences between the sexes make most appropriate the usual division of those roles between the sexes, we have compelling reasons to expect that the decrease in differentiation of adult sex role will not continue to the vanishing point. In our training of children, there may now be less differentiation in sex role than characterizes adult life— so little, indeed, as to provide inadequate preparation for adulthood. This state of affairs is likely to be especially true of formal education, which is more subject to conscious influence by an ideology than is informal socialization at home. With child training being more oriented toward the male than the female role in adulthood, many of the adjustment problems of women in our society today may be partly traced to conflicts growing out of inadequate childhood preparation for their adult role. This argument is nicely supported in extreme form by Spiro's analysis of sex roles in an Israeli kibbutz (7). The ideology of the founders of the kibbutz included the objective of greatly reducing differences in sex role. But the economy of the kibbutz is a largely non-mechanized one in which the superior average strength of men is badly needed in many jobs. The result is that, despite the ideology and many attempts to implement it, women continue to be assigned primarily to traditional "women's work," and the incompatibility between upbringing or ideology and adult role is an important source of conflict for women.

NOTE ON REGIONAL DISTRIBUTION

There is marked variation among regions of the world in typical size of sex difference in socialization. In our sample, societies in North America and Africa tend to have large sex difference and societies in Oceania to have small sex difference. Less confidently, because of the smaller number of cases, we can report a tendency toward small sex differences in Asia and South America as well. Since most of the variables with which we find the sex difference to be significantly correlated have a similar regional distribution, the question arises whether the correlations might better be ascribed to some quite different source having to do with large regional similarities, rather than to the functional dependence we have suggested. As a partial check, we have tried to determine whether the correlations we report in Table 2 tend also to be found strictly within regions. For each of the three regions for which we have sizable samples (North America, Africa, and Oceania) we have separately plotted 2 × 2 tables corresponding to each of the 6 relationships reported in Table 2. (We did this only for the more inclusive sample, since for the more selective sample the number of cases within a region would have been extremely small.) Out of the 18 correlations thus determined, 11 are positive and only 3 are negative (the other 4 being exactly zero). This result clearly suggests a general tendency for these correlations to hold true within regions as well as between regions, and may lend further support to our functional interpretation.

SUMMARY

A survey of certain aspects of socialization in 110 cultures shows that differentiation of the sexes is unimportant in infancy, but that in childhood there is, as in our society, a widespread pattern of greater pressure toward nurturance, obedience, and responsibility in girls, and toward self-reliance and achievement striving in boys. There are a few reversals of sex difference, and many instances of no detectable sex difference; these facts tend to confirm the cultural rather than directly biological nature of the differences. Cultures vary in the degree to which these differentiations are made; correlational analysis suggests some of the social conditions influencing these variations, and helps in understanding why our society has relatively small sex differentiation.

From *The Journal of Abnormal and Social Psychology,* 1957, Vol. 55, pp. 327-332. Reprinted by permission of the authors and the American Psychological Association. Copyright © 1957 by the American Psychological Association.

FOOTNOTES

1. This research is part of a project for which financial support was provided by the Social Science Research Council and the Ford Foundation. We are greatly indebted to G. P. Murdock for supplying us with certain data, as indicated below, and to him and Thomas W. Maretzki for suggestions that have been used in this paper.
2. Most of the societies we used are listed by name in H. Barry III, I. L. Child, and M. K. Bacon, Relation of child training to subsistence economy, *American Anthropologist,* 1959, 61, 51-63.
3. For data and interpretations supporting various arguments of this paragraph, see Mead (2), Murdock (3), and Scheinfeld (6).
4. These data were supplied to us directly by Professor Murdock.
5. Looking (with the more inclusive sample) into the possibility that this

correlation might result from the correlation between fishing and sedentary residence, a complicated interaction between these variables was found. The correlation of sex differentiation with absence of fishing is found only in nomadic societies, where fishing is likely to involve cooperative activity of the two sexes, and its absence is likely to mean dependence upon the male for large game hunting or herding large animals (whereas in sedentary societies the alternatives to fishing do not so uniformly require special emphasis on male strength). The correlation of sex differentiation with nomadism is found only in nonfishing societies; here nomadism is likely to imply large game hunting or herding large animals, whereas in fishing societies nomadism evidently implies no such special dependence upon male strength. Maximum sex differentiation is found in nomadic nonfishing societies (15 with large difference and only 2 with small) and minimum sex differentiation in nomadic fishing societies (2 with large difference and 7 with small difference). These findings further strengthen the argument for a conspicuous influence of the economy upon sex differentiation.

6. We think the reverse of this correlation would be more consistent with our generalization here. But perhaps it may reasonably be argued that the various nuclear families composing an extended or polygynous family are less likely to develop antagonisms which hinder cooperation if they are able to maintain some physical separation. On the other hand, this variable may be more relevant to the first generalization than to the second. Occupation of a cluster of dwellings is highly correlated with presence of herding and with herding of large rather than small animals, and these economic variables in turn are correlated with large sex difference in socialization. Occupation of a cluster of dwellings is also correlated with polygyny rather than monogamy and shows no correlation with sororal vs. nonsororal polygyny.

REFERENCES

1. BENEDICT, RUTH. "Continuities and discontinuities in cultural conditioning." *Psychiatry;* 1938, 1, 161–167.
2. MEAD, MARGARET. *Male and female.* New York: MORROW, 1949.
3. MURDOCK, G. P. "Comparative data on the division of labor by sex." *Social Forces;* 1937, 15, 551–553.
4. MURDOCK, G. P. and WHITING, J. W. M. "Cultural determination of parental attitudes. The relationship between the social structure, particular family structure and parental behavior." In M. J. E. Senn (Ed.), *Problems of infancy and childhood: Transactions of the Fourth Conference,* March 6–7, 1950. New York: Josiah Macy, Jr. Foundation, 1951. Pp. 13–34.
5. PARSONS, R., BALES, R. F., *et al. Family, socialization and interaction process.* Glencoe, Ill.: Free Press, 1955.
6. SCHEINFELD, A. *Women and men.* New York: Harcourt, Brace, 1944.
7. SPIRO, M. E. *Kibbutz: Venture in Utopia.* Cambridge: Harvard Univer. Press, 1956.
8. TERMAN, L. M., and MILES, CATHERINE C. *Sex and personality.* New York: McGraw-Hill, 1936.

THE ABSENT FATHER AND CROSS-SEX IDENTITY

Roger V. Burton/John W. M. Whiting

John Whiting has done much to sharpen the "culture and personality" approach into a genuine psychological anthropology. By this we mean that he sees culture and personality less as analogues of one another, but more as bilaterally interacting and precisely denotable variables. His approach allows for the formulation of hypotheses which can then be tested by scouring the ethnographic literature, as was done in the present study, or by making direct observations in the field, as was done in his subsequent Six Cultures Study *(1963, 1975). Moreover, his approach leads directly to cross-cultural analyses, using statistical techniques as a means of uncovering regularities in cultural patterning.*

The Burton and Whiting study reprinted below examines the course of male sex-role development in those societies in which fathers are typically absent during the first few years of life. In such societies the child has exposure only to a female sex-role model, the mother, during his most impressionable period. Thus the authors raise the question: What measures do these societies take to ensure that boys identify with the male sex role? Their remarkably consistent findings would tend to confirm the validity of cross-cultural statistical methods. On the other hand, one detects a strain in the authors' attempt to extend their conclusions to North American society. It is difficult to compare cultures in which father absence is considered desirable and normative with those, e.g., our own, in which it is not viewed as normative or desirable. Malinowski would have warned that the phenomenon of father absence has different meaning to the adherents of the different cultures, thus undercutting the psychological validity of cross-cultural comparison on this variable.

Roger Burton is professor of psychology and director of the Program in Developmental Psychology at the State University of New York in Buffalo. John W. M. Whiting is professor emeritus of anthropology at Harvard University, where he and his wife Beatrice Whiting have trained many dedicated and competent anthropologists, both there and in their East African field station.

I n this paper, we shall present evidence on the effect of the father's position in the family as it relates to the growing child's learning by identification and to the development of his sex identity. This evidence consists first of a cross-cultural study done at the Laboratory of Human Development, Harvard University,[1] and second, a review of recent research in the United States and Europe, relevant to our theory of identification, on the effect of father absence in the household.

THE STATUS ENVY HYPOTHESIS

Before presenting this evidence, however, we would like to state our view on the process of identification and the development of identity. This view we would like to call the *status envy hypothesis*. This hypothesis may be summarily stated as follows: The process of identification consists of the covert practice of the role of an envied status. Identification consists of learning a role by rehearsal in fantasy or in play rather than by actual performance, and this rehearsal is motivated by envy of the incumbent of a privileged status.

Let us consider the mother-infant relationship in which the mother attempts to satisfy all of the infant's needs. According to our theory, if it were possible for the mother to supply everything the infant wanted, he would not identify with her as he already occupies the privileged status. Some learning does, of course, take place in such a complementary relationship. The child learns to give the proper signals when he wants something and to accept and consume it when it is offered. Furthermore, he learns to predict certain sequences of events determined by his mother's behavior. In other words, he has cognizance of his mother's role. Although this cognizance may provide some savings in later learning, if and when he is motivated to perform her role, we would like to distinguish cognizance of a complementary role from identification with its incumbent.

To clarify our view of the motivation leading to identification, we would like to introduce the concept of a resource. A resource is anything, material or nonmaterial, which somebody wants and over which someone else may have control. Resources include food, water, optimum temperature, freedom from pain, and the derived symbolic resources such as love, solace, power, information, and success. Were these resources inexhaustible, and equally and completely available to all, there would be no such thing as status envy and, by our hypothesis, no learning by identification. Such, however, is not the case. As part of the cultural rules of every society, there is a status system which gives privileged access to resources for some positions in the system and, at the same time, disbars other positions from controlling and consuming them.

Returning to our mother-child example: As soon as the mother withholds a resource from her child and, by virtue of her position in the family, either herself consumes it or gives it to someone else, the conditions for status envy obtain. Even during infancy in societies where an infant occupies the most privileged status, complete nurturance is practically impossible. No matter how much a mother might wish to be ever-loving, the exigencies of life are such that there are times when she must withhold some resource that the child wants.

This is particularly true during the process of socialization. By definition this process involves teaching the child to delay gratification and to defer to the rights of others. More specifically, socialization involves teaching the child the privileges and disabilities which characterize the social structure of his society.

We may now restate our major hypothesis: If there is a status that has privileged access to a desired resource, the incumbent or occupant of such a status will be envied by anyone whose status does not permit him the control of, and the right to use, the resource. Status envy is then a motivational component of status disability, and such motivation leads to learning by identification.

This view differs from some other theories of identification in that we hold that a completely satisfying complementary relation between two people will not lead to identification. By this hypothesis, a child maximally identifies with people who consume resources in his presence but do not give him any. He does not identify with the people he loves unless they withhold from him something he wants. Love alone will not produce identification. Thus, the status envy hypothesis advanced here makes identification with the aggressor just a special case, and the Oedipal situation is also simply a special case.

The actual process of learning by identification consists of the covert practice in fantasy or in play of the role of the envied status. So when the child wants to stay up late, for example, and his parents make him go to bed while they themselves stay up, the child says to himself, "I wish I were grown up. Perhaps if I acted as they do I would be grown up," and he goes to sleep rehearsing, in fantasy, grown-up behavior.

ATTRIBUTED, SUBJECTIVE, AND OPTATIVE IDENTITY

We would now like to present our views on another concept which we believe will be useful in distinguishing housholds with fathers absent from those with fathers present. This is the concept of identity.

In every society, statuses have names or labels. In our society, for example, there are the familiar kinship statuses of mother, father, uncle, aunt, brother, sister; the age-determined statuses of infant, child, adolescent, adult, and aged; the occupational statuses of doctor, lawyer, clerk, workman, etc.; and, especially important to our thesis, the sex-determined statuses of male and female.

We would like to define a person's position or positions in the status system of this society as his identity. Furthermore, we would like to distinguish three kinds of identity: attributed, subjective, and optative. *Attributed identity* consists of the statuses assigned to a person by other members of his society. *Subjective identity* consists of the statuses a person sees himself as occupying. And finally, *optative identity* consists of those statuses a person wishes he could occupy but from which he is disbarred. It is this last kind of identity that is most important for this paper.

Obviously, one's optative identity derives from status envy, and nothing much would be added to our theory by introducing this concept if one's optative identity were always objective and realistic. The wish being father to the thought, however, this is frequently not the case, and people often feel "I am what I would like to be." In such a case, the subjective and optative identities merge and become discrepant with the attributed identity.

It is our thesis that the aim of socialization in any society is to produce an adult whose attributed, subjective, and optative identities are isomorphic: "I see myself as others see me, and I am what I want to be." It is further presumed, however, that such isomorphism can only be achieved by passing through a stage in which there is status disbarment, status envy, and thus a discrepancy between one's optative and attributed identities. That is, to become such an adult, a person must have been deprived of the privileged consumption of resources accorded only to adults. This disbarment results in his wanting to be a member of that class. When society then permits him to occupy this privileged status, there is agreement in what he wants to be, in what society says he is, and in what he sees himself to be.

CROSS-CULTURAL EVIDENCE

Having briefly presented our views on learning by identification and on identity, let us now turn to the consideration of some empirical data which may provide a test of these notions. The first such test will be cross-cultural. The independent variables are judgments as to the distribution of resources during infancy and during childhood. Specifically, social structure of a sample of societies was judged for the degree to which the father and adult males in general, or the mother and adult females in general, occupied privileged or equivalent statuses as perceived by the infant and later by the child. Arrangements in infancy lead to *primary identification;* whereas those in childhood lead to *secondary identification.*

It is our assumption, and this has been supported by a previous study (14), that sleeping arrangements provide the best index of status envy during infancy. The bed seems to be the center of a child's world during the first year or two of his life. This is where the resources of greatest value to him are given or withheld, and those who share this setting with him become the models for his first or primary identification.

In most societies the world over, an infant sleeps during the nursing period either in his mother's bed, or in a crib or cradle right next to it, and within easy reach. Of over 100 societies on which we have data on sleeping arrangements, the American middle class is unique in putting the baby to sleep in a room of his own.

For our purposes, the big difference lies in whether or not the father also sleeps with the mother. In a sample of 64 societies which we would like to report now, 36 of them have the pattern of the father and mother sleeping apart, and the infant thus has the exclusive attention of the mother at night. In the remaining 28 societies, the infant either shares his mother's bed with his father or in a few instances sleeps alone. According to our theory, these two arrangements should be profoundly different in their effect on the infant's first or primary identification.

In the exclusive mother-infant case, the mother should be seen as all-powerful, all-important, and, insofar as she sometimes withholds resources, the person to be envied; and we predict the infant will covertly practice her role, and his optative identity will be female. In societies where the father sleeps with the mother, quite a different picture obtains with respect to valued resources. In this instance, both parents give and withhold important resources. Under these conditions, therefore, we assume the envied status to be that of a parent of either sex. For the infant, the juxtaposition of privilege is seen as between self and adult, rather than between self and female.

Thus the male infant in societies with exclusive mother-child sleeping arrangements should have a primary cross-sex optative identity, whereas the boy reared in societies in which the father sleeps with the mother should have a primary adult optative identity.

After a child is weaned and becomes what Margaret Mead calls a yard child, conditions may change drastically from those of infancy. Privilege may now be defined by marital residence. Three major patterns emerge in our samples of societies: patrilocal, matrilocal, and equilocal.

In societies with patrilocal residence, a man will remain throughout his life in or near the house in which he was born, his wife or wives moving in from another village. In such societies, the domestic unit consists of a group of males closely related by blood, and a group of inmarrying and interloping females. Prestige and power are clearly vested in this group of men, and adult males are the ones to be envied.

Societies with matrilocal residence are a mirror image of the patrilocal case. Here the daughters stay at home and their husbands are the interlopers. In such societies, by contrast with the patrilocal, women occupy the privileged and envied statuses.

Equilocal societies are more familiar to us. Here a young husband and wife set up a household of their own apart from the parents of either, as is generally the case in our own society; or they may choose between, or alternate between, living with the wife's parents and the husband's parents. In this instance, residence does not automatically give advantage to either men or women, and sex identity is thus not an important issue.

Thus residence patterns may provide the conditions for the envy of males or the envy of females; or sex-determined statuses may be relatively unprivileged. This distribution of resources in the domestic unit provides the conditions for what we would like to call secondary identification.

SOME PRIMARY AND SECONDARY OPTATIVE IDENTIFICATION COMBINATIONS

Although the two types of sleeping arrangements and three residence patterns yield six combinations of conditions for primary and secondary identification, we would like here to concentrate on only two of them in contrast to all others. These are, first, the societies which should produce the maximum conflict between primary and secondary optative sex identity: e.g., societies with both exclusive mother-infant sleeping arrangements, which should lead a boy initially to wish he were feminine, and patrilocal residence patterns, which should lead him subsequently and secondarily to want to be masculine. The other societies of interest to us are those which promote feminine identification, both initially and secondarily; that is, societies with both exclusive mother-child sleeping arrangements and matrilocal residence.

Having described our independent variables, let us now turn to the dependent variables which should be predicted by our theory from (a) maximum conflict in optative sex identity and (b) maximum feminine optative sex identity.

INITIATION HYPOTHESIS

In a previous study (14), male initiation rites at puberty were shown to be strongly associated with exclusive mother-child sleeping arrangements and a long post-partum sex taboo. Although cross-sex identification was mentioned in a footnote as a possible interpretation of these findings, the authors' major explanation was based on the assumption that these conditions exacerbated the Oedipal conflict, and that initiation rites were the symbolic expression of resolution of this conflict.

We now believe, and would like to present evidence, that the sex identity interpretation is the more valid and fruitful. We would like to present the cross-sex identity and initiation hypothesis explicitly as follows: In societies with maximum conflict in sex identity, e.g., where a boy initially sleeps exclusively with his mother and where the domestic unit is patrilocal and hence controlled by men, there will be initiation rites at puberty which function to resolve this conflict in identity.

This hypothesis suggests that the initiation rites serve psychologically to brainwash the primary feminine identity and to establish firmly the secondary male identity. The hazing, sleeplessness, tests of manhood, and painful genital operation, together with promise of high status—that of being a man if the tests are successfully passed—are indeed similar to the brainwashing techniques employed by the Communists. Indicating how traumatic these rites may be, one ethnographer (11) reports that boys returning home after initiation did not know their village or recognize their parents.

Native theory also supports our interpretation. In most societies with elaborate initiation rites at puberty, there are two terms labeling one's sex identity which are different from the ones with which we are familiar. One term refers to all women and uninitiated boys, whereas the other refers to initiated males only. In these societies, according to native theory, a male is born twice: once into the woman-child status, and then at puberty he symbolically dies and is reborn into the status of manhood.

Let us now turn to our data. In our sample of 64 societies, there were 13 in which there were elaborate initiation ceremonies with genital operations. All 13 of these had the exclusive mother-infant sleeping arrangements which we predicted would cause a primary feminine identification. Furthermore, 12 of these 13 had patrilocal residence which we predicted would produce the maximum conflict in identity and hence the need for an institution to help resolve this conflict. A chi-square test of the association is fantastically beyond chance. Expressed simply, 87½ per cent of the 64 societies fall in the cells predicted by our hypothesis.

But what of societies where the female status is seen as privileged both in infancy and in childhood, where the infant sleeps exclusively with his mother and in childhood moves into a world controlled by his mother, his aunts, and his tyrannical maternal grandmother? Here our theory would predict that a man would have a strong optative feminine identity, and the society should provide him some means to act out, symbolically at least, the female role.

From the beginnings of ethnographic reporting, a strange custom has been described for various societies over the world. This custom consists of the husband going to bed and undergoing all the same taboos as his wife during the time she in is labor. This custom is known as the *couvade* and has long been a favorite example for undergraduate texts in anthropology to exemplify the curious customs of primitive peoples. As a test of our hypothesis, however, the couvade is most apt. What event more than childbirth defines that part of a woman's role that is uniquely feminine? It seems to us, at least, that when a man attempts to participate in the birth of his child by closely imitating the behavior of his wife, this should be a good index of his wish to act out the feminine role and thus symbolically to be in part a woman.

Our hypothesis is again strongly confirmed by the data. Of the 12 societies with couvade in our sample, 10 had exclusive mother-child sleeping arrangements and 9 had matrilocal residence. Again, the results are highly significant statistically. In this instance, 90 per cent of the cases fall in the predicted cells.

AMERICAN CULTURE EVIDENCE

Cross-culture evidence thus seems to confirm the status envy hypothesis with respect to sex identity. Now let us turn to other studies done within our own cultural context which seem relevant and yet were not specifically designed with this theory in mind. A recent book by Rohrer and Edmonson, *The Eighth Generation*(8), seems especially significant. This study is a follow-up twenty years later of the people described in *Children of Bondage* by Davis and Dollard(2). The problems of identification and identity are stressed throughout, and the importance of what we have called primary feminine identification clearly presented.

The girls raised in the matriarchy, which coincides with our exclusive mother-infant case, are very likely to establish a matriarchal home of their own and to live with their mothers or very close to them. The boys from this kind of household also seem to conform to our theoretical expectations. If the boy finds that he falls under the dominance of older men when he leaves his house, in these cases a gang of older boys, he shows evidence of a sex role conflict in compulsive denial of anything feminine. Rohrer and Edmonson conclude that "the gang member rejects this femininity in every form, and he sees it in women and in effeminate men, in laws and morals and religion, in schools and occupational striving"(8, p. 163).

This compulsive masculine behavior is also described by Walter Miller(6) in his discussion of the "focal concerns" of the lower-class culture. He emphasizes that the "female-based" household and "serial monogamy" are characteristics of the "hard core" of this lower class and closely associated with delinquent gang behavior. He argues that delinquent acts function as means of resolving dominant motivational themes in the lower-class community, which he views as "a long-established, distinctively patterned tradition with an integrity of its own—rather than a so-called 'delinquent subculture' which has arisen through conflict with middle class culture"(6, pp. 5-6).

In Miller's writings and in *The Eighth Generation* are descriptions of the requirements for gang membership, requirements which closely resemble the attributes of the initiation ceremonies of primitive societies, especially the "tests of manhood." Miller specifically relates the focal concern of "toughness" to conflict over sexual identity:

... Among its [toughness] most important components are physical prowess, evidenced both by demonstrated possession of strength and endurance and athletic skill; "masculinity," symbolized by a distinctive complex of acts and avoidances (bodily tattooing; absence of sentimentality; non-concern with "art," "literature," conceptualization of women as conquest objects, etc.); and bravery in the face of physical threat (6, p. 9).

The attributes of this male model are seen in the prototypical "private eye" of television: "hard, fearless, undemonstrative, skilled in physical combat," and irresistible as a Don Juan(6, p. 9). Behavior deviating from this stereotype is evidence of one's being a homosexual. Miller also attributes the genesis of this obsessive concern with masculinity to a cross-sex primary identification and considers the behavior a type of compulsive reaction formation. This interpretation is, of course, closely attuned to the status envy hypothesis we have described.

In their study of delinquency, the Gluecks report that more of the delinquent boys, as compared with the nondelinquents, came from homes "broken by desertion, separation, divorce, or death of one or both parents, many of the breaches occurring during the early childhood of the boys" (3, p. 280). They further indicate that the fathers of the delinquents tend to be irresponsible in family matters and to have far poorer work habits than the fathers of the nondelinquents. If many of these broken homes were actually exclusive mother-infant or female-based households, and it seems from most reports on the lower class that this is a fairly safe assumption, these results are consonant with Miller's interpretation that delinquent acts conform to the focal concerns of boys raised in the mother-child household.

Concentrating on the "good" boy in a high delinquency area, Reckless, Dinitz, and Murray(7), and more recently with Scarpitti(9), found that the nondelinquent boy comes from an intact family which is quite stable. These boys also felt accepted by their parents and expressed acceptance of them. These relationships with their parents were markedly different from those of a group of boys being held in a detention home.

The studies we have just considered found family structure an important factor in the early lives of the subjects. This relationship was found as a result of the analyses of the data which the investigators had gathered in order to study the culture as a whole or with special focus on delinquency. Let us now turn to some investigations which have the presence or absence of the father as the selected variable for study.

FATHER ABSENCE AND PRESENCE

The draft at the beginning of World War II made possible several studies comparing middle-class children from father-absent homes with those from father-present households(1, 10, 12). These studies indicated that boys from father-absent households behaved like girls both in fantasy behavior and in overt behavior, especially with respect to producing very little aggression. Investigating the effect on the child of the father's return, Stolz(12) found that boys whose fathers had been absent but were then returned, continued to be effeminate in overt behavior, but there was a marked change in their fantasy behavior. This group now produced the maximum amount of aggression in fantasy. These conditions of father absence for the initial years and then control by an adult man are the conditions we have indicated should produce conflict over sexual identification.

The influence of father absence on the child has also been studied in Norway(4, 5, 13). The families of sailors were compared with other families of the same social class in which the fathers were present. The absence of these fathers often extended for two or more years. The results showed the wives of the sailors were more isolated from social contacts, more overprotective, and more concerned with obedience rather than happiness and self-realization for their children than were the nuclear household mothers, i.e., mothers whose husbands were not away from the household. The boys of the sailor families tended to be infantile and dependent and to manifest conflict over identification through compensatory or overly masculine behavior as compared with the father-present boys.

These data are suggestive for our theory, but we would also be interested in what happens to those boys later on. It would be interesting to know whether or not these boys themselves tend to become sailors, an occupation which would be suitable for a man who places a high value on obedience and also permits a man to perform acts of the female role in cleaning his quarters, sewing, etc., that are necessary on an extended sea voyage. The age of their first voyage and a description of the treatment accorded them as novitiate seamen would be pertinent. We would not be surprised, according to our theory, if these boys from sailor households themselves became sailors, made their first voyage during adolescence, and underwent a rather severe initiation ceremony on their first trip.

These studies, then, seem generally consistent with our cross-cultural findings in that the absence of the father produces in the boy cross-sex identification which is either acted out or, more usually, defended against by exaggerated masculine behavior. Although the conditions differentiating primary and secondary identification are not as clearly specified in these studies as in the cross-cultural study, it does seem clear that the gang is an institution with a function similar to that of initiation, and that at least certain types of delinquent behavior are equivalent to the tests of manhood in those societies with conflict in sex identity.

FURTHER RESEARCH

Although the general effect of father absence seems evident, the details of the process are not. For example, are there critical periods when the absence of a father is more crucial than other times? How long does it take for a child to establish identity? What are the relative effects of a weak father and an absent father? What is the effect of the absent father on the development of a girl?

Some of these details are being investigated at the Laboratory of Human Development at Harvard University, and others at the National Institutes of Health at Bethesda, Maryland, but these studies are not far enough along to warrant reporting here. It seems to us, however, that the effect of the household structure on the process of identification provides a very fruitful area for research.

From *The Merrill-Palmer Quarterly,* 1961, vol. 7, pp. 85-95. Reprinted by permission of the authors and the Merrill-Palmer Institute.

FOOTNOTE

1. The first portion of this paper constituting the theoretical formulation and supporting cross-cultural material is based on a presentation of the status envy hypothesis given by John W. M. Whiting at Tulane University as part of the Mona Bronsman Sheckman Lectures in Social Psychiatry, March 17-19, 1960.

REFERENCES

1. BACH, G. R. "Father-fantasies and father-typing in father-separated children." *Child Develpm.,* 1946, **17,** 63-79.
2. DAVIS, A. and DOLLARD, J. *Children of bondage.* Washington: American Council on Education, 1941.
3. GLUECK, S. and GLUECK, ELEANOR T. *Unraveling juvenile delinquency.* New York: Commonwealth Fund, 1950.
4. GRØNSETH, E. "The impact of father absence in sailor families upon the personality structure and social adjustment of adult sailor sons." Part I. In N. ANDERSON (Ed.), *Studies of the family.* Vol. 2. Gottingen: Vandenhoeck and Ruprecht, 1957. Pp. 97-114.
5. LYNN, D. B. and SAWREY, W. L. "The effects of father-absence on Norwegian boys and girls." *J. abnorm. soc. Psychol.;* 1959, **59,** 258-262.
6. MILLER, W. B. "Lower class culture as a generating milieu of gang delinquency." *J. soc. Issues;* 1958, 14(3), 5-19.
7. RECKLESS, W. C., DINTZ, S. and MURRAY, ELLEN. "Self concept as an insulator against delinquency." *Amer. sociol. Rev.,* 1956, **21,** 744-746.
8. ROHRER, J. H. and EDMONSON, M. S. *The eighth generation.* New York: Harper and Bros., 1960.
9. SCARPITTI, F. R., MURRAY, ELLEN, DINITZ, S. and RECKLESS, W. C. "The 'good' boy in a high delinquency area: four years later." *Amer. sociol. Rev.,* 1960, **25,** 555-558.
10. SEARS, PAULINE S. "Doll play aggression in normal young children: influence of sex, age, sibling status, father's absence." *Psychol. Monogr.,* 1951, **65,** No. 6 (Whole No. 323).
11. STAUB, J. *"Beitrage zur Kenntais der Materiellen Kultur der Mendi in der Sierra Leone"* (Contributions to a Knowledge of the Material Culture of the Mende in Sierra Leone) Solothurni Buchdruckerei

Vogt-Schild, 1936, p. 61. Translated for the Human Relations Area Files by Cecil Wood.

12. STOLZ, LOIS M. *Father relations of warborn children.* Palo Alto: Stanford Univer. Press, 1954.

13. TILLER, P. O. "Father absence and personality development of children in sailor families: a preliminary research report." Part II. In N. Anderson (Ed.), *Studies of the family.* Vol. 2. Gottingen: Vandenhoeck and Ruprecht, 1957. Pp. 115-137.

14. WHITING, J. W. M., KLUCKHOHN, R. and ANTHONY, A. "The function of male initiation ceremonies at puberty." In Eleanor E. Maccoby, T. M. Newcomb and E. L. Hartley (Eds.), *Readings in social psychology.* New York: Holt, 1958. Pp. 359-370.

15. WHITING, BEATRICE B. (Ed.) *Six Cultures: Studies of Child Rearing.* New York: Wiley, 1963.

16. WHITING, B. B., & WHITING, J. W. M. *Children of Six Cultures: A Psycho-Cultural Analysis.* Cambridge, Mass.: Harvard University Press, 1975.

WOMEN AND MEN

Yolanda Murphy/Robert F. Murphy

Yolanda and Robert Murphy lived among the Mundurucu Indians of central Brazil for one year. During their stay the first author spent her days with the women, while the second author spent his time with the men, in keeping with the sharp sex division among the Mundurucú. In reading the following selection from the last chapter of Women of the Forest, *some background information should be kept in mind.*

The Mundurucú are a small people, consisting of approximately 1,250 individuals. They live under two conditions: some staying in their traditional villages located in the savannah; some living in a new kind of village on the Cururú River where they retain part of their savannah heritage, but are primarily encultured to the economic and social ways of the larger Brazilian society. They are a patrilineal, matrilocal society and, therefore, present quite a different picture from Malinowski's Trobriand Islanders, who are matrilineal and patrilocal.

The Murphys did their field work in 1952 and 1953. However, they wrote their book twenty years later through a sensibility which undoubtedly was leavened by two decades of maturity and sharpened by the emergence of a new feminism which did not exist in the 1950s.

The focus of their study is on the relations between the sexes, not on individual sex differences. Thus, they describe how the officially dominant status of the Mundurucú men is counteracted by the de facto bonding practices of the women, which are a direct outgrowth of the fact of matrilocality. For our purposes, their most interesting finding is that the pattern of relations between the sexes differs according to cultural and economic context. Notice the skill with which the authors move their analysis among the three contexts of savannah village, river village, and North American suburb, using each to understand the human dimensions of the others.

Yolanda Murphy is professor of anthropology at Empire State College, and Robert Murphy's professorship in anthropology is at Columbia University.

The biological differences between men and women intrude upon and shape their social roles most strongly in the spheres of work and, of course, reproduction, and child-rearing. Among the Mundurucú, certain tasks are allocated to the men on the basis of sheer physical prowess. The felling of forest areas for gardens requires great strength, and hunting similarly calls for a kind of athleticism that is usually not found among women. Fishing is not a very strenuous activity, but it involves familiarity with weapons, and it also requires absence, sometimes at great distances, from the village. The latter is a critical factor, for in times past, the forests and rivers far from the settlements could harbor enemy war parties, to which the women would have been easy prey. Beyond that, the women are commonly barred from the more intense and energetic forms of activity by pregnancy, and the need to nurse children keeps them close to home, long after the region has become pacified.

This basic division of labor has been perpetuated in the villages of the Cururú River, with one significant difference—the organization of the work has undergone modification. Whereas the sexes used to perform their respective tasks in substantial isolation from one another, they now work in active cooperation and association. The issue of the organization of labor is fundamental to an understanding of the position of the woman. Writers on the subject of women's work frequently concentrate upon the gross importance of female labor to the economy in the belief that the prestige of the woman will vary directly with her contribution. But this need not be at all true, and we could dredge up endless examples in which the reverse proposition is equally valid and in which women, and children, are held down and exploited exactly because their labor is vital. Certainly, the fact that Mundurucú women do most of the garden work places them at least on an economic par with the men, but their evident autonomy derives not so much from what they produce as from how they produce it and who controls the product.

The principal crop, bitter manioc, lends itself to cooperative work both in its growing and its preparation. This brings the women together in a joint effort and in a common place. Thus, just as the men join in hunting and associate in the men's house, the women make manioc flour together and find a common meeting ground in the farinha shed. There is a true collectivity of women in every traditional village which matches the collectivity of the men and must also be understood, in part, as a defensive reaction to it. The men, as an organized body, are unable to dominate females as isolated individuals, nor does the lone male really find a situation in which he coerces the similarly lone female. Rather, they confront each other as two entities, each having internal organization and cohesion and a sense of identity and common interest.

Women's work among the Mundurucú is largely directed and initiated by women, and the men do not intrude upon their area of responsibility and authority. Farinha making may indeed be the worst task in the society, and it is indeed a drudge job that is relegated to the women, but it is still work that remains under their exclusive jurisdiction and control and it is still central to survival. Superficially, it would seem that grating tubers and standing over a hot oven for long hours is a mark of inferiority, and on one level it is, but to the extent that it draws women together and isolates them from the immediate supervision and control of the men, it is also a badge of independence.

In stratified societies, one must ask who works for whom and who gets what? Among the Mundurucú, however, this is not a real question. Except for rubber production and the sale of small amounts of farinha to traders, production is for immediate consumption by the producers and their dependents. The natural resources from which subsistence is derived, whether forest lands, hunting areas, or fishing grounds, are not the property of any individual or group. The instruments of production, tools and weapons, are hardly a form of capital except in a technical sense; they are accessible to everybody either through trade or their own manufacture, and no individual or group, again save for the traders, is able to exercise control over their availability. These, of course, are the classic ingredients of the classless society, but they also inhibit the development of forms of economic domination of men over women. Gardens are not owned, only their use rights, and these belong to the women just as much as to the men. Houses, we have said, are not real estate, but the consensus of most Mundurucú is that women have primary rights in them. As for artifacts and tools, women have every bit as much right to these forms of private property as do men. And foods, whether produced by men or by women, are usually distributed by the females.

Curiously, it is only in rubber production—so strongly encouraged by the women—that the men are able to obtain sure economic leverage over the women. Men, not women, have rights to rubber trees, and men do the trading. Despite the growing importance of the trade economy, and the marginality of the females in it, wives have surprising success in getting their husbands to buy things for them, though, it must be noted, they now have to ask. It would seem that the essential communality of the household unit, a traditional and valued part of Mundurucú culture, has persisted as a bulwark of female status in a changed situation. What the future will bring, however, is uncertain. In the families that have left the savannah villages, the men now help the women in their labors and associate with them to an extent unimaginable in the past. This has the appearance of growing equality, but it is a situation in which the men really hold the cards, though they do not seem fully aware of it yet. When the men do recognize the implications of their control over property and commerce in rubber, the women may well discover that they have traded the symbolic domination of the men, as a group, over the women, as a group, for the very real domination of husbands over wives.

The degree and way in which women are involved in labor beyond the domestic realm is important to their status in every society. There is a common belief among Americans today that women have just emerged from the household during the past century into the larger workaday world, but in reality industrial society is unique in the extent to which women, until recently, have been freed, or excluded, from subsistence pursuits. Even our own agrarian past saw women take a substantial role in farming and the raising of small stock, and the literature of ethnography gives ample documentation of the significance of women's work beyond child-rearing, cooking, and so forth. They hoe gardens, they tend goats, sheep, and fowl, they gather wild vegetable products, and they even lend a hand in fishing. In a sense, what we are now experiencing in our own society is a reemergence of women into the broader economy after a period of confinement.

The reasons for this change are complex and beyond our scope, and we can point to only a few of the more interesting circumstances of it. First, the entire drift of our technology has diminished the significance of the physical differences between the sexes in production. One may have to be a male to be a hunter but not to be a computer operator, a pilot, an engineer, or a salesperson. Machines have largely replaced hard manual labor, and now machines are beginning to tend machines; there are few occupations left that cannot be held by women. Moreover, the percentage of the labor force engaged in farming and capital production has been decreasing for many years, while the proportion in the administrative and service sectors, which have used female labor most extensively, has increased. The technology of an advanced industrial society erases sex differences in work.

All of these considerations are self-evident, but latter-day industrial society has done more than open up an opportunity to females—it has discovered in women the last large and unused pool of labor. In one sense, the entry of women into the job market may be looked upon as the outcome of a struggle for equality, and so it is. But the increased absorption of women in occupations long predated the women's liberation movement and is a function of post-World War II industrial growth. Women have entered commerce and industry because jobs have expanded faster than the male labor supply. They have been cheap labor, to be sure, just as southern blacks are in this country and Turks in Germany, and the real struggle is to attain parity with men in salary and job advancement. This will indeed occur in time, for one of the tendencies of an industrial economy is to universalize the labor force, to reduce social relations, people, and their labor, to object commodities. The female status and female labor have traditionally been of an ascriptive and particularistic kind—that is, women have been treated in a highly specified way due to the simple fact of birth as a female—but this pattern is incongruent with the needs of an industrial society, which views people as things. Women will undoubtedly achieve much of the status of the male, but with it will come depersonalization of their selves and their work.

There has been, we are often told, a "revolution of expectations" in much of the world that is commonly expressed at the popular level in spiraling consumer demands. Despite gains in industrial productivity, the male worker is hard pressed to satisfy the heightened requirements of his family by his labors alone. The problem is exacerbated by endemic inflation, which is not so much a temporary economic dislocation as a regular concomitant of an expanding economy and increased consumer demand.

The answer to this crunch between increased wants and higher prices is for the European or American wife to go to work, a phenomenon that is more pronounced at the lower economic levels, where the women's movement has been least active. Most women are not so much engaged in finding themselves or escaping from stultifying households as in helping to pay off the mortgage and new car, to buy a summer home, or just to eat. There is a curious parallel here with the Mundurucú, whose deisres for trade items and involvement in a credit system has also altered the division of labor. The Mundurucú woman, following her husband along his rubber avenue, carrying the latex cups, and helping collect them when they are full, shares a true sisterhood with her American counterpart at a typewriter. And both may well feel that doing these things has improved their status, as women. The Mundurucú woman has, however, lost in the process the strength that comes with unity with other women—the American woman never had such a unity but now seeks to find it in a society that offers no practical basis for it either in economoc cooperation or in residence.

The Mundurucú pattern of residence is a bulwark of female status. Again, one has to distinguish between simple appearances and hard reality, for it would seem at first glance that the separation of the sexes, the relegation of women to large noisome households inhabited by squalling babies and nasty dogs, is their ultimate denigration. But the households, we saw, are the only true corporate units within Mundurucú society. Whereas the memberships of the men's houses tend to be diverse with regard both to kinship and place of origin, the households are more stable and cohesive. A woman's residence in a house outlasts her marriages; she may not pass her entire life in the household of her birth, for other contingencies than kinship affect where one lives, but her association with it is stronger and more lasting than any association of men.

The preference for matrilocality is the key to the solidarity of the Mundurucú women. The presence of strong kin ties among the residents of the men's house is adventitious, but among the women of the dwellings it is given within the norms. Mothers and daughters tend to reside together, as do sisters, and the preference is upheld by a strong value upon the integrity of ties between females; there is no such value upon close male kin ties except for the more diffuse attachments that are prescribed between fellow clansmen, and men in general. That this same group of female kinfolk should also be a commensal and productive unit, central in cooperation and sharing, heightens the dependencies between its members. They can do without one or another of their men, confident that he will ultimately be replaced by another, but a fellow woman is central to a work team and must be kept. The household, at the same time, does not become isolated from others, because much work requires a village-wide effort. Women cannot be divided from each other along lines of nuclear family or household and then conquered, for they have a very real and continuing need for one another. They have their rifts, of course, but these tend to be resealed by the exigencies of everyday life. The women present a united front to the men, but, it should be remembered, they do so at the expense of the strength of marriages.

Matrilocality brings us back to one of the issues raised by the notion of the "primitive matriarchy." It was stated that female status is generally higher in matrilineal societies than in those having patrilineal descent. This pattern is so, however, not as a matter of female dominance which somehow perpetuates itself in matrilineal descent, but as a result of the fact that many matrilineal societies are also matrilocal. Descent through females may indeed have some effect upon the woman's public prestige, but far more critical is its association with a residence rule that holds together a core of related women. The Mundurucú are a remarkable illustration of this as they have one of the very few societies that combines patrilineality with matrilocality. As in many patrilineal societies, there is a series of rules and symbolic observances that supposedly guarantees the right of the men over the sexuality and issue of their women, but these, we have seen, are largely illusory. Children do receive the clan names of their fathers, but they stay with their mothers. The men assert a strong show of dominance in sex relations, which has its principal expression in marriage. Otherwise, the women band together in such a way that men cannot intrude upon individual women; premarital love and postmarital philandery are the secure province of female strategy and planning. Mundurucú patrilineality shapes the symbolic expression of relations between the sexes, but it has little impact upon their day-to-day relations. These are molded instead by the presence in the dwellings, and in the village as a whole, of groups of women who are bound by ties of kinship and economic dependency. Under the firm leadership of their senior women, the households must be understood as political units.

Men do not supervise women or order them about, for this would bespeak a greater degree of association of the sexes. Judith Shapiro (1972), in her study of the women of the Yanomamö, a tribe of northern Brazil and southern Venezuela, notes that the kind of sexual division of work and residence that characterizes the Mundurucú is absent. Yanomamö hubands exercise continuing control over their wives, and the very fact that the women are imported through patrilocality leaves them vulnerable, without a close circle of supporting relatives. Mundurucú women experience no such isolation, and their husbands treat them with a deference and caution that is in sharp contrast to the ritual expression of sex relations. Shapiro concludes that although it may indeed be best to be integrated and equal, it is better to be separate and unequal than integrated and unequal. In much the same way, most black Americans find it more palatable to live in a northern urban ghetto than in a southern white man's back alley. The Mundurucú woman, too, has her "turf."

The Mundurucú female stays home, and the male leaves. The woman works in the village or close to it, but the man ranges out in hunting, fishing, trading, and, at one time, warfare. The woman remains in her household when she marries, but the man leaves his to join the village of his wife. The preadolescent girl stays close to her mother, helping care for the babies, and the boy wanders around the savannahs and forests, moving into the men's house as soon as the adults will accept him. This is, in one sense, a severe limitation for the woman, but, in another, it makes her the stable figure in the emotional economy of the society. The men may be the controlling political figures, for whatever that is worth in a classless and rankless society, but the women are the repositories of affective relations. They not only control the attachments of their sons, but they keep their daughters. And despite all the cohesion of the men, the women are bound together by stronger emotional ties.

The very fact that the men are public figures and minor political actors gives a peculiar coloration to their show of solidarity. It results in a characteristic reserve and a careful maintenance of personal distance between them. There is a veneer of fellowship, but one senses that it is maintained by the potential for social disruption if feelings were to be expressed. The women are under no such constraints. They are more open and outgoing, they laugh more easily, they express their hostilities more quickly. The latter fact might lead one to assume that the lives of the women are more invaded with divisiveness, but this is not the case at all. Rather, the strength of their attachments, unlike those of the men, is sufficiently strong to survive easily transient jealousies and disagreements. The men are really far more estranged from each other than are the women.

The women of the Cururú River have moved from this social setting into one that is closer to that of the American female. They are still prisoners of the household, but, to a degree, so also are their husbands. Unlike most American families, the Cururú River couple spends much time together. The American husband may well leave for work at 7:30 in the morning and return at 6:30 in the evening, whereas the Mundurucú man will return in early afternoon from rubber collection, spend some time fishing and while away the rest of his day near the household. On many days, he will not bother going to his rubber avenue at all, and most of his day will be passed in the company of his wife—there is really nowhere else to go. This, and the fact that a small village necessarily places one in continual association with others, has undoubtedly protected the woman from the sting of isolation that might be expected with the move from the savannahs. The American woman, on the other hand, suffers acutely from sheer loneliness and boredom. This was brought home to us vividly one day when a woman asked Yolanda where she went to draw water in her village in America. Yolanda explained that we do not go to a stream, but bring water through a hollow tube, like a long piece of bamboo, right into our houses. The women were not impressed, only dismayed. "But if you don't go with the other women to get water and to bathe, aren't you lonely?" Yolanda thought about it a moment and answered, "Yes, we are."

The modern American woman often confesses to a feeling of entrapment and anomie. She is not only cut off from realizing some of the central values of the culture, such as they are, but she is also cut off from the association of others. Caught in a nuclear family household and in the constant company of small and demanding children, by the time the growth of the young gives her free time, her abiliites are irrelevant to the changing world. And she finds not freedom but abandonment in the departure of the children. The family has been her special province, a jurisdiction that she herself may have carved out and jealously preserved, and the husband has long since found other forms of identification and interest. He has a job, he may hunt or fish, he may dabble in politics, or do any of the countless things that American men do; these are the ways they lose, not find, themselves. The culmination of the long and, for the woman, isolating child-rearing process is that the couple discovers suddenly that they have each other, and only each other, on their hands. This is one reason why so many American marriages break up after twenty or twenty-five years. The American family is self-destructing; it preserves little continuity and it has few extensions.

Unlike the Mundurucú woman, her American counterpart has few bases for structuring relations with other women. The middle-class woman may join clubs or become active in one or another form of community service, but these are of a wholly voluntary nature. She may find pleasant company and quite useful work, but it has none of the strong and compelling economic qualities of Mundurucú female cooperation. The American woman's relations with the opposite sex are usually confined to the one-to-one tie with her husband, except for casual business contacts or family friends and neighbors. And in her interaction with the husband, she has little support from others. Her family of origin is scattered and preoccupied with its own concerns: besides, it shares the American view that such problems are best left to the principals. As for other women, she may find a bit of sympathy or counsel, but little in the way of active and practical help. They, too, are locked into their own little worlds of house, husband, and children.

Certainly, nothing even remotely comparable to the unity of Mundurucú women exists to sustain the American woman. For all the low official status of the Mundurucú woman, there is far less wife beating among them than in the average American suburb, and, indeed, there is far less direct domination and coercion of wives by husbands. The Mundurucú females are protected by their unity, while ours are, at best, separate or, at worst, pitted against one another.

This sense of separation, coupled with increasing awareness of the problems of the female role, has been, of course, one of the forces behind the women's movement. Involvement in the cause, or in consciousness-raising sessions and so forth, may produce short-term results, but there is room for doubt that it will be an effective means, in the long run, of unifying women. In this day and age of mass media and instant communications, such movements exhaust themselves with astounding rapidity. They tend to spin out into ideological realms that, as they depart from the normative centers of the society, repel converts and alienate followers, ending in involuted disputes between leaders of empty phalanxes. We cannot even guess what the resolution will be. Mundurucú women find a cohesive core in work, residence, and the opposing unity of their men. American women do not have even the latter rallying point, for the men are as fragmented, confused, and dissatisfied as they are. Most work at jobs they loathe, and if they are tyrants at home, as so many are, their assertiveness can be understood in good part as a result of their marginality in the life of the family.

The American woman, to an even greater extent than the Mundurucú, holds a firm rein on the distribution of love within the family. She is, in the sociological terms of Talcott Parsons, the "expressive leader" of the family, whereas the husband is the "instrumental leader" (Parsons and Bales, 1955, pp., 35-131). This, however, is too simple a dichotomy, for the woman actually has very important and real instrumental, or practical and administrative, functions in the family. She has a good deal to say about the entire pattern of consumption and expenditures, and much of the discipline and direction of the children is within her sphere. Whatever may be the governing power of the female within the family, we should not place affective ascendancy as secondary in significance. In actuality, governmental agencies, as well as wives, have preempted many of the areas of family decision-making through educational laws, social legislation, and the statutes governing family life; the role of *paterfamilias* is no longer a very awesome one. What is left in our society is the hard core of the family, which, as David Schneider tells us (Schneider, 1968), is based on enduring, diffuse, and intense attachments—or love.

From Yolanda Murphy and Robert F. Murphy. *Women of the Forest.* New York: Columbia University Press, 1974, pages 209–222. Reprinted by permission of the publisher and authors.

REFERENCES

PARSONS, TALCOTT, and ROBERT F. BALES, 1955. *Family, Socialization and Interaction Process.* Glencoe, Ill.: The Free Press.

SCHNEIDER, DAVID M. 1968. *American Kinship: A Cultural Account.* Englewood Cliffs, N.J.: Prentice-Hall.

SHAPIRO, JUDITH. 1972. *Sex Roles and Social Structure Among the Yanamamo Indians of Northern Brazil.* Unpublished Ph.D. dissertation, Columbia University.

PART THREE

THE BIO-ETHOLOGICAL DIMENSION

ETHOLOGY AND SEX DIFFERENCES

Patrick C. Lee

M ost of us have anthropocentric conceits about the uniqueness of *homo sapiens,* and it is true that our symbol-using,
culture-making species has all the appearances of being radically
different from other kinds of animals. But evolutionary theory
teaches us that there is structural continuity among species, including our own, and that this continuity takes both anatomical
and behavioral forms. The evolutionary perspective is critical for
anyone who would comprehend human nature in context. Humanity is viewed, first and foremost, as an integral part of nature and subject to its laws. Second, it is viewed as one product
of an evolutionary process which has spun off many other products (i.e., species) which, since they tend to derive from the
same ancestral forms, are more or less related to one another.
Finally, it specifies parameters of relationship in anatomical
terms, in behavioral terms, and in terms of social
organization—these three are the functional basics of adaptation.
If a given distribution of function appears to have adaptive
payoff for one species, then one may look to another species with
similar adaptive problems to see if it has distributed function
similarly.

For example, if two species were plains-dwelling, carnivorous,
and socially organized (e.g., lions and wild dogs), one would expect them to have developed similar patterns of hunting behavior because they share a common adaptive problem: How to
kill swift, strong, and wary herbivores. If the two species were
phylogentically close relatives (e.g., wild dogs and wolves) we
would expect their patterns of hunting behavior to be even more
similar. However, if one species were not socially organized, then
we would expect patterns of solitary hunting in place of patterns

of group hunting. If one species were not carnivorous, then we would expect food gathering behavior not to follow hunting patterns at all. Observations of animals in the wild tend to confirm expectations such as these, indicating that evolutionary theory has made cross-species behavioral comparison valid. When the species being compared have membership in common ecological and/or phylogentic niches as do the two canine species mentioned above, the comparisons become even more plausible and fruitful.

Ethology, as defined by Lorenz (1970, p. xvi), is "the comparative study of behavior." Let's take a brief look at each term of this definition. By "study" ethologists usually mean direct observation of their subject(s). Ethology is probably one of the more radically empirical sciences, although it has generated its share of amateurish theories and speculations. But in examining the work of reputable ethologists one gets the impression that they spend a great deal of time simply *staring* at animals in the wild state, in partially domesticated arrangements (i.e., zoos and animal preserves), or in laboratory settings (cf., Lorenz, 1970, p. xvi). Ethologists understand the term "comparative" in evolutionary terms, that is, they look for laws of behavior which enable them to group and divide species just as zoologists group them according to laws of anatomical structure. By "behavior" they can mean anything from molecular units of movement to entire adaptive patterns. They may study the behavior of any living creature, ranging from oysters (see Tinbergen selection) to human beings (see Birdwhistell selection). Finally, the target behaviors are usually those which are performed spontaneously by the species in question. This general predilection for "natural" behavior is, of course, inevitably violated in laboratory studies in which either the environment or the physiology of the animal is artificially manipulated (as in the Money and Ehrhardt selection).

The particular behaviors of most interest to us are those which are divided between the sexes, take place at the level of adaptive patterns, and are found in social species. These would include mating, parenting, and other kinds of sex-differentiated labor, such as food gathering, nest building, and territorial defense. For the sake of economy our focus is on mating behavior, although the other types have been studied extensively by ethologists and are equally important.

There are several keys to understanding what mating behavior is all about. First, it has adaptive value, that is, it contributes to the economy of reproduction. In the absence of mating behavior, the sexes often would not recognize each other, copulatory behavior would not take place as often nor would it be as well timed, sexual urges would often translate into nonsexual behaviors, and there would be more cross-species copulation. In general, the efficiency of reproduction would be reduced, thereby negatively influencing a given species' ability to reproduce itself (see Tinbergen selection). The second key is that mating behavior is made up of *sex-specific signals* which, through the process of evolution, have taken on meaning to the members of a given species. These signals tend to be sequentially and reciprocally arranged, so that they guide males and females through whatever steps are necessary for them to become breeding partners at precisely the time that they are physiologically prepared to breed successfully.

Thus it would be entirely erroneous to disregard the puffing, wing spreading, head bobbing, and strutting of many male birds, and the mock retreats, food-begging, and appeasement postures of female birds, for example, as so much random behavior. On the contrary these behaviors are guidance systems which enhance the probability of reproduction and without which reproduction probably would not occur (cf., Tinbergen, 1960). The third key to understanding mating behavior lies in the characteristics of signals which enable them to serve as such effective guidance systems. Sex signals have at least four characteristics. First, they are perceptible to potential breeding partners, i.e., they signal clearly that one is a male or a female. Second, they are relatively unambiguous in meaning, so that each sex "understands" that opposite-sex signals indicate sexual receptiveness and that same-sex signals or no signals indicate non-receptiveness. Third, they increase the probability of physical contact of the genitalia, that is, male signals are attractive to female animals and female signals attract males. Finally, they tend to be imperceptible, meaningless, and devoid of attraction to unacceptible breeding partners, particularly those from other species (see Tinbergen selection).

These are the functional properties and consequences of sex signaling systems. But where do the signals come from? That is, how do they enter the sex-linked behavioral repertoire of a given species, or of a given member of a species? They become integral to a species' mating behavior through many generations of natural selection which favors some signals over others. To the degree that favored signal systems contribute to reproductive economy, they tend to spread throughout the genetic pool of a given species while less economical signals tend to disappear. Eventually all or virtually all females of a given species possess female signals to a marked degree, while all males tend to adopt equally marked male signals.

With respect to individual members of a species, sex signals are transmitted through a combination of genetic programming, timing and type of hormonal secretion, and individual experience. All that need be said about the first transmission device is that each individual is either a genetic male or female and that some individuals are genetically predisposed to emit stronger sex signals than others, but that this predisposition interacts dynamically and in only partially understood ways with hormonal discharges and idiosyncratic experience. Money and Ehrhardt, in their review which follows, discuss the influence of complex hormonal variations as transmitters and shapers of mating behaviors. The research seems to indicate that there is a behavioral bipotentiality in animals like rats, mice, and hamsters. That is, animals of both genders seem able to emit both sets of sex signals and these seem to be associated as much with hormonal status, physical size, status in dominance hierarchies, and transient situational factors as they are with gentically determined gender. Interestingly enough, Lorenz (see his selection) also found this to be true in certain species of fish and birds, indicating the probable existence of a broad bipotentiality factor among species. However, there is a distinct tendency for animals to manifest either one set of sex signals or the other at any given time, and not to blend them androgynously in any one behavioral sequence. Moreover, in the *natural* state (i.e., not in captivity) sex signals are specific to the appropriate gender, particuarly during sexually receptive periods in the estrous cycle. Money and Ehrhardt attribute this to the prenatal or neonatal discharge in normal genetic males of male hormones and to the absence of such discharge in normal genetic females. Lorenz attributes it to the availability of opposite sex partners in the wild which are not always available in captivity. These positions are not mutually exclusive—in the natural state the genders tend to distribute in ecologically sound patterns, and those adults which are hormonally and genetically normal tend to be the ones which signal their sex identity and sexual "intentions" most effectively and, therefore, reproduce most successfully.

The final piece in the mosaic is experience. As one moves up the phylogenetic scale, experience appears to play an increasing role in the transmission of sex-linked signal systems. Money and Ehrhardt found that individual experience was a significant factor in the adoption of standard mating postures and receptive behaviors by female rats, even by those whose neonatal hormonal secretions had been interfered with by researchers. Lonrenz and Tinbergen make it clear that complete sequences of mating behavior do not appear in a vacuum, but that they are released by exposure to reciprocally coordinated signals of opposite sex partners, i.e., by experience. In the absence of such experience it is doubtful that such complex behaviors would emerge, even with the inner urgings of genetic and hormonal predispositions. Harlow's (1962) experiments with rhesus monkeys indicate that atypical early experience can disastrously interefere with the subsequent mating behaviors of physically "normal" adults. In the case of Harlow's monkeys, it does not appear that the key factor was underexposure to signals which "release" behaviors almost in a reflex fashion; rather it appears that as youngsters they never had adequate opportunity for affectional exchange or adequate exposure to proper models of mating behavior. Both males and females simply failed to acquire the attitudes and *learn* the behaviors specific to their roles in a successful mating encounter. Learned behavior, even if abnormal, is *prima facie* demonstration of the role of experience.

At this point it may be useful to raise the question: What does all this have to do with sex differences in human behavior? The ethological research on nonhuman mating behaviors suggests several hypotheses which may help to explain human mating behavior. It suggests that human mating patterns are made up of gender-specific signals which guide males and females toward successful breeding; and that these sex signals have adaptive value in contributing to reproductive economy. It also suggests that these signals have clear meaning to humans and that heterosexual attraction is part of that meaning. Moreover, since human beings are high-order primates, it suggests that the gender differentiation of these signals is primarily learned and secondarily mediated by genetic and hormonal factors. Finally, it suggests that signal systems differ between human groups (i.e., cultural groups) so as to prevent excessive outbreeding with consequent loss of group identity. On the other hand, ethological research does *not* suggest that the mating behaviors of human males and females are similar or analogous to those of infrahuman males and females. It would be a serious mistake to assume that human mating behaviors are as stereotyped as male and female behaviors of most species. Human sex signals are quite variable from culture to culture and from individual to individual, although not so variable as to lose communicable meaning. Within limits, therefore, there probably exists a broad range of behavioral variation without loss of reproductive economy.

Given the variability of human mating behavior, one might be tempted to claim that exceptions tend to be the human rule. But for the moment it would be useful to resist this temptation and admit that there is probably just enough negative evidence available to keep general hypotheses tentative and subject to revision. In the meantime, it may be profitable to raise a few questions about these more general human tendencies.

Given that the earth is dangerously overpopulated, can we continue to assign adaptive value to human reproductive economy? There are two answers to this question. From the perspective of biological evolution, no species has absolute value; species wax and wane and life in one form or another persists and reproduces. From a humanistic perspective, however, it is clear that reproductive economy has become counter-adaptive. It is also clear that in most parts of the world human leadership is aware that continued breeding is dysfunctional and is adopting policies designed to reduce reproduction, although these policies are far from operational.

If human sex signals contribute to reproductive economy, then are they not also counter-adaptive? And, if so, why are they retained? They are retained for two simple reasons: First, they have sexual and aesthetic meanings which continue to be important to the human species. Men and women derive pleasure and satisfaction from each other's sex signals. Second, they have surplus, extrasexual meaning for the division of human function by gender. This second rationale is increasingly vestigial in more industrialized sectors of human society. Industrial advance and concomitant changes in social organization have normatively reduced functional differences between the sexes in all respects except those directly associated with the anatomy of sexuality and the physiology of reproduction. It is fair to expect that this second set of meanings will tend to become more sentimental and less functional with the passage of time.

But the first set of meanings is less likely to wane and there are three bases for this. The first is that humanity is a relatively nonestrous species, that is, its sense of sexual urgency is more or less constant (or at least perceived as constant) and consequently it is sexually active through all seasons. Thus men are more or less perpetually motivated to present sex signals to women and vice versa. The second is that, through the technology of birth control, sexuality is easily separated from reproduction. Thus, in the operational presence of such technology, sex signals are not necessarily counter-adaptive. In fact, to the degree that they are incompatible with aggressive signals, they may play an important role in the suppression of aggressive behavior.

The third reason, as explicated by Birdwhistell in his selection to follow, is that human beings may need sex signals in order to clearly distinguish between the sexes. Birdwhistell postulates a continuum of gender anatomy of species, ranging from the dimorphic at one extreme to the unimorphic at the other. Assuming that his placement of *homo sapiens* toward the unimorphic end is correct, then humanity faces an adaptive problem similar to that of the herring gull (see Tinbergen) and the jackdaw (see Lorenz). In these species males and females look so alike that they cannot identify each other by sex without elaborate patterns of gender-specific sex signals. Birdwhistell suggests that human beings have developed a similar behavioral solution to what is essentially a similar adaptive problem. These "tertiary sexual characteristics" constitute the different behaviors which human males and females have adopted in order to enhance the relatively limited signaling power of their anatomical differences. This may sound preposterous to some, but consider for a moment what adjustments one would make in order to resemble the opposite sex. It is hard to imagine that behavioral adjustments would not be an indispensable part of the project. Thus, Birdwhistell has found that the American woman signals her "femaleness" to men by keeping her arms proximal to her torso and rolling her pelvis slightly forward. American males signal "maleness" by placing their arms at a decided angle from the torso, closing and opening their eyes in a continuous movement, and rolling their hips backward.

Birdwhistell's hypothesis is extremely provocative because it suggests that sex differences in human behavior are not only functional extensions of the physiology of reproduction, as so many anthropologists and psychologists assume; but that they are also feedback systems which reinforce the physiological differences on which they were originally based. Perhaps it is this reciprocal interdependence between genetically given physiology and culturally invented behavior which encourages many of us to confuse what is invented with what is given.

In any event it would appear that sex-differentiated signaling behavior in our species has become functionally autonomous. The technology for separating it from human reproductivity is already available; moreover, it is conceivable that mating behaviors could persist even while other sex-linked human functions diminish in importance.

REFERENCES

HARLOW, H. F. "The heterosexual affectional system in monkeys." *American Psychologist,* 1962, 17, pp. 1–9.
LORENZ, K. *Studies in animal and human behavior* (Vol. 1). Cambridge, Mass.: Harvard University Press, 1970.
TINBERGEN, N. *The herring gull's world.* New York: Harper & Row, 1960.

THE FUNCTIONS OF THE SEXUAL COMPANION

Konrad Lorenz

*There is probably no ethologist better known than Konrad Lorenz,
both within and outside his chosen profession. He has, in a sense,
had two parallel and interacting careers, one as a scientist and
the other as a public figure. As a scientist his work has been conducted in the unobtrusive fashion typical of most scientific endeavor. It led ultimately to his sharing the Nobel Prize for
Physiology in 1973.*

*As a public figure, however, he has drawn his share of adula-
tion and criticism. After the publication of* King Solomon's Ring
*(1952) he was widely regarded as a sensitive observer and lover of
animals, even if he tended to anthropomorphize them as well. But
his subsequent book,* On Aggression *(1966), aroused a great deal of
controversy, some people hailing it as a penetrating analysis of the
human condition, and others criticizing it as an overly instinct-
laden and pessimistic depiction of human potential. Thus Lorenz
has been viewed as one who both "humanizes" animals and
"animalizes" humans.*

*Paradoxically, Lorenz is completely aware of the dangers and
benefits of cross-species generalization, particularly since he defines ethology as "the comparative study of behavior" (1970, p.
xvi). He does not shy away from discussing the behaviors of different species (including* homo sapiens) *as analogues of one
another. On the contrary, he has developed an evolutionary model
of behavioral structure and of its interaction with anatomical
structure. This perspective, like any evolutionary perspective, sees
the behavior of species as characterized as much by continuity as
by discontinuity. The question is which behaviors are continuous
and which are not. Even Lorenz cannot answer this question definitively, although, as one who has spent his life studying animal
behavior, his answers must be given serious consideration.*

The selection reprinted below is taken from what Lorenz calls his "good old companion paper" (1970, p. xviii). It was originally written in 1935 in German and was newly translated with updated footnotes into English in 1970 with the publication of Studies in Animal and Human Behavior. *Lorenz is currently Director of the Abteilung Lorenz of the Max Planck Institute in Bavaria.*

T he instinctive behaviour patterns of a bird pair serving reproductive functions exhibit what Alverdes calls *instinct interlocking*. The factor eliciting a chain of instinctive behaviour patterns in one partner is a behavioural act of the other bird, in many cases only the last element in a behavioural chain performed by the latter. This element, rather like the cue of an actor, provokes the partner to perform a new activity. Presumably, all mating responses of birds, and their reproductive responses in general, are cases of instinct interlocking. Only in animal species in which the female is simply "raped" by the male does one find a lack of reciprocal behavioural patterns on the part of the female sex, so that the term instinct co-ordination does not apply. However, I think it is unlikely that such cases occur among birds.

Demonstrative Behaviour—Many responses which an animal (usually a male animal) exhibits when placed together with a conspecific are quite generally interpreted as courtship patterns. Similarly, conspicuous colours and shapes (*"Prachtkleider"*) found only in the male sex are interpreted as a device exerting an effect on sexual selection by the female. Both interpretations can be correct in individual cases, as Selous (1905) has shown with the Ruff (*Philomachus pugnax*), for example. The explanation of the origin of these instinctive behaviour patterns and morphological characters through sexual selection in its narrowest sense is to some degree a probable one, though it is of course not fully substantiated. On the other hand, it must be remembered that in many animals quite equivalent behaviour and quite similar morphological characters restricted to the male sex obviously elicit responses only from *other males,* as Noble and Bradley (1933) have shown for many lizards. In yet other animal species the behaviour concerned and the correlated organs are not restricted to the male sex at all, though such cases form a definite minority.

In all cases, behaviour and the associated morphological patterns ("Prachtkleider") are to be interpreted as *typical releasers*. Whether they operate on the same or the opposite sex, their effect is similar to the extent that they always provoke the performance of quite specific reciprocal behaviour patterns which are concerned with reproduction, in fact with pair-formation.

Doubtless, the most common (and probably the most archaic) effect of these releasers is represented by *simultaneous* elicitation of a positive response from the female and a "negative" behavioural response from any other male. Heinroth (1918) aptly refers to all behaviour patterns which thus combine threat and courtship effects as *demonstrative behaviour ("Imponiergehaben")*. In the English literature on the subject, this is usually expressed briefly, and probably too generally, as "display." The concept of demonstrative behaviour incorporates the information that such behaviour is predominantly performed only when a receptive spectator is present.

Demonstrative behaviour in its wider sense is extremely widespread in the animal kingdom. It can be seen in presumptive form in the invertebrate world and is present in more or less the same form in all vertebrates, from teleost fish to man. Genuine demonstrative behaviour represents a constituent of the few undeniable instinctive behaviour patterns of man.

In its most generalized and obviously most primitive form, demonstrative behaviour does not consist of specific motor patterns performed only in this context, still less is it accompanied by special organs developed as supplementary features. Primitive demonstrative behaviour is in fact represented by the performance of all normal motor patterns of the species *with a conspicuous expenditure of energy, in excess of that actually necessary to fulfil the purpose of the behaviour.* The behaviour of a courting Greylag gander (*Anser anser*) incorporates this type of demonstrative behaviour in a particularly pure form. Each single movement of such a bird is performed with such an excess of muscular power that even an impartial observer would have the immediate impression of tense, affected behaviour. Both when walking and standing still, the bird sticks out its chest and holds itself upright. The stride becomes longer whilst the walking speed decreases. The normal side-to-side rotation of the body in walking is exaggerated so that it virtually looks as if the bird finds walking more laborious than normal. Whereas Greylag geese otherwise make little use of their wings and only fly off in face of actual danger, the "demonstrative" gander makes use of every opportunity to demonstrate the strength of his wings. At such times, he will fly over quite short stretches which he would normally cover only by swimming or walking. In particular, he will fly headlong towards any actual or apparent opponent and then, after chasing off the intruder, fly back with just as much expenditure of energy to the female he is impressing. He subsequently lands by her with his wings raised and uttering a loud triumph-call. After landing, and following any other occasion for spreading the wings, closure of the wings is not immediate. Even in a goose which does not happen to be exhibiting demonstrative behaviour, we can see that the wings are held out stiffly for a moment before folding. This time-interval is greatly extended in demonstrative behaviour, and the ostentatious gander stands for a period of seconds with wings spread wide every time they are opened. In other Anatidae, exactly this behaviour has developed to produce a specialized display ceremony.

Demonstrative behaviour in man is extremely similar to that of the Greylag goose. Even extremely able men talented with powers of self-criticism can, under circumstances involving physical activity (for example when skiing or ice-skating), become considerably more vigorous and dashing when the number of spectators is increased by one attractive girl. In primitive or not quite grown-up men, this is often accompanied—as in the gander described—by attacking or at least molesting weaker pseudo-opponents. The most remarkable fact to be seen from this, however, is that many men perform the dissipation of energy characteristic of demonstrative behaviour with a *machine,* if they happen to be riding one. I have repeatedly observed that motor cyclists in such cases increase the noise-level and energy consumption of their machines by revving and simultaneously adjusting the ignition, without greatly increasing their speed. Sharp braking and much too rapid acceleration of motor vehicles can often be explained in the same way. The American writer Mark Twain, an extremely acute psychological observer, relates an example of collective demonstrative behaviour on the part of crews of Mississippi steamers. At places where the passage of these ships could be observed from settlements on the shore, the speed always increased and a particularly large volume of smoke was produced by laying on particular kinds of wood.

I am of the opinion that all more highly-specialized forms of instinctive demonstrative behaviour have developed from origins corresponding to the behaviour described above for the Greylag gander. In the same way, I am sure that the supplementary morphological organs have been *secondarily* acquired. The questionable proof of "phylogenetic" series seldom appears so convincing as in the comparison of specific components of demonstrative behaviour of related bird species. For example, the prolonged opening of the wings, as described above for the Greylag gander, has come to form an independent ceremony in other Anatidae. This component of demonstrative behaviour in *Anser* is only performed when the male has just flown or has just exhibited wing-flapping. (Opening of the wings in defense of the young belongs to a quite difference complex of behaviour patterns!) The most that one could say is that a gander, when "in love," is inclined to promote with particular frequency situations in which spreading of the wings occurs. By contrast, the male Egyptian Goose *(Alopochen)* spreads its wings in demonstrative behaviour without any further provocation. In the Orinoko *(Goose Neochen),* the response of flapping the wings with a demonstrative significance has been completely separated from the normal response of wing-flapping. During the demonstrative response, the male rears up to a position far past the vertical, spreads his wings and performs restricted, quivering wing-beats followed by a long pause with the wings spread. This is accompanied by utterance of the "triumph-call" (Heinroth). In addition, *Neochen* has in fact developed a morphological releaser which underlines the operation of this behaviour pattern. The ventral side of the gander's body, which is prominently exposed in the posture described, is conspicuously coloured. The entire ceremony can immediately be recognized as "the same" as the behaviour of a Greylag gander returning to its adored one and uttering the triumph-call, and the two displays are doubtless homologous. In *Neochen,* however, the display is far more specialized and far removed from the original biological function of the motor patterns performed.

Similar relationships are highly probable in a great number of cases. Frequently, it is not possible to draw sharp boundaries between an instinctive behaviour pattern originally performed with a quite different function and a response operating only as a demonstrative behavioural element. In many cases, the relevant factors are not immediately obvious. For example, it is not easy to understand why a threatening cock must "pretend" to peck at something on the ground and why a crane preens behind its wings in the same situation. In the European crane, this ceremony still has the appearance of normal preening, and anybody who is not aware of the significance of the ceremony would regard it as such. With the Manchurian crane, one would scarcely take the corresponding motor pattern as a preening action, although it is certainly homologous with the pseudo-preening of the European crane.[1]

Every thinkable kind of morphological organ occurs for the consolidation of demonstrative behaviour, and such organs, like the behaviour itself, are in many cases restricted to the male animal. These structures carry all of the typical characters of the releaser and are therefore to some degree similar to one another. Above all, it is impossible to recognize from the form of a releasing organ whether it is determined for the elicitation of a reciprocal behaviour pattern from a conspecific male or from a conspecific female. It frequently occurs, in fact, that the same motor pattern and the same organ are used both for intimidation of other males and for elicitation of a female behavioural response. When we are acquainted with the responses of a species, however, we can often separate the organs of an animal "intended for the female" from those serving to intimidate other males. The elongated feathers of the neck-ruff of the Burmese Jungle-fowl and the domestic cock are predominantly employed against male conspecifics, whereas courtship of the female largely entails display of the tail-coverts. Hingston (1932) has expressed the opinion that all vivid colours and conspicuous shapes in the plumage of male birds, and in animals in general, operate exclusively as an intimidatory device. This is an extravagant generalization of a theory which applies only to certain animals, for example to certain lizard species.

It is, however, extremely probable that colours and shapes occurring in only *one* sex should generally be regarded as releasers.

If one is not to take recourse to an entirely transcendental, entelechial explanation, interpretation of male *"Prachtkleider"* (display patterns) as *releasers* is the only theory which can explain the general improbability of the structures involved. The colour patterns restricted to the males are always more regular, more uniform and frequently simpler than the markings of the conspecific females. We have already discussed the combination of uniformity and simplicity in releasers. The colours of the *"Prachtkleid"* as well as the marking pattern can be explained in the same way: reflection of a single, pure spectral colour from the wave-chaos of white light is in itself so improbable that a specific coloration of the feathers could alone become a releaser. The same probably applies to the pure and "beautiful" notes of bird-calls and songs.

Any theory which explains the *details* of various morphological patterns as products of chance, conflicts with the laws of probability. In saying this, I am thinking mainly of the views expressed by Wallace in his publication *Colours of animals*. He maintains that the *"Prachtkleider"* of the males are a "consequence of the greater strength and vigour, together with the greater vitality of males." This can be countered with the observation that in many birds the females bear the *"Prachtkleid"* and not the males. In addition, in those animals where the *"Prachtkleid"* of the males had more or less achieved its greatest degree of development, namely in spiders of the families *Attidae* and *Lycosidae*, the males are much smaller, weaker and less "vital" than the females. The Peckhams (1889) have recognized the true releasing function of the male *"Prachtkleid"* in this case.

My view that the typical appearance of *"Prachtkleider"* is related to their releasing function is supported by the fact that in a veritably overwhelming number of individual cases the conspicuous, brightly coloured areas of the male are employed as an organ in an elicitatory *behaviour pattern*. We do in fact frequently find releasing behaviour patterns which, so to speak, make use of already available material. By means of conspicuous body postures, spreading of wings and tail, ruffling of particular areas of the plumage and so on, a characteristic optical stimulus combination is produced, without particular differentiation of areas of the plumage to generate the stimuli involved. It has also been mentioned that this probably represents the archaic form of such behaviour. However, it would appear that the converse (i.e., markedly differentiated plumage areas which are not employed in specific ceremonies) is never found. In this case too, the impression is gained that the *ceremony is always more archaic than the correlated organ.* For example, in the demonstrative behaviour (displays) of probably all species of dabbling ducks the feathers on the crown of the head, the wing elbows and the rump are rendered particularly conspicuous, since the ducks raise their outline as far as possible above the water by spreading the feathers on the dorsal aspect. This behaviour is also exhibited by males of species which have no specialized display feathers on these dorsal areas. Whenever such specialized feathers occur in a species, however, they are almost always located on one of the three sites named and sometimes occur on all three—as in the Mandarin drake *(Aix galericulata).*

Consequently, whenever elongated, iridescent or conspicuously coloured feathers, conspicuous areas of naked skin, inflatable organs and the like are found in a given bird species, it can be quite reliably assumed that the structures concerned play a part in a specific releasing behaviour pattern. This behaviour pattern need not necessarily be concerned in sexual processes, however—it can also perform a purely social function, as we have seen with the Night Heron. But in cases where conspicuous elicitatory organs are only found in the male bird, they presumably serve either for the elicitation of a female sexual behavioural response or for the intimidation of other males; in many cases both functions are certainly involved. The functions of these releasers and the nature of the instinct interlocking systems which they set in operation vary so widely that they will be discussed in a special section.

The Various Types of Pair-Formation—The conjunction of two individuals for formation of a pair is guaranteed by an interlocking system of responses, which can vary radically from species to species. Nevertheless, the number of possibilities open for such a process appears to be limited, since we can find extremely similar behaviour patterns in different animal species which are taxonomically widely separate (e.g., birds and teleost fish). Of course, these similarities are merely convergent phenomena, as is illustrated by the fact that the pair-formation of the majority of birds is quite reminiscent of the behaviour of labyrinth fish, whilst pair-formation in a number of other birds is remarkably similar to the behaviour of another group of fish—the Cichlidae.

This being the case, there is no apparent justification for pronouncements on the phylogenetic relationships of the various forms of instinct interlocking. However, in order to give some degree of clarity to my account of these behaviour patterns, I shall attempt to select *three* types of such behaviour. In doing this, I shall steer clear of any phylogenetic assumptions, and I emphasize that I do not maintain that no other types of pair-formation can be postulated. The concept of the type incorporates the assumption that no individual concrete case will represent an ideal form of the type, and no more should be expected from the following described types of pair-formation. The purest forms are found among the lower vertebrates—the first type in some reptiles, the second type in labyrinth fish and the third in Cichlidae. These types are found in the birds with so little change in form that I have no hesitation in naming them after the animals mentioned and speaking of a lizard-type, a labyrinth fish-type and a Cichlid-type of pair-formation. This certainly does not mean that *all* representatives of the animal groups from which the names are taken exactly correspond to the relevant type in pair-formation. For example, I suspect that among the labyrinth fish the genus *Anabas* is distinctly different from the type of the Family. Similarly, the genus *Apistogramma* of the Cichlidae appears to have a labyrinth fish type of pair-formation. This said, we can pass on to a discussion of the three selected types of pair-formation.[2]

In many *lizards* the demonstrative behaviour and the "*Prachtkleid*" of the males has no influence whatever on sex-determined instinctive behaviour patterns of the female. The latter in fact responds to the demonstrative behaviour and "*Prachtkleid*" of the male in the same way as a weaker male— she flees. The male exhibits such demonstrative behaviour eliciting flight in females and weaker males towards *any* conspecific, but a male of approximately equal rank will respond with similar behaviour. In the former case, the fleeing animal is pursued and may be "raped," whereas it is only in the latter case that demonstrative behaviour reaches its zenith. If one of the displaying males does not flee in response to the threat of the other, a *fight* follows.

In this case, we are faced with the rare situation where a chain of behaviour beginning in a quite uniform manner can be continued in two different directions. It is as if the responses were moving along a track which forks into two at a set of points. The actual progress of the behavioural chain in one of the two possible directions is exclusively dependent upon the response given by the second animal to the male's demonstrative behaviour. Noble and Bradly (1933) have demonstrated experimentally that the demonstrative behaviour *always* carries on to the response of "rape" unless presentation of demonstrative behaviour on the part of the other animal causes a shift to the track of fighting behaviour. In most species, if the second male is restrained from performing its demonstrative behaviour by fettering, narcosis or some other means it will be "raped." In some species with specialized development of a male *"Prachtkleid,"* however, the coloration of the restrained animal also had to be obscured (at least partially) in order to elicit this response. *In this case, the* "Prachtkleid" *acts like a continuously presented form of demonstrative behaviour.* The male of such reptile species responds in a purely male fashion in all cases, treating *any* conspecific which does not elicit his fighting behaviour with sex-determined *male* elicitatory patterns as a female. The demonstrative behaviour and the *"Prachtkleid"* function exclusively as intimidatory agents and as releasers for reciprocal demonstrative behaviour from males of matching strength. This behaviour can therefore be biologically valuable in two different ways, firstly by preventing pointless fights through intimidation of the weaker opponent and secondly by preventing "erroneous" copulatory behaviour through the elicitation of male responses.

In *labyrinth fish,* the situation is quite different. Whereas in the lizards only the male exhibits demonstrative behaviour, each of these fish will react towards any other of the same species with demonstrative behaviour. The only exceptions occur when one individual is much larger than the other, in which case the reciprocal response of the weaker individual is nipped in the bud.

This also occurs when the development of the sex-determined male demonstrative organs of one fish is far in advance of that of the second fish. In fact, females will often not respond to a much weaker male with reciprocal display and will flee without further ado, as long as the fins of the male are sufficiently developed.[3] Even when the females are not sexually motivated, such that they do not respond to the demonstrative behaviour and *"Prachtkleid"* of the male with female mating invitations, they will permit themselves to be intimidated by both factors, even when they are physically much stronger than the male displaying with its fins.

In labyrinth fish, demonstrative behaviour is similarly followed by fighting and mating responses. In this case, too, the actual type of response which emerges depends entirely upon the behaviour of the second animal. However, there is a vital difference from the behaviour of the lizards in that in labyrinth fish fighting responses are *always* elictied if the second animal does not divert the demonstrative behaviour of the first along the channel of mating responses with *female* elicitatory behaviour patterns. The direction of the continuation of the behavioural chain into fighting or amatory behaviour depends upon the sex and the physiological condition of the second animal. Even a female will be treated as a rival if she does not perform the elicitatory patterns of sexual receptivity. A further important difference between the behaviour of these fish and that of the reptiles described is to be seen from the following: females will also respond to any weaker (more properly, lower-ranking) conspecific with *male* demonstrative behaviour. Conversely, a sexually-motivated male can also be observed to exhibit female instinctive behaviour patterns in response to a stronger conspecific of the same sex. In many birds, this sexually "ambivalent" behaviour is even more pronounced, and we shall need to deal with this in more detail later on.

Thus, demonstrative behaviour and the *"Prachtkleid"* of labyrinth fish have a different function to those of lizards. They are similar in that they serve to intimidate rivals, but they do not prevent mating behaviour involving two males. However, they do perform the important function of suppressing male responses in a female exhibiting ambivalent responses. Further, they function as the eliciting agent for the initial female behavioural responses which switch off the fighting responses of the male and initiate his mating responses.

These latter responses must be considered in more detail at this point. Above all, it must be emphasized that they include prominent behaviour patterns which are adapted for sexual arousal of the female. These "courtship" patterns have nothing to do with threat functions. It is far from my intention to deny this courtship function of these responses and to interpret all sex-determined male elicitatory behaviour patterns as demonstrative behaviour. The co-ordinated behaviour of pair-formation consists of a vast number of highly-specialized instinctive behavior patterns exhibited by both sexes, and nothing would be more erroneous than to incorporate all male elicitatory behaviour under the heading of "demonstrative behaviour."

The first behavioural response which a sexually receptive female labyrinth fish exhibits in answer to male demonstrative behaviour is in every way opposite in form. Whereas the displaying male always spreads his fins and places himself parallel to the other fish, a sexually receptive female always orients her longtudinal axis perpendicular to that of the male's and draws in her fins to lie as close as possible against the body. In addition, the female becomes pale in colour, thus providing another contrast to the bright, saturated colours of the displaying male. The continual attempt of the male to present his broad aspect to the partner whilst swimming along and the female's persistent endeavour to remain perpendicular to the male produce the circling behaviour of labyrinth fish pairs which is well known to any keeper of aquarium fish.

It is easy to see the radical difference between the mating behaviour of the lizards[4] and that of labyrinth fish. It has already been stated that *both* types of behaviour can be found among birds, and that we must therefore be extremely careful about generalization of principles which apply to a particular bird species. Noble and Bradley (1933) oppose the theory that male *"Prachtkleider"* exert any influence on females and that their origin is possibly to be explained as a result of sexual selection. They state: "This wonderful theory is complete nonsense when applied to the lizards, and if this is true for lizards, why not for birds as well?" This last question incorporates a basic misconception. Something which is completely wrong when applied to lizards may nevertheless be perfectly valid when applied to birds. Indeed, one is tempted to give in answer to this question: "Because most birds do not have a functional penis, so that mating without the participation of the female is not possible." This is an answer which can only be challenged on the basis of its causal structure.

One feature in which pair-formation in labyrinth fish corresponds with that of the lizards is that of the dominance relationship between male and female. In both, it is a precondition of pair-formation that the female should rank lower than the male.[5] We have seen that the *"Prachtkleid"* of the male plays a part in the establishment of this relationship. To this extent, Hingston's (1932) hypothesis that all bright colours and conspicuous shapes in the entire animal kingdom function exclusively to intimidate other organisms incorporates an element of truth. Otherwise, this hypothesis is a precipitate generalization from facts which are in themselves correct.

Even the more careful interpretation of the same phenomena given by Schjelderup-Ebbe (1923) is not entirely correct. Although there is an (at least potential) struggle for dominance between the sexes in the majority of birds, there are enough species in which *no* dominance relationship exists between the members of a pair. In such species, the character of the relative rank of an individual is inapplicable in determination of its sex.

We have classified this type of pair-formation as the *Cichlidtype* after the *fish* which exhibit this behaviour in its most pronounced form. In the Cichlid species which I have investigated *(Aequidens pulcher and Hemichromis bimaculatus) the female retains her demonstrative behaviour towards the male throughout the entire cycle of reproductive processes.* If two mutually unacquainted *Hemichromis bimaculatus* are set together, they will circle one another with the fins maximally spread and displaying their finest colours. In doing this, the two fish always remain parallel to one another. In other words, each turns its broad aspect to the other, just as two male (or, more exactly, two mutually threatening) labyrinth fish do. Now if the observer is familiar with the ritualized pairing behaviour of the labyrinth fish, he will often wait in vain for the fin-retraction and perpendicular posturing of the female. When this does not occur, the observer then erroneously expects fighting to take place at any moment, even if he is confronted with an actually compatible Cichlid pair. However, the behaviour which follows, *without* cessation of demonstrative behaviour on the part of the female, is composed of sex-specific elicitatory patterns. In *Hemichromis,* the assumption of markedly different colour-patterns apparently plays a part in this. *These* releasers inhibit the onset of dominance contests *without* rendering the female submissive and without overtly fighting, in contrast to the male demonstrative behaviour of labyrinth fish.[6]

In these fish, collapse of the demonstrative behaviour of the female in response to that of the male signifies the failure of pair-formation: the male then responds unspecifically with pursuit, and possibly killing, of the female. For this reason, it is hardly ever possible to pair off Cichlids of greatly differing size. In particular, it is virtually impossible to induce a smaller female to hold her ground before the demonstrative behaviour of a much larger male without abandoning her reciprocal demonstrative behaviour and fleeing. The normal reciprocal "display" which represents the introduction to Cichlid pair-formation is a typical case of the type of behaviour referred to by English-speaking animal psychologists as "mutual display."

We shall now investigate the extent to which the three described types of pair-formation are to be found among birds.

The purest form of behaviour corresponding to that of the *lizard-type* found in birds is provided by the Muscovy duck *(Cairina moschata)* and possibly in come related forms *(Plectropterus, Sarcidiornis).* Even in *Cairina,* however, the incipient development of female releasers can be demonstrated. In the first place, a female close to egg-laying and ripe for fertilization is in some way recognizable to the male, since one can observe that such ducks are pursued with particular vigour by males. The releasing signal may well be a particular, luminous red coloration of the facial tubercles of the receptive female (Heinroth). In addition, the females exhibit releasing *behaviour patterns* at the peak of receptivity. One can often observe, particularly when there are more ducks than drakes, that a female pursued by a male will abruptly freeze for a moment in the copulation posture before continuing flight from the drake. If the drake has not quite caught on, it can occur that the duck will actually remain crouching and wait for him. A similar phenomenon can be found even in the Class Reptilia. Peracca (n.d.) found with *Iguana tuberculata* that females run away from pursuing males, but nevertheless exhibit a simultaneous female elicitatory pattern in the form of elevation of the tail and extrusion of the cloaca. In the Egyptian Goose *(Alopochen aegyptiaca)* the pursuit by the male and the flight of the female have become entirely "ceremonial." Heinroth states that the mating of this species has the appearance of "prearranged mock rape." In my opinion, many cases where we can observe so-called "coyness" in the female during mating represent instinctive ceremonies based on the vestiges of originally genuine escape patterns. This would indicate that the lizard-type of mating also represents a "primitive" form of behaviour in some birds.

Some ducks, particularly the mallard, exhibit—in addition to their actual highly specialized type of pair-formation based on interlocking releasing ceremonies—an extremely peculiar behaviour pattern whose biological significance is difficult to comprehend. The males attempt to "rape" *any* strange duck which they encounter during the entire breeding season. In contrast to the female *Cairina*, however, the duck really takes to flight and is in fact not normally overtaken by the pursuing drake. Since the female in this case is "not guilty of" exhibiting the slightest responsive pattern, we are faced with the only instance of bird mating behaviour which corresponds to the pure lizard-type. For this reason, I shall consider this in some detail: In his relations with his consort, the drake shows the greatest consideration and will not attempt to copulate without an unequivocal invitation. In fact, he may fail to copulate even when invited. The drake thus behaves in the manner characteristic of most lizards only in response to *strange* females. However, this "raping" response has yet other characteristics in common with that of lizard behaviour. In particular, the response is apparently elicited by any conspecific of either sex and is only inhibited by sex-determined male characters. The most predominant of these characters is evidently the male "Prachtkleid." In 1933, I had a pure-blooded male albino mallard, which I received through the kindness of Frommhold in Essen. It was extremely interesting to observe that this male was pursued by the other drakes and subjected to "rape" attempts. Some years ago, I observed with a wild-coloured

domestic drake that it pursued in the same manner male conspecifics which still bore the female-like juvenile plumage. Wild
drakes never have the opportunity to exhibit such behaviour,
since their breeding season has elapsed before young conspecifics
are sufficiently grown. It must be said, however, that the male
albino drake described was sickly and exhibited no sexual activity whatsoever. The male demonstrative behaviour can apparently replace the *"Prachtkleid;"* since this albino drake was entirely healthy and sexually active the next year and was never
treated as a female by male conspecifics. I should greatly like to
know whether castrated females, which possess the full
"Prachtkleid" but none of the male demonstrative behaviour, are
"raped" by the males. Probably, *"Prachtkleid"* and demonstrative
behaviour operate in exactly similar fashion to deter the "rape"
responses of other drakes and doubtless have no effect on the
female pursued with intent to "rape." The female is not bothered
with the presence or absence of impressive characteristics in the
pursuer and simply attempts to escape in all cases.

All of this only applies to this particular form of duck mating,
however. In the establishment of a lasting pair-bond, the
"Prachtkleid" quite obviously affects the females as well and is
displayed to them in an unmistakable manner. Noble and Bradley's (1933) assumption that the *"Prachtkleid"* of a male bird
generally has the same function as that of the male of the reptile
species which they investigated is thus only partially applicable
even to these ducks and is even less valid in regard to other bird
species.

We now come to those birds whose pair-formation corresponds
to that of the *labyrinth fish-type.* This category includes the
majority of bird species. The parallels with pair-formation in
labyrinth fish extend into quite amazing details, as would be
confirmed by anybody who has observed both male fighting fish
and a Golden Pheasant during courtship of the female. Of course,
this similarity is entirely due to convergence. In the fish, where
external fertilization occurs, the co-operation of the female is just
as important as in the birds, in which "rape" of the female is not
possible for anatomical reasons. It is certainly no chance
phenomenon that the few birds which are known to exhibit the
lizard-type of mating all belong to species in which the male has

a functional reproductive appendage. Whereas the mating type of the labyrinth fish cannot have originated from a lizard-like "rape" of the female, such a source would seem to be probable on comparative anatomical grounds for birds which exhibit extensively similar behaviour.

One property which is possibly latently present in all vertebrates emerges in those birds in which pair-formation occurs according to the labyrinth fish-type. In these birds, each individual possesses not only the complete complement of species-specific, sex-determined instinctive behaviour patterns of its own sex; it also possesses (though normally in latent form) the sexual instinctive behaviour patterns of the other sex. It may appear contradictory to speak of "sex-determined" behaviour patterns at all in the face of such "ambivalence," but male and female instinctive behavioural systems remain sharply separate within a single individual. The animal can respond to a specific partner only in one way—*either* as a female *or* as a male. The behaviour patterns of an "instinctive outfit" are mutually bound as a very cohesive unit and the two units are not generally mixed. The membership of a behavioural component within the male or female behavioural units can therefore be just as exactly determined as if the two units were never exhibited by the same individual.

On the basis of the conditions under which female behaviour patterns can be experimentally elicted in a male (and *vice versa),* we have some knowledge of the factors which under natural conditions induce the emergence of the instinctive behavioural system corresponding to the gonads of the animal and suppress the opposite behaviour, causing it to remain latent.

Above all, it must be borne in mind that in bird species exhibiting the labyrinth fish-type of pair-formation *each* individual exhibits the tendency to perform the *male* behaviour patterns, and that it is the stimuli emanating from the sexual partner which suppress male behaviour patterns in the female and (so to speak) make room for female behaviour. An isolated female deprived of male company always inclines towards exhibition of male demonstrative behaviour (possibly in a fashion analogous to the development of the male *"Prachtkleid"* in a castrated female). The decisive character of the partner which inhibits emergence of male instincts in the female is the *one-sided dominance relationship.* A female can only respond in a feminine way when she is presented with a socially dominant conspecfic. A male can exhibit male responses when in complete isolation, but remarkably cannot do so when *only* accompanied by dominant conspecifics. A. A. Allen (1934) has observed with *Bonasa* that in a large number of males living together in one space the individuals lower in the rank-order not only failed to perform any male demonstrative behaviour, but even failed to enter into reproductive condition at all. If such low-ranking males exhibit any sexual instinctive behaviour patterns at all, then they are female in type. Allen refers to this entire complex of behaviour patterns quite simply as "inferiorism," which expresses the decisive rôle of the dominance relationship.

It can scarcely be doubted that even in a natural society of a bird species whose pair-formation takes place according to the labyrinth fish-type, a female high in the social order will not respond in a female way and that a male standing on the lowest rung of the dominance hierarchy can exhibit no male behaviour.

In spring of 1932, I had four ravens—a pair of adults, which were just preparing to breed, and two one-year-old females. I also regarded these two young females as a pair, however, since they exhibited vigorous courtship behaviour in which the older and stronger of the two sisters always took the male rôle. Because of a disruption in the sequence of instinctive behaviour patterns involved in pair-formation, the adult pair did not go on to breed, and the male eventually drove off the female for good with his persistent pursuits. When I subsequently allowed the two young ravens to join him, I was amazed to see the sibling which I had previously regarded as a male respond to the attempted approaches of the two-year-old male with all of the ritualized female behaviour patterns, such that the two formed a pair. I was particularly interested to see that this female did not at once cease to court her sister in male fashion and only began to treat her aggressively when she was firmly paired with the male.

Similar behaviour was exhibited by my adult jackdaw female Red-Yellow, the only surviving bird from my colony of tame jackdaws, which provided the observational material for my paper *Beiträge zur Ethologie sozialer Corviden*. I at first introduced four new young jackdaws to this surviving female, and in the next spring (1931) she formed a pair with one of the new birds and performed the rôle of the *male*. A normal nest was constructed, but no eggs were laid. In other words, the female responses of Red-Yellow remained completely dormant, for the jackdaw playing the female rôle was not yet mature enough to lay eggs. In 1932, the two birds constructed a peculiar nest reminiscent of Siamese twins, *two* nest-cups were built on a normal foundation. In *Coloeus*, as in the majority of passerines, the male normally constructs the rough foundation of the nest, whereas the preparation of the nest-cup belongs to the specifically female instinctive behaviour patterns. Both cups of this double nest, were used for holding the eggs, though I could not determine their actual number because the nest lay in an extremely inaccessible deep cavity. The eggs were apparently unfertilized, since no young emerged. My suspicion that a female pair had been formed was confirmed by an unexpected event in autumn 1932. One of the jackdaws of my former colony, which I had long since believed to be dead, turned up again after an absence of more than two years. The returned jackdaw immediately behaved as if it had never been away and promptly demonstrated that it was a male by undergoing bethrothal with Red-Yellow in the first few days after arrival. Red-Yellow immediately responded to the advances of the immaculate adult male and, in so doing, confirmed my assumption that the lack of an adequate male had been the cause of female pair-formation. In 1931, Red-Yellow had no male at all available, and in 1932 she had only an immature male born in 1931, in place of which she obviously preferred the female born in 1930 as a partner. The appearance of a competent male immediately evoked the response of all her female behaviour patterns. However, this surprisingly did not lead to a disruption of all relationships between Red-Yellow and her previous female consort. The male was initially very aggressive towards the latter, but gradually became accustomed to his wife's hanger-on. From this time onwards, the birds formed an inseparable trio. I do not know whether the male also copulated with the second female, but this is my suspicion. In spring 1933, the birds built a double nest similar to that of 1932 and filled it with such an enormous clutch that I am convinced that both females had laid, although (as in the previous year) I could not count the number of eggs exactly. The eggs were fertilized, but the small nestlings succumbed because of a disruption of nest-relief caused by the presence of the two females. The females always brooded simultaneously; each on one of the nest-cups, whereas the male (which had to relieve both females alone) was of course only able to cover one of the two nest-cups at a time. This had not affected the eggs, in fact, but it was most probably the cause of the death of the small nestlings.

This behaviour of female ravens and jackdaws plainly shows that the male instinctive behaviour patterns are also latently present in the female and can emerge in the absence of a consort companion of the opposite sex. In these birds, which exhibit little external sexual dimorphism and in which males and females are distinguished only by a gradual non-qualitative difference in the plumage areas employed in demonstrative behaviour, any strong individual with fine plumage will respond to a weaker and less impressively coloured bird by performing the rôle of a male. Nevertheless, formation of unisexual pairs does not appear to occur under natural conditions. In the normal, bisexual pairs, however, *the male is always dominant to the female*. Among the many jackdaw and raven pairs which I was able to observe, there were actually some in which strong, beautifully-developed males had selected disproportionately weak (in fact virtually sickly) females but the converse never occurred.

A. A. Allen (1934) described similar behaviour in the American ruffed grouse *Bonasa umbellus*. In this case, too, strong females exhibited male demonstrative behaviour towards any weaker conspecific, regardless of the sex of the latter. Similarly, weaker males cannot maintain their male behaviour patterns in the face of greatly dominant rivals, and the female "instinctive outfit" then emerges. Allen even succeeded in setting up an "inverted pair" by introducing a weak, frequently defeated male to an extremely strong female which tended to exhibit male demonstrative behaviour, such that pair-formation with reversed rôles took place. Unfortunately, in the summary of the results of his extremely valuable study, Allen presents this observation in the form of inaccurate generalizations, in which he repeatedly writes "the birds" instead of *"Bonasa umbellus."* The sentence "Birds are not sex-conscious" only applies to species in which pair-formation proceeds according to the "labyrinth fish-type." This does in fact include the majority of birds, but by no means all. In any case, introduction of the concept of "consciousness" is unnecessary and misleading.

Wallace Craig had already investigated the phenomenon of sexual reversibility in 1908 and had conducted very impressive experiments with pigeons. Craig kept his experimental animals in isolation cages and studied the mutual influence of sexual behaviour of the birds by placing the cages together two at a time without actually allowing the birds to come together. It then emerged that actual physical domination by one of the opponents is not necessary for the production of what Allen (1934) later called "inferiorism." When Craig gave a courting Barbary Dove *(Streptopelia risoria)* of average strength and normal temperament a particularly strong and vigorous old conspecific as a neighbour, the weaker bird ceased to exhibit courtship and even normal demonstrative behaviour. Soon after this collapse of male responses, the bird exhibited *female* elicitatory behaviour patterns. The fact that in this case demonstrative behaviour *alone*, without the slightest possibility of physical contact, was able to disarm the rival is extremely important. At first, one tends to regard it as improbable that simple display movements combined with bright colours and loud calls should exert a greater influence than sharp claws and a pointed beak. Craig's experiments demonstrate, however, that this is in fact the case. In rivalistic struggles between male animals, physical strength is never the sole deciding factor, and· neither are weapons. Victory is predominantly dependent upon the determination of the fighting animal, or—to put it more exactly—upon the *intensity* of its fighting responses. In fact, the opponent can determine the intensity of this response from the demonstrative behaviour exhibited. In cases where there is a considerable difference in intensity between two mutually displaying animals, the animal responding at a lesser intensity develops an inferiorism, even if it does not have the chance to take part in actual fight.

The reversibility of sexual responses in birds whose pair-formation takes place in agreement with the laybrinth fish-type raises the question of how the formation of unisexual pairs is prevented. We must particularly examine this question with those species in which external signs of sexual dimorphism are absent. From what has been said, it would seem to be quite possible that even under natural conditions a stronger male might extinguish male behaviour in a weaker individual and evoke female behaviour. The fact that this, to all appearances, does not occur is probably closely associated with the process of individual choice of a partner. In other words—using a genuine analogy with human behaviour—the responses of falling in love are involved. Such responses play no part at all in pair-formation of the lizard-type. In the birds which pair according to the Cichlid-type, as will be discussed later, similar phenomena are in fact sometimes found, but in these it is already decided before the choice of the partner whether the animal will subsequently exhibit male or female displays. In a bird undergoing pair-formation according to the labyrinth fish-type, the subsequent performance of male or female behaviour depends upon the individual selection of the love-object. As has been mentioned, the choice of the partner represents the only hormonally governed difference in the behaviour of the sexes: males only fall in love with subordinate animals and females only with dominant animals. If a partner of the opposite sex is lacking, these birds make do with a love-object of the same sex, and the animal immediately begins to exhibit the responses of the other sex. The personal bond to such a partner can be so strong that later arrival of a sexually receptive animal of the opposite sex will not break it. This is, for example, true of pigeons, in which preference of the opposite sex seems quite generally to be less prevalent. They will in fact form male pairs and female pairs even when animals of both sexes are available. This predominance of personal relationship over sexual influences should be regarded as an effect of domestication, however. As we have seen, in jackdaws and ravens a love-relationship with a conspecific of the same sex is immediately broken if an adequate sexual partner appears on the scene, provided that the new arrival exhibits the correct dominance relationship.

Since pair-formation can only occur through a mutual understanding (more exactly, as a result of mutual process of falling in love), under natural conditions the slight, genuinely sexually determined difference in response patterns is sufficient to prevent the formation of unisexual pairs. In particular, the following must be emphasized: If we keep birds of a given species in a group composed exclusively of one sex, the responses of falling in love are oriented towards a substitute object, leading to the formation of unisexual mated pairs. If, however, a few males are present among a much greater number of females, all of the females become so decidedly in love with the few males that the dominant females will not respond to the female mating invitations of their subordinate sisters. Rigid attachment to a love-object once chosen, which has been described by Heinrich Heine in a classically simple fashion in *Ein Jüngling liebt' ein Mädchen,*[7] can be found in mallard, Greylag geese and jackdaws, even when superfluous individuals of the same sex are available. Uninitiated enquirers always respond with disbelief, however, when one maintains that a sexually receptive bird refuses to undergo mating with an equally receptive conspecific simply because it is in love with another individual. I am inclined to the opinion that this "Ritter-Toggenburg behaviour" is in many birds, particularly in social species, the only factor which prevents all superfluous animals of a given sex from pairing with one another.

This portrayal of the factors preventing the formation of unisexual pairs doubtless incorporates a sweeping simplification of the relationships which actually exist, but the description is nevertheless quite accurate for jackdaws and many gallinaceous birds.

We now come to those bird species in which there is *no dominance relationship* between the members of a pair and in which there is therefore no observable competition for dominance between the sexes—in contrast to the views of Schjelderup-Ebbe (1923). This type of pair-formation has been referred to above as the *Cichlid-type.* We have already learnt that the preservation of demonstrative behaviour in the female is a characteristic of this type. In many cases, this in fact dictates the development of cermonies in which the sexes stand opposite one another and behave almost identically. As an analogue to the parallel swimming of Cichlid pairs described previously, I should like to recall the rattling ceremony of the white stork. Similar behaviour is found in herons, cormorants, the petrel relatives and the grebes. This reciprocal demonstrative behaviour has been much discussed in the English literature, where it is called "mutual display."

In very many birds, a dominance relationship within pairs never appears because the partners never have to cope with "differences of opinion." This in itself is not sufficient for us to classify the species concerned as a "Cichlid-type." In very many cases of this kind, a dominance relationship is not only present at the *formation* of the pair but actually indispensable for pair-formation. This dominance relationship reappears at each disturbance of the harmony of the pair in that the female flees without a preceding fight.

The situation is quite different in the dominance-less pairs of the pure Chiclid-type, as in many herons. In the process of pair-formation of these animals, the two potential mates gradually approach one another whilst performing specific ceremonies, which inhibit the normal defensive response. However, threat and demonstrative behaviour of *both* animals repeatedly breaks through this pacific ceremony. Even later on the partners do not exhibit such complete mutual confidence as pigeon or Anatid pairs. A single abrupt movement of one of the birds, for example caused by stumbling or some other loss of balance, suffices to bring the other on the defensive, with the display feathers of the neck ruffled. A moment later, the partners are standing opposite one another, exhibiting the complete threat behaviour of the species and ready to fight. Frequently, a fight does actually ensue, and this (together with the manner in which it ends) deserves more detailed description. Verwey (1930) describes minor disputes, which he refers to as "beak-fencing," in pairs of the heron. He observes that he originally believed that a ceremony was involved, but that he later concluded that serious fighting was actually involved. In the Night Heron, the situation is such that beak-fencing exactly corresponding to Verwey's description begins as serious fighting and then dissipates in the form of an appeasement ceremony. The animals rear up together and momentarily stab at one another with open beaks. Seconds later, beak-stabbing gives away in a smooth transiton to beak-rattling of gradually increasing rapidity. The two birds nibble one another's beaks in "placatory" fashion. Heinroth describes this nibbling beak-rattling as an expression of affection in his isolated hand-reared Night Heron. In actual fact, paired birds often exhibit this behaviour in the same context, *without* preceding beak-fencing. In accordance with what has been said, it appears very probable that affectionate beak-rattling has evolved from originally serious beak-fencing. This represents a typical case of evolution of a ceremony from a behaviour pattern which originally had an entirely different significance. I assume from Verwey's doubts and subsequent change of interpretation that in the heron the process of ceremony-formation from this response is incipiently present. At least, I belive that this author would agree with my interpretation on observing the corresponding behaviour of the Night Heron.

I have described this behaviour of the herons in some detail because, to all appearances, in animals with dominance-less pair-formation *very many* affectionate ceremonies have been derived from threatening demonstrative behaviour. The ceremony always represents a truce without victory of one or other partner. It is characteristic of these pacification ceremonies that they develop from the posture and behavior of threat before actual fighting occurs and before it has been decided which partner is the stronger. The behaviour of both partners of a pair during the process of becoming acquainted with one another is always reminiscent of the behaviour of two dogs during the same process: the tension, the threat posture, the expression of armed neutrality and finally the dissipatory pacification signal (in the case of the dog, tail-wagging). This is markedly different from the behaviour of labyrinth fish and that of most other birds, in which encounters are always accompanied by a fight, which always ends with at least a "moral" victory for one of the animals.

A further vital difference from the labyrinth fish-type is that the individuals involved are not sexually ambivalent at the outset. If they were so, all individuals—males and females alike—would respond in male fashion, since neither of the two partners of a pair would have the opportunity to develop an "inferiorism" (A. A. Allen, 1934). The male Night Heron enters the reproductive cycle without any relationship to a female, and the female never shows the slightest traces of male behaviour.

Apparently, the responses of individuals falling in love play little part in the Cichlid-type of pair-formation. In pairs, either of the partners *can be replaced* at any time by individuals of the same sex and physiological condition, even in those species where persistent pairs are formed. Schüz has demonstrated that this is so for the white stork, and according to Herrick (1935) the same applies to the Bald eagle*(Haliaetus leucocephalus)*. I suspect that pair-formation of the Cichlid-type is present in all birds in which there are on the one hand no sexual differences in the display organs, and on the other no relationships between the partners independent of the reproductive cycle.

The fact that three types of pair-formation have been presented by no means dictates that all forms of pair-formation in birds must fit into these categories[8] This is simply a means of demonstrating the basic differences in pair-formation which can exist and the danger in making precipitate generalizations.

From Konrad Lorenz. *Studies in Animal and Human Behavior* (Volume 1). Cambridge, Massachusetts: Harvard University Press; London: Methuen & Co., Ltd., 1970, pages 188-208. Copyright © 1970 by R. Piper & Co., Verlag. Translated from the German by Robert Martin. Reprinted by permission.

FOOTNOTES

1. This is the first reference to the problem of the displacement activity and, at the same time, to the phenomenon of ritualization.
2. This attempt to distinguish certain types of pair-formation is only partly successful. The lizard type as described here is only characteristic of the Iguanidae described by G. K. Noble. The lizards of the genus *Lacerta* behave quite differently, as they possess typically female releasers. The cichlid type of pair-formation also proved to be a special case only and occurs, I am sorry to say, not in cichlids but only in herons and some other territorial and colony-nesting birds. In cichlids I had missed, at the time of writing, the fleeting stage of rank inferiority in the female. (See Seitz, 1940, 1943; and particularly Oehlert, 1958). What is said about the labyrinth fish type is more or less correct.
3. Exactly the same is true of the blue throat in *Lacerta viridis* (G. Kitzler, 1942). In this reptile, the largest female reacts with submission to the smallest male, provided the latter is in possession of a blue throat.
4. This statement by Noble and Bradley is a typical error arising from generalization. What the authors say here is not even true of all lizards, let alone of all birds.
5. The explanation of this was given in 1958 by B. Oehlert. In the individual which happens to be rank superior, female sexuality is suppressed while, conversely, a dominated individual is unable to activate the patterns of male sexual behaviour.
6. This was a complete error. I had simply missed the period of female submissiveness which, however short, is as indispensable for the pair-formation in these fish as it is in labyrinth fishes.
7. *Ein Jüngling liebt ein Mädchen, die hat einen andern erwählt, der andre liebt eine andre, und hat sich mit dieser vermahlt. Das Mädchen heiratets aus Ärger den ersten besten Mann, der ihr in den Weg gelaufen,*

der Jüngling ist ubel dran. Es ist eine alte Geschichte, doch bleibts sie immer neu, und wem sie just passieret, dem bricht das Herz entzwei.
8. Geese, for instance, do not fit into these categories at all. The complicated mechanism of their pair-formation has been investigated by H. Fischer (1965).

REFERENCES

ALLEN, A. A. "Sex rhythm in the Ruffled Grouse *(Bonasa umbellus* Linn.) and other birds," *The Auk;*51/2, 1934.

CRAIG, W. "The voices of Pigeons regarded as a means of social control," *The American Journal of Sociology*, 14, 1908.

FISCHER, H *"Das Triumphgeschrei der Graugans" Anser anser, Zeitschrift für Tierpsychologie,* 22, 247–304, 1965.

HEINROTH, O.*"Beiträge zur Biologie; namentlich Ethologie und Psychologie der Anatiden,"* Verhandlungen des V. Internationalen Ornithologen-Kongresses; Berlin, 1910

HEINROTH, O, *"Reflektorische Bewegungen bei Vögeln,"* Journal für Ornithologie, 66, 1918

HEINROTH,*"Zahme and scheue Vögel;"* Der Naturforscher, I, 1924

HEINROTH, O, "Uber bestimmte Bewegungsweisen der Wirbeltiere," *Sitzungsbericht der Gesellschaft naturforschender Freunde;* Berlin, 1930

HEINROTH, O, und M. Die Vögel Mitteleuropas; *Berlin-Lichtenfelde,* 1924-8

HERRICK, F. H. Wild birds at home; New York and London, 1935

HINGSTON, R. W. G. The meaning of animal colour and adornment; London, 1932

KITZLER, G. "Die Paarungsbiologie einiger Eidechsen," *Zeitschrift für Tierpsychologie;* **4,** 353, 1942

LORENZ, K. On Aggression. New York: Harcourt, Brace & World, Inc., 1966.

LORENZ, K. Z. King Solomon's Ring. New York: Thomas Y. Crowell Company, 1952.

NOBLE, G. K. and BRADLEY, H. T. "The mating behavior of the lizards: its bearing on the theory of sexual selection," *Annals of the New York Academy of Sciences,* **35/2,** 1933

NOBLE, G. K. and BRADLEY, H. T. "Experimenting with the courtship of lizards," *Natural History,* **34/I,** 1933

OEHLERT, B. "Kampf und Paarbildung einiger Cichliden;" *Zeitschrift für Tierpsychologie;* **15,** 141-74, 1958

PECKHAM, G. W. and E. G. "Observations on sexual selection in spiders of the family Attidae," *Occasional Papers of the National History Society of Wisconsin;* Milwaukee, 1889

PERACCA, M. C. "Osservazioni sulla riproduzione della *Iguana tuberculata* Boll. Mus. Zool. Anat. Comparat. Reg. Univ. Torino; 6/110

SCHJELDERUP-EBBE, TH. "Zur Sozialpsychologie der Vögel," *Zeitschrift für Psychologie;* 1924; *Psychologische Forschung;* 88, 1923

SEITZ, A. Die Paarbildung bei einigen Cichliden. II. Die Paarbildung bei *Hemichromis bimaculatus* Gill; "Zeitscrift für Tierpsychologie; 5, 1943

SELOUS, E. "Observations tending to throw light on the question of sexual selection in birds, including a day to day diary on the breeding habits of the Ruff, *Machetes pugnax;" The Zoologist;* Fourth Series, 10/114, 1905

VERWEY, J. "Die Paarungsbiologie des Fischreihers;" *Zoologische Jahrbücher (Abteilung für allgemeine Zoologie;* 48, 1930

MATING BEHAVIOR

Niko Tinbergen

If ever anyone was born to his profession it was Niko Tinbergen. From a boyhood among the sand dunes of Holland's beaches to the Nobel Prize for Physiology, he has spent his life observing animals. In a sense, he never left the sand dunes. Although he has not avoided the laboratory and has always balanced experimental with field research, Konrad Lorenz once wrote of him, ". . . primarily he is a hunter. He likes to stalk and watch and sit in hides. Unlike myself, he does not want to keep and breed animals, but prefers to study them in their wild haunts, the wilder, the better. In him, the hunting instinct has been sublimated into the search for a deeper understanding of nature." Lorenz wrote this in his introduction to Tinbergen's important book, The Herring Gull's World *(1960), which must stand as a definitive model for how one does a natural history. Because of Tinbergen's lifelong infatuation with the herring gull we probably know more about the behavior of this species than of any other wild animal.*

Tinbergen and Lorenz have collaborated many times during their respective careers. From their first meeting in 1937 to their sharing of the Nobel Prize in 1973, they have mutually influenced each other and are generally recognized as the two seminal figures in ethology as it is known today.

Tinbergen began his professional work at the University of Leiden in Holland, and in 1949 he moved to Oxford where he has since served as professor of animal behavior and has done much to both legitimize and popularize ethology as a branch of zoology. His clear and engaging writing style is evident in the selection below, taken from his book Social Behavior in Animals *(1953). He begins with a simple problem—how to ensure that egg and sperm get to the same place at the same time—and describes how the adoption of sex-differentiated "mating behaviors" within each species functions to solve this problem.*

THE FUNCTIONS OF MATING BEHAVIOUR

Many animals, particularly species living in the sea, ensure the fertilization of the egg cells in such a simple way that we can scarcely speak of mating behaviour. Oysters for instance simply eject their sperm cells in huge numbers at a certain time of the year; for a while each individual is enveloped in a cloud of sperm cells. The egg cells, it seems, cannot avoid being fertilized. Yet even here an important sort of behaviour is involved: fertilization would not succeed if the various oyster individuals did not produce their sperm cells and their eggs at the same time. A certain synchronization therefore is necessary. As I hope to show, this applies equally to land animals.

In many higher animals, particularly land animals, fertilization involves mating, or copulation. This requires more than mere synchronization. It means bodily contact. This is a thing most animals avoid. This avoidance is an adaptation, part of their defence against predators. Being touched usually means being captured. Also, during actual mating the animals, and above all the females, are in a dangerous, defenceless position. In such animals the mating behaviour therefore involves the suppression of the escape behaviour. Since the female carries the eggs for some time, often even after fertilization, and since in so many species the female takes a larger share than the male in feeding and protecting the young, she is the more valuable part of the species' capital. Also, one male can often fertilize more than one female, an additional reason why individual males are biologically less valuable than females. It is therefore not surprising that the female needs persuasion more than the male, and this may be the main reason why courtship is so often the concern of the male. Often the male needs persuasion as well, but for a different reason. The males of most species are extremely pugnacious in the mating season, and unless the females can appease the males, they may be attacked instead of courted.

Further, apart from synchronization, which is a matter of coordinating the time pattern of mating, there must be close spatial co-ordination: the males and females must find each other; during actual copulation they must bring their genital organs in contact with each other; and, next, the sperm must find the egg cell. This orientation is also a task of mating behaviour.

Finally, there is a premium on the avoidance of mating with members of another species. Since the genes, and the highly complicated balanced growth processes started by them, are different in each species, mating between animals of different species brings widely different genes together, and this easily disturbs the delicately balanced growth pattern. Mating between different species therefore often results in fertilized eggs which are unable to live, and which die at the beginning of their growth; in less serious cases the hybrids may live but are less vital, or infertile. This premium on intraspecific mating has led to the development of differences between the mating patterns of different species, so that each individual can easily "recognize" its own species.

Apart from actual insemination, therefore, synchronization, persuasion, orientation, and reproductive isolation are the functions of mating behavior.

Our problem in this chapter is: how are these functions fulfilled? What part does social behaviour play, and how does it attain these results? Let me say right at the beginning that our knowledge is very patchy. We have bits of information on each of these problems, but part of our knowledge applies to one species, and other parts to other species. In not a single species do we know the whole picture. The only thing I can do, therefore, is to present some examples of the various ways in which mating behaviour attains these ends, leaving it to future research to find out to what extent we are entitled to generalize our findings.

One thing seems to be obvious already: all the behaviour involved is of a relatively low "psychological" level, and does not imply foresight of these ends, nor deliberate action with the aim of attaining them. As we shall see, mating behaviour in all animals except Man and, perhaps, some of the apes, consists of immediate reactions to internal and external stimuli. There is no way in which "foreseen" effects of the behaviour can be brought into play as causes of the behaviour, as it does, in some as yet completely mysterious way, in Man.

SOME INSTANCES OF TIMING

The timing of the reproductive behaviour of oysters· *(Ostrea edulis)* has been shown recently[8] to be the work of a rather unexpected outside factor, and therefore it is not, strictly speaking, a sociological problem. Yet it is perhaps useful to discuss it here as an example of the way in which the action of outside factors may often, so to speak, "fake" social co-operation.

About eight days after the oysters spawn, the larvae "swarm." They lead a very short floating life, and soon settle down on a solid substratum. In the muddy estuaries of the Scheldt, in Holland, oyster breeders increase their oyster stock by depositing roof tiles as artificial substrates on the bottom of the sea. This must not be done too much in advance of swarming, since the tiles would then become overgrown with other organisms before the oyster larvae could settle. A zoologist therefore had to find out whether he could forecast when the swarming would take place. His forecast, based upon many years of study, seems astonishing: "The big maximum in swarming is to be expected each year between June 26 and July 10, at about 10 days after full or new moon." This sounds like a fable, yet it is the hard truth. Since swarming takes place eight days after spawning, this means that spawning is to be expected two days after full or new moon. This gives us the key to the factor that is responsible for the timing: the tides. Spawning takes place at spring tide. How the spring tide affects the oysters is not yet known; it is not improbable that it is a matter of water pressure, which reaches its greatest oscillations at spring tide. Also, the intensity of the light penetrating to the bottom shows its maximum fluctuations at that time, and this might also be a factor.

Since the oysters do not spawn at each spring tide, there must be another factor preparing them to be ready in June to react to the spring tides; the nature of this factor is not known yet. It works much less precisely than the tides, for although the maximum of spawning occurs between June 18 and July 2, there are minor peaks during the preceding and the following spring tide. This factor is not known in the oyster, but in other animals we know something about it.

Not only the oyster but several other marine animals are

known to be timed by the tides, among them the famous Palolo worm of the Pacific, and various other worms and molluscs.

Timing in the higher animals is a more complicated affair. Something is known of fish, birds, and mammals of the Northern temperate zone. Reproduction of most of these begins in spring. The first phase is migration towards the breeding grounds. This is done by all individuals at approximately the same time, though there may be weeks between the arrival of the first and the last comers. This rough timing is again due not to social behaviour but to reactions to an outside factor. The main factor here is the gradual lengthening of the day in late winter.[3],[12] Various mammals, birds, and fish have been subjected to artificial day-lengthening. The result was that the pituitary gland in the brain began to secrete a hormone which in its turn affected the growth of the sex glands. These then began to secrete sex hormones, and the action of these sex hormones on the central nervous system brought about the first reproductive behaviour pattern, migration. Often a rise in the temperature of the environment has an additional effect.

As I said, this timing process is not very accurate. The different individuals do not all react to the lengthening of the day with the same promptness. There may be a considerable difference between the male and the female of a pair. It has been found, in pigeons and in other animals, that if the male is further advanced than the female, his persistent courtship may speed up the female's development. This has been found in the following way. When a male and a female are kept separately in adjoining cages so that they can see and even touch each other, but are prevented from copulating, the persistent courtship of the male will finally induce the female to lay eggs.[4],[5] These of course are infertile. It may occur in captivity, when no males are available, that two female pigeons form a pair. Of these two, one then shows all the behaviour normally shown by the male. And although their reproductive rhythms may have been out of step at the beginning, the final result is that they both lay eggs at the same time. Somehow their mutual behaviour must have produced synchronization, not merely of behaviour, but also of the development of eggs in the ovary.

It is possible that this effect may be found in other species as well. It has been suggested by Darling[6] that the communal courtship of birds breeding in colonies may have the same effect.

A further refinement of synchronization however is necessary. In all species that copulate, and in many other species as well, the co-operation between male and female must run according to an exact time schedule, and without exact co-operation no fertilization would be possible. In only very few species can the male force the female against her will to copulate. This means that in many species some form of very accurate synchronization must occur, which is a matter of fractions of a second. This is done by a kind of signal system. As an example I will discuss the mating of the Three-spined Stickleback.[16] In the scheme of mating behaviour there is not merely a temporal sequence, but also a causal relation: each reaction really acts as a signal which releases the next reaction in the partner. Thus the male's zigzag dance releases approach in the female. Her approach in its turn releases leading in the male. His leading stimulates her to follow, and so on. This can easily be shown by the use of models or dummies. When a very crude imitation of a pregnant female is presented to the male in its territory, he will approach it and perform the zigzag dance. As soon as the model is then turned in his direction and "swims" towards him, he turns round, and leads it to the nest.

Pregnant females can be induced in a similar way to react to a model of the male. A crude fish model again is sufficient, provided it is painted red underneath. A bright blue eye will also help, but beyond that no details are necessary. If such a model is moved round a pregnant female in a crude imitation of the zigzag dance, the female will turn towards the model and approach it. If we then let the model swim away, the female follows it, and it is even possible to make her try to "enter" anywhere in the bottom of the aquarium by making the male model "show the nest entrance." No nest is necessary; the movement of the model is sufficient stimulus for the female to react.

Now in these cases the fish do not react exclusively to the partner's movements, but also to certain aspects of shape and colour. If the female dummy does not have the swollen abdomen of the real female, it will not or scarcely stimulate the male to dance. If the model of the male does not show a red underside, the female shows no interest in it. On the other hand, all other details have little or no influence, so that it is easier to release mating behaviour by using a very crude but "pregnant" dummy than with a live but non-pregnant female. However, the swollen abdomen, and the red colour, which are displayed continuously, are not responsible for the timing of the response of the male. It is the movements, which appear suddenly and immediately elicit a response, that are responsible for the exact timing.

The mating behaviour of Sticklebacks is a complicated series of such signal-response sequences, and the end result is that the male fertilizes the eggs immediately after they are laid by the female. It is not at all difficult to observe this behaviour, and to carry out all the model tests described. The Three-spined Stickleback will readily breed in an aquarium of a cubic foot or larger. It should have sand on the bottom, and plenty of green vegetation, including some green thread-algae.

The mating behaviour of many species involves such signal-movements which serve this ultimate refinement of synchronization.

PERSUASION AND APPEASEMENT

Even when an animal is in a sexually active condition, it does not always react immediately to the partner's courtship. It may take a considerable time to overcome the female's reluctance. The zigzag dance of a male Stickleback for instance does not always elicit the female's response at once. She may approach in a half-hearted way, and stop when the male tries to lead her to the nest. In that case the male returns, and again performs his zigzag dance. After a number of repetitions the female may eventually yield, follow him, and enter the nest.

A similar repetition of signals is necessary when the female has entered the nest. The male's prolonged "quivering" is required to make her spawn. When you take the male away just after the female has entered the nest, she is unable to spawn. When you touch such a female gently with a light glass rod, imitating the male's quivering with it, she spawns just as easily as when the male has delivered the stimuli. Both male and rod have to touch her a great number of times.

In many species this repetition of signals is the rule. The copulation of Avocets for instance[10] is preceded by curious antics: both male and female stand and preen their feathers in a hasty, "nervous" fashion. After some time the female stops preening, and adopts a flat attitude. This is the signal indicating that she is willing to mate, and only then does the male mount and copulate. Sometimes he does not react at once, but only after a certain time.

Herring Gulls have a similar introduction to coition. Both male and female bob their heads upwards, uttering a soft, melodious call with each bob. Here it is the male which takes the initiative in copulation: after a series of such mutual head-tossings he suddenly mounts and mates.

Sometimes persuasion has another function. In many birds, and in other species as well, the males become very aggressive in the breeding season. Actually, most of the fighting seen in animals is fighting between rival males in spring. This fighting is essential. Since it is always aimed at a rival male, the female has to differ from the male lest she should be attacked as well. In species such as the Chaffinch, the Redstart, or various Pheasants, the differences in plumage partly serve this purpose. In many other species however, such as the Wren, the plumages of male and female are not very different, or they are even identical, and here the female has to show special behaviour to suppress the male's aggressiveness. The essence of this "female courtship" therefore is to avoid provoking attack. Whereas a strange male may either flee from the displaying male—in which case it immediately elicits pursuit—or strut and threaten in reply (which also provokes the displaying male's aggressiveness), a female does neither. In the Bitterling *(Rhodeus amarus)* the female is at first attacked.[2] She either withdraws quietly or merely avoids the attack by swimming under the male. The male then seems to be unable to attack her, and after a while it ceases to try and begins to court the female. A similar unobtrusive appeasement can be observed in many Cichlids.[1] In other species the female shows infantile behaviour, that is to say, it resorts to the same method of appeasement as employed by the young, which probably stimulates the male's parental drive. That is why in so many species the male feeds the female during courtship. This happens, as we have seen, in the Herring Gull. There are also species in which the appeasing postures used during courtship are different from those used by the young. The female, or in other species both sexes, then show a type of behaviour which in many respects is the exact opposite of the threat behaviour. When, for instance, Black-headed Gulls *(Larus ridibundus)* meet in the mating season, they show the "forward display," lowering the head and pointing the beak towards each other. This threat gesture is emphasized by the brown face, which surrounds the bill, the actual weapon. Mates however show their friendly intentions by "head flagging"; they stretch the neck, and then, by a sudden jerky movement, they turn their faces away from each other.[17] Here, since both sexes are rather aggressive, the male appeases the female, as well as vice versa.

In some web-building spiders, the male visits the female on her web. Here the male has to appease the female, because he might be mistaken for prey.

ORIENTATION

The spatial directing of mating movements is another important function of courtship. The most obvious function to be fulfilled is attraction. Many songbirds, such as the Nightingale, spend the winter far from the breeding grounds. The males, as mentioned above, return from the south well in advance of the females. How do the females find the males? This is made possible by the song. Many birds attract the other sex by some loud noise. In the Nightingale we happen to find this noise beautiful and have called it song. But the spring call of a male Grey Heron *(Ardea cinerea)*, a harsh cry, does not appeal to human ears. Yet it does to the female Heron.[19] It serves exactly the same function as the Nightingale's song. The Night-jar's rattling, the Woodpecker's drumming and the croaking of toads belong to the same category. So exactly is the song of many birds tuned to this function that the song is most intense as long as the males are still unmated, and it stops as soon as a female arrives. This again is due to a conflict between various interests. Song serves the species in that it attracts females (and, as we shall see later, repels rival males), but it endangers the male because it attracts predators as well. Nature, as always, has evolved a compromise:

song is only produced when it is really needed, or at least when the advantages outweigh the disadvantages.

Since most animals are deaf (only the vertebrates and some other groups are exceptions), we find auditory advertisement in relatively few groups. It is well developed in birds, in frogs and toads, and in various insects such as crickets and grasshoppers. Special organs have evolved in such groups exclusively for the production of sound.

Other groups use scent as a means of attracting the opposite sex. Extreme cases are found among moths. The Psychid Moths[11] have been studied to some extent and will be chosen as examples. The females have lost the capacity to fly; they are practically wingless. Soon after hatching, a female leaves the tubular shelter in which she has been living as a caterpillar and as a pupa. She does not move beyond her doorstep however, but remains hanging beneath her shelter. The males can fly. Shortly after hatching they leave their house, and take wing in order to search for a female. This search is guided by a scent which emanates from a virgin female. This attraction by female scent is highly developed in many other moths, such as Saturnia and Lasiocampa species. In such species the male is often able to find a female from a considerable distance, and his organs of smell, situated on the plume-like antennae, are highly sensitive. It is not at all difficult to collect caterpillars of those species, let them pupate and hatch, and watch the wild males come and enter the house in their search for the virgin females.

Visual attraction plays a part in many species. It is beautifully developed in the Sticklebacks. The male Three-spined Stickleback develops its most brilliant nuptial colours after the nest is finished. The red of the underside becomes more brilliant, and the dark shade which has covered his back during nest building becomes a fluorescent bluish white. Simultaneously, his behaviour changes. While during nest building he moved about smoothly, avoiding sudden movements, he now keeps swimming round the territory in a jerky abrupt fashion, which together with his conspicuous dress makes him visible from afar.

Many birds add visual displays to their auditory attraction devices. This is developed most impressively in birds of wide open plains. The waders of the Arctic tundra and many marsh birds in this country specialize in this respect. Again we often find a combination of conspicuous colours and movements. Lapwing, Black-tailed Godwit, Dunlin and other waders are good examples. Other species have entirely specialized on movement, and are lacking in colour; such are found among the more vulnerable songbirds: Pipits, Larks. Specialization on colour has also occurred: the Ruff *(Philomachus pugnax)* has no special song flight, but relies on gorgeous coloration. Yet it has evolved another signal movement: now and then the males on a "lek" lift their wings, the light undersides of which make them very conspicuous. This wing lifting occurs particularly as a reaction to females flying in the distance, and it seems to attract these females. These lek birds apply still another principle, which has been called the "flower-bed principle": by crowding together their individual colour-effects are added together; they form a large gaudy patch somewhat like a flower bed.

In only a few of these cases has experiment proved the attracting influence. The red colour of male Sticklebacks has been proved to attract the females; models lacking red do not attract them. The influence of song has been nicely demonstrated in various locusts, as in the following study. In one cage, hidden in the heather, singing males of Ephippiger were kept; in the next cage there were the same number of males, which were silenced by gluing their stridulation organs together. This is a minor operation, which leaves this wingless form free to pursue all other activities. At a distance of ten yards, females in mating condition were released. They invariably made their way in a short time to the cage containing singing males.[7]

Experiments of this type justify the conclusions drawn in these paragraphs concerning the attracting influence of various types of display. Yet further experimental work is needed.

The orientation task of courtship is not finished when attraction has been effected. In actual copulation, the male has to bring his copulation apparatus into contact with that of the female, and this again requires powers of orientation. This is most obvious in many insects, where the males possess a complicated system of claspers to be fitted into the closely corresponding "negative" counterparts of the females. But in less 'mechanized" animals such as birds this problem exists as well: the male cannot bring its cloaca in touch with that of the female without first reacting to orienting stimuli from the female.

However, very little is known about these behaviour mechanisms.

REPRODUCTIVE ISOLATION

Hybridization between species is exceedingly rare in nature. This is only partly due to differences in habitat preference between different species. Closely related species which breed in entirely separated geographical regions, and species which, though living in the same general region, go to different habitats to breed, are prevented from cross breeding by this spatial separation. But even where there is no such separation, species do not ordinarily interbreed. This is due to the fact that the various signals serving attraction, persuasion, appeasement, and synchronization, are so very different from one species to another. Also, the tendency to react to such signals is specific; every animal is innately equipped with the tendency both to gives its species' signals and to react only to the signals of its own species. Yet one often sees, in nature, sexual relations to other species. The males of the Grayling, which I have studied for several seasons, start their courtship by following the females in flight. This sexual pursuit is not released by females only: butterflies of other species, beetles, flies, small birds, falling leaves, even their own shadow on the ground attracts them. How is it that they never mate with these other species? Similar observations, leading to the same query, can be made on birds, fish, and many other animals.

The answer seems to be found in the chain character of mating and pair formation activities. When a female Grayling is willing to mate, it reacts in a special way to the male's sexual pursuit: it alights. All the other species usually do the opposite: if bothered by a pursuing male, they fly off as fast as they can, and this makes the male abandon its pursuit. Only closely related species react occasionally, but this has never been observed to lead to mating. Sticklebacks show essentially similar behaviour. The male may react to a small Tench entering its territory by zigzag-dancing. For a continuation of his mating behaviour, however, it is necessary that the partner swims towards him.

Even if a Tench does this inadvertently, it has to follow the male to the nest, it has to enter the nest, and it has to spawn there before it can release sperm-ejaculation in the Stickleback. In other words, it must show the correct series of responses to the whole succession of the male's courtship activities, including the final "quivering." And this is so extremely improbable that it has never been observed. The sign stimuli of each separate reaction of the chain may not be sufficient to prevent reactions to other species, but since the separate reactions are each released by different stimuli, these together are sufficiently typical to prevent interspecific mating. This is obvious in species with "mutual" courtship, for here each sex shows a series of courtship activities. But even in a species such as the Grayling, where the female just sits while the male performs his courtship sequence, the female supplies a series of stimuli: experimental analysis has shown that the various activities of the male are released by stimuli which differ from one reaction to the next.

This specificity is particularly needed in closely related species. As we will see later, the behaviour patterns of closely related species are always very similar, just as their morphological characters are. They simply have not had the time for wide evolutionary divergence. But in such species there is always some striking difference between mating patterns, at least if spatial (geographical or ecological) or temporal (differences in breeding season) separation does not render this unnecessary. For instance, the Ten-spined Stickleback's *(Pungitius pungitius)* mating behaviour is rather similar to that of the Three-spined species.[13] It has however evolved very different nuptial colours in the male. The male of the Ten-spined species is pitchblack in spring. Just as the red colour attracts Three-spined females, so the black colour appeals to the females of the Ten-spined species. This, together with some minor behaviour differences, is sufficient to make interbreeding rare.

A systematic study of this problem of reproductive isolation has been undertaken in only one group: the fruit flies *(Drosophilia)*.[14] The first results indicate that mating attempts between diffferent species break off at various stages of the courtship, depending on which species are involved. Whenever such an interruption of courtship is found to be consistent in a series of observations, it is a sign that we are dealing with a specific response which cannot be released by the partner. The results obtained thus far show that in some cases the male fails to give the correct stimulus, in other cases the "fault" is with the female.

CONCLUSION

This very brief and sketchy review may be sufficient to show the intricate nature of behaviour patterns serving co-operation between the members of a pair. It has been shown that we must distinguish between four different types of functions served by courtship. This does not mean that each particular courtship activity serves only one of these ends. The zigzag dance of the male Stickleback for instance certainly serves timing, persuasion, orientation, and isolation, but the difference between the nuptial colours of Three-spined and Ten-spined Sticklebacks can only be understood from the viewpoint of isolation. Also, we know of courtship activities which have to do with timing and persuasion but not with orientation: Grayling females for instance can be timed and persuaded by the courtship of one male, and then mate with another male, which shows that the first male did not orient the female's response towards himself. Similarly, in pigeons, the persistent cooing and bowing of the male does not so much orient the female but it makes her gonads start ovulation. The various closely related "Darwin's Finches" of the Galapagos islands were found to have almost identical courtships.[9] Yet there is no interbreeding. Here reproductive isolation is effected partly by ecological isolation, partly by each species reacting specifically to its own species' type of bill, which, in relation to the type of food taken, is different from one species to another. In this case therefore the courtship activities have nothing to do with reproductive isolation, but they do serve all the other functions.

In all these cases courtship activities, however different their functions may be in detail, have one thing in common: they send out signals to which the sex partner responds.

From Niko Tinbergen. *Social Behavior in Animals*. London: Methuen & Company, 1953, pages 22–39. Reprinted by permission. In reprinting this selection, plates and line drawings contained in the original have been omitted.

REFERENCES

1. BAERENDS, G. P. and BAERENDS, J. J., 1948: "An introduction to the study of the ethology of Cichlid Fishes." *Behaviour, Suppl.*, **I**, I-242.
2. BOESEMAN, M., VAN DER DRIFT, J., VAN ROON, J. M., TINBERGEN, N., and TER PELKWIJK, J., 1938: *"De bittervoorns en hun mossels." De Lev. Nat.* **43**, 129-236.
3. BULLOUGH, W. S., 1951: *Vertebrate Sexual Cycles*. London.
4. CRAIG, W., 1911: "Oviposition induced by the male in pigeons." *Jour. Morphol.*, **22**, 299-305.
5. CRAIG, W., 1913: "The stimulation and the inhibition of ovulation in birds and mammals." *Jour. anin. Behav.*, **3**, 215-21.
6. DARLING, F. F., 1938: *Bird Flocks and the Breeding Cycle*. Cambridge.
7. DUYM, M., and VAN OYEN, G. M., 1948: *"Het sjirpen van de Zadelsprinkhaan." De Levende Natuur;* **51**, 81-7.
8. KORRINGA, P., 1947: "Relations between the moon and periodicity in the breeding of marine animals." *Ecol. Monogr.*, **17**, 349-81.
9. LACK, D., 1947: *Darwin's Finches*. Cambridge.
10. MAKKINK, G. F., 1936: "An attempt at an ethogram of the European Avocet *(Recurvirostra avosetts L.)* with ethological and psychological remarks." *Ardeac* **25**, I-60.
11. MATTHESE, E., 1948: *"Amicta febretta. Ein Beitrag zur Morphologic und Biologie der Psychiden." Mémor. e estudos do Mus. Zool., Coimbra,* **184**, I-80.
12. ROWAN, W., 1938: "Light and seasonal reproduction in animals." *Biol. Rev.*, **13**, 374-402.
13. SEVENSTER, P., 1949: *"Modderbaarsjes." De Lev. Nat.,.* **52**, 161-68, 184-90.
14. SPIETH, H. T., 1949: "Sexual behavior and isolation in Drosophila II. The interspecific mating behavior of species of the willistoni-group." *Evolution;* **3**, 67-82.
15. TINBERGEN, N., 1940: *"Die Übersprungbewegung." Zs. f. Tierpsychol.,* **4**, I-40.
16. TINBERGEN, N., 1951: *The Study of Instinct*. Oxford.
17. TINBERGEN, N., and MOYNIHAN, M., 1952: "Head-flagging in the Black-headed Gull; its function and origin." *Brit. Birds;* **45**, 19-22.
18. TINBERGEN, N. *The Herring Gull's World*. New York: Harper & Row, Publishers, Inc., 1960
19. VERWEY, J., 1930: *"Die Paarungsbiologie des Fischreihers." Zool. Jahrb. Allg. Zool. Physiol.* **48**, I-120.

MASCULINITY AND FEMININITY AS DISPLAY

Ray L. Birdwhistell

Although Ray Birdwhistell was trained as an anthropologist and continues to identify himself as one, he has pursued a distinctly atypical line of research during his career. He has been very instrumental in the development of kinesics, i.e., the science of body movement and gesture, more popularly known as "body language." The basic premises of his approach are that humans communicate through movement as well as through words, and that these communications are learned, relatively precise, and culturally determined.

Why have we included him in our ethological section? The first reason is that his focus is on patterns of behavior, precisely the focus of the ethologist. Secondly, his approach is comparative, involving cross-species as well as cross-cultural comparisons. Third, there is a loving, almost preoccupied quality to his observation of human movement which is suggestive of Lorenz's definition of what constitutes ethological expertise (cf.,Lorenz, 1970 , p. xvi). Finally, many social scientists are convinced that human beings are proper subjects for ethological study, and Birdwhistell has come very close to instrumentalizing that conviction.

In the following selection, drawn from Kinesics and Context *(1970), Birdwhistell posits a continuum among species ranging from those in which the sexes have exaggeratedly different anatomy (dimorphic) to those which show no perceptible anatomical differences (unimorphic). He then locates* homo sapiens *toward the unimorphic end of the continuum and suggests that our species has developed a repertoire of "tertiary sexual characteristics" in order to signal sex meanings which our relatively unimorphic bodies cannot carry. This is a novel and provocative approach to the relationship between gender and sex role in humans, although it has been used by other ethologists in their investigations of nonhuman species.*

Birdwhistell is Senior Research Scientist at the Eastern Pennsylvania Psychiatric Institute and professor of communication at the Annenberg School of the University of Pennsylvania.

Z oologists and biologists have over the years accumulated archives of data which attest to the complex ordering of animal gender display, courtship, and mating behaviour. Until recently, the implications of much of this data have been obscured by the governing assumption that this behavior was, while intricate and obviously patterned, essentially a mechanical and instinctual response to a genetically based program. There has been, however, an increasing realization that intragender and intergender behavior throughout the animal kingdom is not simply a response to instinctual mechanisms but is shaped, structured, and released both by the ontogenetic experiences of the participating organisms and by the patterned circumstances of the relevant environment. Behavioral scientists focusing upon human behavior have been forced to relinquish the ethnocentric assumption that human gender and sexual behavior is qualitatively different from that of other animals. Many have conceded that culture, a human invention, is not interpreted profitably as a device for curbing and ordering "animalistic," "brutal," "bestial," or instinctual appetites. The elaborate regulation of fish, bird, and mammalian courtship and mating behavior has been of particular interest to sociologists and anthropologists. That this interest has not been more productive seems to me to be occasioned by confusion in the ordering of gender-centered behavior. In the discussion to follow, which utilizes certain insights derived from analysis of communication, I wish to focus upon one aspect of gender-related interactional behavior—that of gender identification and response.[1]

Biologists have long been aware that the clear demarcation between the production of ova and spermatazoa in organisms of a bisexual species is not necessarily accompanied by any comparable bifurcation in the distribution of secondary sexual characteristics. In some species there is such extreme gender-linked dimorphism that only the specialist in the particular species can recognize that males and females are conspecial. At the other extreme, some species are so unimorphic that near-surgical techniques are required to determine the gender of isolated individuals. By and large, researchers concerned with human behavior have assumed that in relatively unimorphic species there were subtle differences in the perceptible taxonomy of males and females which were easily recognizable by conspecifics even if they were difficult to detect by humans. However, it would be difficult for any reader conversant with Konrad Lorenz' (1957) description of the difficulties involved in the mating of graylag geese to maintain the fiction that gender differences are always apparent to the membership of a unimorphic species. There is humor and a certain pathos in the situation when two graylag males meet and each acts as though the other were a member of the opposite sex. Only the reproductive rate of graylags gives us confidence that even a goose can solve such a problem.

The social biologist Peter Klopfer has pointed out that even with the incomplete evidence now at hand, it would be possible to establish a spectrum of species rated by the extent of their sexual dimorphism (personal communication). Insofar as I have been able to determine, no such list has been prepared. However, by establishing an ideal typical gamut with an unimorphic species at one end and an extreme of dimorphy at the other, it has been possible to tentatively locate *Homo sapiens* on this scale. Obviously, the position of any particular species on this scale is a function of both the number of species chosen and the special characteristics of the selected species. When, however, the secondary sexual characteristics themselves are stressed (whether visibly, audibly or, olfactorily perceptible), man seems far closer to the unimorphic end of the spectrum than he might like to believe.

Physical anthropologists have long pointed out that if such anatomical markers as differential bone structure or the distribution of body hair are used, the measurement of human population reveals no bimodal curve in the distribution of secondary sexual characteristics. Most authorities agree that instead of a single bimodal curve ⌒⌒, we find two overlapping bell-shaped curves: ⌒⌒ Masculine and feminine traits in aural sound production seem to be distributed in a similar manner following puberty. There is as yet no definitive evidence that there is a significant difference in the odor-producing chemicals released by human males and females. This may be due to the crudity of our avialable measuring instruments, but at the present, odor does not seem to function as a constant gender marker for humans.

The case for the relative unimorphy or the weak dimorphy of man should not be overstressed for the purposes of this argument. The upright position of humans obviously makes for clear visibility of differential mammary development and for the easy display of the genitalia. These may provide sufficient signals in themselves. However, certain pieces of data permit us to discount these as definitive of gender in and of themselves. First, we have long been aware that children do not, even in societies as preoccupied with these organs as ours, immediately note the gender-defining qualities of either the external genitalia or the differential mammary development. I doubt seriously that this represents some psychological denial function in the child's perception of his universe. The near universality of the G-string or other clothing protecting, obscuring, or hiding the genital region, even in societies with minimal shame or embarrassment about genital display, does not seem sufficient evidence for the final importance of genitalia display for gender identification. Furthermore, the fact that the more prominent breasts of females or the less prominent breasts of males do not seem to have universal sexual stimulus value would seem to support our de-emphasis upon mammary dimorphism as gender identifiers. Needless to say, however, until we have more systematic knowledge about clothing and other cosmetological devices, we are not going to be able to settle this particular question. There is no reason to make the *a priori* assumption that uncovered breasts are more or less obvious than covered ones (except of course, to those trained to make these distinctions). It seems permissible to proceed in our discussion while holding this aspect of human dimorphy open for future investigation.

My work in kinesics leads me to postulate that man and probably a number of other weakly dimorphic species necessarily organize much of gender display and recognition at the level of position, movement, and expression. It seems methodologically useful to me to distinguish between *primary* sexual characteristics which relate to the physiology of the production of fertile ova or spermatazoa, the *secondary* sexual characteristics which are anatomical in nature, and the *tertiary* sexual characteristics which are patterned social-behavioral in form. These latter are learned and are situationally produced.

Let me hasten to add that the terms "primary," "secondary," and "tertiary" imply no functional priorities. There seems plenty of reason to believe that these levels are mutually interinfluential. Patterned social behavior seems to be required to permit the necessary physiological functioning requisite for successful and fertile mating. And, we have at least anecdotal evidence and clinical reports that certain of the secondary sexual characteristics respond to both the physiological substratum and the particular social-behavioral context. I hope that premature "explanation" which accounts for this behavior in simplistic psychological or cultural terms does not preclude investigation on other levels.

I have worked with informants from seven different societies. It has been clear from their responses that not only could native informants distinguish male movement from female movement (and the items of what was regarded as "masculine" and "feminine" varied from society to society) but they easily detected different degrees of accentuation or diminution of such movement, depending upon the situation. In all of these societies (Chinese, middle- and upper-class London British, Kutenai, Shushwap, Hopi, Parisian French, and American) both male and female informants distinguished not only typically male communicational behavior from typically female communicational behavior but, when the opportunity presented itself, distinguished "feminine" males and "masculine" females. This does not imply that any informant could make a complete and explicit list of "masculine" or "feminine" behavior. However, each culture did have stereotypes which could be acted out or roughly described. That the behavior described by the informants did not always coincide with the general range of scientifically abstractable gender-identifying behavior should not come as a surprise to any field worker who has tried to elicit microcultural behavior from native informants. One comment should be included here before we turn for examples to the body motion communicational system most intensively studied, the American. Informants from all of these societies either volunteered or without hesitation responded that young children matured into these behaviors and that as people got older they gave up or matured out of them. As might be expected, both the propedeutic period and the duration of the active gender display varied from society to society. Furthermore, while most informants agreed that in their particular society some individuals learned how to accentuate or obscure these signals, informants from all of these societies interpreted the differences as instinctually and biologically based.

I have no data which would permit me to assess the relative emphasis American culture places upon gender display and recognition as compared to other societies. However, it is quite clear that within American society, class and regional variations occur—not so much in the signals themselves as in the age at which such messages are learned, the length of time and situations in which they are used, and the emphasis placed on them in contrast to other identification signals.

As an illustration, I will describe a few of the most easily recognizable American gender identification signals. Two are derived from the analysis of posture, one from "facial expression." The male-female differences in intrafemoral angle and arm body angle are subject to exact measurement. American females, when sending gender signals and/or as a reciprocal to male gender signals, bring the legs together, at times to the point that the upper legs cross, either in a full leg cross *with feet still together,* the lateral aspects of the two feet parallel to each other, or in standing knee over knee. In contrast, the American male position is one in which the intrafemoral index ranges up to a 10- or 15-degree angle. Comparably, the American female gender presentation arm position involves the proximation of the upper arms to the trunk while the male in gender presentation moves the arms some 5 to 10 degrees away from the body. In movement, the female may present the entire body from neck to ankles as a moving whole, whereas the male moves the arms independent of the trunk. The male may subtly wag his hips with a slight right and left presentation with a movement which involves a twist at the base of the thoracic cage and at the ankles.

Another body position involved in gender presentation is made possible by the flexibility of the pelvic spinal complex. In gender identification the American male tends to carry his pelvis rolled slightly back as contrasted with the female anterior roll. If the range of pelvic positioning is depicted as ⌣⟋ , the female position can be depicted as ✕⟋ , the male as ⌣✕ . As males and females grow older or, because of pathology, over- or under-emphasize gender messages, the male and female position can become almost indistinguishable, or become bizarrely inappropriate.

One more example may be sufficient for our point. Informants often describe particular lid and eye behavior as masculine or feminine. However, only careful observation and measurement reveal that the structural components of circumorbital behavior are related, in closure of the lid in males, to prohibiting movement of the eyeballs while the lids are closed. Comparably, the communicative convention prescribes that unless accompanying signals indicate sleepiness or distress, males should close and open their lids in a relatively continuous movement. Let me stress again that these positions, movements, and expressions are culturally coded—that what is viewed as masculine in one culture may be regarded as feminine in another.

I have presented these examples with a hesitation occasioned by past experience. Inevitably, such examples have been interpreted as the messages males and females send to each other when they wish consciously or unconsciously to invite coitus. However, I must emphasize that *no position, expression, or movement ever carries meaning in and of itself.* It is true that in certain contexts gender display, appropriately responded to, is an essential element in the complex, interchange between humans preliminary to courtship, to coitus, and, even, to mating. However, the identical behavior inappropriately presented may have the opposite function, it may prevent the development of the interaction that might culminate in a more intimate interpersonal exchange. For example, a prematurely presenting male may define a situation in such a manner that the female cannot respond without considerable role sacrifice. Thus, the male can prevent coitus and even courtship from occurring by presenting in a manner which defines his action as insufficiently directed to the receiving female. The so-called "sexy" female can by inappropriate gender display effectively protect herself against intimate heterosexual involvement. The male who sends "feminine" or pubescent and awkward "masculine" display signals may in one context be signaling to a male; in another he degenderizes his female respondent by returning a message more appropriate to a female-female interaction than a male-female interaction. Furthermore, while it is not at all difficult to detect in context the message sent by either a male or a female which reads, "I wish to be considered a homosexual," we have been able to isolate no message, masculine or feminine, which is in itself an indicant of homosexuality or heterosexuality when such sexuality is measured by active genital participation.

For the sociologist and the anthropologist, a more important aspect of the possibility of decoding a given society's gender display and recognition system is that such a code provides him with a tool for more adequately studying the division of labor in the day-to-day life of a community. Social role and status theory have been very useful at one level of social investigation. However, when the researcher seeks to relate such theory to problems of social learning, to personality and character development, or to the solution of individual and social problems, he all too often is prevented from testing high-level generalizations in the crucible of behavior. Gender identity and relationship is only one of several nodal points coded into a society's communicational system. Kinesic and linguistic research has demonstrated, at least for American society, that such nodal behavior never stands alone—it is always modified by other identification signals and by the structure of the context in which the behavior occurs. In these complex but decodable behaviors lies the proof that gender behavior is not limited to a sexual response and that sexual behavior is not always *either* genital or uncompleted genital behavior.

In the discussion so far an attempt has been made to demonstrate the methodological correctness and convenience of ordering gender-related phenomena into primary, secondary, and tertiary characteristics. Tertiary sexual behavior has been described as learned and patterned communicative behavior which in the American body motion communication system acts to identify both the gender of a person and the social expectancies of that gender. It has been presented with the fiat that gender display or response is not necessarily sexually provocative or responsive and is probably never exclusively genital in nature.

The paper was introduced with a discussion of the relatively weak dimorphy in the structure of human secondary sexual characteristics. Until more animal societies are studied as societies and until the nature and range of the possibilities for the division of labor have been investigated in these animal societies, we cannot make any final appraisal of unimorphy or dimorphy as base lines for social interaction. However, we are in a position to postulate that for human society at least, weak dimorphy creates an opportunity for the development of intricate and flexible tertiary sexual characteristics which can be variably exploited in the division of labor.

Finally, in a society like ours, with its complex division of labor and with the rapid change in social role as related to gender, we should not be surprised to find that the young have considerable difficulty in learning appropriate intra- and intergender messages. Nor should we be surprised to find that in such a society messages about sex and gender can become a preoccupation. Children who become confused about the meaning of gender messages can become adults who have difficulty comprehending the relationships between male and female roles in a changing society. Only the fact that children can learn in spite of parental teaching protects us from a situation in which accumulating discrepancy could destroy the necessary conditions for appropriate mating. There is no evidence for the popular statement that men in western European society are becoming "weaker" or that women are becoming "stronger"—there is considerable evidence that both are confused in their communication with each other about such matters.

From Ray L. Birdwhistell. *Kinesics and Context: Essays on Body Motion Communication.* Philadelphia: University of Pennsylvania Press, 1970, pages 39-46. Reprinted by permission.

FOOTNOTE

1. Presented to the American Association for the Advancement of Science, in December 1964 under the title "The Tertiary Sexual Characteristics of Man: A Fundamental in Human Communication."

REFERENCES

LORENZ, K. (1957). "The role of aggression in group formation." In B. Schaffner (Ed.) *Group Processes.* Transactions of the 4th Conference of the Josiah Macy, Jr., Foundation, pp. 181 ff.
LORENZ, K. (1970). *Studies in Animal and Human Behavior* (Volume 1). Cambridge, Mass.: Harvard University Press.

FETAL HORMONES AND THE BRAIN: EFFECT ON SEXUAL DIMORPHISM OF BEHAVIOR—A REVIEW

John Money / Anke A. Ehrhardt

Like Tinbergen, John Money and Anke Ehrhardt pose the same initial problem: how to get the sperm and egg to the same place at the same time. They also offer essentially the same solution to the problem: differentiation and complementarity of male and female mating behavior. However, while ethologists like Tinbergen, Lorenz, and Birdwhistell examine the functional consequences of mating behavior, bio-ethologists like Money and Ehrhardt investigate the biochemical precursors to mating behavior. Each strategy focuses on animal behavior. But Money and Ehrhardt concentrate on the inner stimuli which provoke such behaviors, while the others focus on the external signals which elicit reciprocal patterns of behavior. Thus, the two approaches tend to complement one another.

Money has concentrated, during most of this career, on psychosexual behavior, primarily of humans and secondarily of infrahuman species. He has done ground-breaking research on hermaphroditism, transexualism, and other deviations from normative psychosexual development. Moreover, he has always manipulated variables at the interface of human biology and psychology, and traced the developmental interactions of both sets of variables. In the selection reprinted below, he and Ehrhardt review a large body of animal research on the relationships between genetic sex, sex hormones, timing of hormonal treatment, and mating behavior. They conclude that treatment with male sex hormones very early in life tends to "masculinize" the central nervous system in irreversible directions, so that male-typed mating behaviors predominate, even in genetic females. Early treatment with female hormones (or no treatment at all) allows for bipotentiality in adult mating behavior. They are very cautious about generalizing these patterns to humans.

Money is professor of medical psychology and pediatrics at Johns Hopkins School of Medicine. Ehrhardt is associate professor of psychology and pediatrics and co-director of the Psycho-Endocrinology Program at the State University of New York Children's Hospital in Buffalo.

DIMORPHISM OF MATING BEHAVIOUR

The reproductive anatomy is dimorphic. Therefore, it is foreordained, if a species is to reproduce, that sexual behavior must, at a bare minimum, be sexually dimorphic enough to permit conception to take place. It would not much matter whether, instead of the copulatory act as we know it, the male should take his sperm to the female in a membranous bubble, or whether the female's egg, attached to an ovidepositor, should temporarily inhabit a sperm chamber in the male. The issue at stake is whether the male and female each carry out their complement of behavior appropriately. Assuming that they do, then the issue becomes one of the origin of the dimorphism or complementarity of their behavior.[1]

Behavior that is sexually dimorphic is not necessarily sexually exclusive. It may be shared by both sexes—perhaps during an early developmental period, or seasonally, or episodically, or over the long term except for interludes when complementarity is needed. Thus males may play at mounting males as well as females when they are young, and females may mount females and males as well. Then at puberty, the balance may shift, so that males will ordinarily mount only females, and females will ordinarily only be mounted. One exception may be that a male will present his rump to another male, as an invitation to mount, as a sign of deference and subordination. The dominant male may or may not mount him, only rarely with anal intromission, dependent, perhaps, on his state of tension release and the length of time he has been segregated from females. A second exception may be that a female will present and be mounted by another female at a time when agitation and nervous excitability are running high.

Before it can be decided whether sexually dimorphic behavior is strictly exclusive and sex specific, or to some degree shared by both sexes, it is essential to avoid the pitfall of global impressionism. To do so requires differentiating a gross pattern of behavior, like mating, into its component acts. In the mating of the rat, for example, experimentalists follow the convention of differentiating, in the male, mounts without intromission, mounts with intromission, and mounts with intromission plus ejaculation. In the female, they differentiate lordosis, ear wiggling, and darting or hopping. A female can mount. She cannot achieve intromission, but she may exhibit spasmodic movement corresponding to ejaculation. A male can assume the crouched, rump-up, tail-deflected posture of lordosis and also do the copulatory hop or darting movement and the ear wiggle.

Beach's analysis of dimorphic sexual behavior in the rat (Beach *et al.*, 1969) is pragmatic and empirically applicable. The analysis for the female is as follows:

Mount by stimulus male: The criteria here are very strict. It is required that the stimulus male mount directly from the rear, clasp the experimental animal firmly with the forelegs, palpate the subject's sides with the forelegs, and execute vigorous pelvic thrusts. Mounts which are oriented in any other fashion or which are not accompanied by palpation and thrusting are not included.

Ear wiggle: The head is shaken rapidly in the lateral plane and the ears seem to vibrate.

Hop and dart: The rat runs or hops rapidly away from the stimulus male and then comes to an abrupt stop.

Crouch: The rat assumes a motionless pose with legs slightly flexed and back held parallel to the substrate.

Turn: The animal turns around when the stimulus male tries to mount.

Walk: When mounted, the subject walks away.

Flat: The mounted subject assumes a position in which the back is parallel to the floor but neither the head nor tail is elevated.

Arch I: The mounted rat raises both head and tail noticeably but not maximally.

Arch II: Like arch I except that the head is raised with marked neck flexion and the tail is distinctly elevated or deviated laterally.

For the male the analysis is as follows:

Mount or intromission latency: Time from introduction of the female until the first mount or intromission.

Mount and thrust: The same response described earlier for the stimulus males during tests for feminine coital responses.

Intromission pattern: Identical to the mount and thrust response except that contact is terminated by a definite and vigorous backward lunge on the part of the mounting individual. In normal males this pattern almost always signals the occurrence of penile insertion and it is clearly distinguishable from a mount and thrust without intromission.

Ejaculation pattern: The mounted male executes several pelvic thrusts and on the final thrust achieves full insertion, which is maintained for a considerably longer time than during simple intromission. The male then releases his clasp of the female, frequently elevating his forelegs slowly and dismounting in deliberate fashion without a backward lunge. Ejaculation invariably is followed by a pause of approximately 4-5 min. before copulation is resumed.

It is necessary to differentiate the component elements of the mating pattern, species by species. In the rhesus monkey, for example, pelvic thrusts are differentiated from mounting and intromission. Other compenents include grooming and the sexual yawn. There is, as yet, no conventionally agreed upon differentiation of the components of human sexual performance. The lack no doubt reflects contemporary scientific reluctance to watch human beings copulate, as well as the relatively unstereotyped nature of human sexual activity, as compared with that of other primates.

The evidence of animal sexology to date (Beach, 1947; Whalen, 1968) is that sexually dimorphic behavior is not uniquely male or uniquely female, respectively. Rather, it is bisexual in potential, though predominantly male or predominantly female in manifestation. Each sex may, and does, on occasion, display mating behavior, or elements of mating behavior, that belongs primarily to the other sex. The circumstances, conditions, or individual history in consequence of which the reproductively less appropriate patterns may appear have not been catalogued. It is known, however, that excessive crowding may disrupt normal sexual behavior patterns in rats (Calhoun, 1962), as may infantile isolation in rhesus monkeys (Harlow and Harlow, 1965) and chimpanzees (Kollar *et al.,* 1968). It is also known that castration of adult rats followed by treatment with heterotypical (opposite-sex) hormone may release heterotypical sexual behavior patterns (Beach, 1947). Swanson and Crossley (1971) report the same for the male hamster. Such observations are of cardinal importance with respect to the long-term effects of pre-natal or neonatal hormonal treatment on behavior. The dimor-phic type of sexual behavior observed will be a product not only of the early hormonal manipulation, but also of the animal's pubertal hormonal status at the time of testing. To illustrate: the postpubertal sexual behavior of a female rat androgen-treated before 10 days of age will be different if she has been sub-sequently left with her own ovaries intact than if she has been castrated and left untreated, or castrated and later treated with androgen.

The reason for singling out the rat for special mention, here and in what follows, is that this has been the favored laboratory animal in the majority of experiments. The hamster, guinea pig, rabbit, and rhesus monkey have also been used. They are identified when referred to in the remainder of this paper.

MATING BEHAVIOR OF NEONATALLY ANDROGENIZED FEMALE RATS AND HAMSTERS

A neonatally androgenized and surgically ovariectomized female rat, if given no subsequent treatment, will show no puberty and no pubertal sexual behavior. She will, in general, be sexually in-different to males and females alike, and they will be without copulatory interest in her.

The animal that is neonatally androgenized but not ovariec-tomized will not necessarily be sexually indifferent, but she will manifest an inhibition of feminine sexual behavior. It may be either complete or partial inhibition, dependent on the dosage strength and timing of neonatal androgen administration. On a dose as small as 10 mg. administered on the fifth day of postnatal life, the animal might accept the male, but on a bizarre schedule, such as on 9 consecutive days (Barraclough and Gorski, 1962). The normal female rat displays lordosis and the other behavioral components of feminine mating, ear wiggling and darting, on the day of estrus. The neonatally androgenized female rat manifests not cyclic but persistent estrus, as a consequence of being gonadotropically acyclic. Persistent estrus is anovulatory, so that the animal is sometimes referred to by the acronym, TSR, testosterone-sterilized rat. A large dose of neonatal testosterone, as large as 100-500 mg., does the same as a smaller dose in producing persistent estrus of the vaginal mucosa (the vagina is anatomically normal or only mildly deformed). Its inhibiting effect on mating behavior at estrus is more complete, however, for the animal actively rejects and repulses the advances of the male.

This same animal, in the presence of a normal estrous female, will display partial masculine mating behavior, namely, mounting. Since all females do the same, the residual effect of neonatal testosterone, if in evidence, will be a matter of degree. Investigators have been neglectful in statistical reporting with respect to increased frequency of the uncastrated TSR's mounting of other females. This neglect perhaps reflects the habit of thought which biases most people toward juxtaposing male and female, and forgetting about the ambisexual potential of most mammals. Nonetheless, there is sufficient evidence from which to infer an increase in behavior that technically might be called homosexual. The chief effect of neonatal testosterone, however, is to inhibit normal female patterns from expressing themselves under circumstances, and in response to stimuli, sufficient to elicit them from normal control females.

The neonatally androgenized female who is not subsequently castrated has ovaries that secrete female hormone. If these ovaries are removed before puberty, and the animal is later given a replacement injection of estrogen plus progesterone, then her sexual behavior remains essentially the same as without castration. If, however, the injection is with male sex hormone (testosterone propionate, most commonly), then the animal's behavior shows a change. It is the same kind of a change as observed when a normal female is prepubertally castrated and then injected with testosterone, namely, an increase in the manifestation of components of male sexual behavior, particularly mounting. The neonatally androgenized female, however, shows a greater degree of this behavior, and perhaps a more complete form of it. Harris and Levine (1965) reported an increase in the number of mountings in which vigorous pelvic thrusts were followed by a backward fall, with subsequent licking of the genital area, in the manner of the male intromission pattern. Such behavior appears when the experimental animal is tested with a normal estrous female. When she is tested with a normal male, she avoids being mounted, but shows an increase in nosing and exploring the genital area of the male. Harris and Levine (1965) reported that two of their experimental females mounted the male with vigorous pelvic thrusts.

Swanson and Crossley (1971) obtained results from the neonatally androgenized female hamster that are in agreement with those from the rat. They added one new experiment, namely, testing their animals with an estrous female not only after priming with testosterone, but also after priming with estrogen plus progesterone. The female hormones induced the same masculine mounting behavior as did the male, hormone. Exactly the same result was obtained from males that had been neonatally injected with testosterone propionate, castrated later in life, and then tested with estrogen plus progesterone. Males not testosterone-treated neonatally failed to show the response. Their only reaction to estrogen plus progesterone was to display feminine mating behavior (lordosis) in the presence of a stud male. In the hamster, it thus appears, neonatal testosterone injection induces an even stronger degree of masculinization of mating behavior than does androgen from the normal male's own testes. The neonnatally androgenized females were, however, awkward in their mounting. They positioned themselves on the head or side, as well as the rump, and tended to slip off.

The experimental females herein considered are, as a result of having been neonatally injected with androgen and of having been given more of the same again in adulthood following prepubertal castration, likely to manifest a slight virilization of the external genitalia (Beach, 1968; Swanson, 1971), especially enlargement of the clitoris. Levine and Mullins (1964) obtained the same virilizing effect when using a different neonatal masculinizer, estradiol benzoate (see below). One must, therefore, ask the question as to whether neonatal androgen affected behavior only by changing sexual behavior centers in the brain or by potentiating clitoral enlargement and changing neural sensory organization at the periphery. It is quite possible that both the centrum and the periphery are involved. If so, their respective roles have not yet been clearly distinguished.

The same issue arises in converse form with respect to deandrogenization of the male, when the effect is to diminish the penis in size or leave it incompletely formed (Whalen, 1968; Beach *et al.*, 1969; Nadler, 1969). Complete deandrogenization of the male early enough in fetal life results in completely feminine external genitalia and the possibility of copulating as a female (see below). Though the peripheral organs have not been entirely overlooked, so much intellectual excitement has been generated by the idea of finding sex-regulatory centers in the brain that investigators tend to have been biased, in their hypotheses, in favor of the central functions of the brain.

ESTRADIOL SIMULATING NEONATAL ANDROGENIC EFFECT ON MATING BEHAVIOR OF FEMALE RATS

Estradiol benzoate, stilbesterol, and Norlutin have been identified as simulating the neonatal androgenic effect on hypothalamic cyclicity. The first and only one to have been investigated for its effect on the behavior of genetic females is estradiol benzoate.

Levine and Mullins (1964) treated neonatal female rats with estradiol benzoate. They castrated them as adults and injected them with testosterone. A possible complicating factor is that after 9 days on testosterone, they mainfested greater masculinization of the clitoris than the neonatally untreated control animals. They also manifested an increased incidence of the components of masculine mating behavior as compared with control females. One experimental animal is said to have exhibited, on two occasions, a simulation of the male ejaculatory spasm.

Whalen and Edwards (1967) did a similar experiment except for the different timing of ovariectomy, which was performed on the day of birth. The two groups thereupon treated with either testosterone propionate or estradiol benzoate were remarkably similar in response to further treatment with testosterone again in adulthood. They had high mounting scores and low or negative lordosis scores. The reverse occurred in animals that had been either sham-operated or only ovariectomized, neonatally, without neonatal hormonal treatment.

These experiments issue a clear warning that one must not

equate masculine behavior with masculine hormone, nor feminine behavior with feminine hormone. The correct inference is that, in the absence of gonadal steroids in the neonatal period, neural differentiation takes place that will subsequently favor the expression of the component patterns of feminine mating behavior. In the presence of gonadal steroids, administered by injection, feminine neural differentiation is likely to be disturbed. Such disturbance has been proved when the injected gonadal steroid is the androgen, testosterone, or the estrogen, estradiol benzoate. In both cases, the disturbance is in the direction of abolishing a feminine type of differentiation, either by disorganizing it, if the dosage was small, or, if a larger dosage was given, by potentiating a masculinizing trend.

MATING BEHAVIOR OF NEONATALLY ESTRONGENIZED MALE RATS

The same rule that applies to the dimorphic neonatal hormonal effect on gonadotropic cycling in the hypothalamus applies also to the effect on behavior: the antithesis of androgen is not estrogen, but no hormone at all. The evidence in support of this principle comes from experiments in which estrogen has been administered to neonatal males and experiments in which newborn rats have been deprived of their own androgens by being castrated or treated with an antiandrogenic compound.

Levine and Mullins (1964) injected male rats neonatally with 100 mg. of estradiol benzoate. In adulthood, these rats were mating-tested before and after castration, and again after 7 days of replacement therapy. Their performance paralleled that of the oil-injected control males to some extent, rather than being like that of a female. The intromission and ejaculation rate was lowered, perhaps because of poor morphological development of the accessory sex organs after castration and injection with estrogen. Mounting activity was adversely affected. It was, in fact, quite bizarre. The animals tried to mount from the head, the side, or high up on the back of the receptive female.

There is no report on the mating behavior of the normal male toward these animals while they were on substitution treatment with androgen. Nor is there a report on what might have occurred had the animals been given substitution therapy with estrogen and tested with both male and female partners.

MATING BEHAVIOR OF NEONATALLY DEANDROGENIZED (CASTRATED) MALE RATS AND HAMSTERS

Like his female counterpart, a male rat castrated at birth and given no hormone treatment whatsoever will in adulthood be sexually indifferent. The rat is one among many species in which the activation of sexual behavior requires an endogenous sex hormone as well as an exogenous perceptual stimulation. Without the priming effect of the hormone, the perceptual stimuli of sexual arousal, chiefly visual, olfactory, and tactile, are devoid of arousal power. In other species, especially man, the central nervous system, as mediator of perceptual arousal, is somewhat less rigidly dependent on the sex hormones as prerequisties of sexual behavior.

If the neonatally castrated male rat is given sex hormone, either masucline or feminine, after reaching the age of puberty, then it will become apparent that the loss of the testes and the androgen they would have secreted during the critical neonatal period has left a permanent behavioral effect. This effect is not all or none, however, like the companion effect on the hypothalamic cycling mechanism. Loss of the masculinizing principle through neonatal castration does not induce simply a persistence of a primary feminine behavioral prototype. Rather it lays bare that bipotentiality of sexually dimorphic behavior which persists beyond infancy more strongly in the normal female than in the normal male (Whalen and Edwards, 1966; Beach *et al.*, 1969). In the hormonally normal female, this bipotentiality may manifest itself spontaneously in her behavior from time to time in adulthood, especially in mounting behavior, interspersed with her far more frequent lordosis. If this normal, intact female's usual androgen level is exogenously augmented, however, then her latent masculine behavior pattern will be manifested with greater frequency, and augmented to include not only mounting but also the movements that accompany intromission and ejaculation as well.

The neonatally castrated male rat resembles the normal female when he reaches adulthood, with respect to bipotentiality of sexual behavior, except that all behavior will be dormant unless exogenous hormone is administered. Then, as many different investigators have demonstrated (Grady *et al.*, 1965), if he is primed with estrogen followed by progesterone,[2] he will manifest a fairly complete replica of normal female receptive behavior, when placed with a test male that tries to mount him. A normal intact male similarly injected with estrogen and progesterone would show far less receptivity and would continue to show less, even if surgically castrated as well.

Instead of priming with estrogen and progesterone, the other alternative is to prime the neonatally castrated rat in adulthood with androgen. His behavior, when tested with a receptive female in estrus, then resembles that of a control female injected with androgen more than that of a control male. His behavior includes mounting, but intromission and ejaculatory behavior do not match in either frequency or perfection that of a control male castrated in adulthood and treated with testosterone (Whalen, 1964). The neonatally castrated male is at a great disadvantage in having hypoplasia of the penis and seminal vesicles. This is a permanent and irreversible sequel of having been deprived of his own testicular androgens in the early days and weeks of life, which is obviously a period when the future growth program of the sex organs can be permanently affected by absence of the testes.

The caution against a too easy transfer of principles from one species to another needs again to be sounded in connection with the neonatally castrated hamster. Though the findings in this species closely follow those in the rat (Swanson, 1970, 1971), they are not identical. Neonatally castrated male hamsters, later given an ovarian implant, replicated their female controls in cyclic display of feminine mating behavior in the presence of a stud male. By contrast, males castrated in adulthood and given an ovarian transplant displayed lordosis not in cycles but continuously in response to a mounting male. Their own hypothalamic-pituitary mechanism could not make the transplanted ovary function cyclically. When the transplant was removed from the animals of all subgroups and the female hormones, estrogen plus progesterone, were given acyclically by injection, then all were continuously, and not cyclically receptive of stud males. This finding applied to neonatally castrated females as well as males.

Males castrated in adulthood resumed masculine mounting behavior if injected with testosterone propionate and tested with a receptive female, but this behavior could not be induced in neonatally castrated males or females, nor in adult castrated females injected with testosterone.

The resumption of masculine mounting behavior in males castrated in adulthood also occurred, paradoxically enough, if they were tested, as above, with receptive females after receiving an ovarian transplant. Since the same effect could not be achieved by injecting female hormones, one may implicate ovarian androgens as the responsible hormones (Swanson, 1971).

All told, data from the hamster suggest that the primacy of feminine mating behavior is more pronounced in this species than in the rat. Even the normal male reveals a vigorous capacity for mating as a female if he has been castrated, given female hormonal treatment, and paired with a stud male. Uncastrated, it is an absolute prerequisite to his masculine mating behavior that a small amount of androgen should have been present postnatally. The quantity is apparently very small: in the hamster it is experimentally easy to suppress the feminine behavior potential in the female by neonatally androgenizing her. It is also experimentally easy to suppress such manifestations of feminine-type behavior as are displayed by the normal male by neonatally injected extra androgen. The suppression is then more complete than that usually induced by the normal neonatal testes.

To return to the rat—no one has tested the neonatally castrated male with a combination of estrogen, progesterone, and androgen so as to imitate the experiment of injecting androgen into an intact adult female. Pfaff and Zigmond (1971) found that they could obtain the feminine pattern of response to a stud male if they injected the adult experimental male (neonatally castrated) with estrogen and omitted the progesterone, or if they retained the progesterone and substituted androgen for the estrogen.

The story of neonatal (or prenatal) hormonal effects on behavior is like a story in which a juggler throws a ball into the air, where it doubles and returns to him as two balls, each of which also doubles, so that there are four, each of which doubles so there are eight, and so on. The source of all this complexity is, of course, the very dimorphism of sex itself. Thus there are genetic male and female fetuses or neonates, each of which can be castrated and deprived of their natural male or female hormone, or exposed to more of either, or both. Hence, one has already, at the outset, 12 groups.

Each of these 12 groups may at the age of puberty be left untreated or injected with androgen or with estrogen, making a total of 36 groups. Each of the 36 groups may then be behaviorally tested with a partner of the same sex or opposite sex, making a total of 72 groups—to say nothing of testing with special partners themselves subject to experimental hormonal or other treatment. Add to all of this complexity a timing effect, necessitating that some experiments need to be repeated on perhaps as many as ten groups of differing age. Add also such other variables as the substitution of pharmacological for surgical castration, the substitution of one form of androgen or estrogen for another, the substitution of different quantities of hormone administered, and the simultaneous use of a hormone and one of its pharmacological antagonists. No wonder that investigators have had to limit themselves! They have focused their attention on selected programs of treatment and testing to the neglect of others, dependent on their chief theoretical interest and orientation in research. Understandable though it is, this selectivity has left some gaps in information which, hopefully, will be filled.

One of the gaps pertains to variation of the sex of the partner when testing behavior as a sequel to the various hormonal-priming conditions. The standard procedure has been followed of using a normal stud male as the partner when testing an experimental animal for feminine behavior and a normal estrous female partner when testing the experimental animal for masculine behavior.

One exception is in the work of Swanson (1970), already quoted. Another is in the work of Dörner (1969), who has been theoretically interested in the relevance of animal studies to human homosexuality. He reasoned that the homosexual counterpart of man in rat experiments would be the neonatally castrated—and therefore deandrogenized—male rat, subsequently in adulthood maintained on replacement androgen (not estrogen plus progesterone) and mated not only with a normal receptive female in estrus but, alternatively, with a normal stud male. The frequency of mounts on the estrous female could then be compared with the frequency of receptive, lordosis responses given to the stud male.

Making comparisons on the basis of 5-min. testing sessions, Dörner found that neonatally castrated males which had been androgen-injected as adults showed a higher proportion of receptive, lordosis responses toward stud males than of mounting responses toward estrous females, despite the essentially masculine (albeit diminished) configuration of their own genitalia.

A control group of males, normal until adulthood, when they were castrated and treated with androgen, showed no lordosis response toward stud male partners. A control group of females, normal until adulthood, when ovariectomized and treated with androgen, showed a lesser tendency than the experimental male animals to mount estrous female partners and a greater tendency to be mounted by a stud male partner. Thus the neonatally castrated, deandrogenized males did not behave exactly like either males or females that had grown up uncastrated insofar as their scores for dimorphic mating behavior were concerned. In this experiment, as in others involving neonatal castration, a peripheral neural effect from the hypoplastic genitalia cannot, by today's methods, be distinguished from a central, brain effect.

Dörner's data on the rat have not been fully replicated on the hamster, but there are some pertinent findings from the laboratory of Swanson (1971). Female hamsters castrated in adulthood and injected with testosterone propionate show no mating behavior with either a male or female partner. By contrast, normal males castrated in adulthood and given estrogen plus progesterone display feminine mating behavior with a male partner. Neonatally castrated males subsequently injected with testosterone propionate in adulthood show no sexual behavior with either a male or female partner; the same happens in neonatally castrated females injected with testosterone in adulthood.

Dörner (1968) has also experimentally tested a model of female homosexuality. This model deviates slightly from its counterpart for male homosexuality in that female rats were neonatally androgenized and later ovariectomized and primed not with female hormones but with androgen at the age of puberty. They were then test-mated with estrous females *vs.* stud males, so that lordosis *vs.* mounting responses could be compared. In spite of their having a vagina and at most only a slightly enlarged clitoris, mounting of other females occurred significantly more often than lordosis responses to stud males. If androgens were administered prenatally as well as postnatally, the female rat was born masculinized with a penis, and the remainder of the experimental treatment being the same as above, lordosis and other components of female coition were completely suppressed. In these animals the frequency of mountings and ejaculator-like patterns and the refractory periods that followed them did not differ significantly from those manifested by a genetic male control group.

Swanson's data indicate that the female hamster testosterone-injected at birth may be bisexual in mating behavior when later tested with estrogen plus progesterone. She may crouch for the male, but will also try to mount the estrous female. A male similarly treated will also mount, whereas had he not been androgen-treated at birth, he would react only with feminine crouching (lordosis) with a male as a partner. The added testosterone at birth activates a bisexual potential in the female hamster and inactivates or diminishes the routine, normal bisexual potential of the normal male.

As applied to the human condition, studies such as those of Dörner and Swanson cannot be explanatory in studies of human psychosexuality, but only suggestive of new hypotheses to be investigated.

MATING BEHAVIOR OF ANTIANDROGENIZED, HERMAPHRODITIC MALE RATS AND HAMSTERS

Neumann and his colleagues discovered the antiandrogenic properties of the steroid cyproterone acetate. They were engaged in testing a large range of newly synthesized steroids for biological activity. When they injected this substance into newborn male rats, it induced a pharmacological castrating effect, not only on anatomical genital development but also on subsequent sexual behavior. The behavioral effect closely parallels that of neonatal surgical castration (Neumann and Elger, 1966). When their own testes were left intact, the rats were capable, postpubertally, of a masculine type of response to an estrous female. If, however, they were castrated in adulthood and provided with implanted ovaries, they then displayed a marked feminine type of response when approached by a stud male.

This result was quite different from the observation on the control group of males, castrated later than the newborn period, who showed little or no female behavior, even when they were injected with up to 50 times as much estradiol as is sufficient to evoke the female response in males castrated at birth (Grady and Phoenix, 1963).

As in the case of bisexuality in the androgenized female, the theoretical significance of the bisexual potential revealed by Neumann's investigations is considerable: one conjectures the possibility of a pharmacological effect on the human male fetus predisposing it to a potential for bisexual behavior after puberty. The dramatic and heuristic impact of this experiment is less, however, than the experiment in which Neumann and his colleagues began antiandrogenization of the genetic male offspring by injecting the pregnant mother rat with cyproterone acetate during the critical prenatal period when the external sex organs of the fetus are being differentiated and by injecting the newborn male for 3 weeks after birth.

The effect of this treatment is to produce a vagina that in anatomy closely approximates that of the normal female (Neumann and Elger, 1965). The treatment is not effective in feminizing the internal accessory reproductive organs, and it does not change the gonads from testes to ovaries. Thus, it is possible for the genetically male animal with an experimentally produced vagina to reach the age of puberty with two undescended testes which, being undescended, are subject to temperature-induced sterility but secrete their normal quota of male sex hormone.

With their testes intact in adulthood, these animals behaved bisexually (Neumann and Elger, 1966). They were capable of a masculine type of response to an estrous female. They would pursue a female in estrus, sniff and lick her genitalia, and mount her, though with less purposeful behavior than that shown by normal male controls. Their mounting attempts were reduced by 50%, and only a small number of these mounts were normal performances. More than 80% of the attempted mounts were incomplete. The animals tried to mount from one side, over the head of the female, or even fled from the female altogether.

When the same animals were exposed to normal stud males, they were treated as females by their partners. The studs pursued them, sniffed and licked the vagina and perineum, as they would with normal females, and then attempted to mount them. The vaginalized males raised their tails, as a normal female would, but did not crouch in the normal lordosis position to effect copulation, as would a normal estrous female. Nonetheless, they sometimes allowed the stud male to mount. Alternatively, they exhibited the defense postures of a female not in estrus or overtly repulsed the male.

In order to make comparisons, some of the vaginalized males were castrated at the age of 3 months and implanted with the ovaries of infantile female rats. As adults, many of these experimental animals underwent estrus cycles. They were then able to behave in the manner of normal females. They were responded to by stud males as if they were normal females. On the day of estrus, they frequently reacted to the mounting attempts of a stud male by going into the position of lordosis, with elevation of the tail, squeaking, and manifestation of other features typical of the female response.

Because their sexual anatomy was changed, as well as their hormonal priming in adulthood, these animals raise a semantic issue about the definition of homosexuality. Did their behavior qualify as homosexual when they were mounted by the male, or when they mounted the female phallically quite inadequate to accomplish intromission? Common sense says that the anatomical and not the genetic or hormonal sex is primary in this context: the vaginalized genetic males were behaviorally homosexual when trying to mate with another rat that also had a vagina. Nonetheless, when they were mounted by a stud male, one might say that though they did not qualify as anatomically or morphologically homosexual, genetically and gonadally they were homosexual. Whether or not they were also hormonally homosexual depended on their hormonal treatment status at the time.

What Neumann and his colleagues discovered in the rat, Swanson (1970) found to hold true also for the hamster feminized *in utero* and rendered partially hermaphroditic by cyproterone (she used the plain and not the acetate form). Swanson reported that, with their testes intact, cyproterone-treated males attempted to mount receptive females. They could not achieve intromission, however, presumably because of their genital maldevelopment, and frequently slid over the back of the female or attempted aberrant mounts.

After castration, these animals resembled normal males that had been castrated in adulthood, showing loss of mating behavior. They further resembled castrated normal males in that testosterone, but not estrogen plus progesterone, would reinstate male mating behavior. The hormones released by ovarian implants, as contrasted with injected estrogen plus progesterone, were adequate to elicit male behavior toward receptive females. The same effect applied to the castrated normal males.

Female mating behavior in cyproterone-treated males could be elicited under the same conditions as in normal males, namely, when they were given estrogen plus progesterone and tested with a stud male. Some but not all of the cyproterone-treated males manifested feminine mating cycles when given ovarian implants that could be cyclically programmed by the cyclically functioning hypothalamic-pituitary mechanism.

The influence of prenatal cyproterone had a contradictory effect on nonmating dimorphic behavior in the open-field test. Cyproterone-treated males did not show the typical feminine response of uninhibited ambulation. In addition, female littermates who also had been prenatally exposed to cyproterone became reticent instead of free-roaming and obtained low ambulation scores, within the male range.

With respect to aggression, prenatal cyproterone did not make males either more or less aggressive than control males. Both were typically defeated' by females, as is usual among hamsters, females being larger than males.

EFFECT OF HOMOTYPIC NEONATAL HORMONE INJECTIONS ON SUBSEQUENT MATING BEHAVIOR

For the sake of completeness, one wants to know the effect of estrogen added to the neonatal female and of androgen added to the neonatal male. It has been already noted in this review that at least one estrogen, specifically estradiol benzoate, simulates androgen in the female and has a masculinizing effect on behavior (Levine and Mullins, 1964; Whalen and Edwards, 1967).

The effect of androgen administered prenatally or neonatally to the male rat will depend on the type of androgen used. When the testosterone normally produced by the developing testis is augmented by injection of exogenous testosterone, then there is no observable effect on subsequent behavior (Whalen, 1968). If the neonatal rat is castrated prior to the injection of testosterone, then the injected hormone completely replaces the missing testicular secretion.

When the neonatal rat is castrated and given replacement treatment with androstendione instead of testosterone, the injected hormone is not identical in effect with the secretions of the testes. In their subsequent behavior, male rats so treated will be able to display lordosis quite readily when in the presence of a stud male, if given prior injections of estrogen plus progesterone. Conversely, if given prior injections of testosterone propionate, they will display mounting behavior, intromission, and ejaculation when paired with estrous females. This finding was independently demonstrated by Goldfoot et al. (1969) and Stern (1969).

The behavior produced experimentally in rats in the above experiments replicates that which can be elicited from male hamsters that have a normal untreated infancy. If the intact male hamster is castrated in adulthood and then injected with estrogen plus progesterone, he responds readily with lordosis when approached by a stud male. Injected with testosterone propionate, his behavior changes, so that he responds to the estrous female by mounting with intromission and ejaculation (Swanson, 1971).

When testosterone propionate, 300 mg., is injected into the intact male hamster at birth, it is able to have an effect on the lordosis response reported above—one which would have been entirely missed in the design of most experiments. Swanson (1971) was able to discover this effect because she tested her experimental animals with both male and female partners after castrating and hormone-injecting them in adulthood. In this particular instance, the neonatally testosterone-injected males did not show the typical lordosis response when injected with estrogen plus progesterone and paired with a stud male. Instead, they manifested something entirely new: a mounting response in the presence of the estrous female, exactly the same as if they had been injected not with estrogen and progesterone, but with testosterone propionate instead.

The female hamster given parallel treatment responded similarly, that is, with masculine mounting behavior in response to injected female hormones, when in the presence of an estrous female.

In the light of these experiments, one can speak of an ultramasculinizing effect of testosterone treatment of the intact neonatal male hamster. The criterion of ultramasculinism in the male is that he never shows lordosis behavior as the regular male may be induced to do. In his counterpart, the neonatally testosteronized female, the frequency of the lordosis response at the time of estrus, in the presence of a stud male, may be either reduced or unchanged.

These findings, suggesting as they do degrees of early masculinizing, may eventually prove to be of relevance with respect to the differentiation of gender identity in human beings. They may have special reference to the differentiation of gender identity as homosexual.

The dramatic antimasculinizing effects of neonatal castration on the male have no parallel in neonatal castration of the female (Whalen and Edwards, 1967).

EFFECT OF NEONATAL HORMONES ON NONMATING BEHAVIOR

Laboratory rats provided with a running wheel maintain extraordinarily regular daily running schedules. The intact female, as compared with the male, manifests cyclic fluctuations in running time, from day to day, in synchrony with her cyclic estrus. This sexual dimorphism of running scheules can be changed by neonatal hormone injections (see review by Gorski, 1971). Neonatally feminized males with an ovarian transplant secrete ovarian hormones cyclically as do females. They display corresponding cyclic fluctuations in running time. By contrast, rats with persistent estrus do not have cyclic running schedules, though the amount of running activity is not decreased to the male level, unless neonatal hormonal treatment happens to leave the animal, as an adult, in persistent diestrus.

Gorski (1971) also reviews various findings on saccharin preference, open-field behavior, and emergence behavior in rats. Unless the drinking water contains saccharin, water intake is the same for male and female rats. When the water contains saccharin, females drink more. Neonatally androgenized females have a masculine saccharin-preference intake. The estrogen, estradiol benzoate, cannot be used neonatally to produce this effect, even though it will mimic some of the other neonatal effects of the androgen, testosterone propionate.

Placed in an open field, intact female rats move about more freely and drop fewer fecal pellets than do males. Neonatal testosterone propionate treatment changed this behavior in females, making them more reticent, like males. More of these animals than intact females were reticent also with respect to emerging from an enclosed box into an open arena. They thus resembled intact males. Neonatal castration did not, however, make males more venturesome in emerging from the box. These neonatally induced changes in open-field and emergence behavior in the female occur independently of the hormonal status of the animal being tested as an adult.

Open-field and emergence behavior were tested in the neonatally androgenized hamster by Swanson (1967). The findings were the same as above for the rat, namely, reduced ambulation and reduced emergence. The effect could be produced by estradiol benzoate as well as testosterone propionate, neonatally. The change is not observed prior to puberty, but it persists postpubertally, even after gonadectomy and adrenalectomy (Swanson, 1969). There is, however, an interaction effect with experience, for hamsters that had been open-field tested in prepuberty failed to show the sexually dimorphic effect when tested in postpuberty.

Conner and Levine (1969) studied fighting in neonatally castrated male rats treated with testosterone in adulthood. These animals showed a female-like fighting pattern in a fighting test in which two same-sexed animals were placed in a wire cage and given an electric shock. The neonatally castrated males differed significantly from normal males and also from the other males castrated in adulthood and given replacement testosterone. They behaved like ovariectomized females treated with testosterone; that is, they fought less and needed a more intense shock before they displayed fighting.

Fighting for dominance is another pattern of nonmating behavior that may be influenced by the neonatal hormonal history, while not being exclusively dependent on it. Edwards (1969) found that male and female mice given no treatment other than castration at 30 days of age would when full grown attack a juvenile mouse that intruded into the older animal's home cage. When it was experimentally arranged that the intruder would be of the same size, sex, and experimental history, then neonatal hormonal status was found to make a difference (Edwards, 1968, 1969). In particular, females that had been injected with testosterone propionate on the first day of life resembled control males in attacking an intruder—100% of control males attacked, compared to 95.5% of androgenized females and only 20% of control females. All three groups had been similarly injected, as adults, with testosterone propionate prior to the fighting test.

In another experiment, Edwards (1970) found that even if ovariectomy was postponed until day 30, the masculine style of dominance attack could still be testosterone-induced later in 75% instead of the expected 25% of the fully grown females, if a large amount of testosterone had also been injected from day 30 through day 50. Thus it appears that early androgenization of the dominance-attack response has a long sensitive period and is subject to a dose-response effect.

An essential part of the female role, after giving birth, is taking care of the young. Maternal behavior can also be influenced by early manipulation of gonadal hormones and their modification of neural differentiation. As yet, there are very few reports. Neumann and his colleagues observed that antiandrogenized male rats that had been subsequently treated with female sex hormones, to the point where they were capable of lactation, cared for young rats and retrieved them into the nest, a behavior which is normally rarely observed in males. It was not possible to keep the newborns alive for more than a week in the care of antiandrogenized males, since induced lactation was not sufficient to nourish the litter (Neumann *et al.*, 1970).

The building of a nest is hormone-dependent but not sexually dimorphic behavior, according to the evidence of Lisk *et al.* (1969) in a study of mice. They found an estradiol injection to inhibit nest building and a progesterone injection to induce it. The optimal hormonal stimulus appeared to be high progesterone and very low estrogen. Similar reactions were obtained from males as from females, though of lesser degree in males. The difference between the sexes in manifesting nest-building behavior in ordinary life is, on the basis of this evidence, hormonally but not neurally determined, and it is not normally influenced by hormonal events at the time of neonatal sexual differentiation of the brain.

EFFECT OF BEHAVIORAL EXPERIENCE

There is a tradition left over from nineteenth century biological materialism that makes some experimentalists of sexual behavior profoundly embarrassed by the idea that life experience might have any effect on the differentiation of behavioral dimorphism. The preference of such experimental traditionalists is to assume that all sex differences in sexual behavior can be accounted for exclusively in terms of genetic and/or prenatal hormonal or adult hormonal engineering, and to plan their experiments accordingly.

Young (1961), a pioneer in hormones and behavior, was among the first to point out that individual differences among animals, including differences in social history, introduce variability into experimental results. Even so, today's investigators seldom systematically explore the interaction of hormones and past experience in producing a given pattern of sexual response. One exception is an experiment by Clemens *et al.* (1969). These investigators injected 10 mg. of testosterone propionate into newborn female rats. As adults, they were spayed and injected with replacement hormone (estrogen plus progesterone). Then, tested with a stud male, they failed, as expected, to show the lordosis response. This failure was reversible, however, if the experimental animals were given a two-hour adaptation period in the test arena prior to the behavior test. Gorski (1971) conjectures that neonatal androgen may have rendered the females more sensitive to the copulatory environment, possibly to olfactory cues, in the manner that is usually typical of males. Once adapted to the environment, they became disinhibited. The behavior that was then released was not masculine in type, but the feminine response of lordosis.

In a different experiment, Clemens et al. (1970) found that the lordosis quotient of an adult group of neonatally androgen-treated female rats increased when the behavioral test was extended until the stud males had mounted them 50 times (under the conditions of the experiment, the females had been primed with estrogen alone, progesterone having been omitted). Here one sees an increase in lordosis in response to immediately prior experience.

EFFECT OF PRENATAL SIBLINGS AND PRENATAL STRESS

No one knows how many apparently normal genetic females not treated prenatally with hormones and born with normal-looking female genitalia might, in fact, have been subject to prenatal androgen excess insufficient to influence the external anatomy, though perhaps sufficient to influence the brain. A hitherto unsuspected example of such a possible prenatal influence was recently reported by Clemens (personal communication) from Michigan State University. He found that the larger the number of brothers in a litter of rats, the greater the likelihood that the sisters would display masculine mounting behavior when hormonally primed with androgen in adulthood. If the androgens of the brothers had influenced the brains of their sisters, then one has here an effect reminiscent of the freemartin phenomenon in cattle.

The converse of the prenatally androgenized genetic female with normal genital anatomy would be the genetic male with normal genitalia but a prenatal history of androgen deficit. There is another recent discovery by Ward (1971) at Villanova

University that points in the direction of an androgen-deficit effect on the brains of genitally normal males. She exposed pregnant female rats to the extreme stress of constraint under glaring light, in order to test the effect on the offspring of the mother's hormonal response to stress. The result was that the sons grew up to have lessened testicular weight and penis length. They were deficient in male mating behavior as adults when tested with receptive females. They also more readily displayed the lordosis response typical of the female if castrated and treated with estrogen-progesterone substitution therapy. These findings inevitably raise unanswered questions about the origins of masculine failure in some effeminate homosexual men.[3]

PRENATALLY ANDROGENIZED, HERMAPHRODITIC FEMALES: MATING AND NON-MATING BEHAVIOR IN THE GUINEA PIG AND RHESUS MONKEY

The principles of anatomical differentiation as hermaphrodite are two: androgenization of the female and antiandrogenization of the male. The latter is exemplified in the rat experiments of Neumann and his colleagues and the hamster experiments of Swanson and Crossley. Behaviorally, their findings were that prenatally antiandrogenized rats are capable of behaving bisexually in later life, dependent on the type of sex hormone then present in the bloodstream to activate sexual responsiveness and the sex of the test partner.

The opposite experiment is prenatal androgenization of the female. The first experiment of this type done for the purpose of examining subsequent behavior was that of Phoenix *et al.* (1959) on the guinea pig. They reported that hermaphroditic female guinea pigs, completely masculinized prenatally with a penis, were capable in adulthood of a lower feminine and higher masculine component in the bisexualism of mating behavior, as compared with the behavior of normal control females receiving the same adult hormonal injections. Their scores were also less feminine and more masculine than those of other females who received a lesser hormonal dosage prenatally and were therefore able to develop normal female external genitalia. These latter animals did, however, show some defeminizing effect of the prenatal treatment on subsequent mating scores.

These guinea pig experiments are inconclusive with respect to the effect of the anatomy of the external sex organs on adult behavior, since none of the animals was subjected to surgical feminization. They are further inconclusive insofar as all permutations and combinations of sex hormone injection and sex of mate were not tested in adulthood. Nonetheless, they are experiments which occupy a very important place, historically, in opening up the question of prenatal hormonal organizing effect on the central nervous system that will eventually mediate sexual behavior. They led directly to the first study of experimental hermaphroditism in a primate species. The same investigators produced hermaphroditic female monkeys with a penis by injecting the pregnant mother with large doses of testosterone.

The juvenile behavior of hermaphroditized females has shown some hermaphroditic changes, presumably as a sequel to prenatal androgenization and prior to and thus independently of the priming influence of pubertal hormones (Phoenix *et al.*, 1967; Goy, 1970). In the other species heretofore mentioned, changes in childhood behavior have been either not manifested or not looked for. The juvenile macaque female hermaphrodite behaves in a manner reminiscent of tomboyism in girls. More in the manner of her male than her formal female controls, she shows an increased amount of play initiation, rough-and-tumble play, chasing play, and playful threats. The frequency of mounting play is also increased in proportion to the frequency of hind-end presentation as a gesture of sexual invitation. Developmentally, the pattern of mounting also takes on a masculine stance. The juvenile hermaphroditic animal lifts its feet off the ground and clasps them around the shanks of the normal female's hind legs as she presents on all fours and is mounted from behind. When a normal female mounts another, she keeps her own feet on the ground.

Developmental behavioral studies of the first generation of hermaphroditic female macaques continue at the Oregon Regional Primate Center. Retarded by an average of nearly 8 months in the onset of menstruation (Goy, 1970), the nine oldest hermaphroditic females are now postpubertal. The full story of the adult sexual behavior of these animals remains to be investigated. The variables to be manipulated include the hormonal status of the hermaphrodite, replacing her own female hormones with androgen; the anatomy of the external genitalia, with surgical feminization and externalization of the vagina; and the sex of the partner.

FETAL HORMONES, BRAIN DIMORPHISM, AND BEHAVIOR

The experimental task of identifying and tracing brain tracts, with all their tributaries and cross-connections, that mediate sexual behavior is difficult and delicate, regardless of sex. Tracing of the homologous tracts of sexual behavioral activation in the male and female brain is more than has been achieved at the present time. No wonder, then, that little can yet be said regarding the various structures of the brain that are subject prenatally to dimorphism of hormonal organizing influence on subsequent behavior. No wonder, likewise, that little can be said with accuracy regarding the localization of brain changes when prenatal or neonatal male hormone injections change the subsequent balance of manifest sexual behavior in the genetic female—or, vice versa, when antiandrogenization or castration changes the balance of manifest sexual behavior in the genetic male.

The most direct evidence so far available comes from a rat experiment (Nadler, 1968) in which the behavioral changes of the anovulatory, persistent estrus syndrome could be induced by direct implantation of androgen into the hypothalamus of the newborn.

Another method of tracing brain changes related to sexual behavior is by tracing the focalized uptake, in the brain, of radioactively labelled hormone (see review by Gorski, 1971), the animals first having been hormone-treated in infancy or fetal life. So far, this method has yielded no definitive information concerning brain loci that regulate sexually dimorphic behavior.

A large part of today's knowledge of where early hormonal treatments might exert their action on the brain is derived by inference from brain lesion studies in normal males and females that are subsequently treated and tested with extra sex hormone. Lisk (1967) summed up the prevailing point of view with respect to the hypothalamus: in addition to the regulator of the pituitary-gonadal axis, in the region of the median eminence, there is another hormone-sensitive system essential for feminine lordosis behavior in several species. It is situated in the preoptic region of the anterior hypothalamus. This same area, especially its midline structures, must be intact for expression of the sexual behavior patterns of the male.

As for hormone-sensitive centers in other brain structures, the full story is yet to be unraveled. The same is true with respect to prenatal and neonatal influences of sex hormones on neural cells at the periphery.

PRINCIPLE OF DIMORPHIC BEHAVIORAL DIFFERENTIATION

There are two paradigms of differentiation of the sexual anatomy. One applies to the gonads, which differentiate first, and then also to the internal reproductive tracts. In both instances, Nature initially lays down the anlagen for both the male and the female organs, and then allows one set to regress and wither away permanently. The other set proliferates and develops into the adult organs of generation. The chemistry that regulates gonadal differentiation is not known. The differentiation of the internal organs is chemically supervised by hormones released by the embryonic gonads. No gonads, no male. Female differentiation takes place if no male hormone interferes. Moreover, it does not require female hormone or any kind of hormone. Male differentiation takes place only if the embryonic testis releases its chemical messengers.

The same principle of male hormone for male differentiation and no male hormone for female differentiation applies to the external genitalia. Here the second paradigm applies: from the same anlagen, homologous female and male structures differentiate. The end result is fixed and irreversible.

With respect to differentiation of the brain, experimental evidence suggests that the nuclei of the hypothalamus in charge of pituitary-gonadal cycling follow the same paradigm as the external genitalia: without androgen, they differentiate a permanently cyclic, feminine function; with androgen (or a substitute), feminine cycling is irreversibly abolished.

The evidence that emerges from this review suggests that, insofar as brain and behavior are prenatally or neonatally hormone-influenced, differentiation of certain patterns of mating behavior, and by inference of the brain that programs them, follows the paradigm of internal organ differentiation. The rule would appear to be that male-female bipotentiality applies initially, prior to any hormonal infleunce. The original disposition of the organism is to be bisexually competent in mating behavior. The bipotentiality persists in the presence of no hormonal influence during the early, critical period of differentiation. Bipotentiality also continues in existence if the early hormonal environment is feminine, so that either component of mating behavior can be elicited in adulthood, dependent, among other things, on whether the eliciting hormone is androgen or estrogen.

Bipotentiality is resolved in favor of unipolar masculinity of mating behavior if the early hormonal influence at the critical differentiating period is androgenic. The feminine component is inhibited, and once this is accomplished it will manifest itself only in response to special conditions (for example, direct brain stimulation), or not at all. The completeness of inhibition of feminine behavioral potential, in the course of normal differentiation, varies across species. For example, it is more complete in the rat than in the hamster. In man, it is probably not very complete, and is perhaps individually variable, as well.

FOOTNOTES

1. Research support by Grant 5K03-HD18635 and Grant 2R01-HD00325, U.S.P.H.S. This review is an extract (Chap. 5) from a forthcoming book, *Man and Woman: The Differentiation and Dimorphism of Gender Identity,* by John Money and Anke A. Ehrhardt, and is here published by permission of The Johns Hopkins Press, Baltimore, Maryland.
2. In the rat, among other specicies, the induction of estrus requires the presence first of estrogen and then of progesterone, about 4 hr later, on

the day of proestrus. The exact time relationship is relative to the stage of the estrus cycle. See Lisk (1969).

3. Preliminary data from a new pilot study by Dr. Ward reveal that when prenatally stressed males are castrated in adulthood, given replacement testosterone, and then mating-tested with stud males, some will show female behavior, an effect not seen in the control animals.

REFERENCES

BARRACLOUGH, C. A., and GORSKI, R. A. (1962). "Studies on mating behaviour in the androgen-sterilized female rat in relation to the hypothalamic regulation of sexual behavior." *J. Endocrinol.* **25**: 175-182.

BEACH, F. A. (1947). "A review of physiological and psychological studies of sexual behavior in mammals." *Physiol. Rev.* **27**: 240-307.

BEACH, F. A. (1968). "Factors involved in the control of mounting behavior by female mammals." In Diamond, M. (ed.), *Perspectives in Reproduction and Sexual Behavior;* Indiana University Press, Bloomington, Ind.

BEACH, F. A., NOBLE, R. G., and ORNDOFF, R. K. (1969). "Effects of perinatal androgen treatment on responses of male rats to gonadal hormones in adulthood." *J. Comp. Physiol. Psychol.* **68**: 490-497.

CALHOUN, J. B. (1962). "Population density and social pathology." *Sci. Amer.* **206**: 139-148.

CLEMENS, L. G., HIROI, M., and GORSKI, R. A. (1969). "Induction and facilitation of female mating behavior in rats treated neonatally with low doses of testosterone propionate." *Endocrinology* **84**: 1430-1438.

CLEMENS, L. G., SHRYNE, J., and GORSKI, R. A. (1970). "Androgen and development of progesterone responsiveness in male and female rats." *Physiol. Behav.* **5**: 673-678.

CONNER, R. L., and LEVINE, S. (1969). Hormonal influences on aggressive havior. In Garattini, S., and Sigg, E. B. (eds.), *Aggressive Behavior,* Excerpta Medica Foundation, Amsterdam.

DÖRNER, G. (1968). "Hormonal induction and prevention of female homosexuality." *J. Endocrinol.* **42**: 163-164.

DÖRNER, G. (1969). *"Zur Frage einer neuroendokrinen Pathogenese, Prophylaxe und Therapie angeborener Sexualdeviationen." Deutsch. Med. Wochenschr.* **94**: 390-396.

EDWARDS, D. A. (1968). "Mice: Fighting by neonatally androgenized females." *Science* **161**: 1027-1028.

EDWARDS, D. A. (1969). "Early androgen stimulation and aggressive behavior in male and female mice." *Physiol. Behav.* **4**: 333-338.

EDWARDS, D. A. (1970). "Post-neonatal androgenization and adult aggressive behavior in female mice." *Physiol. Behav.* **5**: 465-467.

GOLDFOOT, D. A., FEDER, H. H., and GOY, R. W. (1969). "Development of bisexuality in the male rat treated neonatally with androstenedione." *Physiol. Psychol.* **67**: 41-45.

GORSKI, R. A. (1971). "Gonadal hormones and the perinatal development of neuroendocrine function." In Martini, L., and Ganong, W.F. (eds.), *Frontiers of Neuroendocrinology; 1971;* Oxford University Press, New York.

GOY, R. W. (1970). "Experimental control of psychosexuality." In Harris, G. W., and Edwards, R. G. (eds.), *A Discussion on the Determination of Sex,* Philosophical Transactions of the Royal Society, London, Series B, Vol. 259, No. 828.

GRADY, K. L., and PHOENIX, C. H. (1963). "Hormonal determinants of mating behavior; the display of feminine behavior by adult male rats castrated neonatally." *Amer. Zool.* **3:** 482-483.

GRADY, K. L., PHOENIX, C. H., and YOUNG, W. C. (1965). "Role of the developing rat testis in differentiation of the neural tissues meditating mating behavior." *J. Comp. Physiol. Psychol.* **59:** 176-182.

HARLOW, H. F., and HARLOW, M. K. (1965). "The effect of rearing conditions on behavior." In Money, J. (ed.), *Sex Research New Developments,* Holt, Rinehart and Winston, New York.

HARRIS, G. W., and LEVINE, S. (1965). "Sexual differentiation of the brain and its experimental control." *J. Physiol.* **181:** 379-400.

KOLLAR, E. J., PECKWITH, W. C., and EDGERTON, R. B. (1968). "Sexual behavior of the ARL colony chimpanzees." *J. Nerv. Ment. Dis.* **147:** 444-459.

LEVINE, S., and MULLINS, R. (1964). "Estrogen administered neonatally affects adult sexual behavior in male and female rats." *Science* **144:** 185-187.

LISK, R. D. (1967). "Sexual behavior: Hormonal control." In Martini, L., and Ganong, W. G. (eds.), *Neuroendocrinology,* Vol. II, Academic Press, New York.

LISK, R. D. (1969). "Progesterone: Role in limitation of ovulation and sex behavior in mammals." *Trans. N.Y. Acad. Sci.* **31:** 593-601.

LISK, R. D., PRETLOW, R. A., and FRIEDMAN, S. M. (1969). "Hormonal stimulation necessary for elicitation of maternal nest-building in the mouse *(Mus musculus)." Anim. Behav.* **17:** 730-737.

NADLER, R. D. (1965). "Masculinization of the female rat by intracranial implantation of androgen in infancy." Unpublished doctoral dissertation, University of California, Los Angeles.

NADLER, R. D. (1968). "Masculinization of female rats by intracranial implantation of androgen in infancy. "*J. Comp. Physiol. Psychol.* **66:** 157-167.

NADLER, R. D. (1969). "Differentiation of the capacity for male sexual behavior in the rat." *Hormones and Behavior* **1:** 53-63.

NEUMANN, F., and ELGER, W. (1965). "Proof of the activity of androgenic agents on the differentiation of the external genitalia, the mammary gland and the hypothalamic-pituitary system in rats." In *Androgens in Normal and Pathological Conditions,* International Congress Series No. 101, Proceedings of the Second Symposium on Steroid Hormones, Excerpta Medica, Amsterdam.

NEUMANN, F. and ELGER, W. (1966). "Permanent changes in gonadal function and sexual behaviour as a result of early feminization of male rats by treatment with an antiandrogenic steroid." *Endokrinologie* **50:** 209-225.

NEUMANN, F., STEINBECK, H., and HAHN, J. D. (1970). "Hormones and brain differentiation." In Martini, L. Motta, M., and Fraschini, F. (eds.), *The Hypothalamus;* Academic Press, New York.

PFAFF, D. W., and ZIGMOND, R. E. (1971). "Neonatal androgen effects on sexual and nonsexual behavior of adult rats tested under various hormone regimens." *Neuroendocrinology* **7:** 129-145.

PHOENIX, C. H., GOY, R. W., GERALL, A. A., and YOUNG, W. C. (1959). "Organizing action of prenatally administered testosterone propionate on the tissues mediating mating behavior in the female guinea pig." *Endocrinology* **65:** 369-382.

PHOENIX, C. H., GOY, R. W., and YOUNG, W. C. (1967). "Sexual behavior: General aspects." In Martini, L., and Ganong, W. F. (eds.), *Neuronendocrinology,* Vol. II, Academic Press, New York.

STERN, J. J. (1969). "Neonatal castration, androstenedione, and the mating behavior of the male rat." *J. Comp. Physiol. Psychol.* **69:** 608-612.

SWANSON, H. H. (1967). "Alteration of sex-typical behaviour in hamsters in open field and emergence tests by neonatal administration of androgen or oestrogen." *Anim. Behav.* **15:** 209-216.

SWANSON, H. H. (1969). "Interaction of experience with adrenal and sex hormones on the behavior of hamsters in the open field test." *Anim. Behav.* **17:** 148-154.

SWANSON, H. H. (1970). "Effects of castration at birth in hamsters of both sexes on luteinization of ovarian implants, oestrous cycles and sexual behavior." *J. Reprod. Fertil.* **21:** 183-186.

SWANSON, H. H. (1971). "Determination of the sex role in hamsters by the action of sex hormones in infancy" (paper read at the Society of Psychoneuroendocrinology). In *Symposium on the Influence of Hormones on the Nervous System, June 1970,* S. Karger, New York, in press.

SWANSON, H. H., and CROSSLEY, D. A. (1971). "Sexual behaviour in the golden hamster and its modification by neonatal administration of testosterone propionate." In Hamburgh, M., and Barrington, E. J. W. (eds.), *Hormones in Development;* Appleton-Century-Crofts, New York.

WARD, I. (1971). "Prenatal stress feminizes and demasculinizes the behavior of males." *Science* (in press).

WHALEN, R. E. (1964). "Hormone-induced changes in the organization of sexual behavior in the male rat." *J. Comp. Physiol. Psychol.* **57:** 175-182.

WHALEN, R. E. (1968). "Differentiation of the neural mechanisms which control gonadotropin secretion and sexual behavior." In Diamond, M. (ed.), *Perspectives in Reproduction and Sexual Behavior,* Indiana University Press, Bloomington, Ind.

WHALEN, R. E., and EDWARDS, D. A. (1966). "Sexual reversibility in neonatally castrated male rats." *J. Comp. Physiol. Psychol.* **62**: 307-310.

WHALEN, R. E., and EDWARDS, D. A. (1967). "Hormonal determinants of the development of masculine and feminine behavior in male and female rats." *Anat. Rec.* **157**: 173-180.

YOUNG, W. C. (1961). "The hormones and mating behavior." In Young, W. C. (ed.), *Sex and Internal Secretions,* Williams and Wilkins, Baltimore, chap. 19.

PART FOUR

THE PSYCHOLOGICAL DIMENSION

PSYCHOLOGY AND SEX DIFFERENCES

Patrick C. Lee

There is no definitive "Psychology of Sex Differences." In fact, there is considerable disagreement among psychologists on most aspects of sex differences, including what they are, how they develop, how one should study them, or even whether they are an important area of study in the first place. Most psychologists have scant professional interest in sex differences and probably believe as much and know as little about sex differences as the average educated layman. Thus, the reader who looks to psychology for a final answer to his questions about sex differences is bound to be disappointed. The reader in search of stimulating ideas, well-argued positions, and sometimes convincing, often uneven, concentrations of evidence may find greater satisfaction in the psychological literature. Readers who love ambiguity will be happiest of all. Much of this disputation and ambiguity is evident in the selections to follow. Perhaps a brief (and regrettably oversimplified) sketch of the history of the psychology of sex differences will serve to introduce these selections as well as place them in some meaningful context.

Many of the early psychologists showed little interest in sex differences. They tended to be generalists in search of "universal laws" of behavior, feeling, and thinking which applied to all human beings rather than to certain categories of people. For example, William James, generally recognized as the first great American psychologist, devoted about five pages to sex differences in his 1400 page, two volume classic, *The Principles of Psychology* (1890). In his section on "instincts," he mentioned that women showed greater sexual coyness and parental love than men (pp. 438-440, Vol. 2), but assigned so little importance to the matter that it was omitted entirely in his later abbreviated version written especially for students (1892, 478 pages). Another eminent psychologist, John Dewey, made fleeting mention of sex differences in his many published writings (e.g., Ratner, 1928, p. 283), but apparently conducted a lively personal correspondence with an associate which often included the theme of sex differences. Basically Dewey's position, both privately and publicly, was that women should be accorded the same individual treatment that men get as subjects of scientific inquiry. He maintained that the greatest block to scientific understanding of women was that they were treated as idealized types rather than as varied individuals (cf., Boydston, 1975). It is interesting to contrast this sentiment with that of G. Stanley Hall who wrote in 1904 that "an ideal or typical male is hard to define, but there is a standard ideal woman" (see selection).

Unlike generalists such as James and Dewey, Hall represented a very different point of view, that of "differential psychology." This latter perspective saw differences among various types of human beings as an irreducible reality and as an indispensable factor in the equation of human understanding. The differential school examined psychological phenomena as influenced by differences in age, intelligence, race, social class membership, body type, personality type, cultural background, and sex. Thus, sex was just one among several categories, and, unfortunately, the intervening decades of research on sex differences followed no systematic plan of inquiry; rather they have yielded a chaotic collection of discrete and disjointed findings. These have been periodically drawn together and reviewed by differential psychologists like Anastasi (1937), Tyler (see selection), and Garai and Scheinfeld (1968), almost always with comments about the near impossibility of the task.

However, there was one systematic thrust in the investigation of sex differences, and that was carried primarily by a small number of psychologists who developed what ultimately came to be known as "M-F scales" (Masculinity-Femininity scales). Two of the most comprehensive M-F scales were those developed by Terman and Miles (see selection) and Strong (see Tyler selection). These scales ferreted out an extraordinary range of sex differences and were serious attempts to establish scientifically valid and reliable means for differentiating between the sexes. Terman and Miles' objective was to develop standard measures of masculinity and femininity analogous to the measures of intelligence yielded by I.Q. tests. Strong's purpose was to develop a vocational interest inventory which would enhance the efficiency of vocational preparation and the relevance of vocational counseling for young men and women. Both projects were monumental efforts and were quite influential, beginning in the 1930s and extending through the 1950s. Recent social and political movements have had the effect of reducing the use of these and other M-F scales because the tests are viewed as discriminatory against women and as stereotyping both men and women. However, in all fairness, it should be mentioned that scale builders, including Terman, Miles, and Strong, have always been aware that their work was not free of problems. Their primary concerns have been with methodological and conceptual problems, but, at least in Strong's case, there also appeared to be a sensitivity to the potential misuse of M-F scales in the service of undesirable social ends.

One major problem is that the scales conceptualize aspects of masculinity and femininity as polar opposites on a single continuum. Thus, they tend to rule out serious examination of the co-existence in one person of masculine and feminine characteristics, however these may be defined. Moreover, since the scale items are designed, by definition, to discriminate between males and females, the scales do not include items which fail to discriminate. Thus, they do not reflect the real range of differences and similarities between males and females, but are distillations of an abstract notion of masculinity-femininity as bipolar characteristics. They tend to exaggerate differences and to minimize similarites. Interestingly enough, however, despite this deliberate bias, they yield puzzling irregularities.

Perhaps the most startling and persistent irregularity is the low correlations among the various scales. Correlations are positive, of course, but often dip into the .40s and .50s, certainly not acceptable for well-designed assessment devices. There are probably two reasons for the scales' failure to capture an "airtight" version of M-F differences. First the various scales often measure different aspects of M and F, some, for example, tapping interests (e.g., Strong) and others personality characteristics (e.g., Terman and Miles). A test-taker's personality, in other words, imperfectly predicts his interests, and vice versa. Second, and most fundamentally, the scales assume the existence of a palpable reality, i.e., that there is, in fact, a universe of stable and valid psychological differences between males and females. This assumption probably lies at the heart of the matter—its failure to hold has encouraged some psychometricians to abandon sex differences as a significant factor of human personality. It is almost with a sense of relief and mischief that R. B. Cattell, for example, concludes that "as far as the major source traits are concerned the important observation is apparently that men and women are primarily human personalities and secondarily of a particular sex!" (1965, p. 260). Long ago, in 1911, E. L. Thorndike had come to essentially the same conclusion when he wrote that ". . . it appears that if the primary sex characters—the instincts directly related to courtship, love, child-bearing, and nursing—are left out of account, the average man differs from the average woman far less than many men differ from one another" (1911, p. 30).

Twelve years after his original book on the *Vocational Interests of Men and Women* (1943), E. K. Strong offered this terse summary of scaling M-F differences: "The interests of men and women . . . are more similar than different. If we look for similarity we find it, if we look for dissimilarity we find it. The study of individual differences has pointed out differences and has placed a false emphasis on differences. . . . When the M-F scale is constructed, the interests common to both sexes are eliminated from consideration, being given zero weights, and the items on which the two sexes differ are given significant weights. The M-F scale expresses accordingly the maximum differences to be found between the two sexes. . . ." (1955, p. 121). In his earlier book, Strong reported that the average correlation between the interests of males and females was .69, indicating considerable similarity in interests (1943, p. 92). Ironically, Strong is often remembered as one who prescribed rather than described sex differences in vocational interests. Despite his disclaimers, such as the above, vocational interests labeled as "masculine" came to be viewed as abnormal for women, and vice versa. This was not his intention, but it was an unfortunate consequence of his work, as well as that of others who developed M-F scales.

A second major approach in psychology which eventually focused on sex differences was developmental psychology. As with the study of individual differences, G. Stanley Hall also lent his considerable prestige to the study of children's growth. For many years Arnold Gesell, one of Hall's students, was an important influence in keeping the "child studies" movement a vigorous and fruitful part of psychology. In the 1950s and particularly in the 1960s interest in child development and socialization expanded tremendously until it now stands as one of the major branches of psychology, and probably the fastest growing branch at that. As is usually the case in a burgeoning area of inquiry, specializations have formed in child development, and among these is a specialization in the differential development of sex identity in young males and females. Gesell and Ilg made extensive observations of children at their Yale clinic and established age-linked norms of development for boys and girls, many of which are described in their selection to follow. Their approach came to be known as "Normative-Maturational" theory and their overriding objective (reminiscent of Hall) was to discover the "natural laws of human growth." Thus, for example, they noted certain cycles in child development such as the alternation of periods of consolidation with periods of rapid spurts in growth. But beyond the formulation of such general principles of growth as these, their main contribution has been to leave us with a wealth of normative data on all aspects of child development, including sex-role development. For some time their work has not been given the recognition it once had, but there is a small body of psychologists (e.g., Elkind, 1974) who think that Gesell's work will be resuscitated as psychology gradually discovers that it has fashioned a science of childhood without fully undertaking the prerequisite step of building a natural history of childhood.

Nevertheless, normative-maturational theory does not give an adequate treatment of the etiology of sex-role development, nor does it sufficiently account for either the child's social and physical environment or his emerging capacity for organizing that environment in meaningful ways. The need for more sophisticated theoretical treatment of the development of sex differences eventually was met in the 1950s and 1960s by psychologists of a socialization-identification persuasion. The two most important theories in existence today are Social-Learning Theory, which explains how others shape the child's sex-role socialization, and Cognitive-Developmental Theory, which describes how the child socializes himself.[1]

Social-Learning Theory (see Bandura and Walters selection) is a combination of traditional learning theory and observational learning theory. The first component explains how boys and girls are cued and reinforced to adopt male and female-typed behaviors, respectively. Children are reinforced to adopt "sex-appropriate" behaviors by their parents, other adults, and, perhaps most significantly, by their peers. This last factor has not received as much research or theoretical attention as adult reinforcement has, but the few studies of peer reinforcement indicate that peers tend to reinforce sex-typed behavior more rigidly than adults do (e.g., Fagot and Patterson, 1969).

The second and more important component of Social-Learning Theory is observational learning. Basically this refers to learning of entire sequences of behavior through observing models without receiving direct reinforcement for such learning. The observing child can either imitate, ignore, or counter-imitate an available model. Children tend to imitate models who meet four criteria: They are perceived as similar, as powerful and/or having high status, as friendly or nurturant, and as themselves being rewarded for their behavior. To the degree that these criteria are not met children tend not to imitate; and where none of the criteria are met, children tend to counter-imitate, i.e., behave differently from the model. Thus a young boy, for example, would tend to imitate the mannerisms of a famous male athlete because this model would meet three of the criteria. If he also shook hands with the famous athlete and received his autograph, meeting the criterion of friendliness, the boy might develop a temporary case of hero worship. It is entirely probable that, under the same circumstances, a young girl would also adopt the male athlete as a model because he would meet three of her modeling criteria. However, if she were discouraged from imitating this model by her parents or friends and if she were supplied with an equally acceptable female athlete as a model, then she might shift her imitative responses from the male to the female. The application of negative reinforcement coupled with her perception of the female athlete as being more similar to herself would tend to have this effect.

In real life a child typically imitates a great number of models including parents, relatives, peers, television personalities, fictional characters; in a complex society such as ours the list is almost endless. Each boy and girl synthesizes the results of this multiple modeling process into a blend which is peculiarly his or her own. Due to exposure to effective models of both sexes, children usually do not develop extremely masculine or feminine behavioral repertoires, although the balance is usually one way or the other and, in the great majority of cases, it corresponds with the child's biological gender. Social-Learning Theory, therefore, explains rather well how children are influenced by others to adopt sex-typed behaviors, values, and preferences. It may be that the cumulative effect of countless influences of this type is the formation of a sex-role identity, although one critical ingredient is left out of the social-learning formulation. That ingredient is the *initiative* the child exercises in selecting which models to imitate and which to counter-imitate,[1] and, of those selected for imitation, how the child arranges the timing, order, and priority of his exposure to the selected models; and, having made such arrangements, how he decides which specific behaviors he will imitate and which he will ignore from the full range of behaviors a given model manifests.

Cognitive-Developmental Theory attempts to supply this missing ingredient by postulating stages of cognitive development which determine, first, on what basis the child selects aspects of his interpersonal environment for imitation and, second, the particular form of his imitative responses (see Kohlberg and Zigler selection). This theory holds that sex-role concepts are formed according to the same epistemological laws as all other concepts. Since conceptual development, as formulated by Jean Piaget, passes through an invariant sequence of stages which is universal, then the structural properties (not necessarily the content) of sex-role concepts are also universal. Children are motivated by considerations of cognitive consistency, that is, they selectively recruit information from the world which is consistent with already developed cognitive structures. Thus, their sex-typed preferences, behaviors, values, etc., are selected on the basis of "what is like me." Cognitive-Developmental Theory holds that these child-initiated selection processes tend to override the reinforcement strategies of others; in fact, the child selectively attends to those reinforcements which confirm his emerging cognitive organization of sex-role concepts and tends to ignore those which are disconfirming.

The key element to the child's early cognitive organization is his gender identity. From birth on the child is taught that he is a "boy" or that she is a "girl" and, long before either realizes that these labels are based on genitalia, each selects sex-typed experience which is consistent with his or her own gender label.

Apparently gender identity is accorded great importance by the child because it is the one aspect of self which seems to be stable and unchangeable. This explains why children younger than six or seven years of age tend to be rigidly orthodox in their interpretation of what is and what is not appropriate, respectively, for boys and girls. It is only when the child enters what Piaget calls the "Concrete Operational" stage of development that gender identity becomes a more flexible basis for self definition. The concrete operational child is able to comprehend that some aspects of a given sex-role concept can vary while other aspects remain invariant. Thus, both boys and girls come to associate their gender identity with the constant facts of anatomy while separating it from variable phenomena such as behavior. The confidence that one's gender identity remains constant no matter what one does, what clothes one wears, etc., enables children to become less sex-stereotyped in their preferences, activities, companions, and so forth. After seven or eight years of age their relatively advanced level of cognitive development enables them to enjoy the stability which gender identity contributes to self concept, while becoming progressively freer of its constraints.

While Cognitive-Developmental Theory fills some of the gaps left by Social-Learning theory, it has some problems of its own. It seems to account more accurately for male than for female sex-role development (cf. Kohlberg, 1966). Psychoanalytic theory is also bedeviled by the failure of females to fit the standard theoretical formula. Whatever its faults, Social-Learning theory appears to be the only one of the three major theories equal to the conundrums of female sex-role development. Young girls tend to be decidedly more "masculine" in their interests, knowledge, and preferences than young boys are "feminine" in theirs (cf., Brown, 1957; Lee and Gropper, 1974). Social-Learning theory would explain this by pointing to the higher status which males enjoy in our society. Recall that perceived status or power of a model is one of the criteria against which a model's effectiveness is measured. Since male models tend to have higher status than female models, then the probability of cross-sex imitation for young girls would tend to be greater than that for young boys.

Taken together, Social Learning and Cognitive Developmental theories provide adequate descriptions of the *general* framework of early sex-role development. However, there are many *specific* aspects of sex identity which neither these nor psychoanalytic theory can explain, thus creating a need for other approaches to the study of sex differences. Examples of theoretically independent approaches are found in the following selections by Maccoby and Moss, each of whom has done an intensive analysis of a particular aspect of sex-role development. Maccoby focuses on the complex relationship between sex differences in specific intellectual abilities and sex differences in personality characteristics. Moss examines the differences in reciprocal socialization which occurs between mothers and their male and female infants during the first three months of life. Each creates an explanatory model, in Maccoby's case to summarize her analysis, and in Moss's case to organize his data. There is much to be said for the construction of small-scale models, such as these, which focus on specific sectors of sex differences. They allow for analysis which is simultaneously incisive and comprehensive, which sticks to the point, but draws together whatever empirical observations and/or existing research is relevant to the sector under examination.

The developmental psychology of sex differences, then, forms a somewhat mottled pattern. There is one major descriptive theory, i.e., Normative-Maturational; three major theories which purport to be descriptive and explanatory, i.e., Social-Learning, Cognitive-Developmental, and Psychoanalytic; and a number of small-scale models which tend to be independent of the major theoretical systems. Beyond these theories and models, there is an accumulation of bits and pieces of evidence which sometimes hang together, sometimes cancel each other out, and sometimes stand apart as findings which cannot be assimilated to the main body of findings, but cannot be dismissed. There is something here for readers of every persuasion, and perhaps too much for those who would like definitive answers to their questions about sex differences.

Before closing this introduction to the *Psychological Dimension* of sex differences, it might be instructive to see how well the differences described by G. Stanley Hall in 1904 (see selection) have stood the test of time. Hall's ideas about sex differences were extremely influential early in the century and it should be noted that several of the key researchers who studied sex differences over the ensuing years owed at least part of their intellectual legacy to Hall. Arnold Gesell and Lewis Terman were his students at Clark University, and E. K. Strong was trained by James McKeen Cattell, who was one of Hall's students at Johns Hopkins.

Seventy years after Hall's publication of *Adolescence* (1904), Eleanor Maccoby and Carol Jacklin (1974) published a comprehensive review of the psychological research on sex differences. In their summary chapter they classified alleged sex differences as being "unfounded beliefs"; "fairly well established"; or "open questions." Unfortunately, they did not categorize all the psychological differences specified by Hall, probably because many had dropped from serious consideration in the intervening seventy years. Moreover, due to changes in terminology and in nuance of meaning where terminology remained the same, it is not always easy to determine whether the differences discussed by Hall and those summarized by Maccoby and Jacklin are precisely comparable. Nevertheless, given these caveats, this is how Hall's roster of sex differences holds up after seventy years. Maccoby and Jacklin have classified as unfounded beliefs these sex differences mentioned by Hall: Females are more suggestible than males and more susceptible to influence; females are superior to males in associative and rote learning, while males are "more prone to bring things under general rules"; females are more subject to hereditary influences than males are; females excel in "visual discriminations in the indirect field of vision"; females are more "obtuse in hearing." Maccoby and Jacklin classify as open questions these differences: females are "more prone to fear and timidity"; females are more altruistic than males. There is one psychological sex difference pointed out by Hall which continues to hold. Maccoby and Jacklin agree that females are superior to males in verbal ability or, as Hall phrased it, females "speak quicker . . . are likely to be talkative . . . are superior in arts of conversation . . . in quick reading . . . (and) quick apprehension . . . of a paragraph." Ironically enough, Hall failed to observe that males are more aggressive than females, probably the most consistent finding on sex differences, both in American society and cross-culturally.

In any event, Hall's list of psychological sex differences does *not* appear to have passed the test of seven decades of research.

It would be interesting, however, to find out to what degree his list of sex differences is still part of the popular mentality. There is some intuitive basis for supposing that the average member of our society subscribes to a set of sex differences which approximates those described by Terman and Miles forty years ago (see selection). The average person may no longer share Hall's turn of the century sensibility, but it's doubtful that we have yet entered the skeptical era of Maccoby and Jacklin. With each passing season, however, for reasons mentioned in the Introduction to the present anthology, traditional notions regarding sex differences appear to be breaking down, perhaps to emerge in new patterns as yet unknown.

FOOTNOTE

1. Of course, psychoanalytic theory has been centrally concerned with the internalization of sex identity since the turn of the century and it has had considerable influence on psychological theories of sex-role identification. However, since it is treated in the first section of this anthology, it is not addressed here.

REFERENCES

ANASTASI, A. *Differential Psychology*. New York: Macmillan, 1937.

BOYDSTON, J. A. "John Dewey and the New Feminism." *Teachers College Record*, 1975, *76*, pp. 441-448.

BROWN, D. "Masculinity-femininity development in children." *Journal of Consulting Psychology*, 1957, *21*, pp. 197-202.

CATELL, R. B. *The Scientific Analysis of Personality*. Chicago: Aldine Publishing Co., 1965.

ELKIND, D. *A Sympathetic Understanding of the Child: Birth to Sixteen*. Boston: Allyn & Bacon, Inc., 1974.

FAGOT, B. I., & PATTERSON, G. R. "An in vivo analysis of reinforcing contingencies for sex role behaviors in the preschool child." *Developmental Psychology*, 1969, *1*, pp. 563-568.

GARAI, J. E., & SCHEINFELD, A. "Sex Differences in Behavioral and Mental Traits." *Genetic Psychology Monographs*, 1968, *77*, pp. 169-299.

JAMES, W. *The Principles of Psychology* (Volume 2). New York: Henry Holt & Co., 1890.

JAMES, W. *Psychology: Briefer Course*. New York: Henry Holt & Co., 1892.

KOHLBERG, L. "A Cognitive Developmental Analysis of Children's Sex-Role Concepts and Attitudes." In E. E. Maccoby (Ed.) *The Develop-

ment of Sex Differences. Stanford, California: Stanford University Press, 1966.

LEE, P. C., & GROPPER, N. B. "Sex-Role Culture and Educational Practice." *Harvard Educational Review,* 1974, *44,* pp. 369-410.

MACCOBY, E. E., & JACKLIN, C. N. *The Psychology of Sex Differences.* Stanford, California: Stanford University Press, 1974.

RATNER, J. (Ed.) *The Philosophy of John Dewey.* New York: Henry Holt & Co., 1928.

STRONG, E. K., JR. *Vocational Interests of Men and Women.* Stanford, California: Stanford University Press, 1943.

STRONG, E. K., JR. *Vocational Interests 18 Years After College.* Minneapolis: University of Minnesota Press, 1955.

THORNDIKE, E. L. *Individuality.* New York: Houghton Mifflin, 1911.

BIOLOGICAL AND ANTHROPOLOGICAL DIFFERENCES BETWEEN THE SEXES

G. Stanley Hall

G. Stanley Hall's professional credentials are impeccable. He was the first American to receive a Ph.D. in psychology; he did two years of post-doctoral study under Wilhelm Wundt in Germany; he was founder and first president of the American Psychological Association; and he founded the American Journal of Psychology. *Trained by William James at Harvard, he came from the source and, in turn, became a more bountiful source in his own right. Eleven of the first fourteen and thirty of the first fifty-four American Ph.D.'s in psychology were earned under his sponsorship. Among others he trained Arnold Gesell, Lewis Terman, Joseph Jastrow, and James McKeen Cattell, either in his laboratory at Johns Hopkins during the 1880s or in his "Pedagogical Seminary" at Clark University in the 1890s.*

He was the primary American exponent of "Genetic Psychology" and of the study of the child. Apparently a man of great energy and almost indiscriminate thirst for knowledge, his personal and professional goals were ambitious as he strove to formulate a "true natural history of the soul." Although Arnold Gesell differed completely from Hall in character and methodological rigor, in 1912 he wrote: "the greatest modern student of the child is G. Stanley Hall. When the history of science is seriously recorded, his name will be linked with that of Charles Darwin. . . . Hall is the Darwin of psychology" (1912, p. 20.)

It may be that history's final judgment will vindicate Gesell's high opinion of his teacher, but at the present time Hall's scientific and theoretical work is not considered a serious factor in psychology. He is remembered most as an indefatigable organizer, as a stimulating teacher, and as one who left an indelible stamp on the profession, if not the substance, of American psychology.

The following selection is the first part of Hall's chapter on "Adolescent Girls and their Education" from volume 2 of his monumental work Adolescence *(1904). Despite its title, this selection focuses on the physical and psychological differences between the sexes, as seen from the perspective of 1904 and through Hall's romantic sensibility.*

Our modern knowledge of woman represents her as having characteristic differences from man in every organ and tissue, as conservative in body and mind, fulfilling the function of seeing to it that no acquired good be lost to mankind, as anabolic rather than katabolic, or disposed to assimilate or digest on a higher plane, as normally representing childhood and youth in the full meridian of its glory in all her dimensions and nature so tht she is at the top of the human curve from which the higher super-man of the future is to evolve, while man is phylogenetically by comparison a trifle senile, if not decadent. Her sympathetic and ganglionic system is relatively to the cerebro-spinal more dominant. Her whole soul, conscious and unconscious, is best conceived as a magnificent organ of heredity, and to its laws all her psychic activities, if unperverted, are true. She is by nature more typical and a better representative of the race and less prone to specialization. Her peculiar organs, while constituting a far larger proportion of her body than those of man, are hidden and their psychic reverberations are dim, less localized, more all-pervasive. She works by intuition and feeling; fear, anger, pity, love, and most of the emotions have a wider range and greater intensity. If she abandons her natural naïveté and takes up the burden of guiding and accounting for her life by consciousness, she is likely to lose more than she gains, according to the old saw that she who deliberates is lost. Secondary, tertiary, and quaternary sex qualities are developed far beyond her ken or that of science, in a way that the latter is only beginning to glimpse. While she needs tension that only the most advanced modern psychology sees to be sexual at root, we shall never know the true key to her nature until we understand how the nest and the cradle are larger wombs; the home, a larger nest; the tribe, state, church, and school, larger homes and irradiations from it. Biological psychology already dreams of a new philosophy of sex which places the wife and mother at the heart of a new world and makes her the object of a new religion and almost of a new worship, that will give her reverent exemption from sex competition and reconsecrate her to the higher responsibilities of the human race, into the past and future of which the roots of her being penetrate; where the blind worship of mere mental illumination has no place; and where her real superiority to man will have free course and be glorified and the ideals of the old matriarchates again find embodiment in fit and due degree.

Patrick[1] has summarized the salient points of difference between men and women as follows: The latter are shorter and lighter save for a brief period at about thirteen. Her adult height to that of man is as about 16 to 17, and her weight as 9 to 10. Her form is rounder, she has more fat, more water, less muscle; her dynamometer strength foots up about two-thirds that of man; her trunk is relatively slightly longer; the pelvic bend makes her a little less erect; the head is less upright, and her gait slightly less steady; her plantar arch is flatter; her forefinger is relatively longer than the other three; the thyroid larger; the lung capacity relatively less; the blood has less red corpuscles; her bones a little less specific gravity; she is more anemic, and her pulse is faster. In the United States about 105 boys are born to 100 girls, but through life the male death-rate is higher, so that in nearly every land, after the first year or two, there are more females than males. She is more liable to whooping-cough, scarlet fever, phthisis, diphtheria, but resists diseases best and dies less often than man at nearly every age. Ballod[2] shows that the average increased duration of life in the last decennium is for women and not for men, and that large cities and factories tend to shorten average male longevity. Hegar *(Geschlechtstrieb)* concludes that before forty, married, and after forty, unmarried, women are more liable to die, but that married women outlive unmarried men. He is more prone than she to rheumatism, cancer, brain troubles, sudden death from internal or external causes, can less survive severe surgical operations and grows old more rapidly; his hair is gray earlier and he is more prone to loss of sight, hearing, memory, senile irritability, to deformities and anomalies, is less hardy and less resembles children. Woman's skull is smaller, especially at the base, but large in circumference at the crown, which is flatter and more angular; her forehead is more vertical; the glabella and superorbital ridges are less, as are the occipital and mastoid prominences and the parietal prominence; her face is smaller and a little lower, and she is slightly more prognathic. Her absolute brain weight to that of man is about as 9 to 10, but her smaller size makes her brain about equal, if not heavier, in weight. The lower centers are larger in women, and in nearly all these respects women differ less among themselves than do men. Martin and Clouston found the female brain slightly better irrigated by blood, especially in the occipital regions, although the number of its corpuscles as compared to those of man was as 9 to 10. The anterior regions of the brain were best supplied in man. The specific gravity of the gray matter of all parts of the brain was less in women, but in the white matter there was no difference. The female brain has more bilateral symmetry, i.e., its right and left hemispheres are more alike. In all save the occipital regions the male has more secondary gyri and probably the convolutions are deeper. In most forms of lunacy the male brain is most wasted at death, and four men to one woman die of general paralysis between thirty and fifty. Women are more often insane, but men most often die of insanity, while women who die in lunatic asylums more often die of body diseases. Mental stimulus, according to Warner, more readily lowers their general nutrition. Möbius,[3] on the other hand, who sees danger in the emancipation movement of the feminists, thinks that the fact that they have accomplished so little in the world of art and science is not due to subjection but to inferiority. He lays stress on Rüdinger's results, viz., that in infants the convolutions about the Sylvian fissures are simpler, with fewer bends, that the island of Keil is smaller, less convex, and simpler, as is the third frontal gyrus, and the whole parietal lobe is inferior in females at all ages to that of men, these being the portions most closely connected with mentation. The sexes have the same convolutions, but of different sizes, and the same powers, but in differing degrees.

Women seem slightly more obtuse in sight, touch, and hearing, and less sensitive to pain. Concerning taste disciminations, investigators differ. Ellis and Galton conclude that she has less sensibility but more affectibility and nervous irritability. Only about four-tenths of one per cent of women are color blind as against three and a half per cent of men. In visual discriminations in the indirect field of vision, she excels, indicating that the retinal function is less focused in the fovea. With her eyes fixed straight ahead on the streets she observes persons and things farther right and left than man can do. Bryan found that in rapid movements, she excelled from five to sixteen, except at about thirteen, while in precision boys slightly excel. Gilbert concludes that boys tap fastest at every age, and that reaction time is less at all ages for boys. Ellis concludes that in dexterity, as shown in cotton spinning, woolen weaving, cigar and cigarette making, and other fine work, man excels where opportunity and numbers are equal. In quick reading, where the sense of a paragraph is to be grasped in minimal time and with equal knowledge of the subject, woman excels in quick apprehension of wholes. Women go in flocks, and in social matters are less prone to stand out with salient individuality. They are more emotional, altruistic, intuitive, less judicial, and less able to make disinterested and impersonal judgment. Girls are most likely to know their environment, while the boys oftenest show surprising gaps in knowledge of what is right about them and unexpected acquaintance with something afar, special or unusual.

Miss Thompson[4] found from laboratory tests that men excel women in strength, rapidity, and in rate of fatigue, and slightly in accuracy, but the latter are superior in new motor combinations; that men have the lower sensory threshold for light, and women for distinguishing two points on the skin, in sweet, salt, sour, and bitter taste, in smell, color, and pain by pressure, and in discriminative pitch and color. Men excel in distinguishing lifted weights, sweet, sour, and bitter. Women excel in memory. This writer becomes feministic in crediting abstract deductions and taking Lourbet's jesting remark that the smaller and more agile male cell might better represent the female and the larger ovum the male, seriously, and defies Weismannism by ascribing sexual differences of type of mental action to the differences of the influences that surround the sexes in early years.

Her thought is more concrete and individual and she is more prone to associations in space, and man in time. Men are more prone to bring things under general rules and with regard to symmetry. Her logical thought is slower, but her associations quicker than those of man, she is less troubled by inconsistencies, and has less patience with the analysis involved in science and invention.

Of 483,517 patents recorded in Washington up to October, 1892, 3,458 were by women. In education men have made most of the reforms, while recent developments show that they can excel even in dressmaking and cooking. Woman has rapid tact in extricating herself from difficulties; girls speak quicker than boys; old women are likely to be talkative, old men glum; men progress most after graduation; women are very prone to lose accomplishments and special culture and training, are more punctual in school and college, more regular in attendance, and in higher grades have the best marks, but vary less from the average; they excel in mental reproduction rather than in production; are superior in arts of conversation, more conservative and less radical; their vasomotor system is more excitable; they are more emotional, blush and cry easier; are more often hypnotized; quicker to take suggestions; have most sympathy, pity, charity, generosity, and superstitions. Male crime to female is as 6 to 1, women exceeding only in poisoning, domestic theft, and infanticide. She is about as superior to man in altruism as she is behind him in truth-telling, being more prone to ruse and deception. She is more credulous and less skeptical, more prone to fear and timidity, and has greater fidelity, dependence, reverence, and devotion. She dresses for adornment rather than use. In savage and civilized life, her body is more often mutilated and she is more primitive. Her hair is long; she is more prone to wear ornaments which show wealth rather than to dress solely for protection or concealment; is still fond of feathers, skin, and fur, flowing garments, and partial exposure of person, so that she betrays rank and wealth more often than men. She still pinches her waist and feet; uses pins, powders, and perfumes, neck ornaments, beads, overshoes, and sometimes shoes that are not rights and lefts; is more subject to fashion; her work is far less specialized than that of man and less reduced to mechanism or machinery. Man is best adapted to the present; woman is more rooted in the past and the future, closer to the race and a more generic past. Thus again, in very many of the above traits, woman is far nearer childhood than man, and therefore in mind and body more prophetic of the future as well as reminiscent of the past.

Professor Pearson[5] condemns as a superstition the current idea of the greater variability of man than of woman. He first eliminates everything characteristic of sex and all that is pathological, and focuses on size alone. Even color blindness, which is characteristic of sex, he sets aside. By so doing and measuring the limited number of persons, he finds slighly more variation in females than in males and so excoriates the common belief that the reverse is true. That his method is profoundly mistaken, if it does not indeed prove the contrary, will, I think, be plain to all biologists. Some have thought that every variation from the parental type was slightly abnormal. Certainly, normal and pathological shade into each other by imperceptible degrees, and Professor Pearson merely eliminates those classes of facts on which the whole question rests. As Ellis[6] well says, the real question of organic variational tendencies is untouched. If in size woman is more variable, it may be due to her less severe struggle for existence, or to the fact that male children being larger make greater demands on the mother and, therefore, have harder conditions to surmount. The biometric method, which Pearson so ably represents, miscarries here because the preliminary basis in the selection of facts is fundamentally wrong.

W. K. Brooks,[7] approaching the subject from the standpoint of biology, characterized the female body, instincts, and habits as conservative, devoted to keeping what has been acquired by successive generations as new layers of snow are added to glaciers. Thus woman is best in acting and judging in ordinary matters; man in those that are extraordinary. The male is the agent of variation and progress, and transmits variations best, so that perhaps the male cell and sex itself originated in order to produce variation. Influence is more potent than argument with women. An ideal or typical male is hard to define, but there is a standard ideal woman. Because her mind is, more than that of man, essentially an organ of heredity, we find that, although she may sometimes seem volatile and desultory, the fact that her processes seem to be unconscious emancipates her from nature less than is the case with man. Her thought is a mode of thinking. Brooks presents the following suggestive scheme:

The power of	to foresee the conduct of or to influence	is greater than the power of	to foresee the conduct of or to influence
Women	Women	Men	Men
"	"	"	Women
"	Men	"	Men
"	"	"	Women

Hyatt[8] says that "men and women, like the males and females of most animals, show by their organization that they have been evolved from a type in which both sexes have been combined in the same individual. The separation of the sexes did not destroy this dual nature, as is demonstrated by the development of secondary male characters in the old age of many species of animals, and of women in extreme age, and of feminine characters in aged men. This opinion can also be supported by the structure of the tissue cells in the body, the nuclei of which are made up of paternal and maternal parts. This dual structure enables us to understand the fact that secondary sexual characters are latent in both males and females." He also urges that "in the early history of mankind the women and men led lives more nearly alike and were consequently more alike physically and mentally than they have become subsequently in the lives of highly civilized peoples. This divergence of the sexes is a marked characteristic of progression among highly civilized races. Coeducation of the sexes, occupations of a certain kind, and woman's suffrage may have a tendency to approximate the ideals, the lives, and the habits of women to those of men in these same highly civilized races. Such approximation in the future, while perfectly natural and not in the common sense degenerate, would not belong to the progressive evolution of mankind." They would be convergences, and although they might bring intellectual advance would tend to virify women and feminize men, and would be retrogressive. We find gerontic changes even in the younger stages of adults, when the phylum is declining, or in its epacme. Perhaps, he thinks, a type like an individual has only a limited store of vitality and a cycle, so that we can speak of phylogerontic stages. If man is approaching this stage, it is especially important that every degenerative influence be avoided, because our organisms may be such that we can not rely upon continuous or certain progress, one necessity of which is that the sexes be not approximated, for this would inaugurate retrogressive evolution.

From G. Stanley Hall. *Adolescence* (Volume 2). New York: D. Appleton & Company, 1904, pages 561-569.

FOOTNOTES

1. "The Psychology of Woman," *Pop. Sci. Mo.,* June, 1895. See also Ellis: *Man and Woman.* London, p. 409.
2. *Die mittlere Lebensdaur in Stadt u. Land.* Leipzig, 1897.
3. *Ueber den physiolog. Schwachsinn des Weibes.* Fifth ed. Halle, 1903.
4. *The Mental Traits of Sex.* Chicago Univ. Press, 1903.
5. *The Chances of Death*
6. "Variation in Man and Woman." *Pop. Sci. Mo.;* January, 1903.
7. "The Condition of Woman from a Zoological Point of View." Two articles, *Pop. Sci. Mo,* June, 1897.
8. "The Influences of Woman in the Evolution of the Human Race." *Natural Science,* August, 1897, p. 89.

REFERENCE

GESELL, A., & GESELL, B. C. *The Normal Child and Primary Education.* New York: Ginn and Company, 1912.

SEX AND PERSONALITY: STUDIES IN MASCULINITY AND FEMININITY

Lewis Terman / Catharine Cox Miles

After receiving his doctorate with G. Stanley Hall at Clark University, Lewis Terman joined the faculty at Stanford University where he became the leading American student of intelligence for three decades. He constructed the Stanford-Binet I.Q. test and directed the Stanford longitudinal study of genius and giftedness, clearly the most ambitious project ever conducted in this area.

His later work with Catharine Cox Miles was an outgrowth of the earlier longitudinal study, in which various sex differences were found in preferences and interests. These fortuitous findings encouraged them to undertake a more systematic investigation of sex differences in a broad range of personality characteristics, culminating in the book, Sex and Personality: Studies in Masculinity and Femininity (1936). According to their Preface "The purpose of the investigations here reported has been the accomplishment in the field of masculinity-femininity of something similar to Binet's early achievement in the field of intelligence—a quantification of procedures and concepts" (1936, p. vi). This was an ambitious goal which the authors themselves recognized as beyond them, admitting that "... only the simplest and roughest kind of quantification is at present possible ... any attempt at exact measurement of the traits in question would in the present state of psychometric development, be fatuous and unprofitable" (1936, p. vii).

The following selection includes Terman and Miles' summary discussion of three major concerns of their research: The effect of sex differences on personality, technical and epistemological problems in measuring psychological sex differences, and the relative role of nature versus nurture in the determination of psychological sex differences.

We may now consider two questions to which the present findings give rise: (1) Can we extract from them a single prime principle of sex difference at once not too vague to be ambiguous, and not so particular as to be insignificant? (2) What, so far as our evidence goes, appears to be the relation of the differences we have enumerated to nature and nurture, to endowment and environment? We shall take these questions in succession.

1. *Is there one dominant principle?*

It is obvious that from whatever point we have started, whether from the knowledge shown by the sexes or from their associations or their likes and dislikes for people, vocations, pastimes, books, or objects of travel; or whether we have explored directly or deviously their emotions, tastes, opinions, and inner experiences, we have found ourselves arriving at much the same conclusions—all our ways have led to Rome. But the final scene has two aspects—two sides of the same picture—one showing differences in the direction of interest, the other differences in the direction of emotions and impulses.

From whatever angle we have examined them the males included in the standardization groups evinced a distinctive interest in exploit and adventure, in outdoor and physically strenuous occupations, in machinery and tools, in science, physical phenomena, and inventions; and, from rather occasional evidence, in business and commerce. On the other hand, the females of our groups have evinced a distinctive interest in domestic affairs and in aesthetic objects and occupations; they have distinctively preferred more sedentary and indoor occupations, and occupations more directly ministrative, particularly to the young, the helpless, the distressed. Supporting and supplementing these are the more subjective differences—those in emotional disposition and direction. The males directly or indirectly manifest the greater self-assertion and aggressiveness; they express more hardihood and fearlessness, and more roughness of manners, language, and sentiments. The females express themselves as more compassionate and sympathetic, more timid, more fastidious and aesthetically sensitive, more emotional in general (or at least more expressive of the four emotions considered), severer moralists, yet admit in themselves more weaknesses in emotional control and (less noticeably) in physique.

But we must define some of our terms more precisely, for instance, "aggressiveness" and "self-assertion." The evidence is for initiative, enterprise, vigorous activity, outdoor adventure; "aggressiveness" need not imply selfishness or tyranny or unfair attack. The compassion and sympathy of the female, again, appears from the evidence personal rather than abstract, less a principled humanitarianism than an active sympathy for palpable misfortune or distress. In disgust, in aesthetic judgment, and in moral censure, the evidence is rather for the influence of fashion and of feeling than of principle or reason. Our evidence need not imply the possession of a "truer" taste or a more discerning conscience.

But in asking how deep these sex distinctions go we reach our second question: *What appears to be the relation of our main sex difference to nature and nurture, to endowment and environment?*

The question is not, let us remind ourselves, whether this or that trait is innate or acquired, for every human act or thought is both, but whether the actual sex differences we are discovering are ascribable to biological (genetic) factors dividing the sexes or to sex differences in their training and environment. So far as the evidence of our experiment goes, we are not justified in ascribing the manifest differences to one alternative exclusively. Certainly we do not have enough evidence to exclude the gross physiological differences between the sexes from any part in determining the distinctive preference of the male for heavy muscular work and of the female for less active occupations, or in determining her greater sympathy for the young and weak or her greater interest in home life, with the relegation of outside interests to the male. To actual or anticipated childbearing and motherhood—differences physiologically determined—we have found no reason to deny a part in determing differences in overt habits and emotional dispositions. And in the present state of our ignorance it would be even more rash to deny the possible influence upon sex temperaments of the manifold differences between the sexes in their endocrine equipment and functioning.

Whatever our view as to the innateness of the distinctive tendencies, at least as to maternal tenderness in the one sex and comparative aggressiveness in the other, our experimental evidence is inconclusive. However, when we examine the more direct manifestations of these and other contrasting tendencies in our exercises, and consider how any particular manifestation comes about, the power and reach of what we have named cultural sex bias, its many plain and subtle effects on the upbringing and environment of the sexes within the groups we are considering, keep coming to one's mind. In so many ways too familiar to realize, each sex gives and receives such different treatment as largely to explain the divergences in expression or in fact revealed by the material we have studied. Singularly powerful in shaping our development are other people's expectations of us, past and present, as shown by their practice and their precept. Whether the boy is innately more aggressive and fearless, more handy with the electric lighting than with the cooking stove, more interested and informed about public affairs and about science, more active and enterprising physically; and whether the girl is by nature more sympathetic, gentle, timid, fastidious, more attracted to pots and pans than to rods and guns, more punctilious in dress, personal appearance, manners, and language; at any rate society in the shape of parents, teachers, and one's own fellows of whichever sex expects these differences between the sexes, and literature reflects them. Irresistibly each sex plays the role assigned, even in spite of its own protests. The consequence is that throughout these several exercises, however statistically consistent the distinctive sex responses may prove, we cannot tell how deep the difference lies—or how the deeper and shallower factors combine. And here we must be content to leave the problem, for it is clear that the deciding answer can be wrested, not by a more meticulous struggle with this one set of exercises administered to groups comparatively homogeneous, but from: (1) parallel examinations of socially and racially different groups widely different in social tradition and circumstance, and (2) combined psychological and biological case studies of extreme deviants in sex temperaments within a given culture.

THE SIGNIFICANCE OF M-F DIFFERENCES FOR PERSONALITY

Masculinity and femininity are important aspects of human personality. They are not to be thought of as lending to it merely a superficial coloring and flavor; rather they are one of a small number of cores around which the structure of personality gradually takes shape. The masculine-feminine contrast is probably as deeply grounded, whether by nature or by nurture, as any other which human temperament presents. Certainly it is more specifically rooted in a structural dichotomy than the cycloid-schizoid or the extrovertive-introvertive contrasts. Whether it is less or more grounded in general physiological and biochemical factors than these remains to be seen. In how far the lines of cleavage it represents are inevitable is unknown, but the possibility of eliminating it from human nature is at least conceivable. The fact remains that the M-F dichotomy, in various patterns, has existed throughout history and is still firmly established in our mores. In a considerable fraction of the population it is the source of many acute difficulties in the individual's social and sexual adjustment and in a greater fraction it affords a most important impetus to creative work and happiness. The indications are that the present situation, together with the problems it raises for education, psychology, and social legislation, will remain with us for a long time to come.

As long as the child is faced by two relatively distinct patterns of personality, each attracting him by its unique features, and is yet required by social pressures to accept the one and reject the other, a healthy integration of personality may often be difficult to achieve. Cross-parent fixations will continue to foster sexual inversion; the less aggressively inclined males will be driven to absurd compensations to mask their femininity; the more aggressive and independent females will be at a disadvantage in the marriage market; competition between the sexes will be rife in industry, in politics, and in the home as it is today.

Even if it could be shown that the malleability of personality is such as to make the adoption of a single ideal pattern of temperament feasible, no one knows whether the consequences would be more desirable than undesirable. So far only one single-standard society has been described for us, that an extremely primitive one consisting of but a few hundred individuals living in the wilds of New Guinea. Mead's description[1] of this society, challenging as it is, offers no very convincing evidence that a system of unipolarity reduces the difficulties of individual adjustment. Conceivably, in a more complex society it might increase them. It is possible that in an enlightened culture, no longer held in leash by traditions and taboos, dual patterns of sexual temperament are an aid in the development of heterosexuality.

But it is not our purpose to defend the prevailing ideals with respect to sex temperaments. The irrelevance and absurdity of many of their features are evident enough. That in most cultures they have been shaped to the advantage of the physically stronger sex is obvious. It does not necessarily follow that a dichotomy of temperaments is per se an evil to be got rid of. In any case it is not the business of the scientist either to condemn or to praise any given type of human behavior. His task is to understand it. The application of his findings to social betterment he is willing to leave to the social reformer, but with respect to the personality problems with which we are here concerned, he knows that intelligent reform will have to await the establishment of a substantial body of knowledge which does not now exist.

THE NEED FOR MORE ADEQUATE DESCRIPTION OF SEX TEMPERAMENTS

The first step in the investigation of the sex temperaments is to make possible their more adequate description and more exact identification. We have shown that descriptions based upon common observation are often contradictory and that even a subject's intimate friends register little agreement in rating him for degree of masculinity and femininity. This state of affairs betokens the vagueness of current ideas with respect to what constitutes the masculine or feminine temperament and the chaos of opinion with regard to what is valid evidence of its existence. Three sources of confusion may be briefly mentioned.

1. Erroneous ratings may result from the too ready acceptance of overt behavior as the criterion. In this respect the investigator of personality or character is at a disadvantage in comparison with the investigator of intelligence or other abilities. Subjects do not often try to hide their intelligence and they are unable to

hide very effectively their stupidities, but character and personality can be rather successfully simulated. Within limits the dishonest can simulate honesty, hatred can be hidden under honeyed words, anger can be disguised, the introvert can force himself to behave as an extrovert, the homosexual may deport himself so normally as to remain undetected in our midst.

2. Errors may be due to lack of a sufficiently large sampling of observational data. The teacher's contacts with her pupils are limited to certain types of situations. The same is true of our contacts with most of the people we know.

3. Among the hardest errors to eliminate are those that arise from traditional biases, such as the notion that the masculine temperament nearly always goes with a particular type of voice, physique, carriage, manner of dress, or occupation. There are doubtless other biases more or less peculiar to the individual or to the class to which he belongs, varying according to whether he is male or female, masculine or feminine, young or old, strongly or weakly sexed, etc.

It is evident that no clear delineation of sexual temperaments is possible on the basis of uncontrolled observation. The M-F test is an attempt to remedy this situation. Its scientific intent is to free the concepts of masculinity and femininity from the irrelevancies and confusions which have become attached to them as the result of superficial consideration of everyday behavior. It is necessary to go back of behavior to the individual's attitudes, interests, information, and thought trends, which constitute the real personality behind the front presented to his fellows.

That the purpose of the test has been accomplished only in part hardly needs to be said. Our sampling of the universe of mental attitudes and interests which differentiate the sexes is far from adequate. The sampling used has not been validated by item counts for sufficiently large populations. Numerous questions remain unanswered with respect to the selection of test items, the best method of weighting responses, and the most meaningful kinds of score to employ. The defects of our technique will be remedied by experiment, the technique itself seems to us inescapable however much it may require supplementation by direct experimental procedures.

* * *

NATURE AND NURTURE AS DETERMINERS OF SEX TEMPERAMENT

The nature-nurture problem occupies a central position in any theory of sex temperament. The M-F test rests upon no assumption as to the causes responsible for the individual differences it discloses. The aim has been to devise a test which would measure whatever differences may exist in the hope that this would open the way to an empirical estimation of the relative influence of various determiners. At present no one knows whether the M-F deviant is primarily a problem for the neurologist, biochemist, and endocrimologist or for the parent and educator. The question cannot be answered without thoroughgoing search for the constitutional correlates of M-F deviation. The final answer cannot be obtained until both endocrinology and psychometrics have advanced beyond their present stage, though this is no excuse for delaying the initiation of research on the problem at hand. It should be emphasized, however, that failure to find the sought-for correlates can never be taken as conclusive proof that they do not exist. On the other hand, in so far as any such correlates may be demonstrated the nurture hypothesis is to that extent weakened.

In a recent treatise Mead[2] has presented a mass of descriptive evidence favoring the extreme environmental hypothesis for the causes of sex differences in personality. If her observations and interpretations can be taken at their face value it would not be easy to escape the conclusion that among human beings constitutional factors are distinctly secondary to psychological as determiners of the M and F temperaments. Her book is based upon a study of three primitive tribes in New Guinea. She reports that in one of these, the Arapesh, males and females both exhibit in the main a single temperamental pattern, one that corresponds closely to the feminine pattern of present-day occidental cultures. A similar situation was found with the Mundugumors, except that in this case the single standard is typically masculine. The Tchambuli, on the other hand, present both masculine and feminine patterns, but reversed as between the sexes, males approximating what we should call the feminine in temperament and females approximating the masculine. The author describes in considerable detail the cultural influences which she believes to be responsible for these results.

That Mead's contribution offers impressive evidence of the modifiability of human temperament will be readily conceded, but we are by no means convinced that the case for nurture is as strong as a casual perusal of her book would suggest. Psychologists who have investigated personality by means of observational and rating techniques will inevitably question the accuracy of anyone's estimates of the degree of masculinity or femininity of behavior characterizing either an individual or a group of individuals. It is not to be supposed that the field anthropologist, any more than the psychologist, is immune to error in such estimates; indeed, because the groups under observation by him belong to an alien culture, and because his command of the tribal language is almost invariably limited, the anthropologist who attempts to rate the masculinity or femininity of behavior in a primitive tribal group labors under tremendous disadvantages.

We have shown that when subjects are rated by their teachers or intimate acquaintances either on general masculinity-femininity or on specific aspects of personality related thereto, so little agreement is found that the pooled estimates of several independent judges are necessary to increase the reliability of such ratings to a reasonable figure. Even then we do not rule out the types of constant error that result from a common bias among the raters. When subjective methods are employed, greater or less bias is inevitable, however competent and honest the observer may be; and observers who have had a particular kind of training, whether in anthropology or psychology, are bound to be influenced by the effect of biases common to their group—by the "idols of the den."[3]

Notwithstanding the above criticisms, the book in question is one of the most provocative contributions thus far made to the psychology of sex. Written for the general reader, it naturally does not contain the wealth of specific detail that would be necessary to enable the social scientist to judge the correctness of its conclusions. It does, however, present a number of observations which clearly suggest the operation of a nature as well as a nurture factor. The author admits that the cultural pressures in these tribes have not succeeded in forcing acceptance by all individuals of the personality standards imposed. Concrete examples are given of individuals who have become maladjusted by inability to conform. The author even admits that individual differences within a given sex are about as great as in our own culture, and that the chief result of the pressures has been to shift the location of the distribution of differences on the M-F axis without appreciably diminishing its range.

The literature of anthropology furnishes an abundance of cogent testimony as to the plasticity of temperament and personality. Of the treatises bearing on this question, the above-mentioned book by Mead and another not less notable by Benedict[4] are outstanding examples. Nevertheless, valuable as the anthropological evidence is, it cannot be accepted as a final answer to the nature-nurture problem. Primitive cultures are rapidly becoming more rare; the interpretation of behavior offers many pitfalls to observers unaccustomed to think in quantitative terms; conclusions reached by the anthropologist's field observations are usually not amenable to laboratory checks. For these and other reasons the psychologist, the physiologist, the psychiatrist, and the biochemist need not fear that their contributions to the theory of personality are likely to be rendered superfluous by other approaches.

EVIDENCE OF NURTURE INFLUENCES UPON THE M-F SCORE

Several convergent lines of evidence have been mentioned in preceding chapters which point to the efficacy of nurture factors as at least partial determiners of an individual's M-F score. The latter is definitely, even though not closely, associated with amount of schooling, with age, with occupation, with interests, and with domestic milieu. Perhaps the closest association of all, though its degree is suggested rather than measured, is that between cross-parent fixation and M-F deviation toward the norm of the opposite sex. The data do not define the reasons for these or other deviations. Old men test more feminine than young men, but the casual factor may be either experiential or physiological and endocrinal. Superior culture, in the case of women, tends to be associated with masculinity; in the case of men with femininity; but our data do not tell us whether education causes the change, or whether it merely tends to select the already feminine male and the already masculine female. Similarly for occupational classification, though the selective influence of the occupation is more clearly evidenced than in the case of education. Even in instances of cross-parent fixation it is not easy to rule out all possible selective factors: parents may be more likely to foster such an attachment in that particular opposite-sex child who is already a deviant, or, conversely, the already deviant child may be the only one who is affected by the overcherishing parent. Accordingly, although the evidence in favor of a considerable nurture influence is in our opinion very weighty, it is by no means crucial.

From the point of view of science progress could be made more rapidly if experimental and control groups of infants could be artifically segregated and the effects watched in them of reversing nurture influences. Our method for human study can, however, not parallel the "sacrifical" procedure of the physical sciences. Fortunately advance is not blocked by this condition. Comparison of parent-child resemblance in sex temperament with resemblance between foster parent and foster child can be accomplished, also comparison of resemblance between identical twins on the one hand and between like-sex fraternal twins on the other.

Another approach would be to locate parents who belong to one of two extreme types with respect to the kind of influence they have tried to exert in shaping the sex temperaments of their children: (a) parents who accept the usual dichotomy as desirable and have endeavored to inculcate it in their sons and daughters, and (b) parents who adhere radically to the opposite theory and have done their best to counteract every influence that would develop in their daughters the distinctively feminine, or in their sons the distinctively masculine, personality. If enough parents of the second type could be found to permit reliable determinations, the parental influence would be measured by the M-F score difference separating their sons and daughters as compared to the difference separating the sons and daughters of the other parental group. In such an investigation one would of course need to bear in mind that parental pressures may be largely nullified by subtle pressures of the larger social milieu, including playmates, the school, the newpaper, the theater, literature, industry, government, and innumerable other factors.

Even so, we believe that a careful study of parental influences upon the sex temperament of offspring would be worth making.

As to what the outcome of such investigations might be, we prefer not to hazard a guess. On the one hand is a respectable body of evidence pointing to nurture effects; on the other is the spectacular and ever increasing evidence from animal laboratories on the effects of hormone concentration upon patterns of sexual behavior. To assume a partisan position at the present time with respect to the relative influence of nature and nurture upon human personality is hardly warranted.

From Lewis Terman and Catharine Cox Miles. *Sex and Personality: Studies in Masculinity and Femininity.* New York: McGraw-Hill, 1936, pages 447-454, 460-465.

FOOTNOTES

1. MEAD, MARGARET, *Sex and temperament in three primitive societies,* *335* pp., MORROW, 1935.
2. Ibid.
3. In the specific case at hand, it is no reflection upon Dr. Mead to call attention to the fact, verifiable by examination of her earlier writings, that she entered upon her study of sex and temperament with definite leanings toward the environmental hypothesis in the interpretation of human behavior patterns. If the composite verbal pictures of her three New Guinea tribes had been sketched by an equally competent observer of different bias, there is no way of knowing how they would have differed from the dramatic contrasts presented; we can only be certain that they would have differed. It is regrettable that an investigation of the type in question could not have been carried out by the joint efforts of a number of social scientists of widely varying experiential background, including, say, an anthropologist, a psychologist, a sociologist, and a psychiatrist, all recording their observations and making their interpretations independently. Unfortunately, the rapidly growing contacts of these tribes with European cultures will in a few years render such an investigation meaningless, and the student is left to draw from the ingenious but not infallible work of Dr. Mead whatever conclusions seem to him reasonable.
4. BENEDICT, RUTH, *Patterns of culture,* p. 291, Houghton Mifflin, 1934.

SEX DIFFERENCE IN PERSONALITY CHARACTERISTICS

Leona E. Tyler

During the first half of this century, there was a small number of female psychologists who worked on sex differences. This group included, in approximate chronological order, Leta Hollingworth, Catharine Cox Miles, Anne Anastasi, and Leona Tyler. As scientists, each had a sense for theory, method, and evidence. And as women, it may be conjectured, they brought a perspective to the study of sex differences that never allowed for cavalier or slipshod discussion of the issues. Two of them, Tyler and Anastasi, are still active and have recently served as presidents of the American Psychological Association.

The following selection, drawn from Leona Tyler's book, The Psychology of Human Differences *(1947), is a succinct and readable summary of findings and issues as they were viewed on the threshold of the postwar era. In this particular passage, Tyler concentrates on sex differences in personality characteristics. Note that she draws upon the work of Terman and Miles, Deutsch, and Mead (reprinted elsewhere in this anthology) and incorporates these into her discussion of the results of myriad minor studies, as well as into her interpretation of what these results mean in human terms.*

When we move into the area of personality differences we begin to find large psychological differences between males and females. It is not necessary to use any sort of psychological tests to pick up the most striking of these. Go into any elementary school and ask for a list of the chief trouble-makers with whom the teachers have to contend. There is a high probability that the list will include at least twice as many boys' names as girls'. In Wickman's (24) study, teachers reported boys twice as frequently as girls for such offenses as tardiness, truancy, destruction of property, stealing, profanity, smoking, masturbation, interrupting, overactiveness, physical laziness, disobedience, defiance, cruelty and bullying, rudeness, meddle-

someness, acting smart, nervousness, enuresis, slovenliness, sus-
piciousness, and suggestibility. It is apparent that a good share
of these characteristics are of an active, aggressive sort. Observers agree with practical unanimity that misbehavior of this
kind is more common among boys than among girls. In the
Hartshorne, May, and Maller (7) research on character traits,
girls were slightly more coöperative than boys, and were rated
much higher for "service" by boys, girls, and teachers alike. Girls
also showed better inhibition or self-control and more persistence. It is interesting to note that all these traits in which girls
have been shown to excel would make a good impression on
teachers, and, thus, tend to explain the better grades they receive.

Statistics on delinquency and crime point in the same direction
as the schoolroom observations. A government report (11, p. 245)
indicates that in a recent year (1939-40) the total number of persons committed to federal and state prisons and reformatories
was 62,692. Of this number, 60,083 were males and only 2,609
were females. Although the sex ratios are different for different
offenses and change somewhat with changes in social and
economic conditions, there is no offense for which the number of
females even approaches the number of males. Scheinfeld (11) notes
that killing has become far less a masculine crime than it used
to be. However, fifteen times as many men as women are still
sent to prison for murder, and seven or eight times as many for
manslaughter. The figures on crime agree with the school ratings in showing that aggressive types of anti-social behavior are
more characteristic of males than of females. In interpreting
them, we should remember their limitations as indices of *average*
personality traits for each sex. Fortunately, the vast majority of
both men and women stay out of prison.

Some biological basis for the greater aggressiveness of males
would seem to be indicated by the fact that males tend to be dominant throughout the animal world. Seward (15) has recently
brought together considerable research having to do with the relationship of sex to dominance and the effect of the male sex
hormone in changing dominance status in the social heirarchy.
Even in females, aggressive "masculine" behavior patterns can
be produced by androgen injection. In the higher animals, biological and social factors are inextricably interwoven. Hormone-

induced changes in dominance status may be not so much the direct result of an increase in aggressive motivation as a reaction on the part of other animals in the group to the physical changes produced by the hormone treatment.

When we turn to the more passive type of personality traits related to emotional adjustment or maladjustment, there is general agreement that neurotic tendencies are more marked in females than in males. Wellman (23) summarizes a number of studies on school children indicating that girls are more likely than boys to show nervous habits like nail-biting, thumb-sucking, finger-sucking, and tongue-protrusion. Personality inventories usually rank males somewhat higher than females in traits making for emotional adjustment. On the Bernreuter Personality Scale, for instance, the norms show that women are more neurotic and unstable, less self-sufficient, more introverted, less dominant, less self-confident, and more socially dependent than men. Anastasi (2, p. 441) has shown that all these differences in average score except the last are statistically significant. Critical ratios range from 3.15 for neurotic tendency to 9.62 for self-confidence. Personality scales of the questionnaire type have, of course, definite limitations. Differences like those reported might mean nothing more than that girls are more willing than boys to admit their worries, weaknesses, and embarrassments. However, the results as they stand corroborate the common opinion that women are more likely to be nervous and unstable than men.

Another type of personality test upon which clear-cut sex differences have been found is the Allport-Vernon *Study of Values* (1). Most of the items in this test require the subject to choose between alternatives, each of which is related to a dominant value. Men obtain higher average scores than women in theoretical, economic, and political values, which would indicate more interest in abstract ideas, more emphasis on practical success, and more desire for influence and power over others as goals for living. Women obtain higher average scores than men in the aesthetic, social and religious values, which would indicate more interest in art, more emphasis on religion, and more concern for the welfare of others as goals for living.

The interests typical of the two sexes differ markedly. "Eavesdropping" investigations (3) have shown that in casual conversation, men are most likely to be talking about business, money, sports, and amusements, whereas women are most likely to discuss men, clothes, or decoration. Even as children, sexes differ in their play. As early as kindergarten age boys engage in more active games calling for vigorous physical activity, while girls are more interested in dolls, paper activities, and games calling for skilful movements. In reading, movies, and radio, girls show more interest in sentimental and domestic stories, whereas boys prefer stories of violent action. In a number of studies, Symonds (18) asked boys and girls of different ages in a number of different communities to rank fifteen major areas of interest as a basis for discussion and reading in school. The boys consistently gave the high ranks to money, health, safety, study, recreation, and civic affairs. The girls consistently indicated that they would prefer to discuss personal attractiveness, etiquette, and getting along with people. It is to be remembered in this connection that boys and men score consistently higher than girls and women on general information tests. Findings based on these various types of research give a fairly consistent picture. From kindergarten through adulthood, the interests of males seem to be broader and more active than those of females.

Tests devised especially to measure vocational interests have cast further light on the nature of the sex differences. The Kuder Preference Record (20, 21) gives the subject an opportunity to choose between occupational activites sampling a wide variety of tasks. Scores can then be obtained which show the relative frequency with which scientific, computational, musical, artistic, literary, social service, persuasive, mechanical, and clerical activities are represented in his choices. Boys average higher than girls in the mechanical, scientific, computational, and persuasive preferences, whereas the girls average higher in musical, artistic, literary, social service, and clerical preferences.

By far the most comprehensive research on vocational interests has been carried on by Strong (17). Sex differences have constituted an important part of this work. The technique that has been used is to tabulate the responses of various groups of people to each item on the comprehensive list making up the Strong Vocational Interest Blank. From the differences in percentages of the groups making each response it is possible to give the response a scoring weight. These weights can be totaled for an individual to show how much he is like people in the group from which they were derived. In investigating differences between men and women, the natural procedure was to tabulate responses of representative samples of each sex and attach scoring weights to the items showing large differences between the sexes. The M-F (masculinity-femininity) key for the Strong blank was derived in this way. Strong emphasizes the fact that such a procedure tends to *exaggerate* differences between groups, and reminds us that there are many more ways in which men and women are *alike* in their interests than ways in which they differ. However, certain kinds of items show large and consistent sex differences. The distinctly masculine interests show up on items having to do with: (I) mechanical and scientific activites, (2) physically strenuous, adventuresome activities, (3) legal, political and army occupations, (4) selling activities, (5) certain forms of entertainment such as smokers, rough-house initiations, chess, (6) certain miscellaneous preferences, e.g., for outside work over inside, for working for oneself, etc.

The distinctly feminine interests are indicated on items having to do with: (I) musical, artistic activities, (2) literary activities, (3) certain kinds of people, especially the unfortunate and disagreeable, (4) certain forms of entertainment, e.g., fortune-tellers, full-dress affairs, and social-problem movies, (5) clerical work, (6) teaching, (7) social work, (8) merchandise, that is, looking at shop windows, displaying merchandise, etc., (9) certain school subjects, (10) miscellaneous characteristics. A more detailed description of the items thus classified can be found in Strong's book (17).

When M-F scores based on these discriminating items alone are obtained for representative male and female groups, large and highly significant sex differences are found in all comparisons from adolescence through middle age. Critical ratios of these differences for various age groups run from 16.2 to 22.2. There is some overlapping between distributions, but very little. Only 3 per cent of the adult men, for example, are more feminine in their scores than the average woman. No adult women are above the median for men, and only I per cent are above the 25th percentile.

It is to be expected, since this is the case, that women and men will differ in the scores they obtain in the occupational scales of the Strong test. (An occupational scale shows how much an individual's interests resemble those of a representative group of successful persons engaged in that occupation.) This is found to be true. Girls and women average significantly higher than boys and men on the scales for occupations involving art, personnel or social service professions, and writing. Boys and men are higher on the occupational scales for science and business. Seder (12) found, however, that if you do not compare sample groups representative of *all* men and women, but only groups of men and women who are both *in* the same profession, the interests of the two sexes are practically indistinguishable. Men and women physicians, for instance, share the same interests. Men and women life insurance agents, likewise, are very much alike. The interests of women doctors are probably more like those of men doctors than they are like those of housewives.

Strong had developed a special interest blank for women, before Seder's results suggested that for getting at interests characteristic of an *occupational* group, a special test might not be necessary. Work with this blank has pointed to another very interesting fact. The vocational interests of men and women are differently *organized*. Statistical analysis of relationships between occupational scores has shown that for professional men, at least, there are six main types of interest pattern: (I) the human-science occupations, such as physician, architect, and psychologist; (2) the technical-science occupations, such as chemist and engineer; (3) the social-service occupations, such as minister, personnel manager, or schoolman; (4) the business-detail occupations, such as banker and accountant; (5) the sales occupations; and (6) the language occupations, such as lawyer and writer. When relationships between women's occupational scores are studied, four main types of interest are found, but one of them predominates so strongly over the others that in one study of graduating high-school girls, over 90 per cent of them showed predominant interests of this one type. This interest factor has been called "Interest in Male Association" by Crissy and Daniel (4), who made one of the factor analyses on which these conclusions are based. This name was chosen because it includes the interests common to housewives, office workers, stenographers, and nurses, all of them occupations that involve working for and with men. It would be simpler and probably more correct to call it "Typical Feminine Interests." It doubtless represents the general attitude and outlook of the woman who does not want a career for its own sake, but who is satisfied to pursue any pleasant, congenial activity that offers itself until marriage. There is evidence that elementary teachers also belong to this group. The other three interest factors or types for women are: (I) social-service occupations, such as social worker and Y. W. C. A. secretary; (2) language occupations, such as librarians and authors; and (3) science occupations, such as physician and mathematics-science teacher. The important point to keep in mind is that there is a far more uniform and standardized pattern of feminine interests than there is of masculine. One can get a fairly good idea of what it is by examining the content of one of the standard women's magazines—home, personal attractiveness, amusements, and direct relationships with people. The first thing that an interest test indicates about a girl who has taken it is the extent to which she deviates from this typical feminine pattern. If there is a deviation, the direction which it takes can be evaluated by means of scores in the other interest factors. This interest difference between men and women has been emphasized because of its possible bearing on the problem of the rarity of high professional achievement among women. Discussion of the origin of this and other differences will be reserved for the end of the chapter.

One further statement needs to be made about interest scores in general. Contrary to the common belief, likes and dislikes are *not* fleeting, changeable, or transitory. There is overwhelming evidence that in the large majority of cases, the type of interests that characterize an individual in his late adolescence will go with him through life. Even considerably earlier than this, in the first years of high school, it has been shown that interest scores are fairly stable. Thus, it cannot be expected that non-professional women will suddenly develop professional interests, or that interests predominantly in the direction of verbal activities will be superseded by strong scientific interests. The traits of personality we have been calling vocational interests are *not* developed through engaging in a particular occupation, but are formed much earlier in ways as yet unknown to us.

By far the most comprehensive study of all the personality traits in which sex differences occur is the one made by Terman and Miles (19). The investigation had its origin years before in their discovery while collecting information about gifted children that the boys and girls in their experimental group differed markedly from each other in certain ways. Using these items as leads, they tried out a large number of questions on male and female groups of various ages, selecting for their final assortment those which gave statistically significant differences between group responses. The result is the test which they call the Attitude-Interest Analysis Blank, a nondescriptive title chosen so as not to give the individual taking it any clue as to its purpose. There are seven types of item included: Word Association, Inkblot Association, Information, Emotional and Ethical Response, Interests, Opinions, and Introversive Response. The authors give abundant evidence that scores on this test show up large and statistically significant differences between men and women of all ages, occupational levels, and degrees of education. There is very little overlapping of male and female distributions. Terman and Miles remind us that the method they used tends to exaggerate sex difference since the large number of associations, interests, and opinions on which men and women do *not* differ were discarded in constructing the scale. However, the fact that such a set of items can be selected indicates that there are genuine differences between the sexes in our culture.

The nature of these differences is summarized by Terman and Miles as follows:[1]

From whatever angle we have examined them the males included in the standardization groups evinced a distinctive interest in exploit and adventure, in outdoor and physically strenuous occupations, in machinery and tools, in science, physical phenomena, and inventions; and, from rather occasional evidence, in business and commerce. On the other hand, the females of our groups have evinced a distinctive interest in domestic affairs and in aesthetic objects and occupations; they have distinctively preferred more sedentary and indoor occupations, and occupations more directly ministrative, particularly to the young, the helpless, the distressed. Supporting and supplementing these are the more subjective differences—those in emotional disposition and direction. The males directly or indirectly manifest the greater self-assertion and aggressiveness; they express more hardihood and fearlessness, and more roughness of manners, language, and sentiments. The females express themselves as more compassionate and sympathetic, more timid, more fastidious and aesthetically sensitive, more emotional in general (or at least more expressive of the four emotions considered), severer moralists, yet admit in themselves more weaknesses in emotional control and (less noticeably) in physique.

But we must define some of our terms more precisely, for instance, "aggressiveness" and "self-assertion." The evidence is for initiative, enterprise, vigorous activity, outdoor adventure; "aggressiveness" need not imply selfishness or tyranny or unfair attack. The compassion and sympathy of the female, again, appears from the evidence personal rather than abstract, less a principled humanitarianism than an active sympathy for palpable misfortune or distress. In disgust, in aesthetic judgment, and in moral censure, the evidence is rather for the influence of fashion and of feeling than of principle or reason. Our evidence need not imply the possession of a "truer" taste or a more discerning conscience. (19, pp. 447-448)

It is plain from the data furnished by Terman and Miles that masculinity-femininity, as measured by their M-F scale, is no all-or-none trait. The various occupational groups differ, for instance. Among men, athletes and engineers have the most "masculine" averages; journalists, artists, and clergymen, the least "masculine." Among women, domestic employees are the most "feminine"; athletes and doctors, the least "feminine." Age groups differ also. Eighth-grade girls are more "feminine," eleventh-grade boys more "masculine" than any other age groups. Individuals within any one of the occupational or age groups differ among themselves. What we have is a continuous distribution rather than an exact classification.

* * *

With all the evidence that has been assembled for the existence of measurable sex differences in what one might call basic personality directions, the question of the relative contributions of nature and nurture to these differences cannot be avoided. It must be admitted at the outset, however, that this question cannot be conclusively answered. From earliest infancy, boys and girls are exposed to subtle differences in treatment. Whatever differences in personality tendencies may have been inherent in the structure of their bodies and nervous systems are mixed up with differences in what they have learned by the time they are old enough so that we can measure the characteristics with any success. But there are a few lines of evidence that are at least suggestive, though Terman and Miles avoid drawing any final conclusions. There is one aspect of their work that points rather strongly in the direction of a cultural origin for the differences they obtained. On analyzing the scores of various male and female groups one finds that groups which obtain the same total scores do not necessarily have the same responses to individual items (19, Appendix VII). High-school boys, for instance, and engineers are both very masculine groups, with an average standard score of .75. The high-school boys obtain this score largely from Exercise 5 (Interests) and Exercise 3 (Information). They are below average in "masculinity" as measured by Exercise 4 (Emotional and Ethical Response). It is precisely this Exercise 4 which gives the engineers their high score. In a study by Tyler (22), using the M-F test, high-school girls who were taking a college-preparatory course were compared with their classmates who were planning to go to work after they graduated. The college-preparatory girls appeared to be more "masculine" than the others. Upon analysis of items upon which these total scores were based, it was found that the difference arose almost entirely from a few items in two sections of Exercise 4 (Emotional and Ethical Response). The college-preparatory girls, drawn on the whole from better educated and more favorably situated economic groups, admitted less fear for a number of things and condemned various minor sins less seriously. That is *all* which the apparently significant difference in femininity meant, and it could easily be explained by specific differences in what they had learned while growing up. This finding suggests that analysis of the items on which other average score differences are based might give similar results.

The most widely quoted evidence that sex differences are dependent to a considerable extent on culture is Margaret Mead's study of three primitive tribes (9). Among the Arapesh, both sexes display what we would consider feminine characteristics. They are coöperative, unaggressive, gentle, and sympathetic. Among the Mundugumur, both sexes display what we would consider masculine characteristics. They are violent, aggressive, and competitive, lovers of action and fighting. Among the Tchambuli, the traits as we find them in our society appear to be reversed. It is the women who have the positions of power and take the responsibility for earning the living of the family, while the men engage in artistic and non-essential activities. Consequently, the women are impersonal, practical, and efficient, while the men are artistic, timid, sensitive, and dependent. (We have probably all seen families in our society which resemble this pattern.) Mead shows also that these varied temperamental characteristics seem to be related to methods of rearing children in the different societies. Sex inversions occur, however, in these societies as well as in our own. It seems that whatever the characteristic pattern of masculine and feminine characteristics is some individuals will depart from it.

The psycho-analytic writers have consistently maintained that there are biological differences underlying the differences in temperament and behavior. Probably the most thoroughgoing exposition of what these are believed to be is found in Deutsch (5). The evidence that she cites, based on material obtained from patients undergoing analysis, biographies, and fictional representations from literature, is very difficult to evaluate by any of the methods we are accustomed to use with systematically collected (and especially experimental) data on human differences. Fromm (6) develops the hypothesis that sex differences are based fundamentally on the different rôles men and women must necessarily take in sexual intercourse. Since the woman is passive and dependent for her satisfaction on the man, she develops passive, dependent qualities in her other relationships. It is a little difficult to see how this factor could produce the personality differences that have been observed in young children long before they have a very clear conception of how the sex organs function in adults. One might, perhaps, assume that mothers teach their daughters to be passive and dependent, knowing that these qualities are the ones they will need, but so far, no one has produced any clear evidence to support the assumption.

Johnson and Terman (8), after summarizing the evidence that there are measurable sex differences in temperament and personality, discuss in some detail the physiological characteristics which are ordinarily included under the term homeostasis. They show that in the maintenance of constant body temperature, the acid-base relationship in the blood, constant blood sugar level, and gonadal activity, males are somewhat more stable than females. They propose the hypothesis that there is a difference in what they call "mental homostasis" to account for sex differences. Women tend to be more sensitive to external influences, more easily thrown off balance by them. As evidence that sex differences are not entirely cultural, but may well have a constitutional basis, they cite four facts. First, differences have been found in very young children. (We have already noted, however, that differences in treatment may have some effect from the cradle on up.) Second, neurotic tendencies in women have shown no relative decrease as women have been allowed more freedom. Third, institutional groups such as orphanage children whose environments have been closely similar over long periods of time show the same sort of sex differences as groups in the general population. Fourth, a growing body of research on animals shows plainly that sex hormones *can* influence behavior.

This evidence also is not too impressive. About the most that can be said at present is that biological differences in temperament are not out of the question, but are certainly not proved. The most likely conclusion would seem to be that any degree of "masculinity" or "femininity" *can* occur in any individual of either sex, but for some reason as yet inadequately understood, a girl growing up does find certain attitudes, interests, and personality traits much more congenial than others and tends to acquire them, whereas a boy is likely to prefer another set. This slanting, this difference in tendency to acquire differential characteristics, is the factor which may have a biological basis. At the present stage of the research, there is ample room in the intricacies of the endocrine system for all such hypotheses.

Setting aside the as yet unanswered nature-nurture question, we can still draw certain conclusions from the facts as we find them. In the first place, it seems likely that the sex difference in achievement is based more on differences between the sexes in temperament, attitude, and interests than on differences in any sort of ability. Because women are less aggressive, more personal, more willing to play a minor part in the world's affairs, women's talents are more likely to be used in helping someone else win than in winning for themselves. There is some evidence that women are not even averse to considering themselves inferior. Smith (16) reports an interesting study in which girls and boys in each age group from eight to fifteen were asked to vote as to whether boys or girls possess to a greater degree each of nineteen desirable and fourteen undesirable traits. The striking fact was that the older the groups were, the more favorable all the ratings made by *both* sexes were to boys. This is the more remarkable when we remember that during these school years the girls are consistently behaving better, having less trouble, and getting better marks than the boys. The second conclusion to be emphasized is that even if we could prove that human traits are culturally determined this would *not* mean that we can quickly wipe them out. The differences we have analyzed do exist and will have their effect on what males and females now living will do during the rest of their lives. It is useless for enthusiastic supporters of feminine equality to insist that women *should* go into all types of occupations and assume completely independent positions in society. With the attitudes they now have, it is impossible for them to do this unless drastic circumstances force them to go against their basic impulses.

What is desirable is that we should broaden our concepts of what the sex rôles are so as to make room for more kinds of women and more kinds of men. Our complex, highly differentiated society has a place for many different kinds of individuals, in all sorts of *complementing* relationships, of which the ideal marriage relationship is only the most basic example. If, in addition to clarifying our understanding of what the sex rôles are, we can also keep these individual differences in mind, enrichment of our common life will be the result. Just what changes in the social order we need to produce these improvements is a problem for the sociologist rather than the psychologist. Recent articles by Mead (10) and Seward (14) on sex rôles make some interesting practical suggestions. The fact that there is at present considerable ambiguity as to what the sex rôles are makes for adjustment difficulties in adolescent girls. Seward (13) asked 147 college girls to fill out an attitude scale on sex rôles in postwar society. She then compared the scores made by the fifteen individuals who were most liberal in their attitudes on this subject with the scores of the fifteen who were most conservative, on a number of psychological tests. There was no difference in scholastic aptitude, in dominance, or in attitudes toward sex and the basic biological functions. The liberals obtained more "masculine" scores on the Terman-Miles blank and more "feministic" scores on the Kirkpatrick scale for measuring this attitude. Several background factors also differentiated between the groups. The liberals were more likely to have come from broken homes or homes in which the mother was maladjusted. They were less likely to have had brothers. They were also less religious. Analysis of responses to a projective type of personality test in which they made up stories about pictures indicated somewhat greater insecurity and hostility in the liberals. The interesting finding is that the girls with the conservative attitudes toward woman's place in the world seem to be somewhat happier and better adjusted than those with the liberal attitudes. As many writers on the subject have pointed out, the progress of science and the removal from the home of many kinds of work which were once carried on there makes the restriction of women's activities to home and family increasingly inappropriate. The wide range of abilities in both sexes makes it appear that sex typing of occupations is not appropriate either. But the *attitudes* that both men and women have grown up with fit these practices better than they do the actual economic and psychological facts, and too great a deviation from the accepted attitude makes for maladjustment. There lies our problem.

From *The Psychology of Human Differences* (first edition). New York: D. Appleton-Century Company, 1947, pages 79-87, 89-94. Reprinted by permission of Prentice-Hall, Inc.

FOOTNOTE

1. Reprinted by permission from *Sex and Personality* by Terman and Miles, Copyrighted, 1936, by the McGraw-Hill Book Company, Inc.

REFERENCES

1. ALLPORT, G. W., and VERNON, P. E. "A test for personal values." *J. abnorm. and soc. Psychol.*, 1931, 26, 231–248.
2. ANASTASI, A. *Differential psychology.* New York: Macmillan, 1937. Pp. 615.
3. CARLSON, J. S., COOK, S. W., and STROMBERG, E. L. "Sex differences in conversations." *J. appl. Psychol.*, 1936, 20, 727–735.
4. CRISSY, W. J. E., and DANIEL, W. J. "Vocational interest factors in women." *J. appl. Psychol.*, 1939, 23, 488–94.

5. DEUTSCH, HELENE. *The Psychology of Women.* New York: Grune and Stratton, 1944–45. Pp., Vol. I, 393, Vol. 2, 491.
6. FROMME, E. "Sex and character." *Psychiatry,* 1943, 6, 21–31.
7. HARTSHORNE, H., MAY, M.A., and MALLER, J. B. *Studies in the nature of character;* Vol. II *Studies in service and self-control.* New York: Macmillan, 1929, Pp. 559.
8. JOHNSON, W. B., amd TERMAN, L.M. "Some highlights in the literature of psychological sex differences published since 1920." *J. Psychol.,* 1940, 9, 327–336.
9. MEAD, M. *Sex and temperament in three primitive societies.* New York: MORROW, 1935. Pp. 335.
10. MEAD, M. "Women's social position." *J. educ. Sociol.,* 1944, 17, 453–462.
11. SCHEINFELD, A. *Women and men.* New York: Harcourt Brace, 1943–44. Pp. 453.
12. SEDER, M. A. "The vocational interests of professional women," *J. appl. Psychol.,* 1940, 24, 130–143 and 265–272.
13. SEWARD, G. H. "Cultural conflict and the feminine rôle." *J. soc. Psychol.,* 1945, 22, 177–194.
14. SEWARD, G. H. "Sex rôles in postwar planning." *J. soc. Psychol.,* 1944, 19, 163–185.
15. SEWARD, G. H. *Sex and the social order.* New York: McGraw-Hill, 1946. Pp. 301.
16. SMITH, S. "Age and sex differences in children's opinions concerning sex differences." *J. genet. Psychol.,* 1939, 54, 17–25.
17. STRONG, E. K., JR., *Vocational interests of men and women.* Stanford University: Stanford Univ. Press, 1943. Pp. 746.
18. SYMONDS, P. M. "Sex differences in the life problems and interests of adolescents." *Sch. & Soc.,* 1936, 43, 751–752.
19. TERMAN, L.M., and MILES, C. C. *Sex and personality: studies in masculinity and femininity.* New York: McGraw-Hill, 1936. Pp. 600.
20. TRAXLER, A. E., and MCCALL, W. C. "Some data on the Kuder Preference Record." *Ed. and Psychol. Meas.;* 1941, 1, 253–268.
21. TRIGGS, FRANCES O. "A study of the relation of Kuder Preference Record scores to various other measures." *Ed. & Psychol. Meas.,* 1943, 3, 341–354.
22. TYLER, L. E., "The measured interests of adolescent girls." *J. educ. Psychol.,* 1941, 32, 561–572.
23. WELLMAN, B. L. "Sex differences." In Murchison, C. (Ed.) *Handbook of child psychology.* Worcester, Mass: Clark Univ. Press, 1933. Pp. 956, Ch. 15.
24. WICKMAN, E. K. *Children's behavior and teachers' attitudes.* New York Commonwealth Fund, 1928, Pp. 247.

SELF AND SEX

Arnold Gesell/Frances L. Ilg

Early in the century Arnold Gesell maintained that our knowledge of the developmental differences between the sexes was "partial ... piecemeal ... speculation" (1928, p. 292). However, by 1946 he and his associates at Yale were prepared to describe a large number of developmental sex differences and similarities. They arrived at their findings in characteristic fashion, through painstaking and detailed observations made over many years. Of all G. Stanley Hall's students, Gesell has contributed most to the study of the child and, it should be added, with more rigor, discipline, and modesty than his former mentor. He and Frances Ilg have collected huge quantities of observational data to formulate norms of growth in both the physical and psychological domains. Although their "normative-maturational" approach has proved inadequate for the purpose of building a theory of human development, their data and norms can stand by themselves. They represent a great contribution to the natural history of childhood and are highly regarded in this respect.

Gesell has authored or co-authored over twenty books on child development and has been widely read by both professionals and lay people. Except for his more technical research reports, his writing style is invariably simple and unpretentious and reveals a genuine respect for children. The following selection is taken from the chapter entitled "Self and Sex" in The Child from Five to Ten *(1946). Note that the discussion of sex differences is integrated into a consideration of the child's growing awareness of sexuality itself, and that the latter, in turn, is placed in the context of an emerging sense of self and of one's position in the family.*

Gesell, trained as a psychologist and physician, was Director of the Yale Clinic of Child Development from 1911 to 1948. Ilg, a pediatrician, was Director of the Gesell Institute of Child Development, founded in 1950 as successor to the Yale Clinic.

Many of the child's thinkings and feelings in regard to himself never come to utterance. He likes his name before he can speak it. He could scarcely realize himself if he didn't have a name. In the beginning was his name. He hears it so often that he finally identifies it with himself. Step by step he interprets other names and makes significant distinctions between pronouns in the first, second and third persons, and in nominative and accusative cases. The progress which he makes from the first to the tenth year might be summed up in a series of propositions which reflect his advancing insight:

1. *"Johnny"*—that's me. 2. I am I. 3. That's my mother. 4. That's my father. 5. He is a man. 6. I am a boy. 7. Susan is a girl. 8. She has a father and mother too. 9. I was a baby. 10. I grew. 11. I came from my mother. 12. I am going to get bigger. 13. I am going to school. 14. I am in the first grade. I have a mother and a teacher. 15. I am in the second grade. I hope my teacher likes me. I hope Freddie is not mad at me. 16. I am eight years old. I want to grow up. 17. I am ten years old. I read the . . . . . . magazine. I want to be an engineer when I'm a man, like my father.

In rough outline these statements show how the self expands, differentiates and incorporates new dimensions into its structure. The first differentiations have to do with the *me* and the *not me*. But very early the child has to reckon also with the distinctions of sex; at the age of two he distinguishes boys from girls by clothes, hats, and style of haircut. Soon he detects more fundamental physical differences. All this helps him to understand what he himself is. His early interests in sex are by no means purely sexual; they are part of a wide ranging curiosity which comprehends his whole environment. He cannot get his bearings unless he makes certain elementary observations and inferences, concerning mommies and daddies, boys and girls, animals and persons, men and women.

Of great psychological significance is his gradual realization that he has an *historical* self as well as a *present* self. *He* was once a *baby*! A little recapture of that babyhood by questioning, or even by dramatic revival helps to impart a new dimension to his enlarging self. At four or six his interest expands into the family tree from which he himself stemmed, and so he inquires about his relationships to parents, grandparents and great-grandparents. A 7-year-old observing his newborn brother taking a first meal at the breast, asked with astonishment, "Did I do that? And Mommy, did you do that too; and you too, Daddy?" He was in the throes of assimilating a tremendous fact. His questions reveal how closely the development of the self is intermeshed with the phenomenon of sex.

This does not mean that the whole, far ramifying structure of the self is built about a single framework of sex. The processes of generation and growth, to be sure, are so all important for the perpetuation of the species that they are strongly entrenched in the organism. But sexual functions do not necessarily play a despotic role in the patterning of child development. Instead the vast array of realities and attitudes which directly or indirectly pertain to sex must be assimilated into a yet more intricate complex, namely, the growing self. The problems of sexual hygiene cannot be rationally approached unless we see the facts of sex in perspective and recognize the subtle gradations by which they are incorporated into the total development of the individual self.

"Are you a little boy or a little girl?" This is a question which Binet made famous. One addresses it to a child about the age of three years. Usually he (the boy!) responds correctly. But even at this age many children reply by giving their own names. Others respond in terms of an emphatic negative, "Not a girl!" (Does this vehement denial reflect the traditional jest indulged in by relatives who tease small children by attributing the wrong sex to them?) A bright child may counter with a jokingly incorrect response. An older child may indignantly deny the implication of the wording of the question with "No, I am a *big* boy!" Girls are a little more likely to reply "I'm a boy!" Whether this latter is a masculine protest, we do not know! But the variations and tenor of all these responses show how diversely self and sex are interrelated.

Having made a correct intellectual discrimination as to sex, it will still take years for the child to define and establish his proper role as a boy or a girl. Nothing follows automatically. Some writers even hold that it is the culture which impresses this role. Our own studies indicate that there are differences in temperamental predisposition, in psycho-motor demeanor, and in developmental timing which are intrinsic in nature. The differences may not be great, but they can be decisive and they cast doubt on any hypothesis which derives the sex differences in personality solely from environmental or cultural factors.

But the psychological differences between the two sexes are by no means simple. In children as well as in adults they vary enormously in kind and degree. By means of an elaborate masculinity-femininity test consisting of no less than 456 items Terman and Miles (1936) investigated the sex temperaments of groups of adolescents and adults, and found many statistically distinctive sex responses. To what extent the manifold differences are due to a cultural bias the statistics do not disclose. The bias itself must have been originally produced by innate differences in the sexes. In any event, the end result is that each sex tends to play the role assigned to it.

The child, however, must actively find and adapt himself to the role, which again is not a simple matter, because each individual of each sex has a distinctive equipment of innumerable qualities of maleness and femaleness. These qualities manifest themselves in behavior tendencies, which to some extent compete with each other, at least in the eyes of the culture. The 2-year-old begins to identify his own sex by making elementary distinctions based on dress, haircut, and possibly voice. A few months later he becomes interested in the differences between boys and girls in their mode of micturition. Still later each sex may imitate the other in an effort to understand this difference, and a great many other differences. Many of these imitations are simple dramatic projections, even when they happen to include the genitalia.

A young child when confronted by two rival alternatives, tends to try out both when he is relatively unfamiliar with the behavior in question. And so during the formative pre-school years, before the so-called sex role is well established, the child shifts rather readily from one sex role to another. Our guidance nursery staff is frequently amused to see how often the domestic corner of the nursery is occupied by the dominant males, age two-and-a-half to three years. This corner is equipped with nothing but dolls, beds, brooms, ironing board and general housekeeping facilities; and it is the boys who are doing the housekeeping, including laundry.

Four- and 5-year-old children often play the role of the opposite sex. Many a 4-year-old boy has asked for a doll for Christmas; and the 5-year-old often wants a doll house. The 4-year-old may know he is not orthodox; so he keeps his doll somewhat out of sight. He may also be conscious of the excessive cultural pressure exerted by the disapproval of his parents. (It is easy to overstress the virtues of masculinity and gallantry at this age.) Girls from five to six years old may want to wear boys' clothes and tuck in their hair. By the age of seven, the shifting in roles becomes less frequent. The assigned sex role is usually established, a little earlier in girls, who at about this time are likely to object to having their hair cut. This too is the time when girls in particular may manifest an intense desire to simply hold a baby, and to have a baby in the family. Which reminds us again that the area of sex-interests is wide and growing. It is not limited to the so-called sex act; but relates to the whole complex network of interpersonal relations, and especially those of family life.

The problem of the parents is to help the child, be it boy or girl, to find his or her role in this broader family setting—a role which is progressing toward marriage. The child needs guidance all along the way. Parents sometimes think they will wait until the child can understand, and then they will tell him the whole story! And that will be that! But it is never so simple and decisive. Something unexpected is likely to occur; and fortunately it often is much less serious than it appears to be at first blush. To be forearmed the parent should know in advance the sort of things which do happen at least to other children. The growth gradients and maturity traits deal with the concrete situations.

Even before the age of four, questions about marriage begin. The 4-year-old may ask questions about how a specific baby arrived into the family. He may not accept too factual information. He may think the baby is really born through the navel. Or he may prefer to think the baby was purchased. At five years his curiosity is less intense than at six years. At six his questions become more specific, and may show some interest in the mechanics of mating in animals. At seven these interests are less openly expressed; but the child reflects and muses on sex relationships as he does about many other aspects of life. If he has heard about "seeds" he thinks about one or two seeds. At eight his interest in the father's function in procreation becomes more realistic. He is more aware of the marital relationships of his mother and father; and perhaps more susceptible to a jealousy reaction. At nine and ten he naturally feels a deepening identification with his family. He displays it, paradoxically, by withdrawal tendencies, and by a heightened sense of shame at any shortcomings on the part of the household. *He is now tragically sensitive to disharmonies and antagonisms between his mother and father.* And this may have a more devastating effect upon the development of his personality than some minor and unintelligent sex episode on his part.

The period from five to ten years is not a dormant or a latent sexual period. It is a period of progressive organization. Unremitting elaborations of the self and sex attitudes are laying the foundation for the more acute developments of puberty. The guidance during this pre-critical period should consist in progressive orientation. Information must be skillfully imparted and also skillfully withheld; because it should be graduated to suit the occasion and the child's maturity. The same story needs to be told and retold in changing versions. Some facts should be given in advance as a buffer against misinformation. The chief goal, however, should be to preserve easy, mutual confidence between mother and child, father and child (sometimes the latter relationship is the more vital). If sex exploration or an adventure in nudity is reported or discovered, the parent should so far as possible rationalize it calmly in her own mind as well as in that of the child. Orientation, rather than mere instruction or discipline is the key to a solution. Often the supreme psychological moment for effective "sex" guidance arises when there is no sex problem at all. The child is taught by suggestion and by indirection. The two extremes to be avoided are over-protection through silence and evasion; and over-reliance on excessively candid information.

The reticences and the securities of wholesome family life are the best long range guarantee of a normal development of self and sex. Reticence as well as information has a role in sex education.

There are enormous individual differences with respect to the strength of sexual characteristics among adults as well as children. Sheldon (1942), for example, states that the viscerotonic temperament is "notably greedy for routine outward affection by members of his family." The attitude of parents will naturally color their outlook on the problems presented by the child. Misdirected emotion can be avoided only if the parent carefully interprets the individuality and developmental background of the child, as each problem arises. Intelligent, outgoing, factual children want and comprehend many facts early. Other children are so slow or naive that they must be told a little at a time, with much repetition, and sometimes even a little skillful prodding. Some children again assimilate best by making their own deductions from a realistic knowledge of reproduction in animals. Sometimes the father is a better channel of information than is the mother.

A few children of both sexes seem blind to the implications of sex until a relatively advanced age. Boys are more likely to get sex "information" from non-parental sources. They are more active and persistent in experimental play and exploration. They bring home tales they have heard, new "bad" words they have learned. They ask for specific explanations; and parents can be of service in helping the boy to a suitable vocabulary. Comparing boys and girls as groups, girls tend to show a more precocious interest in sex than boys. Their questions are more comprehensive, and less dependent upon the stimulus of information picked up from other children. The questions seem to come from a more integrated curiosity.

It is evident, then, that the acquisition of a mature sense of self is an extremely intricate process in which the sphere of sex figures importantly, but not omnipotently. The younger the child the less developed the self, even though the vigor of self-assertion may be strong. With increasing age and social experience this self becomes less shallow; it grows in depth; it consolidates the past; it orients to the future.

GROWTH GRADIENTS IN SEX

18 MONTHS—*Sex interest and differentiation* Affectionate towards
mother when tired, in trouble or when pants are wet.
Uses general term "baby" for both boys and girls.

2 YEARS—*Sex Interest and Differentiation* Shows strong affection toward
parents: "My mommy," "My daddy." Kisses at bedtime.
Names genitals by word used for urination.
Distinguishes boys from girls by clothes and style of haircut.
Differentiates adults by general words, "lady" or "man," but continues
to call children by specific names: "Jacky" or "Mary."
Babies Interest in the appurtenances of baby sibling: powder, soap,
clothes, crib.

2½ YEARS—*Sex Interest and Differentiation* Conscious of own sex organs
and may handle them when undressed.
Inquires about mother's breasts.
Knows that he is a boy like father and different from girls and
mothers (and vice versa).
Non-verbalized generalization that boys and fathers have distinctive
genitalia, and stand when they urinate; girls and mothers do not.
Shows interest in different postures of boys and girls when urinating.
Differentiates sex of children by general term "boy" and "girl."
If questioned about his sex, negates opposite sex, "I'm not a girl."
Beginning of interest in physiological differences between sexes.
Boys may prefer girls' toys.

3 YEARS—*Sex Interest and Differentiation* Expresses affection by "I like"
(3½ years—"I love").
Affirms own sex if questioned—"I am a boy."
Verbally expresses interest in physiological differences between sexes
and in different posture for urinating. Girls attempt to urinate
standing up.
Desire to look at or touch adults, especially mother's breasts.
Interest in marriage and marrying; proposes to either parent and
others; thinks you can marry either sex.
No distinction between sexes in play.
Temporary and shifting attachment to some "friend" of the opposite
sex (3½ years).
Babies Beginning of interest in babies, wants family to have one.
Asks questions: "What can the baby do when it comes?" "Where does
it come from?"
Most do not understand mother when she answers that the baby
grows inside of her.

4 YEARS—*Sex Interest and Differentiation* Extremely conscious of the
navel.

Under social stress grasps genitals and may need to urinate.

May play the game of "show"; verbal play about eliminating and calling names relating to function.

Interest in other people's bathrooms; may demand privacy for himself, but extremely interested in bathroom activities of others.

Some segregation along sex lines.

Babies Questions about where babies come from. May believe mother's answer that the baby grows inside of the mother's "tummy," but may cling to the notion that the baby is purchased.

Questions about how the baby gets out of the mother's "tummy." May spontaneously think the baby is born through the navel.

5 YEARS—*Sex Interest and Differentiation* Familiar with, but not much interested in physical differences between the sexes.

Decrease in sex play and game of "show."

More modest and less exposing of themselves.

Less bathroom play, less interest in strange bathrooms than earlier.

Aware of sex organs when adult seen undressed and may wonder why father doesn't have breasts or sister a penis.

Boy may reject girls' toys such as dolls, although he may make a doll's bed in carpentry, or take part in house play.

Takes opposite sex largely for granted, little distinction between sexes in play. Frequent boy-girl pairs.

Babies Interest in baby and in having a baby of their own; may dramatize this.

Some boys as well as girls may relate back to when they were in mother's stomach, or to future when they will have a baby of their own.

Re-asks, "Where do babies come from?" and accepts "mother's stomach" as an answer.

Some cling to the idea that you buy the baby at a hospital.

Make little connection between size of pregnant woman and presence of a baby.

6 YEARS—*Sex Interest and Differentiation* Marked awareness of and interest in differences in body structure between sexes. Questioning.

Mutual investigation by both sexes reveals practical answers to questions about sex differences.

Mild sex play or exhibitionism in play or in school toilets. Game of "show."

Some children are subjected to sex play by older children.

May play hospital and take rectal temperatures.

Calling names, remarking or giggling involving words dealing with elimination functions.

Some confusion in differentiation of male and female. May dress in attire of opposite sex.

Interest in marriage to someone of opposite sex, often to a relative.

Strong interest of older boy for younger girl.

Babies Interest in origin of babies, pregnancy and birth.

Vague idea that babies follow marriage.

Interest in how baby comes out of mother and if it hurts.

Some interest in knowing how baby started. Accepts idea that baby grows in mother's stomach and started from a seed.

If told of intercourse by older playmates, child may be disturbed and usually questions mother.

Wants a new baby in the family.

Wants to hold baby after it is born.

7 YEARS—*Sex Interest and Differentiation* The child has long since satisfied interest in differences in physique between the sexes. Less interest in sex.

Some mutual exploration, experimentation and sex play, but less than earlier.

Interest in sex role and characteristics of boys and girls.

May be last age when boys and girls play together regardless of sex lines.

Strong and persistent boy-girl love affairs with the idea of marriage usually strong.

Babies Intense longing for a new baby in family usually of own sex.

Knows that having babies can be repeated and that older women do not have them.

Interested in mother's pregnancy. Excited about baby's growth. Wants to know how it is fed, how big it is, how much it costs.

Interest in literature, such as *The Story of a Baby*, by Marie Ets (1939).

Associates size of pregnant woman with presence of baby.

Satisfied to know that baby came from two seeds (or eggs), one from mother and one from father.

May ask details of birth. Just where mother will be, how baby will get out.

8 YEARS—*Sex Interest and Differentiation* Interest in sex rather high, though sex exploration and play less common than at six. Girls may be unusually responsive to touch and rough play with boys.

Interest in peeping, smutty jokes, provocative giggling; whisper, write or spell "elimination" and "sex" words.

Girls begin to question about menstruation.

Boys recognize pretty girls and girls, handsome boys.

A boy may have several girls but he knows he is going to marry only one of them. But fewer boy-girl twosomes.

Plan to have own home when married.

Sexes begin spontaneously to draw apart in play.

Babies Warm and loving interest in babies.

Understands slow process of growth of baby within mother; connects appearance of pregnant woman with a baby.

Wants more exact information as to where baby is in mother's abdomen. Confused by use of word "stomach."

Some girls may ask about father's part in procreation.

9 YEARS—*Sex Interest and Differentiation* May talk about sex information with friends of same sex.

Interest in details of own organs and function; seeks pictorial information in books.

May be self-conscious of exposing body.

May not wish parent of opposite sex to see him nude.

Sex swearing; sex poems.

Division of sexes in play; if mixed, may stimulate kissing games; teasing about "girl" or "boy" friends.

Babies May relate selves to process of reproduction, "Have I a seed in me?"

Some NINES may still think that baby is born by Caesarian section.

From Arnold Gesell and Frances L. Ilg (in collaboration with Louise Bates Ames and Glenna E. Bullis). *The Child from Five to Ten.* New York: Harper & Row, 1946, pages 311-317, 322-325. Reprinted by permission of Harper & Row, Publishers, Inc. Copyright © 1946 by Arnold Gesell and Frances L. Ilg.

REFERENCES

ETS, M. H. *The Story of a Baby.* New York: Viking Press, 1939.

GESELL, A. *The Mental Growth of the Preschool Child.* New York: Macmillan Company, 1928.

SHELDON, W. H. (In collaboration with S. S. Stevens) *The Varieties of Temperament: A Psychology of Constitutional Differences.* New York: Harper, 1942.

TERMAN, L. M., & MILES, C. C. *Sex and Personality: Studies in Masculinity and Femininity.* New York: McGraw-Hill, 1936.

THEORIES OF IDENTIFICATION AND EXPOSURE TO MULTIPLE MODELS

ALBERT BANDURA / RICHARD H. WALTERS

The work of Albert Bandura and Richard Walters represents the "social-learning" approach to sex-role development. Unlike psychoanalytic and cognitive-developmental theories, this approach does not postulate the existence of psychosexual stages of development. On the contrary, it holds that sex-role development is a function of continuous learning, whereas the other two theories maintain that what children learn about sex identity varies according to their developmental stage.

Social-learning theory is an amalgam of two components: learning theory and social identification theory. The first component simply holds that children will learn to behave as they are expected and reinforced to do, and that such learning is in accord with well-established principles of generalization, discrimination, and mediation. The social component explains the learning of elaborate, complex, and novel behaviors by invoking principles of modeling, imitation, observational learning, and vicarious reinforcement.

Bandura is professor of psychology at Stanford University and a past president of the American Psychological Association. He is probably best known for his research on the effects of filmed and televised aggressive models on children's behavior, although his compass has been much wider than that, covering sex-role identification, behavior modification, and the development and treatment of deviant behaviors. Walters was professor of psychology at the University of Toronto and founded the Psychology Department at the University of Waterloo in Ontario. His primary research interests were in modeling, aggression, and punishment.

The selection reprinted below is drawn from Chapter 2 of Social

Learning and Personality Development *(1963). In this selection the authors discuss processes of identification, the characteristics of effective models, and the results of multiple modeling, with particular reference to sex-role acquisition.*

During their life history children are exposed to a series of models, the relative strength of whose influence depends on their availability, their homogeneity or heterogeneity, their interrelationships, and the extent to which each of them has received rewarding or punishing consequences for his behavior.

During the child's early years the family constitutes the child's basic reference group; at this stage, the range of available real-life models is restricted to family members, particularly the parents, who serve as the source of biological and conditioned rewards for the child. Consequently, theoreticians who accept the psychoanalytic view that a child's early experiences are crucial for determining his future development and behavior have focused on the role of intrafamily dynamics in determining the direction and extent of a child's imitation of the same-sex and opposite-sex parent, a topic which is customarily labeled as the problem of "identification."

Psychoanalytic theory has provided the most widely accepted explanation of the identification process. According to Freud, there are two quite different sets of antecedent conditions, both fear-inducing, that result in a child's identification with a parent. *Anaclitic identification* (Freud, 1925 [1917]) occurs when a nurturant adult, usually the mother, to whom the child has developed a nonsexual dependent attachment, commences to withhold rewards that she has previously freely dispensed; the resulting threat of loss of the loved object then motivates the child to "introject" her behavior and qualities. *Defensive or aggressive identification* (Freud, 1924b [1912], 1949 [1945]), which received increasing emphasis in Freud's later writings, occurs only for boys. The mechanism of identification with the aggressor depicts introjection as the outcome of the resolution of the Oedipus complex in which the child adopts the characteristics of the rivalrous like-sex parent, thereby reducing anxiety over anticipated punishment by castration for his incestuous wishes toward his mother and at the same time vicariously gaining the affectional gratifications of the opposite-sex parent. Fear of punishment, rather than fear of loss of love, thus provides the primary incentive for a boy to identify with his father.

Different aspects of Freud's identification theory have been emphasized by subsequent writers on the topic, several of whom have attempted reinterpretations in terms of learning-theory concepts. Mowrer (1950) describes two forms of identification, developmental and defensive, parallel to those outlined by Freud. However, Mowrer focuses on the developmental form in both his theoretical elaboration and his laboratory analogues of the identification process. According to Mowrer, developmental identification occurs because the caretaking adult, ordinarily the mother, mediates the young child's biological and social rewards, and thus her behavior and attributes take on secondary reward value. On the basis of stimulus generalization, responses that parallel those of the caretaker attain reward value for the child in proportion to their similarity to those made by the caretaking adult. Consequently, the child can administer positively conditioned reinforcers to himself simply by matching as closely as possible the caretaker's positively valenced behavior.

This process is well illustrated by Mowrer's account of the acquisition of language responses (1950, 1958). For example, in the first step of training a bird to talk, the trainer emits words in conjunction with the presentation of food, water, physical contact, and other primary reinforcers. As the formerly neutral word stimuli take on secondary reward value, the bird is motivated to reproduce them. However, in later expositions of the process of learning by observation, including language acquisition, Mowrer (1960a, 1960b) has placed more emphasis on the role of positively conditioned proprioceptive feedback and imaginal mediating responses in the facilitation of imitative behavior.

Sears (1957) has, like Mowrer, placed most emphasis on anaclitic identification and regards a nurturant interaction between a caretaking adult and a child as a necessary precondition of identification. Through this interaction the child learns to want and value his mother's presence and nurturant activities and by the end of the first year of life acquires a dependency drive. However, the mother cannot always be present to mediate the child's rewards; moreover, she may at times withhold or withdraw her attention and affection as a disciplinary or training technique. The consequent dependency frustration and insecurity concerning parental affection and approval leads the child to adopt the method of role practice as a means of reinstating the parent's nurturant responses. Imitative responses may bring direct rewards from parents, who are likely to be pleased, and even flattered, when the child emulates their behavior. Moreover, through role-playing in fantasy the child can perform the parent's nurturant acts himself and thus vicariously obtain rewards that the parent is at the time unable or unwilling to bestow. Thus, through the repeated association of imitation with direct or self-administered reward, identification becomes an acquired drive for which the satisfying goal response is acting like another person. A similar account of identification is offered by Whiting and Child (1953).

More recently, Whiting (1959, 1960) has proposed a theory of identification that places primary emphasis on the defensive aspects of the process. His status-envy theory represents an extension of the Freudian hypothesis that identification is the outcome of a rivalrous interaction between the child and the parent who occupies an envied status. While Freud presents the child as in competition with the father only for the mother's sexual and affectional attention, Whiting regards any forms of reward, material or social, as valued resources around which rivalry may develop. He further assumes that the more a child envies the status of another person in respect to the consumption of resources of which he feels himself to be deprived, the more he will play the role of that person in fantasy. Thus, when a child competes unsuccessfully with an adult for affection, attention, food, and care, he will envy the adult consumer and consequently identify with him.

In contrast to Whiting, other writers (Maccoby, 1959; Mussen and Distler, 1959; Parsons, 1955) appear to assume that the controller, rather than the consumer, of resources will be the primary model for children's imitative role-playing. This power theory of social influence has received considerable attention in

social psychology, though not in the context of theories of identification.

Social power has been defined as the ability of a person to influence the behavior of others by controlling or mediating their
positive and negative reinforcements. French and Raven (1959)
have distinguished five types of power, based on expertness, attractiveness, legitimacy, coerciveness, and rewarding power, each
of which is believed to have somewhat differential effects on the
social-influence process. For example, the use of coercion, in
which the controller derives power from his ability to administer
punishments, not only creates and supports avoidance behavior
toward the controller but also decreases his attractiveness and
hence his effectiveness in altering the behavior of others beyond
the immediate social-influence setting (French, Morrison, and
Levinger, 1960; Zipf, 1960). The use of reward power, in contrast,
tends to elicit and strengthen approach responses toward the
power figure and to increase his attractiveness or secondary-
reward value through the repeated association of his attributes
with positive reinforcement. Attractiveness is assumed also to
extend the controller's power influence over a wide range of behavior (French and Raven, 1959).

Relevant data are available concerning two issues raised by
theories of identification, since both the role of nurturance and
the role of power in facilitating imitation and determining the
source of imitative behavior have been subjects of investigation.
Research cited in earlier sections demonstrates that a wide range
of imitative responses, deviant and conforming, social and nonso-
cial, in the presence or absence of the model, may be elicited
without the necessity of first establishing a nurturant-dependent
relationship between the model and the observer. Although this
research indicates that nurturance is not a necessary antecedent
of imitative learning, other studies provide some evidence that it
can foster imitation.

In an experiment by Bandura and Huston (1961), one group of
nursery-school children experienced a highly nurturant and rewarding interaction with a female model, whereas for a second
group of children the same model behaved in a distant, nonrewarding manner. Following the social-interaction sessions, the
model and the child played a game, the object of which was to
guess which of two boxes contained a picture sticker. In execut-

428 / SEX DIFFERENCES

ing each trial, the model exhibited relatively novel verbal, motor, and aggressive responses that were totally irrelevant to the game to which the child's attention was directed. A measure was obtained of the number of imitative responses the child reproduced while performing his trials. Except for aggressive responses, which were readily imitated regardless of the nurturant quality of the model, children who experienced the rewarding interaction with the model imitated her behavior to a substantially greater extent than did children with whom the same model had reacted in a distant and nonrewarding way. Moreover, the children in the model-rewarding condition also displayed more behavior that was only partially imitative of the model's social responses. This study indicates that exposure to a model possessing rewarding qualities not only facilitates precise imitation but also increases the probability of the occurrence of responses falling within the same class as those made by the model but which the model does not in fact emit.

The association between rewarding parental characteristics and imitative behavior has been demonstrated in a number of studies in which reward and punishment have been assessed from interview material or thematic responses. Mussen and Distler (1959) selected two groups of kindergarten boys, one displaying a high degree of male-role preference and the other a low degree of male-role preference, on the basis of their responses to a projective test (Brown, 1956). The boys were then required to complete nine incomplete stories, involving parent-child relations, during the course of individual doll-play sessions. In comparison to the boys who received low male-role-preference scores, the children with strong masculine-role preferences perceived their fathers as relatively powerful sources of both reward and punishment, a finding which the authors interpret as primarily supporting a social-power theory of imitative learning. In a later study, Mussen (1961) compared senior high-school boys who displayed strongly masculine vocational interests with boys of the same age who obtained strongly feminine vocational-interest scores. As in the Mussen and Distler study, boys with strong masculine interests were more likely than boys with weak masculine interests to depict their fathers as rewarding and positive in their attitudes toward them; however, the strongly masculine adolescents also tended to portray their fathers as nonpunitive and nonrestrictive, a discrepancy between this and the earlier study which could be attributable to the age difference between the subjects. However, since the relationship between punitive power and sex-role preference that was found in the earlier study was of borderline significance, it is perhaps not surprising that this result was not replicated. Mussen's findings for adolescents indirectly corroborate results previously reported by Payne and Mussen (1956), in whose study boys with high and low father-son similarity in responding to items on a personality inventory were required to construct story endings involving father-son relationships. Analysis of the data revealed that boys with high father-identification perceived their fathers as highly rewarding and affectionate persons.

Further evidence of an association between parental characteristics and children's imitative behavior is provided by P. S. Sears (1953), who found that boys of warm affectionate fathers tended to assume the father role in doll-play activities more frequently than did boys of fathers who were relatively cold. Sears' study also revealed the importance of the quality of interactions between models when more than one model is involved, since boys who more strongly adopted the mother role had mothers who were both warm and affectionate toward their children and devaluated their husbands.

Bandura and Walters (1959) reported that nonaggressive boys exhibited greater father-preference and more frequently perceived themselves as thinking and acting like their fathers than did aggressive boys. Comparisons based on parent interviews revealed that the fathers of the aggressive boys were relatively nonnurturant and nonrewarding of their sons' behavior in the home. Moreover, the aggressive boys' fathers were much more punitive than those of the nonaggressive boys, a finding that suggests that the punitive coercion favored by the former group of fathers had in most respects decreased their effectiveness as models for their sons to emulate.

In a comparative study of the status envy, social-power, and secondary-reinforcement theories of imitative learning, Bandura, Ross, and Ross (1963) utilized three-person groups, representing prototypes of the nuclear family. In one condition of the experiment an adult assumed the role of controller of resources and positive reinforcers. Another adult was the consumer or recipient of these resources, while the child, a participant observer in the triad, was essentially ignored. In a second treatment condition, one adult controlled the resources; the child, however, was the recipient of the positive reinforcers, while the other adult was assigned a subordinate and powerless role. An adult male and female served as models in each of the triads. For half the boys and girls in each condition the male model controlled and dispensed the rewarding resources, simulating the husband-dominant family; for the remaining children, the female model mediated the positive resources as in the wife-dominant home. Thus, the experimental design permitted a test of whether power inversions would promote cross-sex imitation. Following the experimental social interactions the two adult models exhibited divergent patterns of behavior in the presence of the child, and a measure was obtained of the degree to which the child patterned his behavior after that of the models.

In both experimental treatments, regardless of whether the rival adult or the children themselves were the recipients of the rewarding resources, the model who possessed rewarding power was imitated, when the models were subsequently absent, to a greater extent than was the competitor or the ignored model. To the extent that the imitative behavior elicited in this experiment may be considered an elementary prototype of identification within a nuclear family group, the data fail to support the interpretation of the identification process as a child-initiated defensive maneuver. Children clearly identified with the source of rewarding power rather than with the competitor for the rewards. Moreover, power inversions on the part of the male and female models produced cross-sex imitation, particularly in girls. Compared to boys, the girls showed a greater readiness to imitate the behavior exhibited by an opposite-sex model. This difference probably reflects both the differential cultural tolerance for cross-sex behavior displayed by males and females and the relatively greater positive reinforcement of masculine-role behavior in our society.

Failure to develop sex-appropriate behavior has received considerable attention in clinical psychology and psychiatry and has customarily been interpreted as a manifestation of underlying psychodynamic processes, especially latent homosexuality. To present these processes as internal causal factors does little to clarify the genesis of sex-inappropriate behavior. On the other hand, to identify the influence of external social-learning variables, such as the distribution of rewarding power within the family, on the formation of deviant sex-role behavior both assists in the understanding of the development of deviant sexuality and directs attention to the manner in which culturally approved patterns may be formed.

Theories of identification have usually assumed that within the family setting the child's initial identification is confined to his mother, and that boys during early childhood are forced to reject the mother as the primary model and to turn to the father as the main source of imitative learning. However, throughout the course of development most children are provided with ample opportunities to observe the behavior of both parents.

When a child is exposed to a variety of models, he may select one or more of them as the primary source of behavior, but he rarely reproduces all the elements of a single model's repertory or confines his imitation to that model. In the experiment by Bandura, Ross, and Ross (1963), although children adopted many of the characteristics of the model who possessed rewarding power, they also reproduced some of the elements of behavior exhibited by the model who occupied the subordinate role. Consequently, the children were not simply junior-size replicas of one or the other model; rather, they exhibited a relatively novel pattern of behavior representing an amalgam of elements from both models. Thus, within one family even same-sex siblings may exhibit quite different patterns of behavior, owing to their having selected for imitation different elements of their father's and mother's response repertories.

From Albert Bandura and Richard H. Walters. *Social Learning and Personality Development*. New York: Holt, Rinehart and Winston, Inc., 1963, pages 91-99. Reprinted by permission of the publisher. Copyright © 1963 by Holt, Rinehart and Winston.

REFERENCES

BANDURA, A., & HUSTON, ALETHA C. "Identification as a process of incidental learning." *J. abnorm. soc. Psychol.*, 1961, 63, 311-318.

BANDURA, A., ROSS, DOROTHEA, & ROSS, SHIELA A. "A comparative test of the status envy, social power, and the secondary-reinforcement theories of identificatory learning." *J. abnorm. soc. Psychol.*, 1963, 67, 527-534.

BANDURA, A., & WALTERS, R. H. *Adolescent aggression*. New York: Ronald, 1959.

BROWN, D. G. "Sex role preference in young children." *Psychol. Monogr.*, 1956, 70, No. 14 (Whole No. 421).

FRENCH, J. R. P., JR., MORRISON, H. W., & LEVINGER, G. "Coercive power and forces affecting conformity." *J. abnorm. soc. Psychol.*, 1960, 61, 93-101.

FRENCH, J. R. P., JR., & RAVEN, B. "The bases of power." In D. Cartwright (Ed.). *Studies in social power*. Ann Arbor, Mich.: Inst. Soc. Res., 1959, pp. 150-167.

FREUD, S. "The dynamics of transference." In E. Jones (Ed.). *Collected papers*. Vol. II. London: Hogarth, 1924, pp. 312-322. (First published in *Zentralblatt*, Bd. II, 1912.)

FREUD, S. "Mourning and melancholia." In E. Jones (Ed.). *Collected papers*. Vol. IV. London: Hogarth, 1925, pp. 152-170. (First published in *Zeitschrift*, Bd., IV, 1917.)

FREUD, S. *An outline of psychoanalysis*. New York: Norton, 1949. (First published in *Internationale Zeitschrift für psychoanalyse und Imago*, Bd. XXV, 1940.)

MACCOBY, ELEANOR, E. "Role-taking in childhood and its consequences for social learning." *Child Develpm.*, 1959, 30, 239-252.

MOWRER, O. H. *Learning theory and personality dynamics*. New York: Ronald, 1950.

MOWRER, O. H. "Hearing and speaking: An analysis of language learning." *J. Speech Dis.*, 1958, 23, 143-152.

MOWRER, O. H. *Learning theory and behavior*. New York: Wiley, 1969 (a).

MOWRER, O. H. *Learning theory and the symbolic processes*. New York: Wiley, 1960 (b).

MUSSEN, P. H. "Some antecedents and consequents of masculine sex-typing in adolescent boys." *Psychol. Monogr.*, 1961, 75, No. 2 (Whole No. 506).

MUSSEN, P. H., & DISTLER, L. "Masculinity, identification, and father-son relationships." *J. abnorm. soc. Psychol.*, 1959, 59, 350-356.

PARSONS, T. "Family structure and the socialization of the child." In T. Parsons and R. F. Bales. *Family, socialization, and interaction process*. New York: Free Press, 1955, pp. 35-131.

PAYNE, D. E., & MUSSEN, P. H. "Parent-child relations and father identification among adolescent boys." *J. abnorm. soc. Psychol.*, 1956, 52, 358-362.

SEARS, PAULINE S. "Child-rearing factors relating to playing sex-typed roles." *Amer. Psychologist*, 1953, 8, 431 (abstract).

SEARS, R. R. "Identification as a form of behavioral development." In D. B. Harris (Ed.). *The concept of development.* Minneapolis: Univer. of Minnesota Press, 1957, pp. 149-161.

WHITING, J. W. M. "Sorcery, sin, and the superego." In M. R. Jones (Ed.). *Nebraska symposium on motivation.* Lincoln: Univer. of Nebraska Press, 1959, pp. 174-195.

WHITING, J. W. M. "Resource mediation and learning by identification." In I. Iscoe & H. W. Stevenson (Eds.). *Personality development in children.* Austin: Univer. of Texas Press, 1960, pp. 112-126.

WHITING, J. W. M., & CHILD, I. L. *Child training and personality.* New Haven: Yale Univer. Press, 1953.

ZIPF, SHEILA G. "Resistance and conformity under reward and punishment." *J. abnorm. soc. Psychol.*, 1960, 61, 102-109.

PHYSIOLOGICAL DEVELOPMENT, COGNITIVE DEVELOPMENT, AND SOCIALIZATION ANTECEDENTS OF CHILDREN'S SEX-ROLE ATTITUDES

Lawrence Kohlberg / Edward Zigler

The "cognitive-developmental" approach to the acquisition of sex-role attitudes and concepts is primarily associated with Lawrence Kohlberg. Actually it is only one product of his effort over the last decade and a half to construct a theory of human social and personality development which corresponds to Jean Piaget's theory of human cognitive development. Kohlberg's most recent work has focused on the development of stages of moral judgment in children, but his earlier work included sex-role development, the development of competency and mental health in children, the interface between cognitive development and education of children, and, more broadly, a cognitive-developmental approach to the larger issue of human socialization.

In the middle 1960s Kohlberg's ideas about sex-role development had a tremendous impact on the study of psychological sex differences almost as soon as they were published. With amazing quickness his theory, through its manifest persuasiveness and originality, was given approximately equal status with more established approaches, such as psychoanalytic theory (see Part I of this anthology), normative-maturational theory (see Gesell & Ilg), and social-learning theory (see Bandura & Walters). Moreover, it has maintained that status to the present time.

Kohlberg is professor of psychology and education and Director of the Center for Moral Education at Harvard University. Edward Zigler is professor of psychology and chairman of the Psychology Department at Yale University. During 1970-1972 he was Director of the U.S. Office of Child Development in the federal government, a position of considerable policy-making responsibility.

The excerpt reprinted below is taken from a large research report published in 1967 in Genetic Psychology Monographs. *Notice that the authors view the child's social and physical concepts as belonging to parallel cognitive systems which interact, develop at approximately the same rate, and follow the same laws of cognitive organization.*

While almost all views of intelligence suggest important social correlates of intelligence, it is not clear that these correlates of I.Q. should include basic sex-role attitudes. The most influential theory of sex-role development, psychoanalytic libido theory, would predict that general growth trends in children's sex-role behavior would be tied to the maturational sequence of instinctual drives. The most important age-developmental trend postulated by Freudian theory is the maturation of phallic sexuality at about age 3 to 5, its expression in a sexualized or Oedipal attachment to the opposite-sex parent, and the decline of sexuality and this attachment during the latency period (ages 7 to 11). Freud expected the timing of these developmental trends to be "lawful" or "periodic" and to parallel chronological age and physical maturation: "It seems certain that the newborn child brings with it the germs of sexual feeling which continue to develop for some time and then succumb to a progressive suppression. . . . Nothing is known concerning the laws and periodicity of the oscillating course of development. It seems, however, that the sexual life of the child mostly manifests itself in the third or fourth year in some form accessible to observation" (5, p. 583).

Freud viewed both the onset and inhibition of sexuality as largely the product of such maturational forces: "It is during the period of total or at least partial latency that the psychic forces develop which later act as inhibitions on the sexual life. . . . We may gain the impression that the erection of these dams in the civilized child is the work of education, and surely education contributes much to it. In reality, however, this development is organically determined and can occasionally be produced without the help of education" (5, p. 583).

The Freudian view then suggests that psychosexual developmental trends are a function of chronological age and the physiological development associated with age. Various additional maturational factors besides sheer age might be expected to lead to general advance or retardation in "anatomical preparation" and consequent psychosexual attitudes. There is relatively clear evidence that the early onset of puberty is associated with the early arousal of genital sexual fantasies and behaviors (4). Onset of puberty is in turn predictable from knowledge of the child's earlier level or rate of physiological maturity (15). It might be plausible to expect physiologically advanced children to be advanced in psychosexual attitudes, if such attitudes reflected instinctual maturation.

The psychoanalytic view of libidinal maturation does not, however, lead to the expectation of psychosexual advance in intellectually advanced children. While it might be plausible to attribute advance in instinctual sexual maturation to children who are generally advanced in physiological development, there is no reason to expect such advance in children generally advanced in intellectual development. Physiological and mental maturity measures do not correlate with one another to any appreciable degree. When social class and chronological age are controlled, very small or zero correlations have been found between measures of physiological and mental maturity (1, 2, 3, 13). In light of the absence of a relationship between intellectual and physiological advance, there is little reason to expect purely maturational sexual development to be advanced in bright children.

Freud later added a footnote to the paragraph previously quoted saying, "The *complete* synchronization of anatomical preparation and psychical development is naturally not necessary." Psychoanalytic theory, however, does not suggest that the discrepancies between anatomical preparation and psychical development should be due to cognitive development. These discrepancies would rather be interpreted as the result of differences in "education": i.e., of the socialization pressures of the family and culture and of differential opportunities for, and restrictions upon, identification with parents.[1] It seems unlikely that the timing or severity of sexually repressive training by the adult culture would be systematically determined by the child's relative intellectual maturity. Insofar as there were age-regularities in sex-role socialization, they would be more likely to be related to chronological age grading, to the child's bodily maturity, and to the physiological maturation of his sexual instincts.

These considerations of the timing of cultural training suggest that intellectual maturity would also not be an important factor in social learning theories of psychosexual development (7, 10, 11, 14). While these theorists have not given clear-cut considerations to intellectual factors in sex-role development, their research use of age-related sex-role measures without making use of controls for I.Q. suggests that they do not consider it a major factor in such development. In these theories psychosexual development is defined as appropriate sex-role identification: i.e., as increased learning of the attitudes and behaviors typed by the adult culture as sex-appropriate. Such development is seen as the product of adult and peer labeling and reinforcement of role-appropriate behavior and of identification with sex-appropriate parental behavior. From this point of view, bright children might be expected to show advance in acquisition of verbal sex-role labels and norms. Since discrimination of adult sex-role labeling and reinforcement and of adult sex-role behavior would appear to be relatively simple, these effects of intelligence would probably not be expected to be major, however. The reinforcement learning and identification mechanisms postulated by these theories do not involve much cognitive complexity, so that the timing of this learning should be determined more by environmental timing than by the child's cognitive capacities. As mentioned earlier, it seems likely that such environmental timing of sex-role socialization should be determined primarily by chronological age-grading, with cultural adjustment of timing to the individual child being influenced more by his physical than by his intellectual maturity.

In contrast to maturational[2] and social learning theories of psychosexual development, a theory based on Piaget's notions of the structural development of intelligence and of social-cognitive parallelism clearly leads to the expectation of developmental advance in the psychosexual attitudes of bright children. As elaborated and empirically documented elsewhere (8, 9), such a cognitive-developmental theory implies the following considerations.

1. The concrete, physicalistic, and symbolic nature of the child's thought and interests leads him to conceive of interpersonal relationships in terms of body actions and to define social roles in terms of physical characteristics and differences. The elaboration of the physical bases of sex-role concepts in the con-

crete thought of the child leads to a core of common meaning to these concepts, regardless of cultural and family variations in sex-role definition.

2. Accordingly, there are "natural" developmental trends or sequences in sex-role attitudes, trends not directly structured by cultural teaching, which are the products of cognitive development. Because of the universal physical dimensions of sex-role concepts and because of culturally universal developmental transformations in modes of conceptualizing, it is plausible to expect some relatively invariant developmental trends in sex-ole concepts and attitudes.

3. The fact that sex-role concepts have physical dimensions suggests that the formation of a sex-role identity is in large part the comprehension and acceptance of a physical reality rather than a process primarily determined by sexual fantasies, social reinforcement, or identification with models. The child's basic sex-role identity is largely the result of a self-categorization as a male or female made early in development. While dependent on social labeling, this categorization is basically a cognitive reality judgment rather than a product of social rewards, parental identifications, or sexual fantasies. The reality judgment, "I really am and will always be a boy" or "I really am and will always be a girl" are judgments with a regular course of age development relatively independent of the vicissitudes of social labeling and reinforcement.

4. The motivational forces implied in such reality judgments are general "drive-neutral" motives of effectance, or competence, which orient the child both toward cognitive adaptation toward a structured reality and toward the maintenance of self-esteem. Accordingly sex-typed preferences in activities and social relationships (masculinity-femininity) are largely the product of such reality judgments of sex-identity. The boy, having labeled himself as male, goes on to value masculine modes because of the general tendency to value positively objects and acts consistent with one's conceived identity.

5. To a large extent, the value of social reinforcers to the child is determined by his sex-identity rather than the reverse. As opposed to a social learning sequence, "The boy wants rewards, the boy is rewarded by boy things, therefore he wants to be a boy," a cognitive theory assumes a sequence, "The boy asserts he is a

boy. He then wants to do boy things; therefore the opportunity to do boy things and the presence of masculine models is rewarding."

6. The tendency to value positively and imitate self-like objects tends to radiate out in the child's development in the form of imitation and liking for the same-sex parent. The boy's preferential attachment to the father as against the mother proceeds from, rather than causes, basic sex-role identity and basic tendencies to imitate the father preferentially.

7. The formation of a stable sex-role identity, and its channelization into patterns of parent identification, are dependent upon complex modes of cognitive organization and development. As an example the stabilization of sex-role identity implied in the judgment, "I really am and will always be a boy" or "I really am and will always be a girl," is apparently dependent upon the types of cognitive reorganization discussed by Piaget. Stabilization of these judgments apparently is not completed until age 6 to 7, at a time when other forms of physical constancy or physical conservation become fully stabilized. The stabilization of judgments of sex-role constancy and of physical constancy closely parallel one another in terms of individual development as well as age group norms. The radiation of sex-role identity into identification with the same-sex parent also seems dependent upon complex cognitive reorganizations (at least in boys). As an example, the boy's increased identification with the father doll in doll play appears to be associated (both in terms of age groups and of individual differences) with the development of abstract cognitive categories of likeness involved in the boy's inclusion of himself and his father in a category of "we males."

8. Because of such cognitive mediators, then, regular developmental trends in sex-role attitudes are to a considerable extent linked to rate of cognitive growth, rather than to physiological or chronological development.

While a cognitive-developmental theory of psychosexuality suggests that cognitive advance should have an important impact on sexual attitudes in the early school years, it also suggests that this impact should be greater for boys than for girls. For both boys and girls, the mother is the earliest and most available and meaningful adult model. In the normal course of development, the boy shifts to preferring the father as a model. This shift occurs as a result of a variety of cognitive conceptual mechanisms consolidating the boy's sex-role identity, leading to common categorization of the self and the father and giving meaning and prestige to the father's work role. In contrast, the girl's psychosexual development does not appear to require a radical shift in parental model mediated by complex cognitive mechanisms.

In addition to demanding radical shifts in model based on various conceptual equations, the urban boy's father-identification must be based largely on rather abstract forms of behavioral equivalence. A large part of the male adult role is a work role which is distant and vague in meaning. The boy is given little opportunity to observe this role and less opportunity to imitate it overtly. Furthermore, the boy has little reason to expect that he will play an adult work role that will be concretely like his father's, so that the elements of the father's role relevant to his own identity must be quite general and abstract. In contrast, the girl's mother-identification involves very concrete forms of domestic behavior which the girl has an opportunity to observe and practice, and which she expects to perform when she grows up. A cognitive-developmental interpretation of I.Q.-personality correlates, then, suggests that I.Q. should be more determining of the development of sex-role attitudes of boys than of girls because the girl's parental identification can be based on more concrete imitative learning processes under conditions of greater exposure to the model, and because such identification does not require a radical developmental shift in model.

From Lawrence Kohlberg and Edward Zigler. "The Impact of Cognitive Maturity on the Development of Sex-Role Attitudes in the Years 4 to 8." *Genetic Psychology Monographs*, 1967, vol. 75, pages 100-105. Reprinted by permission of the authors and the Journal Press.

FOOTNOTES

1. The importance of these forces has been especially elaborated and stressed by modern psychoanalytic thinking, which sees sex identity as the outcome of a complex of psychosocial forces. However, insofar as psychoanalysts conceive of timetables or age trends in sex-role development for the normal population, these trends are derived from classical libido theory.

2. While Freudian theory stresses psychosexual maturation as an instinctual phenomenon, other maturational theories (6, 12) have stressed the notion that intellectual, physical, and psychosexual development are all facets of the general maturation of the organism. Since there is no empirical warrant for grouping physical and intellectual advance into a general "developmental quotient" or "organismic age" concept, however, the maturational view would not really support an expectation of psychosexual maturity associated with purely intellectual advance, with physical growth held constant.

REFERENCES

1. ABERNATHY, E. H. "Relationships between mental and physical growth." *Monog. Soc. Res. Child Devel.*, 1936, *1*, No. 7.
2. BAYLEY, N. "Factors influencing growth of intelligence in young children." *Yearbook Nat. Soc. Stud. Educ.*, 1940, *39*, 49-79.
3. BLOMMERS, P., KNEIF, L., & STROUD, J. B. "The organismic age concept." *J. Educ. Psychol.*, 1955, 46, 142-150.
4. DENNIS, W. "Adolescence." In L. Carmichael (Ed.), *Manual of Child Psychology*. New York: Wiley, 1946.
5. FREUD, S. "Three contributions to the theory of sex." In *The Basic Writings of Sigmund Freud*. New York: Modern Library, 1938 (originally published in 1905).
6. GESELL, A., & ILG, F. *Infant and Child in the Culture of Today*. New York: Harpers, 1943.
7. KAGAN, J. "The acquisition and significance of sex-typing and sex-role identity." In. M. & L. Hoffman (Eds.), *Review of Child Development Research* (Vol. 1). New York: Russell Sage Foundation, 1964.
8. KOHLBERG, L. "Stage and sequence: The developmental approach to moralization." In M. Hoffman (Ed.), *Moral Processes*. Chicago, Ill.: Aldine Press, in press.
9. KOHLBERG, L. "Stages in the development of physical and social concepts in the years four to eight." Unpublished paper, Chicago, Illinois, 1967.
10. LYNN, D. "A note on sex differences in the development of masculine and feminine identification." *Psychol. Rev.*, 1959, *66*, 126-136.
11. MUSSEN, P., & DISTLER, L. "Child-rearing antecedents of masculine identification in kindergarten boys." *Child Devel.*, 1960, *31*, 89-100.

12. OLSON, W. C., & HUGHES, B. O. "Growth of the child as a whole." In R. Barker, I. Kounin, & H. Wright (Eds.), *Child Behavior and Development.* New York: McGraw-Hill, 1943.
13. PATERSON, D. G. *Physique and Intellect.* New York: Century, 1930.
14. SEARS, R. R., RAU, L., & ALPERT, R. "Identification and child-rearing." In press, 1965.
15. TANNER, J. *Education and Physical Growth.* London: Univ. London Press, 1961.

POSSIBLE CAUSAL FACTORS OF SEX DIFFERENCES IN INTELLECTUAL ABILITIES

Eleanor E. Maccoby

Of all psychologists active today, Eleanor E. Maccoby may have the most encyclopedic grasp of developmental and socialization patterns in childhood. She has turned her hand to a number of different areas and has invariably produced conceptual products of a definitive character. In addition to her most recent recognition as the foremost contemporary expert on psychological sex differences, her work in the past has covered such disparate areas as the development of moral values and behavior, the influence of television and other mass media on children, the development of patterns of aggression, dependence, attachment, and separation in children, role-taking in childhood, and the relationship between intelligence and noncognitive variables.

We have selected the second half of her chapter, "Sex Differences in Intellectual Functioning," from The Development of Sex Differences *(1966). After reviewing a variety of intellectual sex differences in the first half of the chapter, she offers the interpretative analysis reprinted below. Note how she raises and considers in turn a number of explanatory hypotheses, before settling for one which appears to be most plausible. Her conclusion is that there are optimal interactions between certain personality characteristics and certain kinds of intellectual performance, but that boys and girls approximate the optimum in different ways; moreover, that, within biological and cultural limits, these differences seem traceable to variations in childhood patterns of experience.*

Maccoby is professor of psychology and chairperson of the Psychology Department at Stanford University.

The research summarized so far has shown that (1) there are a number of aspects of intellectual performance on which the sexes differ consistently in the average scores obtained, and that (2) whether or not there is a difference in average performance on a given task, there are some substantial sex differences in the intercorrelations between intellectual performance and other characteristics of the individual or his environment. We turn now to an examination of several possible explanations for these differences.

DEVELOPMENTAL TIMETABLE

Physiologically, girls mature faster than boys. And because certain aspects of intellectual development cannot occur until the relevant physical structures are complete, we might expect girls to develop some abilities earlier than boys. For example, at birth the cortical structures relevant to speech are not fully formed. Insofar as speech must wait until they are, we might expect girls to talk sooner than boys. The physiological timetable, of course, determines not only the individual's rate of development in early life but also the age at which he reaches his optimum level, the duration of his stay at this level, and the time of onset and the rate of the aging process. The fact that females mature faster during the first part of the life cycle does not necessarily imply that they begin to age sooner, although they may, despite their greater average longevity.

The sex differences found in general intelligence during the early part of the life span, insofar as these differences may be determined from tests standardized to minimize them, do seem to parallel the physiological trends. That is, girls get off to a faster start in language and in some other aspects of cognitive performance. Moreover, parent-child resemblances in intelligence set in earlier for girls than boys. The sexes are very similar during the early and middle school years, and then boys begin to forge ahead in some ability areas during the high school years. But Bayley (1956) has shown that the rate of intellectual growth is unrelated to the rate of physical growth if one scores both in terms of the per cent of mature growth attained. Hence it does not appear that there is any single developmental timetable controlling both physical and mental growth.

As noted earlier, the evidence concerning sex-related I.Q. changes during adulthood is neither extensive nor entirely consistent, though there is some indication that a gradual decline in some aspects of intellectual functioning sets in earlier among women. There is no evidence whether these changes parallel other aspects of aging. In any case, even if some of these differences could be accounted for in terms of different developmental timetables, it is doubtful whether some of the major differences we have noted could be so explained. It is difficult to see, for example, why maturational factors should produce greater differences between the sexes in spatial than verbal performance. Nor why a fast-developing organism should show different kinds of relationships between intellectual functions and personality traits than a slow-developing organism. We must therefore turn to different explanatory concepts.

DIRECT EFFECTS OF SEX-TYPED INTERESTS

Perhaps the explanation for the differences we have noted is very simple: members of each sex are encouraged in, and become interested in and proficient at, the kinds of tasks that are most relevant to the roles they fill currently or are expected to fill in the future. According to this view, boys in high school forge ahead in math because they and their parents and teachers know they may become engineers or scientists; on the other hand, girls know that they are unlikely to need math in the occupations they will take up when they leave school. And adult women, most of whom become housewives or work at jobs that do not make many intellectual demands, decline in measures of "total intelligence" because such tests call upon skills that are not being used by adult women as extensively as they are used by adult men. As far as women's lack of creativity and intellectual productivity is concerned, we could argue that women are busy managing households and rearing children, and that these activities usually preclude any serious commitment to other creative endeavors. Undoubtedly, matters of opportunity and life setting play a very large role in the relative accomplishments of the two sexes. That this is not the whole story, however, is suggested by a study of Radcliffe Ph.D.'s (1956), in which it was found that the women Ph.D.'s who had taken academic posts had published substantially less than their male counterparts, and that this was just as true of unmarried academic women as it was of married ones. Thus women who are as well off as men (or perhaps better off) with respect to alternative demands on their time are nevertheless less productive. It is difficult to attribute this fact to anything about the professional roles they currently occupy. If their behavior is role-determined, it must be determined by sex roles established or anticipated earlier in life.

Some of the major sex differences we have noted—some appearing at a fairly early age—do not appear to have any direct relevance to adult sex roles, actual or anticipated. Does a girl of nine do poorly on an embedded-figures test because she thinks that this kind of skill is not going to be important for her later on in life, and well on a spelling test because she thinks this kind of skill is going to be important? It is doubtful whether either children or adults see those ability areas where we have detected the greatest sex differences as sex-role specific. This is not to say that sex-typing is irrelevant to intellectual development. But it is doubtful whether the sex differences in spatial ability, analytic style, and breaking set can be understood in terms of their greater direct relevance to the role requirements of one sex or the other.

OPPORTUNITIES TO LEARN

Do the sexes differ in their opportunities to learn the skills and content of the ability areas where stable sex differences have been found? It has been widely assumed that girls' early verbal superiority might be due to their spending more time with adults, particularly with their mothers. From research on birth order and experimental studies of the effects of verbal interaction with adults in language acquisition, it may be safely inferred that the amount of a child's contact with adults does influence his language development. Preschool girls are kept at home with their mothers, the argument goes, while boys are allowed to go out to play with age-mates. As a result, girls have more opportunity to develop language skills. But when children enter school, and boys are exposed to intensive stimulation from the teacher, they catch up. A weakness of this argument is that it does not explain why boys catch up in vocabulary and reading comprehension, but not in fluency, spelling, and grammar. And furthermore, we lack direct evidence that preschool girls are kept at home more. Although it fits our stereotypes of the two sexes to think of girls as more protected, we must consider the possibility that girls may actually be given more freedom than boys. Because girls mature faster, perhaps parents can trust them sooner than boys to play away from home with little adult supervision. We simply lack information on this point.

Similarly, it has been suggested that boys acquire greater spatial and perceptual-analytic ability because they have more opportunity to explore their environment at an early age—more opportunity to manipulate objects. Again, we have no evidence that this is so. It is true that if one watches nursery school children at play, one is more likely to find boys building with blocks and girls placing doll furniture in a doll house or pretending to cook with beaters and bowls; but it is difficult to see why one of these kinds of object manipulation should lead to greater spatial ability than the other. We know little about what kinds of learning experiences are involved when a child dissects stimuli (as the analytical, field-independent child does) instead of responding to them globally, but it is difficult to see why sheer quantity of stimulus exposure should make a difference beyond a certain point. That is, it is reasonable to suppose that a child who is subjected to severe stimulus deprivation may find it difficult to make fine perceptual discriminations, and hence might perceive more globally. But normally reared children of both sexes have considerable opportunity to move about in space and explore a variety of objects. We suspect that exposure to a variety of stimuli is a necessary but not sufficient condition for the development of an analytic cognitive style, and that children of both sexes, if they grow up in a normal environment, will have enough stimulus contact to permit, if not ensure, this development.

"IDENTIFICATION" AND MODELING

It has been thought that girls may be more verbal and boys more quantitative because children tend to model themselves primarily upon the same-sex parent (Carlsmith, 1964). Since mothers are typically more verbal and fathers typically more skilled at quantitative tasks, the argument goes, modeling the same-sex parent will produce differential patterns of abilities in boys and girls.

There are a number of difficulties with this explanation of the typical sex differences in ability profiles. Not all aspects of intellectual functioning are susceptible to modeling. Vocabulary and verbal fluency are aspects of a parent's intellectual equipment that a child can copy. Normally, his spelling is not. Yet girls maintain superiority throughout the school years in spelling and fluency, though not in vocabulary. Much of a parent's quantitative reasoning is done covertly, so that it is not accessible for copying, and very little spatial thinking is communicated from parent to child. Yet it is in spatial performance that we find the most consistent sex differences.

Sex differences in verbal ability occur at a very early age, long before the child is able to identify which parent is the same sex as himself, and long before he begins to copy same-sex models differentially (see Kohlberg 1966). Sex differences in verbal ability decline during the age period when the rise of identification and differential modeling ought to increase them. And consistent sex differences in quantitative ability do not appear until adolescence, long after the time when boys and girls have begun to prefer same-sex models. For these reasons we do not believe that the identification hypothesis provides an adequate explanation of the sex differences in ability profiles noted at the beginning of this chapter.

SEX-TYPED PERSONALITY TRAITS AS MEDIATING PROCESSES

Numerous studies have shown that girls are more conforming, more suggestible, and more dependent upon the opinion of others than boys. And as mentioned earlier in this chapter, a number of studies have demonstrated that these very personality traits are associated with (1) field dependency (global perceiving), and (2) lack of ability to break set or restructure in problem solving. Witkin et al. (1962) have suggested that herein lies the explanation of sex differences in field independence and analytic style— that girls are more field-dependent and less analytical because of their greater conformity and dependency.

Why should there be any relationship between the cluster of personality dispositions that we may call the dependency cluster and individuals' characteristic modes of dealing with a stimulus array? Two possible reasons suggest themselves. First, an individual who is dependent and conforming is oriented toward stimuli emanating from other people; perhaps he finds it difficult to ignore these stimuli in favor of internal thought processes. Analytic thinking appears to require more internal "processing"; Kagan et al. (1963) have shown it to be associated with longer reaction times than global responding. Dependent children have been shown to be more distractible (Rau, 1963); their internal processing is interrupted, perhaps because of their greater orientation toward external interpersonal cues. This orientation probably helps them in certain kinds of intellectual performance; they should do better in recognizing names and faces, for example. But tasks calling for sequential thought may be hindered by a heavy reliance on external, interpersonal cues.

A second and related reason why one might expect to find a connection between the independence-dependence personality dimension and the mode of dealing with a stimulus array in problem solving has to do with activity. The dependent-conforming person is passive, waiting to be acted upon by the environment. The independent person takes the initiative. Intellectual tasks differ in how much activity they require, so that the passive person is more at a disadvantage on some tasks than others. Vocabulary tests, for example, depend upon previously established associations, and therefore involve less trial and error than tasks that require restructuring or finding the answer to a previously unsolved problem.

We are postulating, then, that dependency interferes with certain aspects of intellectual functioning. But there are other aspects of intellectual performance that dependency may facilitate—achievement, for example. Sears (1963) has found that, among girls, projective measures of "need affiliation" are positively related to academic achievement; in other words, achievement efforts can be motivated by a desire for social approval, and in the Sears work this proved to be true to a greater degree for girls than boys.

On the basis of the above considerations, we find it plausible to believe that some sex differences in intelligence may be traced to boys' greater independence and activity, girls' greater conformity and passive-dependency. We do not know whether these personality differences between the sexes are in any degree innate, or whether they are entirely a product of the social learning involved in the acquisition of sex roles; but we do suggest that the existence of the differences may have a bearing upon the intellectual development of the two sexes.

A second theory concerning the origins of sex differences in intellectual functioning may be derived from MacKinnon (1962). We noted earlier that high I.Q., and more particularly creativity and originality, appear to be associated with cross-sex-typing in both sexes. MacKinnon has suggested that this may be due to the absence of repression. He argues that a man can only achieve a high degree of "masculinity" (as our culture defines it) by repressing the feminine character elements that all men possess. And presumably the converse would be true of women: ultrafemininity is only achieved through the repression of masculine tendencies. Repression, MacKinnon argues, has a generalized impact upon thought processes, interfering with the accessibility of the individual's own previous experiences. An individual who is using repression as a defense mechanism cannot be, to use MacKinnon's term, "fluent in scanning thoughts." MacKinnon has evidence that creativity is in fact associated with the absence of repression (as indicated through personality-assessment tests), and Barron (1957) reports that originality is associated with "responsiveness to impulse and emotion." Witkin (1962) reports that his field-independent people are less likely to use repression as a defense mechanism than his field-dependent people. If MacKinnon is right, this should mean that field-independent men are somewhat more feminine than field-dependent men. There is some evidence from Bieri's (1960) study that this is indeed the case.

If MacKinnon's hypothesis is to be used to explain sex differences in intellectual performance, we would have to assume that women typically repress more than men, since they are more "field-dependent" and less adept at breaking set than men. It is difficult to see why a girl should have to repress her masculine tendencies more strongly than a boy does his feminine tendencies; on the contrary, social pressure is much stronger against a boy who is a sissy than against a girl who is a tomboy. Furthermore, women are freer to express feelings (with the exception of hostility) than men in our society. Hence it is difficult to characterize women as generally subject to repression. Furthermore, while it is true that they are more field-dependent, women are not any less "fluent in scanning thoughts," if we take their performance on divergent thinking and verbal-fluency tests as an indicator. Some aspects of women's intellectual performance, then, could be attributed to repression if there were evidence of greater repression in women, but others could not.

There appears to be some contradiction between the prediction that we could make on the basis of MacKinnon's repression theory and the prediction from Witkin's theory about dependency. To be creative, MacKinnon says, a man must be able to accept and express the feminine aspects of his character. Surely, one element of this femininity would be passive-dependency. Yet, passive-dependency, we have argued earlier, interferes with analytic thinking and some aspects of creativity. It would appear that the correlation between intellectual performance and cross-sex-typing ought to be stronger for women than for men, since among women masculinity implies both independence and absence of repression—two positive factors in intellectual performance. For men, however, femininity implies absence of repression (a positive factor) and passive-dependency (a negative factor). As we noted earlier, the evidence for cross-sex-typing as a correlate of intellectual abilities is stronger for women than for men.

So far, we have been discussing two mediating factors—repression and passive-dependency—which presumably affect both sexes in the same way. We noted earlier, however, that there were several traits, such as impulsiveness, aggression, and hyperkinesis, which appeared to be positive correlates for girls and negative ones for boys. Kagen, Moss, and Sigel (1963) first called attention to these differences, saying, "It is possible that analytic and nonanalytic responses are the product of different causal agents in boys and girls. Specifically, motoric impulsivity may be one of the primary antecedents of nonanalytic, undifferentiated conceptual products for boys, but of less relevance for girls' conceptual responses " (p. 111).

How can a mediating process facilitate or inhibit intellectual growth for one sex and not the other? We do not think it necessary to suppose that different psychological principles govern the intellectual development of the two sexes; therefore we would like to explore two alternative possibilities to explain these opposite-direction effects. The first is that we have not been measuring comparable processes in the two sexes, and that when we specify the variables more exactly, same-direction correlations will emerge. For example, when we measure total activity level, we might get opposite correlations for the two sexes between activity level and measures of intellectual performance, because a high total activity level may have a different "meaning" for the two sexes, in the sense that it forms part of a different constellation of attributes. There is some indication from a recent study on activity level (Maccoby et al. 1965) that this is the case. But if we measure a selected aspect of activity, such as the ability to inhibit motor movement or the amount of intersituational variation in activity, we can and do obtain correlations with intellectual performance that are similar for both sexes. It is also possible that scores on total aggression will not relate clearly to intellectual performance, while scores that reflect whether the aggression is directed and instrumental would do so. If these distinctions were made in the measurement of aggression, the sex differences in the way aggression correlates with cognitive performance might well disappear.

The second possible explanation of these opposite-direction correlations involves an assumption of curvilinearity. Let us assume that there is a single personality dimension, running from passive and inhibited at one end of the scale to bold, impulsive, and hyperactive at the other. A tentative hypothesis might be that there is a curvilinear relationship between this dimension and intellectual performance, so that both the very inhibited and the very bold will perform less well, while those who occupy the intermediate positions on the inhibited-impulsiveness dimension will perform optimally. We suggest further that boys and girls, on the average, occupy different positions on the dimension we have described. There is reason to believe that boys are more aggressive, more active, and less passive than girls. Whether the differences are innate or the outcome of social learning is not so important here. The important point is that these temperamental differences do exist. The situation that we hypothesize may be graphed as follows:

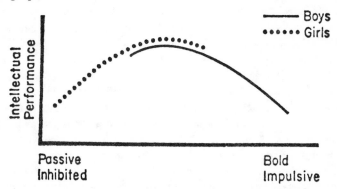

If the hypothesis holds, it would follow that for optimum intellectual performance, most girls need to become less passive and inhibited, while most boys need to become less impulsive. However, for those girls who do happen to be highly impulsive (as much so as the average boy, or even more so), impulsiveness should be a negative factor, as timidity should be for those boys at the passive end of the scale.

A parallel analysis may be made of anxiety as it affects intellectual performance in the two sexes. There is substantial evidence (beginning with the theoretical formulation of the problem by Taylor and Spence, 1952) that the relation of anxiety to performance is curvilinear. Either very high or very low levels of anxiety interfere with performance on a variety of tasks; intermediate levels facilitate performance. If women and girls have a high base level of anxiety, then increases in anxiety above their base level will frequently carry them past the optimum point of the curve, and result in inhibition or disorganization of performance. If boys and men have a low base level of anxiety, increases in anxiety will more often either improve performance, or move them through the middle portions of the curve where changes in performance would not be found.

In evaluating this hypothesis, we must first ask whether the two sexes do in fact differ in their base level of anxiety. As may be seen from the summary in the Oetzel bibliography (1966), there is very strong evidence for greater anxiety in girls when anxiety is measured with paper-and-pencil tests like the CMAS[1] or TASC.[2] However, the tendency for girls to score higher in anxiety on these tests has been attributed to their greater willingness to admit to such feelings, and is not conclusive evidence that any more basic difference exists. The answer to the question will no doubt depend upon how anxiety is defined. In two studies that measure physiological reactions to stress (Sontag, 1947, Berry and Martin, 1957), females were found to have greater autonomic reactivity. Jersild and Holmes (1935) presented standardized fear situations in a laboratory situation to children of nursery school age, and obtained higher average "fear" scores for girls than boys. Some unpublished work by Kagan done with infants during the first year of life shows that when girls are set down on the floor in a strange room, they cling to the mother's leg longer before crawling away to explore objects; also they are more upset when placed behind a barrier so that the mother is visible but inaccessible. Harlow's (1962) finding that monkeys go to the mother for contact comfort when presented with fear stimuli gives us some basis for inferring that the behavior of the infants in Kagan's study was motivated by timidity—i.e., that the girls are more frightened than the boys by the strange situation in which they have been placed. With these various pieces of evidence in mind, we believe it to be a reasonable hypothesis that girls do have a higher base anxiety level than boys, so that increments from this base level might be expected to have a different effect for the two sexes.

We have so far discussed two "personality" dimensions that might bear a curvilinear relation to intellectual performance: anxiety, and a dimension running from inhibited-passive to bold-impulsive. Neither of these dimensions is precisely defined; if we wish to test the validity of the formulation, we must specify more exactly the behavioral dispositions that distinguish the sexes and bear the hypothesized curvilinear relation to intellectual performance. We must note, for example, that although the sexes do differ on such aspects of "impulsivity" as frequency of temper tantrums, aggression, and activity, they do not consistently differ on the "reflectivity-impulsivity" dimension (Kagan et al., 1964), so that this aspect of impulsivity would not be relevant to the explanation of sex differences offered here. Further differentiation will also be needed on the "intellectual performance" dimension. It is quite possible, for example, that "analytic style" and performance on spatial tests are related to impulsiveness or anxiety in the manner described, while certain aspects of verbal ability are not.

GENETIC VERSUS ENVIRONMENTAL CONTRIBUTIONS

In the preceding section, we have discussed sex differences in personality traits as possible mediators of differences in intellectual performance. Assuming that the evidence is sufficient to convince the reader that there is indeed a substantial probability that such attributes as fearfulness, impulsiveness, independence, etc., do have a bearing on intellectual functioning, then it may be valuable to consider briefly the origins of the sex differences in these personality traits, with a view to discovering if the intellectual characteristics of either sex are likely to change as cultural conditions change. To what extent are boys more active or more aggressive because they are trained to adopt these socially defined sex-appropriate characteristics, and to what extent are they more active because of a substratum of biological determination with which environmental inputs must interact? Mischel (1966) has taken a social-learning point of view, arguing that the known socialization inputs to the two sexes are sufficiently different in the appropriate ways to produce known sex differences in dependency and aggression (and by implication in other personality traits as well). Hamburg (1966), on the other hand, has presented evidence that in primates sex-specific hormones govern not only specifically sexual behavior, but also various kinds of social behavior. Male-hormone treatment administered to a pregnant animal increases the incidence among the female offspring of rough-and-tumble play, and decreases the tendency to withdraw from the initiations, threats, and approaches of others. An interesting point emerging from Hamburg's report is that sex differences in social behavior may be related to endocrine influences even though there is no detectable sex difference in hormone concentrations at the time the behavior is observed. This point is important because of the fact that present methods of measurement do not reveal any differences between young boys and girls in the concentration of male or female hormones present in their bodies, even though their social behavior might suggest the presence of such a difference. This might be taken to mean that the differences in social behavior could not be a product of differential hormonal factors in the two sexes. Hamburg points to the possibility that hormonal "sensitization" during the prenatal period may contribute to the arousal of sex-appropriate behavior later in the life cycle, when the specific hormone concentrations are no longer present.

D'Andrade (1966), analyzing cross-cultural evidence, notes that certain temperamental differences seem to be cross-culturally universal, and are found even in societies where most of the usual environmental pressures toward sex-typing are absent (e.g., the Kibbutzim in Israel). He also suggests that certain differential behavior in the two sexes is directly conditioned by such physical differences as size, strength, and biological role in the bearing and suckling of children these differences are then generalized to similar activities and become institutionalized in occupational roles and other cultural prescriptions, in preparation for which anticipatory sex-typing occurs in childhood.

Let us assume, then, that the sex-typed attributes of personality and temperament which we have found to be related to intellectual functioning are the product of the interweaving of differential social demands with certain biological determinants that help to produce or augment differential cultural demands upon the two sexes. The biological underpinnings of the social demands for sex-typed behavior set modal tendencies for cultural demands, and set limits to the range of variation of these demands from one cultural setting to another. Still, within these limits considerable variation does occur, between families, between cultures, and in the nature of the behavior that a social group stereotypes as "feminine" or "masculine." Is there any evidence that such variations are associated with the nature or quality of intellectual performance in the two sexes?

In an attempt to measure cultural influences outside the home, Minuchin (1964) compared the performances of boys and girls in "modern" and "traditional" schools. In this study, an effort was made to control for social class and intellectual ability of the children, in order to isolate the effects of the two school atmospheres. In the traditional school, behavior was more sex-typed during play sessions than in the modern school. And in intellectual tasks, there were greater sex differences in problem solving and coding tasks in the traditional schools than in the modern ones. These findings would be consistent with the hypothesis that strong social demands for sex-typed behavior, such as aggression in boys and conformity-passivity in girls, play a role in producing some of the sex differences we have seen in intellectual performance. The proof of this point, however, would rest on experimental attempts to change the nature of intellectual performance through changes in the social expectations for sex-typed behavior. Only one attempt of this kind has been reported. Carey (1955) attempted to improve problem-solving behavior by changing "attitudes" toward such behavior. Group discussions directed toward improving the subjects' self-confidence in problem-solving tasks were held; these discussions emphasized the fact that it was socially acceptable to excel at problem solving. The discussion sessions improved the performance of college women but not of college men, suggesting that beliefs that skill in problem solving was not appropriate behavior had been an impediment to the normal performance of women but not of men. More such experimental evidence is needed to provide information on the difficulties and possible effects of influencing culturally prescribed behavior. It would be valuable, too, to have information on the extent of sex differences in intellectual performance in societies with high sex-role differentiation, and to compare these findings with similar findings for societies in which sex-role differentiation is minimized.

The findings on socialization practices within families, as they relate to intellectual development in the two sexes, point first of all to the fact that the environmental factors embodied in parent-child interaction do indeed make a difference in the child's intellectual performance. But more importantly, these findings indicate that the same environmental input affects the two sexes differently, and that different factors are associated with optimal performance for boys and girls. The brighter girls tend to be the ones who have not been tied closely to their mothers' apron strings, but have been allowed and encouraged to fend for themselves. The brighter boys, on the other hand, have had high maternal warmth and protection in early childhood (Moss & Kagan, 1958; Baley & Schaefer, 1964). We find, then, that environmental effects are not merely something added to, or superimposed upon, whatever innate temperamental differences there are that affect intellectual functioning. Rather, there is a complex interaction. The two sexes would appear to have somewhat different intellectual strengths and weaknesses, and hence different influences serve to counteract the weaknesses and augment the strengths.

FOOTNOTES

1. Children's Manifest Anxiety Scale
2. Test Anxiety Scale for Children

REFERENCES

BARRON, F. (1957) "Originality in relation to personality and intellect." *J. Pers.*, 25, 730–42.

BAYLEY, NANCY. (1956) "Individual patterns of development." *Child Develpm.*, 27, 45-74.

BAYLEY, NANCY, and E. S. SCHAEFER. (1964) "Correlations of maternal and child behaviors with the development of mental abilities: data from the Berkeley Growth Study." *Soc. Res. Child Develpm. Monogr.*, 29, No. 6, 3-79.

BERRY, J. L., and B. MARTIN. (1957) "GSR reactivity as a function of anxiety, instructions and sex." *J. abnorm. soc Psychol.*, 54, 9-12.

BIERI, J. (1960) "Parental identification, acceptance of authority, and within-sex differences in cognitive behavior." *J. aborm. soc. Psychol.*, 60, 76-79.

CAREY, GLORIA L. (1955) "Reduction of sex differences in problem solving by improvement of attitude through group discussion." Unpublished doctoral dissertation, Stanford University.

CARLSMITH, LYNN. (1964) "Effect of early father absence on scholastic aptitude." *Harvard educ. Rev.*, 34, 3-21.

D'ANDRADE, R. G. (1966) "Sex differences and cultural institutions." In E. E. Maccoby (Ed.) *The development of sex differences.* Stanford: Stanford University Press, 1966.

HAMBURG, D. A., & LUNDE, D. T. (1966) "Sex hormones in the development of sex differences in human behavior." In E. E. Maccoby (Ed.) *The development of sex differences.* Stanford: Stanford University Press, 1966.

HARLOW, H. (1962) "The heterosexual affectional system in monkeys." *American Psychologist, 17, 1–9.*

JERSILD, A. T., and F. B. HOLMES. (1935) "Children's fears." *Child Develpm. Monogr.*, No. 20, 1-356.

KAGAN, J., H. A. MOSS, and I. E. SIGEL. (1963) "The psychological significance of styles of conceptualization." In J. C. Wright and J. Kagan (eds.), Basic cognitive processes in children. *Soc. Res. Child Develpm. Monogr.*, 28, No. 2.

KAGAN, J., BERNICE L. ROSMAN, DEBORAH DAY, J. ALBERT and W. PHILLIPS. (1964) "Information processing in the child: significance of analytic and reflective attitudes." *Psych. Monogr.*, 78, No. 1.

KOHLBERG, L. (1966) "A cognitive-developmental analysis of children's sex-role concepts and attitudes." In E. E. Maccoby (Ed.) *The development of sex differences.* Stanford: Stanford University Press, 1966.

MACCOBY, ELEANOR E., EDITH M. DOWLEY, J. W. HAGAN and R. DEGERMAN. (1965) "Activity level and intellectual functioning in normal preschool children." *Child Develpm.*, 36, 761–70.

MACKINNON, D. W. (1962) "The nature and nurture of creative talent." *Amer. Psychologist*, 17, 484-95.

MINUCHIN, PATRICIA. (1964) "Sex role concepts and sex typing in childhood as a function of school and home environments." Paper presented at American Orthopsychiatric Association, Chicago.

MISCHEL, W. (1966) "A social-learning view of sex differences in behavior." In E. E. Maccoby (Ed.) *The development of sex differences.* Stanford: Stanford University Press, 1966.

MOSS, H. A., and J. KAGAN. (1958) "Maternal influences on early I.Q. scores." *Psychol. Rep.*, 4, 655-61.

OETZEL, R. M. (1966) "Classified summary of research in sex differences." In E. E. Maccoby (Ed.) *The development of sex differences.* Stanford: Stanford University Press, 1966.

RADCLIFFE COMMITTEE ON GRADUATE EDUCATION FOR WOMEN. (1956) *Graduate education for women.* Cambridge: Harvard University Press.

RAU, LUCY. (1963) "Interpersonal correlates of perceptual-cognitive functions." Paper presented at Society for Research in Child Development, San Francisco.

SEARS, PAULINE S. (1963) "The effect of classroom conditions on the strength of achievement motive and work output of elementary school children." Final report, Cooperative research project No. 873, Stanford University.

SONTAG, L. W. (1947) "Physiological factors and personality in children." *Child Develpm.*, 18, 185–89.

TAYLOR, JANET A., and K. W. SPENCE. (1952) "The relationship of anxiety level to performance in serial learning." *J. exp. Psychol.*, 44, 61-64.

WITKIN, H. A., R. B. DYK, H. F. FATERSON, D. R. GOODENOUGH, and S.A. KARP. (1962) *Psychological differentiation.* New York: John Wiley & Sons.

SEX, AGE, AND STATE AS DETERMINANTS OF MOTHER-INFANT INTERACTIONS

Howard A. Moss

Howard Moss's work, as represented in the selection below, is a clear case of how difficult it can be to label a given approach to studying sex differences. His focus is on dyadic human interaction, therefore psychological; his method is to observe his subjects in the natural habitat, therefore ethological. His inductive empiricism would make him appear to be atheoretical, but it is equally apparent that he recruits his findings to a bidirectional, dyadic model of early infant-mother interaction. Moreover, he is interested in change over time, therefore his orientation is developmental, although not embedded in any of the standard developmental frameworks presented earlier. Of the approaches already considered, Moss probably comes closest to Gesell. Like Gesell, he relies heavily on detailed, first-hand observation and his findings contribute to the natural history of childhood. But, unlike Gesell, he does not formulate explicit norms of development.

Moss's primary interest is in the mother-child dyad as a socialization network. For our purposes there are several fascinating components to his study. First, he examines the infant as socializer of the mother's behavior, as well as the converse. Second, he underscores the role that the child's sex plays in this reciprocal socialization process. Third, he discovers sex differences in social patternings and temperamental dispositions as early as three weeks of age. Fourth, he finds that the patterns of differences and similarities change rather markedly by three months of age. And finally, he teases causal relationships out of correlational findings which help to make sense of early male-female differences.

Moss is Research Psychologist and Chief of the Section on Parent-Infant Behavior at the National Institute of Mental Health in Washington, D. C. We have reprinted below that part of his study which deals specifically with sex differences.

A major reason for conducting research on human infants is derived from the popular assumption that adult behavior, to a considerable degree, is influenced by early experience. A corollary of this assumption is that if we can precisely conceptualize and measure significant aspects of infant experience and behavior we will be able to predict more sensitively and better understand adult functioning. The basis for this conviction concerning the enduring effects of early experience varies considerably according to the developmental model that is employed. Yet there remains considerable consensus as to the long term and pervasive influence of the infant's experience.[1]

Bloom (1964) contends that characteristics become increasingly resistant to change as the mature status of the characteristic is achieved and that environmental effects are most influential during periods of most rapid growth. This is essentially a refinement of the critical period hypothesis which argues in favor of the enduring and irreversible effects of many infant experiences. Certainly the studies on imprinting and the effects of controlled sensory input are impressive in this respect (Hess, 1959; White and Held, 1963). Learning theory also lends itself to support the potency of early experience. Since the occurrence of variable interval and variable ratio reinforcement schedules are highly probable in infancy (as they are in many other situations), the learnings associated with these schedules will be highly resistant to extinction. Also, the pre-verbal learning that characterizes infancy should be more difficult to extinguish since these responses are less available to linguistic control which later serves to mediate and regulate many important stimulus-response and reinforcement relationships. Psychoanalytic theory and behavioristic psychology probably have been the most influential forces in emphasizing the long-range consequences of infant experience. These theories, as well as others, stress the importance of the mother-infant relationship. In light of the widespread acceptance of the importance of early development, it is paradoxical that there is such a dearth of direct observational data concerning the functioning of infants, in their natural environment, and in relation to their primary caretakers.

Observational studies of the infant are necessary in order to test existing theoretical propositions and to generate new propositions based on empirical evidence. In addition, the infant is an ideally suitable subject for investigating many aspects of behavior because of the relatively simple and inchoate status of the human organism at this early stage in life. Such phenomena as temperament, reactions to stimulation, efficacy of different learning contingencies, perceptual functioning, and social attachment can be investigated while they are still in rudimentary form and not yet entwined in the immensely complex behavioral configurations that progressively emerge.

The research to be reported in this paper involves descriptive-normative data of maternal and infant behaviors in the naturalistic setting of the home. These data are viewed in terms of how the infant's experience structures potential learning patterns. Although the learning process itself is of primary eventual importance, it is necessary initially to identify the organizational factors, *in situ*, that structure learning opportunities and shape response systems.

A sample of 30 first-born children and their mothers were studied by means of direct observations over the first 3 months of life. Two periods were studied during this 3-month interval. Period one included a cluster of three observations made at weekly intervals during the first month of life in order to evaluate the initial adaptation of mother and infant to one another. Period two consisted of another cluster of three observations, made around 3 months of age when relatively stable patterns of behavior were likely to have been established. Each cluster included two 3-hour observations and one 8-hour observation. The 3-hour observations were made with the use of a keyboard that operates in conjunction with a 20-channel Esterline-Angus Event Recorder. Each of 30 keys represents a maternal or infant behavior, and when a key is depressed it activates one or a combination of pens on the recorder, leaving a trace that shows the total duration of the observed behavior. This technique allows for a continuous record showing the total time and the sequence of behavior. For the 8-hour observation the same behaviors were studied but with the use of a modified time-sampling technique. The time-sampled units were one minute in length and the observer, using a stenciled form, placed a number opposite the appropriate behaviors to indicate their respective order of occurrence. Since each variable can be coded only once for each observational unit, a score of 480 is the maximum that can be received. The data to be presented in this paper are limited to the two 8-hour observations. The data obtained with the use of the keyboard will be dealt with elsewhere in terms of the sequencing of events.

The mothers who participated in these observations were told that this was a normative study of infant functioning under natural living conditions. It was stressed that they proceed with their normal routines and care of the infant as they would if the observer were not present. This structure was presented to the mothers during a brief introductory visit prior to the first observation. In addition, in order to reduce the mother's self-consciousness and facilitate her behaving in relatively typical fashion, the observer emphasized that it was the infant who was being studied and that her actions would be noted only in relation to what was happening to the infant. This approach seemed to be effective, since a number of mothers commented after the observations were completed that they were relieved that they were not the ones being studied. The extensiveness of the observations and the frequent use of informal conversation between the observer and mother seemed to contribute further to the naturalness of her behavior.

The observational variables, mean scores and sample sizes are presented in Table 1. These data are presented separately for the 3-week and the 3-month observations. The inter-rater reliabilities for these variables range from .74 to 1.00 with a median reliability of .97. Much of the data in this paper are presented for males and females separately, since by describing and comparing these two groups we are able to work from an established context that helps to clarify the theoretical meaning of the results. Also, the importance of sex differences is heavily emphasized in contemporary developmental theory and it is felt that infant data concerning these differences would provide a worthwhile addition to the literature that already exists on this matter for older subjects.

The variables selected for study are those which would seem to influence or reflect aspects of maternal contact. An additional, but related consideration in the selection of variables was that they have an apparent bearing on the organization of the infant's experience. Peter Wolff (1959), Janet Brown (1964), and Sibylle Escalona (1962) have described qualitative variations in infant state or activity level and others have shown that the response patterns of the infant are highly influenced by the state he is in (Bridger, 1965). Moreover, Levy (1958) has demonstrated that maternal behavior varies as a function of the state or activity level of the infant. Consequently, we have given particular attention to the variables concerning state (cry, fuss, awake active, awake passive, and sleep) because of the extent to which these behaviors seem to shape the infant's experience. Most of the variables listed in Table 1 are quite descriptive of what was observed. Those which might not be as clear are as follows: *attends infant*—denotes standing close or leaning over infant, usually while in the process of caretaking activities; *stimulates feeding*—stroking the infant's cheek and manipulating the nipple so as to induce sucking responses; *affectionate contact*—kissing and caressing infant; *stresses musculature*—holding the infant in either a sitting or standing position so that he is required to support his own weight; *stimulates/arouses infant*—mother provides tactile and visual stimulation for the infant or attempts to arouse him to a higher activity level; and *imitates infant*—mother repeats a behavior, usually a vocalization, immediately after it is observed in the infant.

The sex differences and shifts in behavior from 3 weeks to 3 months are in many instances pronounced. For example, at 3 weeks of age mothers held male infants about 27 minutes more per 8 hours than they held females, and at 3 months males were held 14 minutes longer. By the time they were 3 months of age there was a decrease of over 30% for both sexes in the total time they were held by their mothers. Sleep time also showed marked sex differences and changes over time. For the earlier observations females slept about an hour longer than males, and this difference tended to be maintained by 3 months with the female infants sleeping about 41 minutes longer. Again, there was a substantial reduction with age in this behavior for both sexes; a decrease of 67 and 86 minutes in sleep time for males and females, respectively. What is particularly striking is the variability for these infant and maternal variables. The range for sleep time is 137-391 minutes at 3 weeks and 120-344 minutes at 3 months, and the range for mother holding is 38-218 minutes at 3 weeks and 26-168 minutes for the 3-month observation. The extent of the individual differences reflected by these ranges

TABLE 1   MEAN FREQUENCY OF MATERNAL AND INFANT BEHAVIOR
AT 3 WEEKS AND 3 MONTHS

Behavior	3-week observation		3-month observation [a]	
	Males [a] (N = 14)	Females (N = 15)	Males [b] (N = 13)	Females (N = 12)
Maternal Variables				
Holds infant close	121.4	99.2	77.4	58.6
Holds infant distant	32.2	18.3	26.7	27.2
Total holds	131.3	105.5	86.9	73.4
Attends infant	61.7	44.2	93.0	81.8
Maternal contact (holds and attends)	171.1	134.5	158.8	133.8
Feeds infant	60.8	60.7	46.6	41.4
Stimulates feeding	10.1	14.0	1.6	3.6
Burps infant	39.0	25.9	20.9	15.3
Affectionate contact	19.9	15.9	32.8	22.7
Rocks infant	35.1	20.7	20.0	23.9
Stresses musculature	11.7	3.3	25.8	16.6
Stimulates arouses infant	23.1	10.6	38.9	26.1
Imitates infant	1.9	2.9	5.3	7.6
Looks at infant	182.8	148.1	179.5	161.9
Talks to infant	104.1	82.2	117.5	116.1
Smiles at infant	23.2	18.6	45.9	46.4
Infant Variables				
Cry	43.6	30.2	28.5	16.9
Fuss	65.7	44.0	59.0	36.0
Irritable (cry and fuss)	78.7	56.8	67.3	42.9
Awake active	79.6	55.1	115.8	85.6
Awake passive	190.0	138.6	257.8	241.1
Drowsy	74.3	74.7	27.8	11.1
Sleep	261.7	322.1	194.3	235.6
Supine	133.7	59.3	152.7	134.8
Eyes on mother	72.3	49.0	91.0	90.6
Vocalizes	152.3	179.3	207.2	207.4
Infant smiles	11.1	11.7	32.1	35.3
Mouths	36.8	30.6	61.2	116.2

[a]Four of the subjects were unable to participate in the 3-month observation. Two moved out of the area, one mother became seriously ill, and another mother chose not to participate in all the observations.

[b]One subject who had had an extremely difficult delivery was omitted from the descriptive data but is included in the findings concerning mother-infant interaction.

seems to have important implications. For instance, if an infant spends more time at a higher level of consciousness this should increase his experience and contact with the mother, and through greater learning opportunities, facilitate the perceptual discriminations he makes, and affect the quality of his cognitive organization. The finding that some of the infants in our sample slept a little over 2 hours, or about 25% of the observation time and others around 6 hours or 75% of the time, is a fact that has implications for important developmental processes. The sum crying and fussing, what we term irritability level of the infant, is another potentially important variable. The range of scores for this behavior was from 5-136 minutes at 3 weeks and 7-98 at 3 months. The fact that infants are capable through their behavior of shaping maternal treatment is a point that has gained increasing recognition. The cry is a signal for the mother to respond and variation among infants in this behavior could lead to differential experiences with the mother.

Table 2 presents t values showing changes in the maternal and infant behaviors from the 3-week to the 3-month observation. In this case, the data for the males and females are combined since the trends, in most instances, are the same for both sexes. It is not surprising that there are a number of marked shifts in behavior from 3 weeks to 3 months, since the early months of life are characterized by enormous growth and change. The maternal variables that show the greatest decrement are those involving feeding behaviors and close physical contact. It is of interest that the decrease in close contact is paralleled by an equally pronounced increase in attending behavior, so that the net amount of maternal contact remains similar for the 3-week and 3-month observations. The main difference was that the mothers, for the later observation, tended to hold their infants less but spent considerably more time near them, in what usually was a vis-à-vis posture, while interacting and ministering to their needs. Along with this shift, the mothers showed a marked increase in affectionate behavior toward the older infant, positioned him more so that he was required to make active use of his muscles, presented him with a greater amount of stimulation and finally, she exhibited more social behavior (imitated, smiled, and talked) toward the older child.

TABLE 2   CHANGES IN BEHAVIOR BETWEEN 3 WEEKS AND 3 MONTHS
($N = 26$)

Maternal variables	t-values	Infant variables	t-values
Higher at 3 weeks:		*Higher at 3 weeks:*	
Holds infant close	4.43****	Cry	2.84***
Holds infant distant	.56	Fuss	1.33
Total holds	4.00****	Irritable (cry and fuss)	1.73*
Maternal contact		Drowsy	9.02****
(holds and attends)	.74	Sleep	4.51****
Feeds infant	3.49***		
Stimulates feeding	3.42***		
Burps infant	3.28***		
Rocks infant	1.08		
Higher at 3 months:		*Higher at 3 months:*	
Attends infant	5.15****	Awake active	2.47**
Affectionate contact	2.50**	Awake passive	5.22****
Stresses musculature	3.42***	Supine	1.75*
Stimulates/arouses infant	2.63**	Eyes on mother	3.21***
Imitates Infant	4.26****	Vocalizes	3.56***
Looks at infant	.38	Infant smiles	6.84****
Talks to infant	2.67**	Mouths	3.69***
Smiles at infant	4.79****		

* $p<.10$ ** $p<.05$ *** $p<.01$ **** $p<.001$

The changes in maternal behavior from 3 weeks to 3 months probably are largely a function of the maturation of various characteristics of the infant. However, the increased confidence of the mother, her greater familiarity with her infant, and her developing attachment toward him will also account for some of the changes that occurred over this period of time.

By 3 months of age the infant is crying less and awake more. Moreover, he is becoming an interesting and responsive person. There are substantial increases in the total time spent by him in smiling, vocalizing, and looking at the mother's face, so that the greater amount of social-type behavior he manifested at three months parallels the increments shown in the mothers' social responsiveness toward him over this same period. The increase with age in the time the infant is kept in a supine position also should facilitate his participation in vis-à-vis interactions with the mother as well as provide him with greater opportunity for varied visual experiences.

Table 3 presents the correlations between the 3-week and the 3-month observations for the maternal and infant behaviors we studied. These findings further reflect the relative instability of the mother-infant system over the first few months of life. Moderate correlation coefficients were obtained only for the class of maternal variables concerning affectionate-social responses. It thus may be that these behaviors are more sensitive indicators of enduring maternal attitudes than the absolute amount of time the mother devoted to such activities as feeding and physical contact. The few infant variables that show some stability are, with the exception of vocalizing, those concerning the state of the organism. Even though some of the behaviors are moderately stable from three weeks to three months, the overall magnitude of

TABLE 3   CORRELATIONS BETWEEN OBSERVATIONS AT 3 WEEKS AND AT 3 MONTHS ($N = 26$)

Maternal variables	$r =$	Infant variables	$r =$
Holds infant close	.23	Cry	.28
Holds infant distant	.04	Fuss	.42**
Total holds	.18	Irritable (cry and fuss)	.37*
Attends infant	.36*	Awake active	.25
Maternal contact		Awake passive	.26
(holds and attends)	.25	Drowsy	.44**
Feeds infant	.21	Sleep	.24
Stimulates feeding	.37*	Supine	.29
Burps infant	.20	Eyes on mother	-.12
Affectionate contact	.64****	Vocalizes	.41**
Rocks infant	.29	Infant smiles	.32
Stresses musculature	.06	Mouths	-.17
Stimulates/arouses infant	.23		
Imitates infant	.45**		
Looks at infant	.37*		
Talks to infant	.58***		
Smiles at infant	.66****		

* $p<.10$ ** $p<.05$ *** $p<.01$ **** $p<.001$

the correlations reported in Table 3 seem quite low considering that they represent repeated measures of the same individual over a relatively short period.

TABLE 4   SEX DIFFERENCES ON FREQUENCY OF MATERNAL AND INFANT
BEHAVIORS AT 3 WEEKS AND 3 MONTHS

Maternal variables	*t-values*		Infant variables	*t-values*	
	3 weeks	3 months		3 weeks	3 months
Male Higher:			*Male Higher:*		
Holds infant close	1.42	1.52	Cry	1.68	1.11
Holds infant distant	2.64**		Fuss	2.48**	3.47***
Total holds	1.65	1.12	Irritable (cry		
Attends infant	2.66**	1.10	and fuss)	2.23**	2.68**
Maternal contact			Awake active	1.66	.57
(holds and attends)	2.09**	1.57	Awake passive	2.94***	1.77*
Feeds infant	.06	.27	Drowsy		.41
Burps infant	1.67	.69	Supine	2.30**	1.07
Affectionate contact	.90	1.00	Eyes on mother	1.99*	.75
Rocks infant	1.21		Mouths		.64
Stresses musculature	2.48**	1.67			
Stimulates/arouses					
infant	2.20**	1.53			
Looks at infant	1.97*	1.36			
Talks to infant	1.02	.79			
Smiles at infant	.57				
Female Higher:			*Female Higher:*		
Holds infant distant		.05	Drowsy	.03	
Stimulates feeding	.62	1.47	Sleep	3.15***	2.87***
Rocks infant		.82	Vocalizes	1.34	.23
Imitates infant	.80	1.76*	Infant smiles	.02	.08
Smiles at infant		.44	Mouths		2.57**

* $p<.10$ ** $p<.05$ *** $p<.01$

Table 4 presents *t*-values based on comparisons between the sexes for the 3-week and 3-month observations. A number of statistically significant differences were obtained with, in most instances, the boys having higher mean scores than the girls. The sex differences are most pronounced at three weeks for both maternal and infant variables. By 3 months the boys and girls are no longer as clearly differentiated on the maternal variables although the trend persists for the males to tend to have higher mean scores. On the other hand, the findings for the infant variables concerning state remain relatively similar at 3 weeks and 3 months. Thus, the sex differences are relatively stable for the two observations even though the stability coefficients for the total sample are low (in terms of our variables).

TABLE 5 SEX DIFFERENCES AFTER CONTROLLING FOR IRRITABILITY AND SLEEP TIME THROUGH ANALYSIS OF COVARIANCE[a]

Maternal or Infant Behaviors	Sleep time controlled for		Sex with higher mean score	Irritability controlled for		Sex with higher mean score
	3 weeks	3 months		3 weeks	3 months	
Variables	t	t		t	t	
Holds infant close	.30	1.22		.64	1.70	
Holds infant distant	.59	−.20		.92	−.20	
Total holds	.43	.88		.86	1.08	
Attends infant	1.12	1.36		1.91*	.94	Males
Maternal contact (holds and attends)	.62	1.04		1.20	1.12	
Stimulates feeding	.55	−1.12		−.09	−1.06	
Affectionate contact	−.46	.91		.56	1.27	
Rocks	.35	−.70		.44	−1.44	
Stresses musculature	1.84*	.71	Males	1.97*	1.40	
Stimulates/arouses infant	2.09**	1.82*	Males	2.43**	2.31**	Males
Imitates infant	−.91	−2.73*	Females	−.63	−2.14**	Females
Looks at infant	.58	1.35		1.17	1.02	
Talks to infant	−.48	.24		.70	.59	
Infant supine	.82	−.03		1.36	.69	
Eyes on mother	.37	.58		1.76*	−.37	Males

* $p<.10$ ** $p<.05$

[a]A positive t-value indicates that males had the higher mean score, and a negative t-value indicates a higher mean score for females.

In general, these results indicate that much more was happening with the male infants than with the famale infants. Males slept less and cried more during both observations and these behaviors probably contributed to the more extensive and stimulating interaction the boys experienced with the mother, particularly for the 3-week observation. In order to determine the effect of state we selected the 15 variables, excluding those dealing with state, where the sex differences were most marked and did an anaiysis of covariance with these variables, controlling for ir ritability, and another analysis of covariance controlling for sleep. These results are presented in Table 5. When the state of the infant was controlled for, most of the sex differences were no longer statistically significant. The exceptions were that the t-values were greater, after controlling for state, for the variables "mother stimulates/arouses infant" and "mother imitates infant." The higher score for "stimulates/arouse" was obtained for the males and the higher score for "imitates" by the females. The variable "imitates" involves repeating vocalizations made by the child, and it is interesting that mothers exhibited more of this behavior with the girls. This response could be viewed as the reinforcement of verbal behavior, and the evidence presented here suggests that the mothers differentially reinforce this behavior on the basis of the sex of the child.

In order to further clarify the relation between infant state and maternal treatment, product-moment correlations were computed relating the infant irritability score with the degree of maternal contact. The maternal contact variable is based on the sum of the holding and attending scores with the time devoted to feeding behaviors subtracted out. These correlations were computed for the 3-week and 3-month observations for the male and female samples combined and separate. At 3 weeks a correlation of .52 ($p < .01$) was obtained between irritability and maternal contact for the total sample. However, for the female subsample this correlation was .68 ($p < .02$) and for males only .20 (non. sig.). Furthermore, a somewhat similar pattern occurred for the correlations between maternal contact and infant irritability for the 3-month observation. At this age the correlation is .37 ($p < .10$ level) for the combined sample and .54 ($p < .05$ level) for females and $-.47$ ($p < .10$ level) for males. A statistically significant difference was obtained ($t = 2.40$, p $< .05$ level) in a test comparing the difference between the female and male correlations for the 3-month observation. In other words maternal contact and irritability positively covaried for females at both ages; whereas for males, there was no relationship at 3 weeks, and by 3 months the mothers tended to spend less time with the more irritable male babies. It should be emphasized that these correlations reflect within group patterns, and that when we combine the female and male samples positive correlations still emerge for both ages. Since the males had substantially higher scores for irritability and maternal contact than the females, the correlation for the male subjects does not strongly attenuate the correlations derived for the total sample, even when the males within group covariation seems random or negative. That is, in terms of the total sample, the patterning of the males scores is still consistent with a positive relationship between irritability and maternal contact.

From these findings it is difficult to posit a causal relationship. However, it seems most plausible that it is the infant's cry that is determining the maternal behavior. Mothers describe the cry as a signal that the infant needs attention and they often report their nurturant actions in response to the cry. Furthermore, the cry is a noxious and often painful stimulus that probably has biological utility for the infant, propelling the mother into action for her own comfort as well as out of concern for the infant. Ethological reports confirm the proposition that the cry functions as a "releaser" of maternal behavior (Bowlby, 1958; Hinde, et al., 1964; Hoffman, et al., 1966). Bowlby (1958) states:

It is my belief that both of them (crying and smiling), act as social releasers of instinctual responses in mothers. As regards crying, there is plentiful evidence from the animal world that this is so: probably in all cases the mother responds promptly and unfailingly to her infant's bleat, call or cry. It seems to me clear that similar impulses are also evoked in the human mother. . . .

Thus, we are adopting the hypothesis that the correlations we have obtained reflect a causal sequence whereby the cry acts to instigate maternal intervention. Certainly there are other important determinants of maternal contact, and it is evident that mothers exhibit considerable variability concerning how responsive they are to the stimulus signal of the cry. Yet it seems that the effect of the cry is sufficient to account at least partially for the structure of the mother-infant relationship. We further maintain the thesis that the infant's cry shapes maternal behavior even for the instance where the negative correlation was noted at 3 months for the males. The effect is still present, but in this case the more irritable infants were responded to *less* by the mothers. Our speculation for explaining this relationship and the fact that, conversely, a positive correlation was obtained for the female infants is that the mothers probably were negatively reinforced for responding to a number of the boys but tended to be positively reinforced for their responses towàrd the girls. That is, mothers of the more irritable boys may have learned that they could not be successful in quieting boys whereas the girls were more uniformly responsive (quieted by) to maternal handling. There is not much present in our data to bear out this contention, with the exception that the males were significantly more irritable than the girls for both observations. However, evidence that suggests males are more subject to incosolable states comes from studies (Serr and Ismajovich, 1963; McDonald, Gynther, and Christakos, 1963; Stechler, 1964) which indicate that males have less well organized physiological reactions and are more vulnerable to adverse conditions than females. The relatively more efficient functioning of the female organism should thus contribute to their responding more favorably to maternal intervention.

In summary, we propose that maternal behavior initially tends to be under the control of the stimulus and reinforcing conditions provided by the young infant. As the infant gets older, the mother, if she behaved contingently toward his signals, gradually acquires reinforcement value which in turn increases her efficacy in regulating infant behaviors. Concurrently, the earlier control asserted by the infant becomes less functional and diminishes. In a sense, the point where the infant's control over the mother declines and the mother's reinforcement value emerges could be regarded as the first manifestation of socialization, or at least represents the initial conditions favoring social learning. Thus, at first the mother is shaped by the infant and this later facilitates her shaping the behavior of the infant. We would therefore say that the infant, through his own temperament or signal system, contributes to establishing the stimulus and reinforcement value eventually associated with the mother. According to this reasoning, the more irritable infants (who can be soothed) whose mothers respond in a contingent manner to their signals should become most amenable to the effects of social reinforcement and manifest a higher degree of attachment behavior. The fact that the mothers responded more contingently toward the female infants should maximize the ease with which females learn social responses.

This statement is consistent with data on older children which indicate that girls learn social responses earlier and with greater facility than boys (Becker, 1964). Previously we argued that the mothers learned to be more contingent toward the girls because they probably were more responsive to maternal intervention. An alternative explanation is that mothers respond contingently to the girls and not to the boys as a form of differential reinforcement, whereby, in keeping with cultural expectations, the mother is initiating a pattern that contributes to males being more aggressive or assertive, and less responsive to socialization. Indeed, these two explanations are not inconsistent with one another since the mother who is unable to soothe an upset male infant may eventually come to classify this intractable irritability as an expression of "maleness."

From *The Merrill-Palmer Quarterly*, 1967, vol. 13, pages 19-36. Reprinted by permission of the author and the Merrill-Palmer Institute. Only that part of the article which deals specifically with sex differences, i.e., pages 19-30, is reprinted.

FOOTNOTE

1. Presented at The Merrill-Palmer Institute Conference on Research and Teaching of Infant Development, February 10-12, 1966, directed by Irving E. Sigel, chairman of research. The conference was financially supported in part by the National Institute of Child Health and Human Development. The author wishes to express his appreciation to Mrs. Helene McVey and Miss Betty Reinecke for their assistance in preparing and analyzing the data presented in this paper.

REFERENCES

BECKER, W. C. "Consequences of different kinds of parental discipline." In M. L. Hoffman & Lois W. Hoffman (Eds.), *Review of child development research: I*. New York: Russell Sage Found., 1964. Pp. 169-208.

BLOOM, B. S. *Stability and change in human characteristics*. New York: Wiley, 1964.

BOWLBY, J. "The nature of a child's tie to his mother." *Internat. J. Psychoanal.*, 1958, 39, 350–373.

BRIDGER, W. H. "Psychophysiological measurement of the roles of state in the human neonate " Paper presented at Soc. Res. Child Develpm., Minneapolis, April, 1965

BROWN, JANET L. "States in newborn infants." *Merrill-Palmer Quart.*, 1964, 10, 313-327.

ESCALONA, SIBYLLE K. "The study of individual differences and the problem of state." *J. Child Psychiat.*, 1962, 1, 11-37.

HESS, E. H. "Imprinting." *Science*, 1959, 130, 133-141.

HINDE, R. A., ROWELL, T. E., & SPENCER-BOOTH, Y. "Behavior of living rhesus monkeys in their first six months." *Proc. Zool. Soc., London*, 1964, 143, 609-649.

HOFFMAN, H., et al. "Enhanced distress vocalization through selective reinforcement." *Science*, 1966, 151, 354-356.

LEVY, D. M. *Behavioral analysis.* Springfield, Ill.: Charles C Thomas, 1958.

MCDONALD, R. L., GYNTHER, M. D., & CHRISTAKOS, A. C. "Relations between maternal anxiety and obstetric complications." *Psychosom. Med.*, 1963, 25, 357-362.

SERR, D. M. & ISMAJOVICH, B. "Determination of the primary sex ratio from human abortions." *Amer. J. Obstet. Gyncol.*, 1963, 87, 63-65.

STECHLER, G. "A longitudinal follow-up of neonatal apnea." *Child Develpm.*, 1964, 35, 333-348.

WHITE, B. L. & HELD, R. "Plasticity in perceptual development during the first six months of life." Paper presented at Amer. Ass. Advncmnt. Sci., Cleveland, Ohio, December, 1963.

WOLFF, P. H. "Observations on newborn infants." *Psychosom. Med.*, 1959, 21, 110-118.

OTHER BOOKS OF INTEREST PUBLISHED BY URIZEN

LITERATURE

Ehrenburg, Ilya
The Life of the Automobile, novel,
   192 pages
Cloth $8.95 / paper $4.95

Enzensberger, Hans Magnus
Mausoleum, poetry, 132 pages
Cloth $10.00 / paper $4.95

Hamburger, Michael
German Poetry 1910-1975, 576 pages
Cloth $17.50 / paper $6.95

Handke, Peter
Nonsense & Happiness, poetry,
   80 pages
Cloth $7.95 / paper $3.95

Hansen, Olaf (Ed.)
*The Radical Will, Randolph Bourne
(Selected Writings) 1911-1918*
   500 pages
Cloth $17.50 / paper $7.95

Innerhofer, Franz
Beautiful Days, novel, 228 pages
Cloth $8.95 / paper $4.95

Kroetz, Franz Xaver
Farmyard & Other Plays, 192 pages
Cloth $12.95 / paper $4.95

Montale, Eugenio
Poet in Our Time (essays), 96 pages
Cloth $5.95 / paper $2.95

Shepard, Sam
*Angel City, Curse of the Starving
   Class, & Other Plays,* 300 pages
Cloth $15.00 / paper $4.95

FILM

Bresson, Robert
Notes on Cinematography, 132 pages
Cloth $6.95 / paper $2.95

Bresson, Robert
The Complete Screenplays, Vol. I,
   400 pages
Cloth $17.50 / paper $6.95

PSYCHOLOGY

Borneman, Ernest (Ed.)
The Psychoanalysis of Money, 420 pages
Cloth $15.00 / paper $5.95

Doerner, Klaus
Madmen and the Bourgeoisie, 384 pages
Cloth $15.00 / paper $5.95

Patrick C. Lee and Robert S. Stewart
Sex Differences, 500 pages
Cloth $17.50 / paper $5.95

Moser, Tilman
Years of Apprenticeship on the Couch,
240 pages / Cloth $10.00

ECONOMICS

De Brunhoff, Suzanne
Marx on Money, 192 pages
Cloth $10.00 / paper $4.95

Linder, Marc
Anti-Samuelson Vol. I, 400 pages
Cloth $15.00 / paper $5.95
Anti-Samuelson, Vol. II, 440 pages
Cloth $15.00 / paper $5.95

SOCIOLOGY

Andrew Arato/Eike Gebhardt (Eds.)
The Essential Frankfurt School Reader,
544 pages / Cloth $17.50 / paper $5.95

Pearce, Frank
Crimes of the Powerful, 176 pages
Paper $4.95

Van Onselen, Charles
Chibaro (African Mine Labor in Southern
Rhodesia), 368 pages / Cloth $17.50

Shaw, Martin
Marxism Versus Sociology
   (A Reading Guide), 120 pages
Cloth $6.95 / paper $2.25

Shaw, Martin
Marxism and Social Science, 125 pages
Paper $2.95

Thönnessen, Werner
The Emancipation of Women, 185 pages
Cloth $10.00 / paper $4.95

Write for a complete catalog to:
Urizen Books, Inc., 66 West Broadway, New York, N.Y. 10007